Gadamer's *Truth and Method*

Gadamer's *Truth and Method*

A Polyphonic Commentary

Edited by
Cynthia R. Nielsen and Greg Lynch

ROWMAN & LITTLEFIELD
Lanham • *Boulder* • *New York* • *London*

Published by Rowman & Littlefield
An imprint of The Rowman & Littlefield Publishing Group, Inc.
4501 Forbes Boulevard, Suite 200, Lanham, Maryland 20706
www.rowman.com

86-90 Paul Street, London EC2A 4NE

Copyright © 2022 by The Rowman & Littlefield Publishing Group, Inc.

All rights reserved. No part of this book may be reproduced in any form or by any electronic or mechanical means, including information storage and retrieval systems, without written permission from the publisher, except by a reviewer who may quote passages in a review.

British Library Cataloguing in Publication Information Available

Library of Congress Cataloging-in-Publication Data Available

Names: Lynch, Greg, editor. | Nielsen, Cynthia R., editor.
Title: Gadamer's Truth and method : a polyphonic commentary / edited by Greg Lynch and Cynthia R. Nielsen.
Description: Lanham : Rowman & Littlefield, [2022] | Includes bibliographical references and index.
Identifiers: LCCN 2021059551 (print) | LCCN 2021059552 (ebook) |
    ISBN 9781538167946 (cloth) | ISBN 9781538167960 (paperback) |
    ISBN 9781538167953 (ebook)
Subjects: LCSH: Gadamer, Hans-Georg, 1900-2002. Wahrheit und Methode. |
    Hermeneutics. | Humanities—Methodology. | Philosophy, Modern—20th century.
Classification: LCC BD241.G33 G33 2022 (print) | LCC BD241.G33 (ebook) |
    DDC 121/.68—dc23/eng/20220211
LC record available at https://lccn.loc.gov/2021059551
LC ebook record available at https://lccn.loc.gov/2021059552

Contents

Introduction   vii
Cynthia R. Nielsen and Greg Lynch

The Basic Structure and Argument of *Truth and Method*   xv
Jean Grondin

PART I: ART   1

1   *TM* I.1.1: Gadamer on the Significance of the Humanist Tradition for the Human Sciences, or Truth and Edification   3
Theodore George

2   *TM* I.1.2: Gadamer's Astonishing Question: Engaging with Gadamer's Critique of Kant's Aesthetics   19
Nicholas Davey

3   *TM* I.1.3: Re-claiming Art's Claim to Truth   39
Daniel L. Tate

4   *TM* I.2.1: Gadamer on Play as Ontological Explanation   59
Jessica Frazier

5   *TM* I.2.2: Gadamer and the Plastic Arts   79
Cynthia R. Nielsen

PART II: TRADITION, HISTORY, AND THE HUMAN SCIENCES   101

6   *TM* II.1.1: Schleiermacher's Hermeneutics and Historical Meaning   103
Kevin M. Vander Schel

7	*TM* II.1.2-3: Phenomenology's Essential Role in the Hermeneutic Tradition *David Vessey*	125
8	*TM* II.2.1: The Historical Situation of Thought as a Hermeneutic Principle *Carolyn Culbertson*	143
9	*TM* II.2.2: "The Recovery of the Fundamental Hermeneutic Problem": Application and Normativity *David Liakos*	165
10	*TM* II.2.3: The Finitude of Reflection *Greg Lynch*	187

PART III: LANGUAGE AND LINGUISTICALITY — 207

11	*TM* III.1: Language as Medium of Hermeneutic Experience *Carlo DaVia*	209
12	*TM* III.2: Gadamer and the Concept of Language *Gert-Jan van der Heiden*	227
13	*TM* III.3: On Language and the Universality of Hermeneutics *James Risser*	245

Index — 263

About the Contributors — 269

Introduction

Cynthia R. Nielsen and Greg Lynch

Hans-Georg Gadamer's *magnum opus*, *Truth and Method,* was first published in German in 1960, translated into English in 1975, and is widely recognized as a ground-breaking text of philosophical hermeneutics. Unsurprisingly, this text has generated an extensive secondary literature, including a number of excellent studies and commentaries. This volume brings to bear on this familiar text what might be thought of as an experimental interpretive approach: that of a *polyphonic* commentary. The term *polyphonic* means many-voiced, and it is first and foremost a musical term. In choral polyphony, for example, multiple voices sound together in a complex, back-and-forth musical dialogue. Similarly, the commentary presented in this volume consists of the voices of multiple authors, each of whom covers a portion of *Truth and Method* following the order of the text itself. Some of these voices are those of established writers who are familiar staples of the literature on Gadamer, others belong to the rising younger generation of Gadamer scholars. In organizing the text in this way, our aim was to simultaneously pursue two interpretive goals. First, in adopting a commentary format, the volume aims to shed light on *Truth and Method* as a whole. It ensures both that the discussion covers the entire text (including those parts that have tended to receive scant attention) and also that it discusses the major themes of the work in the logical sequence in which Gadamer himself developed them. Second, in making the commentary polyphonic, we aim to highlight the wide range of ways in which the text has been understood and to give the reader a sense of where there are debates and conversations yet to be had. The result, we hope, is a volume that meshes unity and diversity in a distinctive way: the many voices are united in the common focus of allowing the text to speak in a way that is meaningful today.

    The approach of a polyphonic commentary could, of course, be applied to any text, but we think it is particularly appropriate to *Truth and Method*. For

Gadamer, reading a text is *always* a polyphonic endeavor because it inevitably includes the voices of others who have read the text before and alongside us. As he puts it,

> Our historical consciousness is always filled with a variety of voices in which the echo of the past is heard. Only in the multifariousness of such voices does it exist: this constitutes the nature of the tradition in which we want to share and have a part.[1]

The present approach, then, can be seen as an attempt to make structurally explicit what, on Gadamer's view, is implicitly true of all hermeneutical engagement: that it is necessarily communal and dialogical.

Another aspect of a polyphonic commentary that reverberates with Gadamer's hermeneutics is the idea that significant texts and works of art will necessarily yield multiple valid interpretations. As Gadamer observes, there is no

> single interpretation that is correct 'in itself,' precisely because every interpretation is concerned with the text itself. The historical life of a tradition depends on being constantly assimilated and interpreted. An interpretation that was correct in itself would be a foolish ideal that mistook the nature of tradition. Every interpretation has to adapt itself to the hermeneutical situation to which it belongs (*TM*, 415).

Though there is, of course, considerable overlap, each contributor to the volume occupies a unique hermeneutic situation and is motivated by distinctive questions and concerns, and as a result, each interprets the text differently. In some cases, these differences are complimentary, like voices singing different parts of a harmony; in others, there is genuine disagreement, and dissonance is the more appropriate musical metaphor. But in each case, the differences bring out the always-ongoing inner *movement* that, on Gadamer's account, belongs essentially to the meaning of any text. Every jazz quartet, for example, will perform its own version of "Stella by Starlight," and not even two consecutive performances by the same ensemble will ever be exactly alike. Yet in each successful performance—and only there—we recognize what we are hearing *as* "Stella by Starlight." In the same way, as Gadamer famously puts it, we always "understand in a *different* way, *if we understand at all*" (*TM*, 307)—not because understanding always falls short of the one true meaning-in-itself, but because the meaning exists nowhere else than in the variety of interpretive voices in which it comes to presentation. The structure of a polyphonic commentary creates a communal interpretive space in which, we hope, the inner diversity of Gadamer's masterpiece—and of the *Sache* it discusses—can come to the fore.

One potential pitfall of a polyphonic commentary is the loss of the forest for the trees. If each contributor offers their distinctive take on a specific section of the text, the reader might lack a sense of how the text hangs together.

To help counter this, Jean Grondin's introductory chapter, "The Basic Structure and Argument of *Truth and Method*," aims to provide an overview of the text as a whole. As Grondin presents it, *Truth and Method* is a text that, as it were, overflows its own bounds. The text was originally envisioned to be (and initially presents itself as) a defense of the humanities' claim to provide us with genuine knowledge. Yet as the text develops, it becomes clear that something broader is at stake. Gadamer's reflections concern not just the nature of the understanding that operates in academic disciplines like history and philology; rather, they concern the nature of understanding in general and as such. The three main sections of *Truth and Method* can thus be seen as a series of three concentric circles, each spilling over into the next. Gadamer begins in Part I by arguing that in the experience of art, we encounter a kind of truth that cannot be captured by or reduced to the objectifying grasp of things that characterizes modern science. The discussion then broadens out in Part II to show that this sort of truth is characteristic not just of art but of the whole of the human sciences. Lastly, in part III, Gadamer contends that this truth that is otherwise than method is ultimately rooted in the linguisticality that characterizes human experience in general.

Theodore George begins the section-by-section exposition of *Truth and Method* with a consideration of Gadamer's discussion of the humanist tradition in TM I.1.1. Gadamer's main contention in this section, George argues, is that the humanist tradition articulates a (largely forgotten) *normative ideal* for theorizing—that is, an account of the goal toward which inquiry is directed and in terms of which it is to be evaluated. In contrast to the Enlightenment's ideal of *method*, for the humanists inquiry aims at *edification*. Gadamer argues that the latter, non-methodological ideal is the one the human sciences properly pursue. As George points out, in making this move, Gadamer is not only distancing himself from thinkers like Dilthey (who sought to discover a method appropriate to the human sciences), he is also subtly challenging Heidegger's famous dismissal of humanism as inextricably tied to a problematic essentialism. While perhaps an apt critique of forms of humanism centered around *formatio*, George argues, this objection does not apply to humanism as such. Specifically, the notion of *Bildung* (edification or cultivation) escapes this charge and thus opens the way for the anti-essentialist humanism that Gadamer will develop over the course of *Truth and Method*.

In chapter 2, Nicholas Davey examines the "astonishing question" that Gadamer poses in his interaction with Kant—whether aesthetics itself serves to conceal the true nature of art. Gadamer, Davey argues, answers this question in the affirmative. Insofar as aesthetics focuses merely on the perceivable features of art and the feelings these features generate in us when we represent them, it overlooks what Gadamer takes to be art's defining characteristic: the fact that it *says something* to us. In this way, the aesthetic tradition not only misunderstands the nature of art, it misunderstands our relationship to it. In conceiving of our encounters with art in terms of *Erlebnisse* (lived experiences), aesthetics alienates us from our basic experience of art as meaning. Gadamer aims to correct this by replacing traditional aesthetics with what Davey calls an *Erfahrung-Ästhetik*, an account of art organized around the de-centering experience of being addressed.

In the third chapter, Daniel Tate articulates Gadamer's positive program for moving beyond "aesthetic consciousness" and restoring the connection of art and truth. Central to this program, Tate observes, is the idea that the truth of art is a "happening" that befalls us when we encounter it and not a matter of a subject accurately representing some pre-given object. Looking forward to the next section of the text, Tate unpacks Gadamer's phenomenological analysis of this happening in terms of the notion of play. For Gadamer, *play* designates a back-and-forth movement and, as Tate shows, this movement appears in different forms in Gadamer's analysis of truth in art. First, play characterizes the artwork itself, in which the various parts of the work dynamically interact with one another. Second, it characterizes the relationship of the artwork to the audience who questions and is questioned by it. Third and most centrally, through these movements the subject matter of the work itself emerges from hiddenness into presence, that is, into truth. The result, as Tate explains, is not only that we come to better understand the artwork's subject matter but also that what presents itself becomes "more truly what it is."

The theme of play is also the central focus of chapter 4, in which Jessica Frazier explores the ontological implications of Gadamer's account of art. In the movement of play, Frazier argues, one is caught up in a "constantly transforming medial structure" that encompasses and reshapes both oneself and the item one is experiencing. This structure is thus phenomenologically prior to the division of subject and object. While Gadamer first identifies this structure in his analysis of art, Frazier argues that it is of far wider significance for his project. As the argument of *Truth and Method* develops play is revealed also to be the basic structure of history, and, eventually, of phenomenality as such. In fact, Frazier argues, the centrality of play stretches beyond *Truth and Method* into Gadamer's later work, as well, particularly his work on the nature of health.

As developed to this point, Gadamer's analysis of artworks as events faces a fairly obvious objection. However well it might fit the phenomena of the performing arts, the idea of art as an ontological "happening" does not seem to apply to the plastic arts and so does not seem to hold for art in general. In chapter 5, Cynthia Nielsen articulates Gadamer's response to this objection. While works of painting, sculpture, and architecture are obviously not 'performed' in the same sense that a drama or concerto is, neither, Gadamer contends, are they to be understood as mere inert objects for aesthetic contemplation. What makes something a portrait, for example, is the fact that it *presents* its subject matter to the viewer, and this presentation is fundamentally different from the sort of reference we find in copies, signs, and even symbols. Works of plastic art do not point away from themselves toward an independent signified; they draw their subject matter into themselves and effect an "increase" in its being. Just like the performances of a symphony, these increases are different each time they occur, and yet the plastic artwork *qua* artwork has no being apart from them.

A genuinely *polyphonic* commentary ought to be more than just a chorus singing Gadamer's praises, and in chapter 6, Kevin Vander Schel voices a critical note. Vander Schel takes up Gadamer's interpretation of Schleiermacher's hermeneutics and its subsequent impact on the history of hermeneutics, and, like a number of other recent scholars, Vander Schel finds this interpretation to be deeply flawed. He argues that Gadamer's reading of Schleiermacher distorts the latter's views in two fundamental ways. First, it focuses almost exclusively on Schleiermacher's account of "psychological" (or "technical") interpretation and largely ignores the "grammatical" dimension of interpretation that, for Schleiermacher, is equally important. As Vander Schel demonstrates, for Schleiermacher, interpretation is not a mere matter of diving into an individual author's mind but of grasping the author's views in their wider historical and linguistic context. Second, Gadamer errs in presenting Schleiermacher's views as an anticipation of Dilthey's project of centering the human sciences on hermeneutics. Though his contributions to the discipline were important, hermeneutics was never the primary focus of Schleiermacher's work. Rather, his hermeneutics grows out of his more fundamental concerns with ethics and dialectics. Despite Gadamer's misrepresentations, Vander Schel argues, Schleiermacher's work represents a promising approach to hermeneutical questions, one that differs from Gadamer's, but perhaps not quite so sharply as Gadamer himself supposed.

After his account of Schleiermacher, Gadamer's critical history of hermeneutics turns to Dilthey's work, and this is the focus of David Vessey's chapter. Though Gadamer sees Dilthey as taking an important step beyond Schleiermacher in his emphasis on the historicity of human life and understanding, his account remains "entangled" in the "aporias of historicism." As Vessey explains, Gadamer has two related difficulties in mind here. First, historicism's claim that all understanding is bound to a specific historical context seems to undermine itself insofar as it purports to state something universally and transhistorically true. Second, the claim seems to be incompatible with the further historicist thesis that an objective, scientific understanding of history is possible. Gadamer, as Vessey explains, argues that first Husserl and then Count Yorck make important headway in resolving these issues, but ultimately it is not until Heidegger that the genuine solution becomes apparent:

the transcendental insight that historicity is itself a condition of the possibility of understanding.

In chapter 8, Carolyn Culbertson articulates two opposed and highly influential contemporary attitudes toward the nature of knowledge. On one hand, proponents of the "transcendence argument" hold that genuine knowledge requires the knower to break free from the constraints of history and tradition and rely wholly on her own reason. On the other hand, proponents of the "immanence argument" contend that this sort of transcendence is impossible and that genuine knowledge is instead a matter of immersing oneself in and submitting oneself to the wisdom of the past. Culbertson argues that Gadamer's account of the historicity of understanding breaks with both of these influential attitudes. On Gadamer's view, both the Enlightenment disdain for tradition and the Romantic idolization of it stem from a common underlying assumption: that reason and tradition are "abstract opposites" of one another. Gadamer argues that this is a mistake. Because critical thinking can never occur apart from preconceptions that we inherit from history, there can be no reason without tradition. At the same time, however, inheriting tradition is never mere passive reception; it is a matter of creatively and critically appropriating what has been handed down. Thus, there can be no tradition without reason. For Gadamer, genuine knowledge is a matter neither of escaping our prejudices nor of uncritically embracing them but of putting them in play and at risk in the course of experience.

Gadamer describes the "putting in play" of our prejudices in hermeneutic experience in terms of the *application* of what is understood to the interpreter's own situation, and he argues that understanding is possible only on the basis of this application. As David Liakos observes in chapter 9, this claim has been the target of a perennial and influential critique of Gadamer's hermeneutics: the charge that Gadamer is unable to account for the *normativity* of interpretation. This is mobilized on two fronts. First, critics argue that Gadamer's hermeneutics precludes us from identifying any criterion by which to evaluate whether a given interpretation of a text is correct or incorrect. Second, they argue that Gadamer's insistence on the need for "openness" to the text leaves interpreters without a standard by which to evaluate the truth or falsity of what tradition says. Liakos argues that these criticisms rest on a misunderstanding of Gadamer's position—specifically, a misunderstanding of the dynamic interplay between the first-person and third-person dimensions of application. To apply a text to one's own situation is not simply to take it to mean whatever one wants to. Application, rather, is about holding oneself accountable to two different but complimentary sets of norms: those that stem from the hermeneutic situation in which one finds oneself and those that stem from the claim to meaning embodied in the text itself. While it is true that, on Gadamer's view, there is no pre-given formula or decision procedure that can tell us how to navigate these considerations, that does not mean that "anything goes." Rather, it means that interpreting correctly, like living well, is a matter of judgment, discernment, and wisdom that cannot be formalized.

In TM II.2.3, Gadamer responds to an objection to his central notion of "historically effected consciousness," and Greg Lynch presents a reconstruction of this argument in chapter 10. It is part of the nature of consciousness that it can rise above its objects, recognizing and endorsing the conditions that make those objects possible. For Hegel and the tradition of "reflective philosophy," this entails that consciousness cannot be *necessarily* limited in the way it would be if it were, as Gadamer claims, historically effected. As Lynch interprets it, Gadamer's response is to claim that the reflective philosophers have misunderstood the nature of reflection itself. Reflection is possible only on the basis of questions that arise from specific contexts of motivation. Since these contexts are ever-changing, the task of reflection must constantly begin anew. Thus, while Hegel is right that reflection is a necessary component of any experience, he is wrong to think that this entails that experience is teleologically directed toward a state of total self-transparency. Instead, Gadamer contends, it leads toward an attitude of *openness* that recognizes the inexhaustibility of what experience has to teach us.

In Part III of *Truth and Method,* Gadamer makes explicit a theme that has been operating below the surface throughout the text: the *linguisticality* of human understanding. Gadamer begins this part of the text by defending the theses that language determines the hermeneutic *object* and that it determines the hermeneutic *act*. These claims appear to be, if not simply obvious, at least unoriginal, as a number of earlier hermeneutical thinkers—most notably Schleiermacher—make seemingly identical claims. As Carlo DaVia argues in chapter 11, however, properly understanding Gadamer's theses reveals them to be anything but platitudinous. This is because, unlike most of his hermeneutic predecessors, for Gadamer the essence of language is its ability to disclose the world, not its ability to express the attitudes of speakers and authors. To say that language determines the hermeneutic act and object, then, is not merely to say that it is only through words that past meanings are preserved for us. The claim, rather, is that the meaning we encounter in tradition is never exclusively *past* in the first place. The paradigmatic objects of hermeneutics are always "contemporaneous" with us; they speak to us in the present just as directly as they did to their original readers. Accordingly, for Gadamer, understanding tradition is not a matter of seeking the original meaning that is encoded in the text but of participating in a present "hermeneutical conversation" with it.

In chapter 12, Gert-Jan van der Heiden walks us through Gadamer's reading of the history of the concept of language in Western philosophy. In contrast to Heidegger's narrative of philosophical decline, for Gadamer this history is one of both forgetting and rediscovering the "proper being of language." As van der Heiden brings out, Gadamer diagnoses how the now predominant conception of language as a mere system of instrumental signs can be traced back to Plato's attempt, in the *Cratylus*, to combat the sophists' deceptive abuse of language. At the same time, however, Gadamer identifies in Plato himself, in the medieval doctrine of the inner word, and in Renaissance humanism resources for resisting instrumentalism and recovering a more authentic understanding of language as the medium in which the world manifests itself.

In our last chapter, James Risser examines the final section of *Truth and Method*, "Language as Horizon of a Hermeneutic Ontology." Here we encounter some of Gadamer's most famous and most difficult claims, most notably the thesis that "being that can be understood is language" (*TM*, 490). Risser argues that the ontology voiced here should not be understood as a kind of linguistic idealism or even as a claim that all experience unfolds in words. Rather, what is at stake in this chapter—and, indeed, throughout the text of *Truth and Method*—is the *self-presentation* of what is. This self-presentation is linguistic in two primary respects. First, being shows itself to us as an objective (*sachlich*) *world* with an "independent otherness" that transcends our subjective opinions about it. On Gadamer's view, it is precisely language that creates the "open space" in which this independence can appear as such. Second, the self-presentation of being always emerges from the "middle" of a wider, linguistically constituted horizon of meaning. This, Risser notes, marks the finitude of self-presentation, in that this wider horizon on which self-presentation depends is never itself brought to full presence. The fact that language characterizes self-presentation as such is what underwrites Gadamer's claim to the "universality" of hermeneutics. In taking language as its subject matter, hermeneutics necessarily concerns itself with more than just the human sciences; its questions embrace the nature of appearance and intelligibility in general.

These studies, we hope, will be beneficial both to readers who are new to Gadamer and those long familiar with his work. To the former, they can offer helpful guides through the often circuitous paths of Gadamer's thinking in *Truth and Method*. To the latter, they offer a diverse set of new contributions to the ongoing conversation about the significance of this seminal text. In either case, we hope this polyphonic commentary will convey a sense of the richness and complexity of Gadamer's own philosophical voice and its continued relevance to the conversation that we are.

NOTE

1. Hans-Georg Gadamer, *Truth and Method*, 2nd ed., trans. Joel Weinsheimer and Donald G. Marshall (New York: Bloomsbury, 2013), 296. Hereafter cited in text as *TM*.

The Basic Structure and Argument of *Truth and Method*

Jean Grondin

Truth and Method is certainly a classic of twentieth-century philosophy, but the huge volume is by no means an easy read. It often deals with issues, authors, and concepts that will not be familiar to the average non-specialized reader. In a sense, this is unfortunate because the book does address fundamental questions that every contemporary mind can understand, such as: To what extent is our outlook on the world and ourselves too permeated by modern science and technology in such a way that it makes us forgetful of other experiences of truth? This question has only gained urgency over the last decades with our unchecked techno-euphoria and internet addiction. Gadamer also asks: What is the point of the humanities and their role in general education? What is a true humanist? What do we discover in the encounter with an artwork? Are artworks somehow deprived of their meaning when they are only seen as the focus of an aesthetic experience? What is the point of historical knowledge? Does the acknowledgment of the historical nature of all opinions lead to relativism? Can we get rid of all our prejudices and should we always view authority and tradition with suspicion? What can the classics, which the ambient woke-culture often wants to dismiss, teach us? To what extent can we know ourselves and what kind of philosophical wisdom can we hope for? What are the limits of our understanding and in what way is all our understanding tied to language? To all these important questions, *Truth and Method* has challenging answers to offer.

1. A LITTLE-KNOWN THINKER UNTIL THIS BOOK

It is one of the basic tenets of Gadamer's thinking and of hermeneutic thinking in general that one can only understand the parts of a book out of an idea of its whole, which is provisional and needs to be corrected as one advances further in the study of the book. We will be concerned here with this whole and will try to see how its parts articulate its basic ideas.

How do we grasp this whole? The first thing one reads in a book is usually the name of its author and its title. Hans-Georg Gadamer (1900–2002) was not a widely known author when the book came out on February 11, 1960, on the occasion of his 60th birthday. He was, to be sure, a well-respected professor of philosophy at the prestigious University of Heidelberg, but he was not seen as a particularly productive scholar, compared to, say, Martin Heidegger, who was his teacher, or Karl Jaspers, who was his predecessor in Heidelberg. The only real book he published before 1960 was his habilitation thesis on *Plato's Dialectical Ethics*, which came out in 1931. Writing was not his strong suit, he feared. He had had the good fortune to count among his mentors very prolific authors such as Paul Natorp, Nicolai Hartmann, Rudolf Bultmann, Paul Friedländer, and Martin Heidegger. They were all great minds with an impressive body of written work. Gadamer felt he was more of a teacher, whose strength resided more in his classes and seminars and in his discussions with students and the main thinkers of the philosophical tradition. In Frankfurt, where he taught from 1947 to 1949, and in Heidelberg, where he taught from 1948 until his retirement in 1968 and well beyond, he had brilliant students, such as Dieter Henrich, Konrad Cramer, Reiner Wiehl, Wolfgang Wieland, Rüdiger Bubner, and many others. When they went to other universities, they were always asked who they were working with in Heidelberg. When they said "Gadamer," most would reply: "Never heard of him, what has he written?" Knowing that their teacher had many things to say, they urged him to finally publish some meaningful book, and this is how Gadamer began working on *Truth and Method*.[1] Gadamer published it when he was sixty and only after working toward it for at least ten years, the way great books used to be written and perhaps the only way they still can. This ten-year incubation period reminds one of the ten years it took for Kant's *Critique of Pure Reason* (1781) and Heidegger's *Being and Time* (1927) to be written. The rest is history, as the saying goes: thanks to this book, Gadamer became a household name in intellectual circles.

2. HOW THE TITLE CAME ABOUT

Truth and Method was not the original title. When Gadamer submitted his long manuscript under the heading *Outlines of a Philosophical Hermeneutics*, the publisher understandably expressed reservations about the term *hermeneutics*, which was not well-known at the time. (Those who were versed in theology or jurisprudence might have known it as the art of understanding which provided guidelines for the interpretation of difficult texts.) A title, as the rhetorically well-schooled Gadamer also understood, had to be catchy. So Gadamer first considered the title *Art and History*, which corresponded to the topic of its first two parts but also to the title of a lecture course on *Art and History: Introduction to the Humanities* that he had been teaching at German universities since 1936 and on which the manuscript was based. In September 1959 he toyed with another title which was quite a mouthful: *The Truth of the Objective Spirit and the Limits of Method in the Humanities*,[2] where at least the two terms of the final title, *Truth* and *Method*, were present. At the end of the year, he thought about a title like *Geschehen und Verstehen* (*Event and Understanding*). (This title, which reminds one of a book title of Rudolph Bultmann, *Faith and Understanding*, finds an echo in the Introduction of *Truth and Method*: "When in the following I shall demonstrate how much there is of *event* effective in all *understanding*, and how little the traditions in which we stand are weakened by modern historical consciousness, it is not my intention to make prescriptions for the sciences or the conduct of life, but to correct false thinking about what they are.")[3] It is only in early January 1960, a few weeks before the publication of the book, that Gadamer came up with *Truth and Method*, which was perhaps reminiscent of Goethe's *Dichtung und Wahrheit* (*Poetry and Truth*). The original title, *Outlines of a Philosophical Hermeneutics*, was demoted to the subtitle. Again, the rest is history: the slow, sleeper-like success of the book soon turned hermeneutics, which sounded exotic when Gadamer submitted his manuscript, into something of a buzzword.

3. THE AIM OF THE BOOK AND ITS THREE INTERLOCKING PARTS

The stated aim of the book is to provide a philosophical account and justification of the truth-experience we encounter in the *Geisteswissenschaften*—a term which can be translated as *humanities*, *human sciences* or, more literally, *sciences of the spirit* (paging Hegel, which never displeased Gadamer). As it will turn out, the book will tackle many other issues and even make a point of going *beyond* its original question when it will raise a universality claim at the end of its journey (more on this later). As a reflection on the truth claim of the humanities, the book did have something to do with what hermeneutics used to be, at least in the tradition of Dilthey, for whom the guiding question was: In light of the undeniable successes of the exact sciences, what is it that makes the humanities scientific, and how can their truth or validity be secured? Since the exact sciences owed their successes to the stringency of their methods, it seemed natural to expect that the humanities would have methods of their own. This is how hermeneutics, at least in the Dilthean tradition as Gadamer frames it,[4] became a reflection on the methods that would ground the validity claim of the humanities. Dilthey was a subtle thinker and too versed in the *Geisteswissenschaften* to argue that the humanities should copy the exact sciences, but Gadamer believed he remained under the spell of their model when he wanted the reflection on the humanities to be first and foremost a reflection on their methods. Gadamer has a better proposition. Instead of understanding the truth claim of the humanities out of the idea of method, he believes one can give a more accurate account of their contribution to knowledge by relying on the experience of truth as it emerges out of the experience of art. Gadamer will, of course, have to help us see to what extent art procures an experience of truth. In a nutshell, it will be Gadamer's contention that art provides an experience of knowledge by confronting us with the lasting truth of things, as it is presented for instance by a picture or a play, yet in such a way that this involves an encounter with our own selves. The input of the spectator or reader is not to be viewed as a deplorable "subjective" addition, which in the case of the humanities could endanger objectivity; it is part and parcel of the truth that comes out of the art experience. Gadamer's conclusion will be that this art experience is not primarily an aesthetic affair but a cognitive one since it opens our eyes and reveals a reality we could not discover otherwise.

The discussion of the art experience thus leads into the second part of the book, which returns to the issue of the humanities. How are we to understand the understanding that the humanities bring about? Gadamer's argument will be that the hermeneutic reflection on their type of understanding, conducted by figures like Schleiermacher, the Historical School (Ranke, Droysen), and Dilthey, wanted to keep in check the subjectivity of the interpreter by providing specific methods to prevent its intrusion. Here, Gadamer argues, the obsession with method—influenced by the exact sciences and the inferiority complex they instill in the humanities—tended to obscure the plain truth of the humanities, namely, that they productively and positively involve the understander in their understanding. This would only have been acknowledged by Heidegger and his insight into the positive significance of the hermeneutic circle, that is, the notion that we always understand out of a guiding preunderstanding which has been shaped by our intentions and the work of tradition. It is this positive significance that Gadamer will sort out in his more constructive theory of the hermeneutic experience (TM II.2). He argues that our preunderstanding and prejudices are not only obstacles but also conditions of knowledge, which leads him to provocatively rehabilitate tradition and authority as sources of knowledge. Understanding, he will contend, is always embedded in an encounter of traditions, so much so that understanding takes on the form of a "fusion of horizons" between the text and its reader, the object and the subject. To become aware of this, one needs to develop a consciousness of effective history, that is, of the way history is at work in all our understanding. We can become aware of this work of history (*Wirkungsgeschichte*), yet there are limits to the consciousness we can develop of it, since to be a historical being means that we can never become fully transparent to ourselves. The consciousness of effective history will also have to be a consciousness of those limits, thus an experience of our finitude and as such a true hermeneutic experience that is more something that happens to us than something we could control. To become aware of one's finitude means that one learns to raise questions, fundamental questions, that challenge what we thought we knew. At this pivotal point of his book, at the end of its second part, Gadamer points out that this raising of questions occurs in language. What if all understanding was couched in the medium of language? This question will be the guiding thread of the third and final part of the book that will follow the lead of language to bestow upon hermeneutics a universal dimension, a thesis which goes beyond the book's original aim to provide an account of the truth of the humanities.

Truth and Method is hence a three-part book that starts off with a simple question—an inquiry into the knowledge claim of the human sciences—and ends up moving, as if by design, far beyond its original question. Its three parts are devoted respectively to the experience of art (TM I), that of history and the humanities (TM II), and that of language (TM III), which will endow hermeneutics with a universal outlook. The first two parts of the book, which formed the primary focus of his work under the title "Art and History," are themselves divided into two main sections: a critical (TM I.1 and TM II.1) and a more constructive part (TM I.2 and TM II.2). The critical part will strive to uncover what prevents us from seeing the true experience of art (in part I, the culprit will be aesthetic consciousness) and of history (in part II, the adversary will be historicism). These obstacles of understanding need to be "overcome," or "destroyed" in Heideggerian parlance, and understood out of their silent and often unacknowledged positivistic origins, if one is to rediscover the truth about art and history. On the ashes of this eye-opening destruction, Gadamer will then in the second section of the first two parts go on to unfold his more constructive account of the truth of art and history. The third and final part of the book does not expressively follow this two-pronged approach (i.e., the need to overcome a misunderstanding of art and history in TM I.1. and II.1., followed by the unfolding of an ontology of the proper experience at stake in TM I.2. and II.2.), but it too will want to overcome a short-sighted view of language, one that sees it as a mere instrument of thinking. Gadamer will argue that language is far more than that; it discovers the ways things are and is thus an ontological experience.

In a schematic form, the architecture of the book looks like this:

	Initial aim of the book: to justify the truth claim of the humanities
TM I.1	Overcoming of aesthetic consciousness
TM I.2	Ontology of the artwork and its truth-experience
TM II.1	Overcoming of historicism
TM II.2	Outlines of a theory of hermeneutic experience
TM III	Ontological turn of hermeneutics following the lead of language
Final outcome: the universality-claim of hermeneutics and linguistic understanding	

The three parts are interlocking and form concentric circles[5] that lead us to an ever-larger universality. The art experience, part I argues, is actually an experience of understanding so that aesthetics has to make way for a hermeneutics in part II. By reaching the element of language, this hermeneutics finally leads us to an ontology in part III. There is thus an undeniable progression and an element of suspense in the secret thriller that is *Truth and Method*:

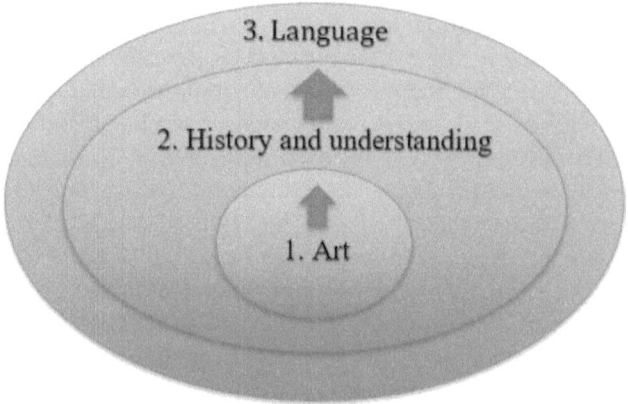

4. PART I: THE QUESTION OF TRUTH AS IT EMERGES IN THE EXPERIENCE OF ART

It is often believed, and Gadamer at times says, that the book starts off with the experience of art. As a matter of fact, Part I does take some time before reaching the art experience (e.g., in TM I.2). It only gets to it after a long and instructive detour. Its very first chapter is entitled "*Das Methodenproblem*," which I would be tempted to over-translate by "The Problem with Method." Gadamer recalls how the entire discussion surrounding the logic of the human sciences has been dominated by the notion of method, as seemed obvious in the work of Dilthey and many others. Gadamer then unearths a largely forgotten Heidelberg lecture of 1862 by the natural scientist Hermann Helmholtz. Helmholz tried to sort out the different methods of the sciences of nature and spirit by suggesting that the first observed is the method of induction, whereas the second appeared to follow something like an "artistic induction," which was more akin to a form of tact or tactfulness. What if, Gadamer provocatively asks, the specificity of the humanities resided more in this notion of tact than in the spellbinding idea of method (*TM*, 7)? In the human sciences, is everything a matter of method, as the model of the exact sciences and the bad conscience it seems to inflict on the humanities would seem to suggest? Here Gadamer has a better solution to offer, which is not primarily related to the art experience: Instead of being seduced by the idea of method, the humanities would be well advised to take their cue from humanism and its guiding concepts.

Humanism? What is that? Under the spell of the idea of method, our time has forgotten what it is all about. This is why Gadamer, in one of the most valiant anamnetic accomplishments of his book, will have to reacquaint us with its basic tenets, which form the true starting point of *Truth and Method*. Actually, this starting point would seem to be a no-brainer since the humanities have after all received their name from this humanist tradition, where they were called the *humaniora*, literally the "more human" disciplines, since the Latin word is a comparative. That is, compared to the "divine studies" of scripture, the "more human" studies deal with basic human sciences such as to name the three fundamental disciplines of the *trivium*, grammar, rhetoric, and dialectic (which incidentally all have to do with language). The problem is that the link to this tradition, which has dominated our intellectual tradition, has been ruptured. Gadamer will thus have to teach us two things: (1) in what this tradition consists and (2) why it has fallen out of favor.

Gadamer masterfully sums up the humanist tradition by recalling four of what he calls its guiding concepts: *Bildung*, common sense, judgment, and taste. *Bildung* is the first concept because it reminds us that the purpose of knowledge and the humanities is to "build" the individual by providing it with an education, a formation, and a culture (three terms one can use to translate *Bildung*). The truths of the humanities are truths of *Bildung*, that is, they contribute to the formation of the mind and the personality. This is already a notion one can contradistinguish from the prevailing methodical model of knowledge, according to which truth has to be independent of the knower. No, Gadamer subtly recalls, the point of humanistic *Bildung* is precisely to "build" the individual. By relying on models and the lessons of history, *Bildung* provides common sense, a capacity of judgment, and taste. *Taste* might sound strange to our ears because we are accustomed to treat matters of taste as merely subjective, deprived of any objective value. Not so, recalls Gadamer, since taste understood as the ability to discern the good in a precise situation and at the right moment is a capacity which a good humanist education can indeed foster. This sense of what is opportune even used to be the centerpiece of morals, as evidenced by the strong tradition of *moral taste* (Hutcheson) which extends to the early Kant, who planned to write a *Critique of Moral Taste*. This moral dimension survives when we continue to speak today of an action or utterance so utterly and objectively despicable as to be called "disgusting" (*gustus* is the Latin word for taste). There is nothing subjective about this moral judgment since it can be universally shared.

This humanist tradition has by and large become unfamiliar to us. Why is that so? In a name: because of Kant. According to Gadamer, Kant is responsible for the estrangement of the humanist tradition because he would have established, in his *Critique of Pure Reason* (1781), the exact sciences of nature as the sole form of reliable knowledge. Everything that does not correspond to their objectifying criteria is not knowledge and must be excluded from the realm of truth. To what realm do they then belong? The answer, which also begins to gain traction with Kant, is that they pertain to some *aesthetic* realm, one that would merely provide playful pleasure. This is what Kant aims to show in his third *Critique*, the *Critique of Judgment* (1790), where he argues that sensus communis, judgment, and taste only have a subjective value and no objective one. It will dawn on the reader that these three concepts were among the four guiding notions of humanism singled out by Gadamer and may well explain why he precisely chose them in the first place in his analysis. Whereas for humanism, sensus communis, judgment, and taste served to describe what *Bildung* aimed to develop, Kant excluded them from the realm of knowledge on the grounds that they did not conform to the methodical model whose monopoly he sought to establish. The loss was momentous, especially for the human sciences, since they lost the bedrock on the basis of which they could have understood themselves on an equal footing with the natural sciences. Kant's relegation of these notions to the aesthetic sphere also had the misfortune of forcing the human sciences, which did not recognize themselves in the methodical straitjacket, to understand themselves out of an aesthetic model. According to this model, which, according to Gadamer's penetrating diagnosis, was the secret upshot of the methodical, the humanities would not provide knowledge or truth; they would devote themselves to something like "expressions" and "life experiences" (*Erlebnisse*)—say, those of a poet, a philosopher, or a composer—and would strive to recreate (*nacherleben*) them. Hence, the fondness in the emerging *Geisteswissenschaften* of the nineteenth century for historical analyses of the genesis and evolution of works and great personalities (understood as "geniuses"). The humanities would only understand "expressions," not truths, and would strive to relate them to the lived experience from which they stem. What is forgotten in this aesthetic self-understanding, Gadamer contends, is the notion that the humanities convey truth and knowledge, not only, nor even primarily, an acquaintance with expressions and lived experience.

This aesthetic vocabulary also pervaded the new understanding of art itself. Art would be nothing but a matter of expression; it would be a subjective and playful affair, having nothing to do with knowledge and truth. The artists would be creators of imaginary realities which would have nothing to do with the real world. Artists would be marginal and cultivate this marginality. Gadamer believes it is tragic since it deprives art of its truth and its important place in the world.

After this long historical "detour" (TM I.1), it is this truth-experience Gadamer wants to rediscover in the second, more constructive section of part I (TM I.2). Gadamer speaks pointedly of an "*ontology* of the artwork and its hermeneutical significance" to hammer home the point that it is an *increased experience of Being* that the artwork conveys, not an experience that would content itself with illusion and appearance as the new aesthetic consciousness likes to believe. Gadamer provocatively starts by picking up a key notion of Kant and of aesthetic consciousness itself: that of play (*Spiel*). Aesthetic consciousness used it to stress that art is merely playful, catapulting us in a sphere of illusion, not of actual reality. Not so, Gadamer argues. His insightful ontology of play reveals that in play we are taken up into a heightened experience of Being which enables the world and the reality of things to represent themselves in their forgotten presence. The artwork is for Gadamer a presentation (*Darstellung*) of reality by virtue of which this reality even receives an increase of Being (*Seinszuwachs*), that is, an accrued reality. Gadamer stresses this augmented encounter with reality to counter the insistence of aesthetic consciousness on the somehow liberating unreality of the art experience and its notion that it would have nothing to do with truth and knowledge. On the contrary, Gadamer argues, the artwork has to be seen as the emanation of the Being of something that receives an increase in Being through its presentation in art. By revealing the essence of things, the one that remains, the artwork confronts us at the same time with our own situation. His prime example is that of tragedy where we cannot but be taken by the tragedy of life which is presented and confronts us with ourselves. He shows that this is also true of the picture which reveals the essence and significance of a person or a situation. This truth has the form of a happening (*Geschehen*), that is, it takes us up into its realm, upending our previous assumptions and thus delivering a truth experience that cannot be severed from our existence. It is an analogous form of truth that Gadamer will seek to retrieve in the human sciences and its encounter with history.

5. PART II: THE EXTENSION OF THE QUESTION OF TRUTH TO UNDERSTANDING IN THE HUMAN SCIENCES

The basic thrust of part I is that the art experience, contrary to popular belief and even to the conception that artists have of themselves, is not primarily an aesthetic one, but a hermeneutic one. It is an experience of understanding. But how is one to understand understanding and its theory, hermeneutics? The first, more historical section of part II (TM II.1) will strive to overcome a conception of understanding and of hermeneutics that Gadamer deems inadequate in order to lay the groundwork for his own hermeneutic theory in the second section (TM II.2), which is the most discussed and constructive portion of his book. The contours of the conception of understanding and hermeneutics that he wishes to overcome are clear. It is the conception that was pursued in the nineteenth century by authors such as Schleiermacher (a theologian, classicist, and philosopher), Ranke and Droysen (both historians), and Dilthey who viewed himself as their heir. According to Gadamer, Schleiermacher construed understanding as the re-creation or reconstruction of the mind of an author (the *mens auctoris*). Here Gadamer takes issue with the romantic notion that understanding is primarily directed toward the soul or mind of an author and not to what she or he has to say, hence the truth of what is said. For Schleiermacher, it would only be the subjective opinion of the author that understanding would seek to recreate, and it does so by reconstructing it out of its constitutive parts. (This is how the circle of the whole and the parts came to play a role in the hermeneutics of the nineteenth century.) As for hermeneutics—that is, the *theory* of this understanding—it mostly followed the methodical model by searching for means to keep in check the subjectivity of the interpreter, which could endanger the objectivity of interpretation. Geared toward the *mens auctoris*, hermeneutics would also have tacitly followed the aesthetic model by assuming that what we seek to understand are merely expressions (which one would seek to reconstruct out of the psychology of the author or the times), not truths.

Husserl and Heidegger helped turn things around. Husserl did so by urging a return to the things themselves, which signifies for Gadamer a step back from the prevailing epistemological model and a return to understanding as it unfolds in our life-world. Heidegger did so by challenging the truth-conception of the epistemological model, according to which truth has to be completely independent from the observer if one wants to avoid the vicious circle of an interpretation that would be contaminated by preunderstandings. No, Heidegger argued, preunderstandings guide all understanding.

Gadamer's grand thesis in the second section of part II (TM II.2) is that this insight paves the way to a more adequate conception of understanding and of hermeneutics that would do justice to the productive historicity of understanding. By elevating historicity in TM II.2.1 to a hermeneutical principle (instead of an obstacle to be overcome), Gadamer hopes to rediscover the fundamental problem of hermeneutics (TM II.2.2) and to analyze the renewed consciousness of finitude that arises from it (TM II.2.3).

This second section (TM II.2) is certainly the most original and provocative one of the book. It is provocative because Gadamer aims to show that prejudices are conditions and not obstacles of understanding! This contention seems to fly in the face of the basic tenet of the Enlightenment: that we should overcome at all costs all prejudices stemming from tradition and authority, since this is the only way to attain objective, scientific knowledge. Gadamer subtly shows that the Enlightenment, which proudly pretends to be free of prejudices, is actually the victim of an unacknowledged prejudice—namely, the prejudice against prejudices. Contrary to a widespread belief, Gadamer doesn't argue here *against* enlightenment, since he provides an enlightenment of the Enlightenment itself and its hidden prejudice against prejudice which fails to acknowledge that prejudgments handed down by tradition and authority can contain a recognizable element of reason. The issue is not whether we should be free of prejudices or not, since they are always at play in our understanding. Reason is always situated. The issue, rather, is how we can come to develop the prejudices that are valid, that is, conducive to understanding, and distinguish them from bad prejudices that lead us astray.

The best answer to this question in *Truth and Method* is that temporal distance is most helpful in carrying out this task (*TM*, 309)—that is, over the long run, bad prejudices will come to be proven false because they would be unstainable. Gadamer seems to display here a lot of confidence in the work of history, which is certainly a Hegelian trait of his. His strong conviction is indeed that all our understanding is carried and rendered possible by this work of history, the *Wirkungsgeschichte*. A hermeneutically schooled consciousness thus needs to take into account this working of history and at the same time, as alluded to above, become conscious of the limits of such a consciousness. This is the grand double, if not triple and even quadruple meaning of his famous *wirkungsgeschichtliches Bewusstsein*, "historically effected consciousness," that is, (1) the consciousness of the work of history that precedes our understanding, that makes it possible and *that we can sort out*; (2) the *consciousness of the limits* of this raising-to-consciousness of this work of history; (3) the notion that *our consciousness* itself or openness to the world is *always a product of the work of history*; and (4) the *awareness of this fact* and thus of the limits of consciousness in general. To be historical, Gadamer concludes, means that one's being cannot become fully transparent in self-knowledge (*Geschichtlichsein heißt, nie im Sichwissen aufgehen*) (*TM*, 313/307). This historically effected consciousness is, as Gadamer felicitously says (at least in German, since much is lost in translation), *mehr Sein als Bewusstsein*,[6] more a matter of what we are (*Sein*) than of what we can become conscious (*Bewusstsein*) of, and this is precisely what one should be conscious of.

This consciousness leads us to rediscover the main and forgotten problem of hermeneutics—namely, that of application (TM II.2.2). Gadamer's idea is that every understanding involves an element of application to the present, whether this understanding occurs in the humanities or in everyday life. (The difference between the two types of understanding will increasingly fade in the rest of the book, in the process of the expanding universality of the hermeneutic question.) Understanding of the past always occurs in the here and now, by an interpreter that is as much the product of the past at work in its understanding as of his or her own times. To anticipate what Part III will stress, this element of application shows itself in the fact that understanding must always explain and translate in its own words what it understands. One needs, however, to correct a common misunderstanding related to this stress on the applicative element of understanding: Gadamer never says that one should *strive* to apply what we understand to the present or that we should be on the lookout for contemporary applications of what we understand in order to give it more resonance, relevance, or actuality. His point is more basic: Even when we seek to understand what an author of the past has said or what a past event means, as do all philologists and historians, there is an element of application involved, in that it is *we* who bring out this meaning in a language we understand. This application happens "over and above our wanting and doing" (*TM*, xxvi), as Gadamer's rightly famous phrase has it.

Nonetheless, one might fear that this insistence on the present might lead to some form of relativism. This is why Gadamer relies on two important models to suggest that an understanding that recognizes this involvement of the present *and* history can achieve binding truth: the ethics of Aristotle and the wisdom of jurisprudence. The interest of Aristotle's ethics is that it shows that ethical virtue (*phronesis*) always has to do with what needs to be done in the here and now. Its task is not theoretical or epistemic. It is practical—it is concerned with what it is that needs to be done—and tied to the present situation because we never act in the abstract. Nonetheless, the distinction between what is right and what is wrong can still and must always be made, and it will be recognized as such by the prudent person. It is important for Gadamer to stress that this ethical virtue of prudence can never be detached from the being of those who are involved in that situation. Ethical virtue is also more Being (and acting) than consciousness: it is more a matter of what we are and how we act than it is something of which we are abstractly conscious. It can never be severed from our interest in the matter—we are always concerned by what is good—nor from our sense of what is good.

For jurisprudence, the issue of application is also front and center since the task of the judge is to apply the law to a given situation. A just ruling is one that does justice to the particular situation at hand that needs to be resolved. To fail to take into account the specific requirements of the present case would be to commit a grave injustice.[7] For this jurists rely on their good judgment but also on the productive bearing of precedent applications of the law that is wisely called jurisprudence. The fact that the law has been applied differently in the past is not a testimony to the "relativism" of judicial decisions; it is, on the contrary, a sign that justice, and binding justice with practical consequences, was sought in each specific case. The different application of the law in each case is not an impediment to truth; it is how truth happens.

Having thus rediscovered the fundamental hermeneutical problem—that of application and its positive historical dimension—Gadamer goes on to draw philosophical lessons from this historically effected consciousness (TM II.2.3). He is mistrustful of the philosophy of reflection (without always naming who he is thinking of in this regard) that would be quick to stigmatize the relativism and the self-contradiction that his position would seem to imply. The reflective argument goes something like this: Gadamer appears to claim that all understanding involves application and is thus relative, but this claim wants to hold universally and thus refutes itself. These are mere intellectual games, Gadamer contends, that do not affect the reality of our Being and its historically situated consciousness.[8]

It is more important for him to stress that the insights of historically effected consciousness impart to us a specific type of experience—that of our own historicity and finitude. Its quintessence was expressed by the tragic Aeschylus, a silent muse throughout all Gadamer's thinking,[9] in his saying *pathei mathos*, "one learns through suffering." This, Gadamer pointedly says, is the essence of the hermeneutic experience. It calls into question everything that we thought we knew and leads us to ask questions. In this questioning Gadamer also sees the fruits of a true humanist upbringing: it consists less in providing us with easy, one-size-fits-all answers than in enabling us to raise questions and to question everything we think we know. Here we find in Gadamer an echo of the Socratic way of questioning. It also leads him to his final theme—namely, language. If questioning occurs in language, might it not be that the fusion of horizons that happens in all understanding is the silent work of language?

6. PART III: THE ONTOLOGICAL SHIFT OF HERMENEUTICS GUIDED BY LANGUAGE

When Gadamer explores the thicket of language in Part III, he is fully aware that he is approaching one of the most difficult and obscure themes, one which was also a relatively new territory in philosophy at the time. Philosophy was more preoccupied with concepts and issues of epistemology and did not pay much attention to language. Language was seen as a mere instrument of thought or communication, and thus as secondary to thinking itself. There is a reason, a *fundamentum in re*, for the fact that language did not become thematic, and Gadamer names it at the outset of his inquiry: the linguistic element is our thinking so "uncannily near" (*TM*, 386) that it doesn't appear as a distinct object and so conceals its own Being out of itself.[10] This "self-forgottenness" is part and parcel of the way language is and how it operates.

Gadamer's guiding thread is that the fusion of horizons that happens in understanding is actually the accomplishment of language (*TM*, 386). Gadamer immediately shows this by focusing on his two favorite examples of understanding, the one that happens when we understand a text and the one that happens in a dialogue or conversation (when one reaches an "understanding"). When I understand a text, I make it speak. There is thus a fusion between understanding and my explanation or interpretation of it. Negatively put, I don't understand unless I can put this understanding into words. The same thing happens when two persons come to an agreement or an understanding: something 'speaks' for the agreement and the interlocutors themselves understand what 'speaks' for it. In both instances, Gadamer observes, understanding necessarily unfolds in a linguistic manner, however, not in the sense that the understanding "is subsequently put to words," but in such a way that understanding realizes itself in the coming-to-language of the thing itself (*vielmehr ist die Vollzugsweise des Verstehens . . . das Zur-Sprache-kommen der Sache selbst*) (*TM*, 386/384).

This thesis has two far-reaching consequences: (1) there is an essential link, indeed a fusion, between understanding and its linguistic unfolding, and (2) there is a fusion between what is understood (Being or the thing itself) and its linguistic expression. The grand thesis is thus that language determines the hermeneutic process (i.e., understanding) and its object (i.e., Being). Negatively put, there is no understanding without the linguistic dimension, and Being is itself linked to language (an idea that is perhaps less intuitive than the first). Both ground the universality claim of hermeneutics, which has to be understood as a thesis on the essentially linguistic character of (1) understanding and (2) Being itself.

One has to note that Gadamer speaks here less of language (*Sprache*) than of the linguistic element or dimension (*Sprachlichkeit* or linguisticality). What he understands by linguisticality is not only the language of words and actual sentences, it is also the language of gestures, non-verbal expressions, and silences. Linguisticality pertains to any meaningful articulation that can be followed and understood because it means something. Our relation to the world, Gadamer argues, is one of understanding and is thus *sprachlich*, geared toward language and searching for language.

Let's decompose Gadamer's thesis into its two decisive parts, as a thesis on the linguistic nature of understanding and of Being:

(1) Is all understanding geared toward language? What about the limits of language to say what we feel or want to convey? Gadamer considers this objection and even uses it to proclaim for the first time the universality of hermeneutics. He points out, first of all, that any objection or queries about language and its limits can only be expressed in the medium of language. Language thus forestalls (*überholt*) any objection to its competence, so that its universality keeps pace with the universality of reason (*TM*, 419). Like reason, language can account for, express, and encompass all that we strive to understand. He argues, second, that queries about the alleged limits of language only single out the limits of given expressions—that is, of expressions that are too sclerotic, wooden, or ideologically loaded—and we can always attempt to overcome these by finding better expressions.

The link between the universality of hermeneutics and that of reason is here important since it entails, and Gadamer states it in remarkably clear terms, that "there are basically no limits to our understanding" (*TM*, 420) and to the linguistic expression of this understanding. Instead of focusing on the boundaries and constraints of language, which are real but can be overcome, Gadamer stresses the opposite: Language, and hence our understanding (since all understanding is oriented toward language), is open to everything that can be understood. This generous view entails the universal *possibility* of understanding, of mutual understanding, and of translation: Every foreign meaning can, to a certain degree, be translated into a language we understand, just as our stammering language can be rendered in other ways. This also implies, refreshingly, that cultures can understand one another and open themselves to what is foreign. In this age of globalization and intercultural dialogue, this is one of the precious insights of the class act that is *Truth and Method*.

(2) Yet Gadamer's universal thesis is not only a *thesis on the essentially linguistic dimension* of our understanding and its openness to everything that can be understood; it is also a *thesis on Being*, which Gadamer expresses in his famous dictum "*Being that can be understood is language*" (*TM*, 490, emphasis original). It is a more difficult thesis since Gadamer becomes here more speculative, drawing heavily on the metaphysical tradition, especially the medieval doctrine of the transcendentals and its sources in Plato's metaphysics of light and the Beautiful.[11] These are sources that are generally not too familiar to contemporary specialists in continental philosophy, many of whom mistakenly think that hermeneutics is post- if not anti-metaphysical.

Gadamer does here take a metaphysical turn of sorts, already indicated in the title of Part III that heralds an "*ontological* shift [*Wendung*] of hermeneutics following the lead of language" and in the title of the final section of

Part III, "Language as the horizon of a hermeneutical *ontology*." In what does Gadamer's ontology or thesis on Being consist?

It is obvious enough that here Gadamer goes beyond the original focus of his book—namely, that of an appropriate hermeneutics of the humanities. He already did so by defending his thesis on the necessarily linguistic nature of our understanding in Part III. He now ventures beyond this thesis on human understanding to speak of Being, since, as he states *right after* his famous dictum *Being that can be understood is language*:

> The hermeneutical phenomenon [i.e., understanding] projects (*wirft zurück*) as it were [*gleichsam*, not translated in the English version] its own universality back unto the ontological constitution of what is understood, by determining it in a universal sense as language and determining its own relation to beings as interpretation. (*TM*, 490/478)

This is an all-important sentence since it explains the meaning of Gadamer's dictum it immediately follows.

The idea that Being *is* language is thus something of (*gleichsam*!) a retro-projection (*zurückwerfen*) on Being on the part of our understanding. This might raise the question that Gadamer is not really leaving the scope of understanding after all. Actually, his focus is on the *belonging together* of language and Being, of I and world (*TM*, 490). In order to explain what this means, Gadamer relies on the medieval metaphysics of the transcendentals and Plato's metaphysics of the Beautiful. From the first, he learns that the universal attributes of Being, that is, truth, unity, beauty, and oneness, are not qualifications that our understanding would bestow or project upon Being but predicates of Being itself. For medieval thinkers, this was the case *because* Being had been *created* as such by God. Gadamer does not (nor can he from his premises) take up the notion that Being was created as such by God (even though this was an *essential* component of the medieval doctrine). He only retains the insistence of the medieval doctrine on the fact that our knowledge or understanding, when it speaks of Being, does not, as it were, stand in front of or apart from Being; rather, it is inserted (*einbezogen*) into it, and what it says springs from it. Our language, he says after explaining his notorious dictum, is thus the language of things (*TM*, 490) more than it is that of our thinking.[12] What is said of Being would not primarily be an injection on the part of our understanding (say, by the framing of our linguistic or conceptual schemes), it is Being as it presents itself in our understanding.

This is precisely the element that Gadamer's reliance on Plato's metaphysics of the Beautiful means to highlight. For Plato, it is in the nature of the Beautiful to shine through things, indeed to be the *ekphanestaton*, which is the most radiant of all. Gadamer recognizes—with a tinge of Plato, Hegel (as the *Logic of Essence* puts it: Being presents itself and is reflected in its essence), and Heidegger (Being as *aletheia* or self-uncovering)—this shining capacity in Being itself by saying, in the simplest of terms really, that Being is presentation and thus language: *"Being is language, i.e., self-presentation"* (*TM*, 502, emphasis original). And this language happens to be the language that we apprehend when we speak (*TM*, 492).

This is indeed a strong universal and ontological thesis. Gadamer's risky maneuver consists here in defending a thoroughly metaphysical thesis (i.e., Being is language and it is Being itself that presents itself in our language) by relying massively on metaphysics (i.e., the medieval transcendentals and Plato's metaphysics of light and the Beautiful) without explicitly taking up the metaphysics that underpins his argument. It is, as I have argued elsewhere,[13] a difficult balancing act, and it is to Gadamer's credit that he attempted it, especially given that he was a pupil of Heidegger, whose misgivings about metaphysical thinking are well-known.

Yet, after this brave and at the same time timid incursion into metaphysical thinking, Gadamer finally recoils, in the sacred name of finitude, from the metaphysics that supports his claim and appears content with its hermeneutical translation, that is, the notion that it is Being that shines forth in our understanding and language. His thesis is finally not one on Being itself but on the *belonging together* of understanding and Being, of I and world (*TM*, 490), of subject and object (*TM*, 477). The universal ontology he offers is that of this *Zusammengehörigkeit* or togetherness of Being and understanding. Just as the artwork has to be seen ontologically as an emanation from its model, language would be the self-presentation of Being in our understanding. Modernity, he argues, put the emphasis too much on our understanding and its ordering capacities. To counter its constructivism he relies, on the one hand, on medieval metaphysics and its emphasis on the insertion of the subject into Being. On the other hand, against a too strong emphasis on Being or Being itself, he highlights the notion that this language of Being is "not the *logos ousias* (the language of Being itself), but the language that our finite, historical nature apprehends when we learn to speak" (*TM*, 492). The courageous breakthrough here lies in the recognition that our understanding, knowledge, and language are not, as moderns like to profess, constructions of the subject but rather reflections of Being itself. Hermeneutics thus leads to an ontology, even to a metaphysics.

NOTES

1. See Jean Grondin, *Hans-Georg Gadamer: A Biography* (New Haven: Yale University Press, 2003), 277.

2. See Martin Avenarius, "Universelle Hermeneutik und Praxis des Rechtshistorikers und Juristen. Die Entwicklung ihres Verhältnisses im Lichte der Diskussion zwischen Gadamer und Wieacker," in *Juristische Hermeneutik zwischen Vergangenheit und Zukunft*, ed. Stephan Meder/Gaetano Calizzi/Christoph-Eric Mecke/Christoph Sorge (Baden-Baden: Nomos Verlag, 2013), 66.

3. Hans-Georg Gadamer, *Truth and Method*, 2nd ed., trans. Joel Weinsheimer and Donald G. Marshall (New York: Bloomsbury Publishing, 2013), xxii. Hereafter cited in text as *TM*. Where the German is cited or the translation has been altered, the page number of the original is indicated after the slash. The latter refer to Hans-Georg Gadamer, *Wahrheit und Methode*, Gesammelte Werke I (Tübingen: Mohr Siebeck, 1990).

4. That Dilthey's project can be seen differently has always been stressed by the specialists of his work. On this, see Jean Grondin, "Dilthey's Hermeneutics and Philosophical Hermeneutics," in *Interpreting Dilthey. Critical Essays*, ed. Eric Nelson (Cambridge: Cambridge University Press, 2019).

5. This was first seen by Pierre Fruchon: "The three parts of TM are embedded into one another like three concentrical circles: the first is embedded into the second by showing that art is not a sensual enjoyment but a temporal encounter with meaning, whereas the second is logged into the third by discovering that understanding occurs as language." "Herméneutique, langage et ontologie. Un discernement du platonisme chez H.-G. Gadamer," *Archives de philosophie* 36 (1973): 532.

6. Hans-Georg Gadamer, "Rhetorik, Hermeneutik und Ideologiekritik," in *Gesammelte Werke, Bd. 2: Hermeneutik II* (Tübingen: Mohr Siebeck, 1993), 247.

7. See Jean Grondin, "Gadamer's Interest for Legal Hermeneutics," *Law's Hermeneutics: Other Investigations*, ed. Simone Glanert and F. Girard (New York: Routledge, 2017).

8. One should not in a panicked hurry to defend Gadamer against the charge of relativism, as is common in the literature. There is such as a thing as a *healthy relativism*, that is, one that recognizes the obvious fact that different persons and different times can understand differently. Human cohabitation would be much enhanced if everyone would recognize this. But this is not the same as claiming that there is no truth or no justice and that hence "all is relative."

9. One has to think of Gadamer's important lecture "Prometheus and the Tragedy of Culture," in which he ponders Aeschylus' take on the myth of Prometheus. ("Prometheus und die Tragödie der Kultur," in *Gesammelte Werke, Bd. 9: Ästhetik und Poetik II: Hermeneutik im Vollzug* [Tübingen: Mohr Siebeck, 1993], 151–60.) Aeschylus' idea is that it is by making them forget about the hour of their death that Prometheus really brought culture and the arts to the humans, thus liberating them and enabling them to project themselves in the future. Gadamer speaks of a *tragedy* of culture since it is built on a form of forgetfulness of fatality. Published in 1946, the lecture was delivered in 1944 in Dresden, of all places. In a strong formulation, he says that *pathei mathos* expresses "in its metaphysical significance the inner historicity of experience" (*TM*, 365)—that is, Aeschylus understood it better than all those in the nineteenth and twentieth centuries who reflected on historicity and tried to circumvent it.

10. The English translation of this passage needs to be corrected. It states that language "conceals its Being from us." The text does not say "from us" (*von uns*), but *von sich aus*, "from itself." One must thus read: "conceals its Being out of itself."

11. To understand the important significance of these ideas and the extent to which Gadamer relies on them, see Jean Grondin, "The Universality of Hermeneutic Understanding: The Strong, Somewhat Metaphysical Conclusion of *Truth and Method*," in *The Gadamerian Mind*, ed. Ted George and Gert-Jan van der Heiden (London: Routledge, 2021).

12. See also the piece he published in 1960, "The Nature of Things and the Language of Things," in *Philosophical Hermeneutics*, trans. David E. Linge (Berkeley: University of California Press, 1976).

13. Grondin, "The Universality of Hermeneutic Understanding."

Part I

ART

Chapter 1

TM I.1.1

Gadamer on the Significance of the Humanist Tradition for the Human Sciences, or Truth and Edification

Theodore George

Gadamer's concern in *Truth and Method*, as he tells us in the introduction to the first edition, is to clarify the legitimacy of a certain kind of knowledge—one that, as he puts it, arises from an "experience of truth that transcends the domain of scientific method."[1] He characterizes this other experience of truth as 'hermeneutical.' Hermeneutics, as we recall, is the study of how we are able to understand something as a result of interpretation. In this context, when we say that we understand, what we mean is that our efforts to interpret something have really gotten to matters at issue (in German, *die Sachen*). Likewise, when we say that we do not understand, we mean that our efforts to interpret something have not yet brought such matters fully into focus. For example, in our interpretation of a conversation we have with a friend, we may come to understand something about, say, mortality in result of our efforts to interpret the significance of her decisions about end-of-life care. Gadamer's concern for the hermeneutical experience of truth is thus the truth of interpretive understanding.[2]

It is precisely Gadamer's concern for such hermeneutical experience of truth that guides his philosophical considerations of the human sciences. The English term *human sciences* is a somewhat strained translation of the German *Geisteswissenschaften*, so that the term designates about the same family of academic disciplines as John Stuart Mill first designated in English with the term *moral sciences* or that is designated today by the French *lettres* or the English *humanities*. The human sciences, then, comprise disciplines such as philosophy, the arts and literature, and the study of history, as well as certain humanistic areas of inquiry in disciplines like anthropology or psychology. Gadamer's philosophical concern for the 'hermeneutical' experience of truth leads him to a consideration of the human sciences because it is precisely these disciplines that focus on truths that we come to understand through interpretation. In the study of art or history, for example, the truths we discover, if we discover them at all, are discovered through the interpretation of an artwork or of the available testimonies of a historical person or event.

Yet, as Gadamer maintains, the prestige of modern science has led to the neglect—even the disregard—of the experience of truth at issue in the human sciences. Today we typically measure the truthfulness of knowledge claims by the normative ideal of what goes by the name of *scientific method*. In this, we take the gold standard of knowledge to be a belief whose truth has been secured through scientific methodological procedures such as a repeatable experiment; any other measure of truth is at best a silver standard, at worst, fool's gold. Given this view of the gold standard for knowledge, the experience of truth at issue in the human sciences comes to be obscured, since, after all, as Gadamer points out, the human sciences are "connected with modes of experience ... in which a truth is communicated that cannot be verified by the methodological means proper to science" (*TM*, xxi). Gadamer observes that in philosophy, too, the prestige of modern science has had an influence. In philosophy, the normative ideal of the scientific method has attained such "dominance" that "in the philosophical elucidation and justification of the concept of knowledge and the concept of truth" the question of the experience of truth at issue in the human sciences "does not" even "appear legitimate" at all (*TM*, xx).

Gadamer believes that because of the current neglect of, even disregard for, the experience of truth at issue in the human sciences, his concern to justify this experience of truth has to begin with a step back, providing a preliminary recovery of the sense of this experience of truth. It is precisely the purpose of section I.1.1, "The Significance of the Humanist Tradition for the Human Sciences," to initiate this recovery. Gadamer, as we shall see, maintains in this section that we can start to recover a sense for the experience of truth at issue in the human sciences through a consideration of the "guiding concepts" of the humanist tradition—namely, the concept of education or edification (*Bildung*) and the related ideas of common sense, judgment, and taste.[3] In this, as I shall argue, Gadamer recovers a sense for the hermeneutical experience of truth that, far from being inspired by the normative ideal of the scientific *method*, is instead made possible precisely by *edification*.

1. UNDERSTANDING THE HUMAN SCIENCES

Gadamer, then, maintains that we can begin to recover a sense for the experience of truth at issue in the human sciences through a return to the guiding concepts of the humanist tradition. He believes that this recovery is necessary because, over the course of the nineteenth century and into our times, the human sciences have themselves lost touch with this sense of truth. The issue, as Gadamer maintains, is that the human sciences have lost touch with this experience of truth because they have attempted to understand themselves on "the model of the natural sciences" (*TM*, 3). With this, the human sciences have become obsessed with the concern, typical of the natural sciences, to justify the validity of their claims in terms of firm methodological foundations. Gadamer's position is that the recovery of the experience of truth at issue in the human sciences through a return to the humanist tradition will, at the same time, save them from themselves—from their misguided attempt to understand themselves on the basis of a comparison with the natural sciences, as well as their normative idealization of method.

Gadamer develops his position in reference to the German tradition of the human sciences since the nineteenth century in particular, but it is not difficult to extrapolate that his point has significance for the wider range of humanistic inquiry in the modern Western world. He suggests, in any case, that the obsession in the German tradition with the model of the natural sciences is discernible already in the German translation of John Stuart Mill's 1843 *System of Logic*. In this translation, the German term *Geisteswissenschaften* is used for Mill's English term *moral sciences* (*TM*, 3). Much more is imported into the German tradition, however, than just an English term. With this import comes a significant assumption from the tradition of British empiricism about the very purpose of the human sciences themselves. This is the assumption that, on the model of the natural sciences, the purpose of the human sciences, too, is to explain, or, more specifically, to provide explanations that will allow us to predict the behavior of objects of inquiry on the basis of inductive methods of research. As Gadamer puts it, the human sciences come to be misguidedly "concerned with establishing similarities, regularities, and conformities to law which would make it possible to predict individual phenomena and processes" (*TM*, 4–5).

To import the purpose of the natural sciences into the human sciences, however, fully misses—or worse, alters or distorts—the very point of inquiry in the human sciences. In the natural sciences, the purpose of explaining, and, in turn, predicting the behavior of objects of inquiry presupposes that these objects are members of a class of objects with the same relevant properties. In natural science, an individual phenomenon is treated as a token or 'an instance of.' For example, in celestial mechanics, the "favoured paradigm for the origin of the solar system," which itself traces to scientific models developed by Immanuel Kant and Pierre-Simon Laplace, involves the formation of the sun through a process that begins with the collapse of a portion of an interstellar cloud.[4] Here the purpose of the model is to explain the current form that the sun takes, as well as to predict the origination of other stars and perhaps also to predict related phenomena, such as the expiration of the sun or other stars. But in this we interpret our power to explain and to predict as dependent on our consideration of the sun as a star—that is, as a member of a class of objects that have the same relevant properties. The sun is 'an instance of ' a star.

The purpose of the human sciences, however, is different. Whereas the purpose of the natural sciences is to provide an explanation that will allow us to predict the behavior of something, itself grasped as 'an instance of,' the purpose of the human sciences, by contrast, is to understand a human experience precisely as a unique phenomenon, a *this*. Gadamer writes that in the human sciences, such as the study of history,

> The individual case does not serve only to confirm a law from which practical predictions can be made. Its ideal is rather to understand the phenomenon itself in its unique and historical concreteness. However much experiential universals are involved, the aim is not to confirm and extend these universalized experiences in order to attain knowledge of a law—e.g., how men, peoples, and states evolve—but to understand how this man, this people, or this state is what it has become or, more generally, how it happened that it is so. (*TM*, 4)

The purpose of the human sciences is not to explain or predict human behavior as 'an instance of ,' but, instead, to understand *this* unique human situation. Indeed, as Gadamer suggests, the model of the natural sciences anticipates, and better suits, modern social science than the human sciences. In the social sciences, the purpose really is, typically, to explain regularities in human society that will allow us to predict human behavior. In this, human individuals are treated precisely as 'instances of' human beings; or, if the inquiry concerns a human group, then, the group is treated as an 'instance of' human groups. The purpose of the human sciences, by contrast, is not to explain human behavior but to understand a unique human situation, precisely in its unique concreteness.

Gadamer recognizes that not all German intellectuals of the nineteenth century attempt to import the purpose of the natural sciences into the human sciences. But even for those who do not, the model of the natural sciences still looms large—this time, as a model of the justification of beliefs on the basis of method. In modernity, the natural sciences are distinguished not only by the purpose of providing explanations that allow us to predict the behavior of their objects of inquiry. The natural sciences are also distinguished by a certain normative ideal—namely, that the validity of a belief is to be measured by the method through which that belief was attained. Gadamer observes that even if some German intellectuals of the nineteenth century recognize the distinct purpose of the human sciences, they nevertheless introduce this methodological ideal as a measure for humanistic inquiry. Gadamer cites as an early example of an 1862 lecture given by the renowned German physicist Hermann von Helmholtz. Helmholtz lauds the significance of the human sciences, and, moreover, introduces an important, if underdeveloped, claim by arguing that research in the human sciences depends on tact and historical memory. But in Helmholtz, the human sciences nevertheless come to be defined negatively because they fail to meet the "methodological ideal of the natural sciences." Because the human sciences fail to meet this ideal, they remain inexact, as claims made in the human sciences derive from methods that are not "logical" but rather "artistic-instinctive" (*TM*, 5).

Helmholtz, it seems, embodies a sentiment that still echoes today. The human sciences, as we sometimes hear now, concern matters that are, without question, of great importance; but, given that they do not meet the methodological ideal of the natural sciences, the results of humanistic inquiry remain imprecise and thus also less conclusive, perhaps even partial or subjective.

Gadamer suggests that in Germany of the nineteenth century, the concern to replicate the methodological ideal of the natural sciences within the context of the human sciences reaches a summit in the so-called historical school (*TM*, 5). By this school, Gadamer has in mind a nineteenth- and early twentieth-century intellectual movement that no longer treated "human nature, morality, and reason as absolute, eternal, and universal," but sought, instead, to grasp these as "relative, changing, and particular" because shaped by historical context.[5] Gadamer observes that in order to replicate the methodological ideal of the natural sciences, important but now largely neglected intellectuals, such as J. G. Droysen and Wilhelm Dilthey, sought to establish the methodological independence of the human sciences. Especially influential was Dilthey's attempt to establish this methodological independence through a (never completed) critique of historical reason that would secure the epistemological foundations of research in the human sciences.[6]

Even in this, though, Dilthey continues to uphold the methodological ideal of the natural sciences. Gadamer provides only cursory evidence of his claim against Dilthey, but the idea is that Dilthey retains tell-tale signs of the methodological ideal of the natural sciences, such as the idea that research methods should ensure detachment from objects of inquiry in order to safeguard objectivity and that methods should enhance our control over the world we find ourselves in (*TM*, 6–7). Gadamer concludes that, attempts of the historical school notwithstanding, very little came of the concern to replicate the methodological ideal of the natural sciences. He writes, for example,

> However strongly Dilthey defended the epistemological independence of the human sciences, what is called "method" in modern science remains the same

everywhere and is only displayed in especially exemplary form in the natural sciences. The human sciences have no method of their own. (*TM*, 7)

Yet for Gadamer, this failure of the historical school does not call for the renewed pursuit of a methodological ideal distinctive to the human sciences. Quite to the contrary, this failure is evidence that the attempt to determine such a methodological ideal is misguided in the first place. What is called for, instead, is a justification of the human sciences that remains more attentive to the distinctive character, the scope and limits, of humanistic inquiry in the first place. Gadamer maintains that in the nineteenth-century Germany, the human sciences retain traces of such a justification. But, as he argues, these traces are owing to the legacy of humanism passed down from the German classicism of the previous century. Of nineteenth-century Germany, he writes that "possessed of the intellectual heritage of German classicism," the human sciences "carried forward the proud awareness that they were the true representatives of humanism" (*TM*, 8). In view of this, Gadamer believes that the justification of the human sciences turns not on any methodological ideal, but rather should be sought in a very different ideal—one that humanists of the previous century believed should guide humanistic inquiry in the first place. This is the ideal of *edification* (*Bildung*), the "concept which is the atmosphere breathed by the human sciences in the nineteenth century" (*TM*, 9).

2. TRUTH AND EDIFICATION

Gadamer clarifies the humanist ideal of edification (*Bildung*) in reference to the fuller meaning that the concept acquired in eighteenth-century German classicism. He observes that, outwardly at least, the German *Bildung* is comparable to *Kultur*, a German word derived from the Latin *cultura*. *Bildung*, like *Kultur*, refers primarily to "the properly human manner of developing one's natural talents" (*TM*, 10). Yet, as Gadamer argues, in German classism, *Bildung* comes to signify much more than the education necessary for competency in one vocation or another, say, as with the Latin *cultura*, competency in agriculture. Rather, *Bildung* concerns something more holistic that, with Wilhelm von Humboldt, is at once "higher and more inward"—namely, our vocation as human beings (*TM*, 10). In German classicism, then, the humanist entreaty to elevate ourselves up into our humanity can be understood as a matter of the pursuit of our vocation as human beings in *Bildung*.

Yet in this, the German *Bildung* differs not only from *Kultur* and its Latin origin, *cultura*, but, moreover, from the Latin *formatio*. The Latin *formatio* suggests, almost of itself, that the entreaty to elevate ourselves into our humanity is concerned with a form—that is, a pre-established form of the human being, so that the purpose of *formatio* is to make of ourselves 'an instance of' that form. Gadamer argues, however, that the German *Bildung* resists this idea, stressing instead a complex ambiguity involved in the process of the elevation of ourselves into our humanity. The word *Bildung* is derived from the verb *bilden*, to form, fashion, shape, or mold. But it also contains the related noun *Bild*, a picture or image, and is related to *Vorbild*, a model or example, and *Nachbild*, a copy or imitation (*TM*, 10). Accordingly, the German *Bildung* suggests not an education determined in advance by a pregiven form, but instead a process, one that shapes us through a complex interplay of images, examples, and imitation.

Gadamer's differentiation of the humanist concept of *Bildung* from that of *formatio* speaks to one of the most important interpretive difficulties of *Truth and Method*—namely, Gadamer's relation to Heidegger. On the one hand, Gadamer tells us that his project in *Truth and Method* is none other than to develop further Heidegger's existentialism. Yet, on the other hand, Gadamer develops Heidegger's discovery in reference to the very tradition of humanism that Heidegger's existentialism leads him to reject. What can we make of this? Heidegger, in his "Letter on Humanism," argues that the humanist entreaty to elevate ourselves into our humanity is typically founded on a pregiven form or essence of the human being.[7] When humanists call upon us to elevate ourselves, what they typically mean is that we should make of ourselves 'an instance of' an essence, whether this essence is identified as a rational animal or in some other manner.[8] Gadamer's differentiation of the humanist concept of *Bildung* from *formatio* suggests a rather subtle, and perhaps even overly diplomatic, reply to his mentor. It may be that a humanism of *formatio*, of molding ourselves into the form of the human being, is essentialist. But a humanism of *Bildung* is different. Even if the humanists in German classicism themselves only partially grasped the implications of this difference, the word involves an ambiguity of meaning that opens up the possibility of humanism that is otherwise than essentialist.[9]

Gadamer maintains that the elevation of ourselves to our humanity through *Bildung* represents a kind of growth. This becomes especially evident in his claim that "it is not accidental that . . . the word Bildung resembles the Greek physis" (*TM*, 10). The Greek *physis* is difficult to translate. The word is usually put into English as *nature*, but *physis* brings into focus the potency, dynamism, and vitality we associate with nature, so that it connotes especially the unbidden force and movement of natural phenomena, of birth, growth, and death. While *Bildung* is a process that we consciously undertake and not one that happens unconsciously, *Bildung* is nevertheless comparable to a process of natural growth. For, as in natural growth, "Bildung has no goals outside of itself" (*TM*, 11).

Bildung can therefore be contrasted with aspects of our lives that we can form or cultivate technically. In such matters, when we reach our end, the means we have used to reach it proves to be unnecessary and is readily forgotten. Gadamer, in illustration, considers the end of forming or cultivating a foreign language. In order to reach this end, we may employ as means any number of technical devices, from tables of verb conjugations to pneumonic tricks. Once we reach our end and actually acquire fluency in the foreign language, however, we are no longer in need of these means, and we leave them behind. By contrast, in *Bildung* the process by which we learn something is preserved, becoming a part of who we are. For example, if I come to understand, say, the *hubris* of some of my poorer life decisions by reading a Greek tragedy, what I thus learn (if I have really learned it) remains with me, and it becomes part of who I am: it helps to shape my understanding of myself, who I have been and who I wish to become, and, moving forward, it can even help me to make different, perhaps better, decisions. Gadamer writes,

> In Bildung . . . that by which and through which one is formed becomes completely one's own. . . . What is absorbed is not like a means that has lost its function. Rather, in acquired Bildung, nothing disappears, but everything is preserved. (*TM*, 11)

Even if *Bildung* can be understood as akin to *physis* or natural growth, however, *Bildung* is a "genuinely historical idea" (*TM*, 11). Because in *Bildung* what we acquire becomes our own and thus preserved, the process of *Bildung* is cumulative, a matter of memory that takes on historical proportions. When I come to understand something about the *hubris* of my life decisions by reading a Greek tragedy, its remaining with me is a figure of memory. But this memory itself has a historical dimension. What remains with me has been acquired through my reading of a Greek tragedy, an artwork that has been preserved thanks to a process of historical transmission that spans millennia. In this, what stays with me from my reading of the Greek tragedy is really something that has stayed with the community, and the tradition that informs it, from the distant past.

Gadamer clarifies the concept of *Bildung* as a historical reference, initially at least, on the model of G. W. F. Hegel's philosophy. Hegel, like others in German classicism, is concerned for our elevation of ourselves to humanity through *Bildung*. Hegel conceives of this elevation to humanity as becoming conscious of a universal perspective, one that allows us to see ourselves in light of the general conditions encompassing our individual existence. *Bildung* is precisely the process of becoming conscious of this universal perspective. Within this context, *Bildung* proceeds through experiences of the world that, initially at least, frustrate our interests and perspectives so that, by steps, we wrest ourselves from our limited perspective and slowly become conscious of ourselves in light of the universal conditions of our existence. The process of becoming conscious of these universal conditions is historical, however, because in our encounter with this universality in our experience of the world outside us, the world itself is shaped by tradition. Gadamer writes,

> Every single individual who raises himself out of his natural being to the spiritual finds in the language, customs, and institutions of his people a pre-given body of material which, as in learning to speak, he has to make his own. (*TM*, 13)

Here the elevation of ourselves to our humanity unfolds as a process of becoming conscious of an increasingly universal perspective through our experiences of tradition.

Gadamer's name for the ideal of our elevation of ourselves to a universal perspective through edification is, simply enough, the edified person (*das Gebildete*). Yet this ideal is not the completion of our edification, at least not in the sense of a conclusion of our edification. Indeed, in this Gadamer departs from Hegel. Hegel holds that the completion of edification is the achievement of absolute knowledge. There is much debate in Hegel studies about what he means by this term. But Gadamer, in accord with a consensus of continental European intellectuals of his era, takes Hegel to mean the achievement of a conclusive universal perspective, one that ends our need for further edification because it is unconditioned, giving us an intellectual mastery over the world. Gadamer, by contrast, believes that the idea of being an edified person is better grasped as a transition to a "mature state" (*TM*, 14). In reaching this mature state we become so edified that edification itself becomes what the ancient Greeks would have called an *ethos*, the basic organization of our character, our core beliefs and our way of being. Thus, in this mature state, when edification has become our *ethos*, we come to be in full possession of our possibilities to pursue further edification. Certainly, we are, even as children, able by degrees to pursue our own edification. But it is only once we have reached a certain maturity, a certain *Niveau* of edification, that we are fully able to learn and learn again.

Gadamer's position is that this mature state, the *ethos* of the edified person, makes possible the experience of truth at issue in the human sciences. In the human sciences, this *ethos* takes shape as what he, again with Helmholtz, initially describes as the "*tact*" of humanistic inquiry (*TM*, 14). In this, the universal perspective achieved through edification is conceived not as a form of absolute knowing but instead as a sense that grants us a "special free mobility," or, in Helmholtz's words, a "readiness" to understand the "most varied" of human experiences (*TM*, 14).[10] Indeed, this universal sense, grasped in terms of tact, becomes the "element" in which humanistic inquiries "move." Gadamer explains,

> It is precisely in this sense that the human sciences presuppose that the scholarly consciousness is already formed and for that very reason possesses the right, unlearnable, and inimitable tact that envelops the human sciences' form of judgment and mode of knowledge as if it were the element in which they move. (*TM*, 14)

Edification, grasped as the *ethos* of the edified person, affords scholars who have it a universal sense—this is what Gadamer, following Helmholtz, calls tact. This universal sense frees scholars, in the sense of enabling them to achieve validity in their interpretations of the human experience. Accordingly, whereas the ideal of the natural sciences is to justify universal knowledge claims on the basis of method, the ideal of the human sciences is to justify interpretations of concrete, singular human experience through the universal sense afforded by edification. Thus, if it is the ideal of the natural sciences to establish a *method* that can guarantee universally valid knowledge, the ideal of the human sciences is to become *edified* persons with a universal sense that allows us to experience the truth at issue in humanistic inquiry in the first place.

3. COMMON SENSE, JUDGMENT, AND TASTE

Gadamer maintains that the universal sense afforded by edification is given further contour by other concepts from the humanist tradition: the *sensus communis* (common sense), judgment, and taste.

The first of these motifs that Gadamer treats is that of *sensus communis* or common sense. Generally, the humanist concept of common sense resonates with the way the concept is typically used today. In this, common sense concerns a type of judgment that is purportedly available to all human beings and that is sound even as it is independent of scholastic sophistication, scientific knowledge, and technical expertise. Likewise, common sense concerns the related ability of human beings to conduct themselves judiciously in civic life and society, one that, again, is purportedly available to all human beings, independent of station. The humanist concept of common sense differs from that found in a tradition of philosophy derived from Aristotle. In Aristotle's *De Anima*, common sense is not about sound judgment and judicious conduct in the context of civic life and society but instead refers specifically to a function of perception (*koine aesthesis*) that unites the five senses.[11] In the humanist tradition, the concept of common sense refers to an entire manner of knowing and being that takes the social context of human life into account.

Gadamer, in any case, elucidates the humanist concept of common sense in reference to figures and themes in seventeenth- and eighteenth-century Europe. He focuses perhaps especially on Giambattista Vico's contributions to the concept of common sense, though he treats Lord Shaftsbury with some care, as well. He also mentions the use made of the concept of common sense in the Scottish Enlightenment, and he reflects on the important role played in French thought and culture by the concept of *le bon sens*. Gadamer's account reads a bit like a grand tour of European ideas from the period, but his basic claim is that whereas the concept of common sense became highly developed in a number of European contexts, in Germany, by contrast, the concept remained comparatively impoverished. With the qualified exception of pietism, and in particular the pietist Friedrich Oetinger, in Germany the concept of common sense "was emptied of all political content" characteristic of the concept in other European contexts. Instead, in Germany there prevails a tendency to treat common sense merely as a form of purely theoretical cognition (*TM*, 25).

Gadamer's concern, in any case, is to shed further light on the universal sense afforded by edification through a return to the humanist concept of common sense. His account is nuanced, but a couple of points may be drawn out in particular. First, this universal sense, as a matter of common sense, originates from civic life and society and, in virtue of this, from tradition. He observes that in Vico, for example, common sense concerns knowledge of universals that give orientation to human life. In common sense, however, such universality is not grasped in terms of abstract principles that can be determined independent of context, as, perhaps, a principle like Mill's principle of utility can be (i.e., roughly, the principle that actions are right if they tend to promote happiness and wrong if they tend to lead to the contrary). Rather, common sense is concerned with a universality that only finds expression in and through concrete, communally and historically determined meanings, as with, say, civic laws and customs. He writes,

> Sensus communis obviously does not mean only that general faculty in all men but the sense that founds community. According to Vico, what gives the human will its direction is not the abstract universality of reason but the concrete universality represented by the community of a group, a people, a nation, or the whole human race. (*TM*, 19–20)

The universal sense afforded by edification, as a matter of common sense, is a universality determined through social and historical context.

Common sense, as concerned with concrete universals that orient human life, is, second, ethical in nature. In this, as Gadamer observes, common sense is closely related to the virtue of *phronesis*. But, as a manner of knowing and being that is rooted in communal and historical context, common sense concerns more than the ability to pursue our interests or inclinations through instrumental calculation. Common sense is as much about the proper purposes, or ends, of our agency, about what is good and right for us to do in concrete circumstances, as it is about the means to such ends. Gadamer, again this time on the example of Vico, writes,

> The sensus communis is the sense of what is right and of the common good that is to be found in all men; moreover, it is a sense that is acquired through living in the community and is determined by its structures and aims. (*TM*, 21)

For Gadamer, the universal sense afforded by edification not only turns on a concrete universality that is determined through social and historical context, but this universality is also itself ethical in orientation.

Gadamer maintains that in the humanist tradition the concept of common sense is closely connected with that of judgment. His account of the humanist concept of judgment is cursory, but this should not be taken to mean that the issue is inconsequential to him. Quite to the contrary, perhaps one reason he gives the concept shorter shrift in this introductory chapter is that the theme of judgment is closely related to what, later, he calls the "fundamental hermeneutical problem"—namely, the problem of application.[12]

The point of Gadamer's discussion of the humanist concept of judgment at the outset of his project, though, is to connect it up with the concept of common sense. Common sense concerns knowledge of concrete universality. In this, common sense concerns not the determination of a universal in the abstract, but a universal made available from the social and historical context in which we find ourselves. But common sense therefore depends on an ability for the discernment of universals within a particular social and historical context. *Judgment* is the name for this ability. Accordingly, judgment is not foremost concerned with universal knowledge *per se* but is rather the good sense required for us to put whatever knowledge we already possess to proper effect. He writes, "The difference between a fool and a sensible man is that the former lacks judgment—i.e., he is not able to subsume correctly, and hence cannot apply correctly what he has learned and knows" (*TM*, 28). Judgment, as the ability to discern a universal in a concrete particular, is brought into further focus by the fact that it cannot be learned in the manner of abstract scientific or technical knowledge. Gadamer writes that judgment "cannot be taught in the abstract but only practices from case to case, and is therefore more an ability like the senses. It is something that cannot be learned, because no demonstration from concepts can guide the application of rules" (*TM*, 29). This is because good judgment is nothing else than being able to put scientific or technical knowledge to proper effect in the first place; thus, we would also need to have good judgment to put any such scientific or technical knowledge to use at all.[13]

German Enlightenment philosophy, as Gadamer argues, did not take kindly to the humanist concept of judgment. In this age that celebrated scientific rationality, an ability that cannot be treated in terms of scientific knowledge came to be considered one of the "lower powers of the mind" (*TM*, 29). With this, the pride of place that judgment had always held in practical philosophy began to fade, and judgment came to find a home, now reduced in scope, in aesthetics. In the humanist tradition, however, the concept of judgment continues to be conceived in terms of civic life, society, and so also ethical life. Common sense, as we saw, concerns the knowledge of proper ends as well as the means to achieve them, and accordingly, judgment is an ability to discern ends that will guide our calculations about means in the first place. Gadamer writes,

> Common sense is exhibited primarily in making judgments about right and wrong, proper and improper. Whoever has sound judgment is thereby enabled to judge particulars under universal viewpoints, but he knows what is really important—i.e., he sees things from the right and sound point of view. (*TM*, 30)

In the humanist tradition, judgment maintains a privileged position among our manners of knowing and being. In coordination with common sense, judgment is not considered to be a lower power of the mind but instead the encompassing ability required for us to comprehend and conduct ourselves sensibly.

The last of the humanist concepts that Gadamer considers is taste. Gadamer suggests that to the universal sense afforded by edification, taste contributes a sense for the ideal of humanity, one that is no less embodied, perhaps even intuitive, than it is communal in nature. This humanist viewpoint is, of course, at odds with views typical of our times. Today we usually conceive of taste in relativistic terms, perhaps as a matter of personal preference that differs from individual to individual. In the humanist tradition, however, taste has been conceived in ethical terms as a sense for the ideal of humanity on the basis of which we can differentiate what is fitting, what is appropriate in human relations and affairs. On the one hand, taste is a sense that we experience in the intimacy of our own embodied existence, in innermost affects. Gadamer observes that in Balthasar Gracian, for example, taste was grasped as "the most animal and most inward of our senses" (*TM*, 33). But, on the other hand, because taste involves a sense for our *common humanity*, this most 'inward' nevertheless has an outward, social significance. Gadamer writes,

> The concept of taste undoubtedly implies a *mode of knowing*. The mark of good taste is being able to stand back from ourselves and our private preferences. Thus taste, in its essential nature, is not a private but a social phenomenon of the first order. (*TM*, 33)

Taste has ethical import as a sense that treats the ideal of humanity as a measure for decision making within the context of civic and social life. Gadamer observes that taste is "curiously decisive," in that it is an "acceptance or rejection that involves no hesitation, no surreptitious glance at others, no searching for reasons" (*TM*, 34). Yet the fact that taste is thus decisive without reasons does not mean that it simply succumbs to societal pressures to conform. Taste, as Gadamer argues, is not "fashion," grasped as something that "has no other norm than that given by what everyone does" (*TM*, 34). Quite to the contrary, while taste functions always within the context of concrete societal relations, it remains in a free relation to the societal pressure to conform. This is because taste functions from a holistic perspective given by the ideal of humanity and not merely on the basis of the ever-changing fashions of society. Indeed, in this, taste remains above the societal pressure to conform just as style remains above fashion. He writes, "One maintains one's own 'style'—i.e., one relates the demands of fashion to a whole that one's own taste keeps in view and accepts only what harmonizes with this whole and fits together as it does" (*TM*, 35). Taste, on Gadamer's view, plays an important role in ethical life because, prior to any deliberation or decision-making, it takes the ideal of humanity as a measure for an embodied, perhaps even intuitive differentiation of what is fitting, what is appropriate.

4. CONCLUSION

Gadamer, as we have seen, maintains that the human sciences are a veritable home of the hermeneutical experience of truth. In the human sciences, the concern is with the experience of truth had when we come to understand something through an interpretation, for example, a work of art or literature, or some testimony from history. Because of this, Gadamer believes that the human sciences harbor insight that will help us to clarify and, in turn, justify this hermeneutical experience of truth. Yet, as he believes, in our times, it has become difficult to recover this insight from the human sciences because they have become obscure even to themselves. The human sciences have come to be, as it were, spellbound by the successes of the natural sciences, so much so that they have too much come to impose the purpose and methodological ideal of the natural sciences on humanistic inquiry. Gadamer, as I have tried to show, attempts to restore clarity to the experience of truth at issue in the human sciences through a return an important source of humanistic inquiry—the tradition of humanism. In this, Gadamer's return to the humanist tradition reveals that while the purpose of the natural sciences concerns knowledge of universals that is secured by the ideal of the scientific method, the purpose of the human sciences, by contrast, is with an experience of the truth of objects of inquiry in their concrete uniqueness—and, crucially, that this experience of truth is not secured by method but made possible by edification, itself related to common sense, judgment, and taste.

Gadamer's belief that the hermeneutical experience of truth cannot be justified on the basis of the ideal of method has led critics to question what role Gadamer sees for norms in interpretive experience at all.[14] Gadamer's elucidation of the relation of the hermeneutical experience of truth and edification suggests, however, a normative ideal that gives a certain orientation to interpretive practice. His approach suggests that we should become and, in turn, remain edified through ongoing and diverse interpretive experience. This ideal, as we have seen, is embodied in what Gadamer names edified persons—those who have achieved a universal sense because edification has become nothing less than their *ethos*. But Gadamer fills out what he means by this ideal later in *Truth and Method*, too—there in reference to what he calls persons of experience. In this, Gadamer brings into focus that the universal sense achieved by the edified person brings with it a heightened openness to new and further interpretive experience. Gadamer writes,

> The experienced person proves to be . . . someone who is radically undogmatic; who, because of the many experiences he has had and the knowledge he has drawn from them, is particularly well equipped to have new experiences and to learn from them. The dialectic of experience has its proper fulfillment not in definitive knowledge but in the openness to experience that is made possible by experience itself. (*TM*, 364)

In Gadamer's hermeneutics, the ideal of edification is closely related to an ideal of experience, one oriented by openness to and readiness always for more experience.

NOTES

1. Hans-Georg Gadamer, *Truth and Method*, 2nd ed., trans. Joel Weinsheimer and Donald G. Marshall (New York: Bloomsbury Publishing, 2013), xx—xxi. Hereafter cited in text as *TM*. Where the German is cited or the translation has been altered, the page number of the original is indicated after the slash. The latter refer to Hans-Georg Gadamer, *Wahrheit und Methode*, Gesammelte Werke I (Tübingen: Mohr Siebeck, 1990).

2. See Theodore George, "Hermeneutics," *The Stanford Encyclopedia of Philosophy* (Winter 2020 Edition), Edward N. Zalta (ed.), https://plato.stanford.edu/archives/win2020/entries/hermeneutics/.

3. As Dennis Schmidt observes, "One notes immediately that the four basic features of humanism that Gadamer singles out seem to be much more easily recognized as the cornerstones of Kant's *Kritik der Urteilskraft* than as the hallmarks of any humanism." Dennis Schmidt, "Gadamer, Humanism, and the Humanities," in *The Gadamerian Mind*, ed. Theodore George and Gert-Jan van der Heiden (London: Routledge, 2021), 40. While Gadamer's relation to Kant comes into focus later in Part I of *Truth and Method*, it plays a subtle role in Gadamer's treatment of the significance of the human sciences.

4. Tobais Chant Owen, "Origin of the Solar System", in *Encyclopedia Britannica*, https://www.britannica.com/explore/space/origin-of the-solar-system/.

5. Frederick C. Beiser, *The German Historicist Tradition* (Oxford: Oxford University Press, 2011), 1.

6. See Jean Grondin, *Introduction to Philosophical Hermeneutics* (New Haven: Yale University Press, 1994), 84–90; Charles R. Bambach, *Heidegger, Dilthey, and the Crisis of Historicism* (Ithaca, NY: Cornell University Press, 1995), 127–85; and Rudolf A. Makkreel, *Orientation and Judgment in Hermeneutics* (Chicago: University of Chicago Press, 2015).

7. Martin Heidegger, "Letter on Humanism," trans. Frank A. Capuzzi, in *Pathmarks*, ed. William McNeill (Cambridge: Cambridge University Press, 1998), 244.

8. Heidegger, 244–45.

9. See Theodore George, *The Responsibility to Understand: Hermeneutical Contours of Ethical Life* (Edinburgh: Edinburg University Press, 2020), 29–46.

10. Here Helmholtz is talking about history and philology in particular.

11. Aristotle, De Anima, in *The Complete Works of Aristotle*, Vol. 1, ed. Jonathan Barnes, 424a27ff.

12. See TM II.2.2, discussed by David Liakos in chapter nine of this volume.

13. Gadamer makes the same point, if in a slightly different manner, in reference to Kant (*TM*, 29).

14. George, "Hermeneutics." For a recent consideration of the distinction between methodological and ontological hermeneutics, see Kristin Gjesdal, "Hermeneutics and the Human Sciences," in *The Cambridge Companion to Hermeneutics*, ed. Michael N Forster. and Kristin Gjesdal (Cambridge: Cambridge University Press, 2019), 354–80.

Chapter 2

TM I.1.2

Gadamer's Astonishing Question: Engaging with Gadamer's Critique of Kant's Aesthetics

Nicholas Davey

Truth and Method is an exemplary hermeneutical text. Its surface arguments betray the presence of underlying conceptual commitments. To judge the early sections of Gadamer's *magnum opus* solely as an attack on Kant's aesthetics misses the point. They attempt to retrieve what Kant's *Critique of Judgment* blocks off; the possibility of re-thinking our experience of art as a potent transformative and hermeneutical force. This chapter tracks the underlying arguments of Gadamer's criticisms to discern in them the grounds for the hermeneutical aesthetic they suggest. Gadamer sublates rather than negates Kantian aesthetics. Whereas Kant makes the aesthetic object dependent upon the epistemological categories applied by a cognitive subject, Gadamer insists that it is the cognitive subject that is subjectivized through its engagement with art and its ontological structures. For Gadamer, "the experience of art" demonstrates that, contrary to Kant's position, the knowing subject is not "the experiencing (*erlebende*) center from which everything considered art is measured."[1] *The plausibility of Gadamer's hermeneutical orientation to art exposes the implausibility of Kant's subjectivist reduction of aesthetics.* If Kant is right, art cannot address us hermeneutically and is deprived of its transformative capacity. Should the critical presuppositions of philosophical hermeneutics be valid, however, Kantian aesthetics is rendered an implausible solipsism.

To protect aesthetic judgment against Hume's mechanical reductionism, Kant proposes that judgments concerning the beautiful have their origin in the "free" (unconditioned) *a priori* structures of our understanding. Gadamer grasps the consequences of this position. In aesthetic judgment, the cognitive subject is not responding to anything external but solely to its own responses to a given sensual manifold. The price of aesthetic autonomy is that subjective consciousness cannot escape itself. If aesthetic judgment only exhibits an inward state of feeling, art's ability to transform the knowing subject from "outside" is disrupted. This challenges the very possibility of a hermeneutic relation to art. Both self- and hermeneutical understanding occur only through understanding something *other* than the self (*TM*, 87). In other words, to free the Kantian subject from the constraints of its fixed repertoire of *a priori* responses and to make it amenable to transformational and educational development, Gadamer has to dismantle the autonomy of the Kantian subject. If that subject has no fixed identity, how is Gadamer to account for the development of a subject-identity able to respond to the hermeneutical challenges of art?

Section 1 of *Truth and Method* is entitled "Die Transzendierung der ästhetischen Dimension," but what does the term *aesthetic* mean? In Kant's *Critique of Pure Reason*, *aisthesis* refers to the realm of sight and sound. In his *Critique of Judgment*, the aesthetic is directly linked to judgments of the beautiful. Though Gadamer seeks to escape from aesthetics which marginalize questions of meaning in favor of pleasure, he cannot escape *aisthesis* with regard to the sensuous embodiment of ideas in art. Yet despite his reservations, Gadamer repeatedly uses variants of the term "aesthetic" in phrases such as "aesthetic distanciation," "aesthetic consciousness," and "aesthetic differentiation."[2] Nor is it clear what he means by "transcending the aesthetic dimension." To escape Kantian aesthetics is one thing, but to approach the question of art without any reference to the aesthetic is another. Gadamer has no intention of abandoning the aesthetic dimension but rather seeks to redeploy it in a broader ontological context. The aim is to establish a hermeneutics of aesthetic transformation by sublating Kant's aesthetic epistemology with an ontology of aesthetic interaction. The following distinction is helpful.

Aesthetics negatively conceived is frequently associated with *Erlebnis* (the lived moment), whereas aesthetics positively articulated as *Erfahrung* expresses a relation to a broader hermeneutic (poetics) of the aesthetic focused on meaning transmission rather than on an analysis of pleasurable sensation. *Erfahrung* relates to a process of interaction which is both ongoing and forever showing new aspects of itself. Gadamer associates this with the "experience of art," an experience which is far from momentary but continuous and ongoing. As an unfinished event, the experience of art demonstrates the virtue of the efficacy of a questioning, polyphonic approach: we never finish with an artwork because, like ourselves, it can always be understood more completely.

The *Erlebniss/Erfahrung* distinction maps onto another that clarifies the conceptual character of Gadamer's approach to the question of the "experience of art." This is entailed in the formula that *Bewußtsein* (consciousness) is more being than knowing. The experience of art (*Erfahrung*) is grounded in ontological processes which extend far beyond what knowing consciousness can be aware of, whereas *Erlebnisse* relate to what consciousness is immediately aware of.[3] As we shall see, the sublation of *Erlebnis* by *Erfahrung* establishes the possibility of a hermeneutical aesthetic.

Why is Gadamer intent on decrying Kant's *Critique of Judgment* as an impotent aesthetics of subjectivism? (*TM*, 504). Gadamer's dense defense of the transformative and educative power of art requires that the key categories of Kant's aesthetics discourse be stripped of their epistemological connotations and be considered instead as the ontological forms of our encounter with art. Aesthetics can no longer be the rhapsody of a Kantian subject entranced by the quality of its own representations. The experience of art shows how such a subject can be de-subjectivized and released from its epistemic self-enclosure. The experience of art always goes beyond itself: "it does not know what it is and cannot say what it knows" (*TM*, 91). "It cannot present the full truth of what it experiences in terms of definitive knowledge. There is no absolute progress and no final exhaustion of what lies in a work of art" (*TM*, 90). In relation to these limitations, the subject of such experiences—*Dasein*—only comes to understand itself in relation to its own radical temporality (*TM*, 90). Involvement in the experience of art is the condition of such understanding, whereas for Kant, it is the transcendental subject that is the condition of our aesthetic judgments of art. Other issues shape Gadamer's response to Kant.

Hume's empiricism shades Kant's philosophical anxieties about the status of aesthetics. To prevent aesthetic judgments from being reduced to a purely mechanical reaction to pleasurable stimuli, Kant claims that aesthetic judgments are *freely* made by a rational subject applying its norms of the beautiful upon a complex body of sensations. This returns a degree of autonomy to aesthetic judgment insofar as it can be seen as the spontaneous expression of the subject's own intrinsic forms of aesthetic reasoning. Gadamer is quick to perceive the limitations of attributing an autonomy of aesthetic reasoning to the cognitive subject. Judging representations as beautiful tells us a good deal about a subject's preferences but reveals to us nothing of the artwork itself. Kant's fundamentally phenomenalist aesthetic epistemology never engages with the artwork *per se* but only with the subject's representations of it. This is the basis of Gadamer's claim that Kant's aesthetics offers us no actual knowledge of the object judged but only access to the feelings of the judge. Kant's reduction of aesthetic response to a question of feeling nullifies art's educative content and disables its capacity for enabling hermeneutic transformation. To retrieve that content, Gadamer has to free aesthetics from its enclosure in the knowing subject and establish it as a mode of interaction between modes of *Dasein*. A bold philosophical maneuver is required and is initiated at the end of section I.2 of *Truth and Method*.

Gadamer asks what is by all accounts an astonishing question: "Is the aesthetic approach to a work of art the appropriate one?" (*TM*, 73). The question implies that aesthetics—traditionally conceived as the science of pleasurable sensations—has to be turned on its head in order to do justice to our experience of art. Following Heidegger, Gadamer rejects the idea that our experience of art entails us being presented with pleasant sensations which we subsequently judge to be beautiful. On the contrary, art speaks to us directly, and so accordingly "aesthetics has to be absorbed into hermeneutics" (*TM*, 164). Gadamer must free aesthetics from its limiting concern with the qualities of sensation (*Erlebnis*) so as to address questions of meaning (*Erfahrung*) which cannot be limited to questions of immediate sensation. Less formally stated, are our responses to art reducible to a trivial liking for the arabesque (form and pattern), or are they indicative of transformative concerns which grapple with the disturbing existential and moral subject matters which can be life shaping? Here we begin to see how Gadamer marshals his terminologies. *Erlebnis* demarcates the subjective territory of "aesthetic sensation," whilst *Erfahrung* addresses what transcends the subjective—namely, the experience of art and its questions of meaning. The contrast appears belligerent. "Traditional aesthetics" is accused of aestheticizing if not anaesthetizing our experience of art by marginalizing the issue of its meaning. The editorial themes of this volume—the idea of the polyphonic and the strategy of questioning—are well chosen. I shall argue that as tactical devices, they unfold Gadamer's strategic end—that is, *the hermeneuticizing of our experience of art*. This brings the latter under the category of *Erfahrung*—that is, as a temporal process of unfolding.

The linking of the polyphonic with Gadamer's *magnum opus* suggests a carefully calibrated way of reading capable of discerning the diverse voices at play within the text. Gadamer's book is composed by "many voices": those of Plato, Aristotle, Nicholas of Cusa, Kant, Humboldt, Hegel, and Heidegger, to name but a few. More important, actively partaking in a polyphonic performance and developing its juxtapositions of voice brings forward harmonic variations and developments which can only emerge through a plurality of voices. The "eventual" nature of polyphonic emergence emphasizes the speculative aspect of Gadamer's language-ontology. Just as the vocal blending of a polyphonic performance lights up and anticipates unsounded figures of musical development, so the entanglement of language with the infinite speculative dimensions of meaning allows words and concepts to invoke constellations of ideas beyond what they immediately state. Both the eventual nature of aesthetic experience hermeneutically conceived and its speculative charge are themes we will engage with below.

Questioning is a means to unfolding the subject matters (*Sachen*) or contents of *Erfahrungen*. Questioning relates directly to our experience of art, in that it endeavors to draw out what it discloses over time. Gadamer notes that "to ask a question means to bring into the open" (*TM*, 371) and that "*to understand the questionableness of something is already to be questioning*" (*TM*, 383). The practice of questioning is not opposed to the experience of art but is a means of clarifying within the hidden and obscure. Questioning is a performative process: it brings about. Within philosophical hermeneutics it is not the answer to a question that is important but rather what arises in the pursuit of an answer. To raise a question is not so much to challenge or refute but to find one's way deeper into the unfolding figures that constitute a way of thinking. Questioning contains elements of both negation and affirmation. To see the limits of a subject matter is to see what it is not (negation), but to grasp what it is not inevitably raises the question of what it might possibly be or yet become (affirmation). The *Erfahrung*, its subject matter, and the artwork have the same constitution as unfolding events—all have infinitely more determinations of meaning than finite understanding can grasp. To question aesthetics understood as our experience of art is thus to participate in a movement of thought and to draw out its prior determinations of meaning, many of which are unspoken.

The preliminary motifs of the polyphonic and questioning figure-modes of thought are what guide Gadamer's reflections on the aesthetic and its controversial place in our understanding of art. The polyphonic announces Gadamer's perspectival approach to artistic images. Conceptual explication is never able to exhaust the content of a poetic or artistic image.[4] The status of images as indefinables does not place them beyond thought but, to the contrary, emphasizes the need to approach them with multiple modes of perspective. This allows an image in the history of its reception to become more fully what it is. The arguments announce Gadamer's poignant re-working of the classical concept of *mimesis*: questioning deepens the perspectival polyphony surrounding our experience of an artwork, enabling it to become within our collective understanding more fully what it is. This clarifies that hermeneutical reflection about the aesthetic neither starts at a zero point (it has always been underway) nor culminates in infinity.[5] What emerges in reflection as "the aesthetic" rests upon the unsaid, that is, those concealed conceptual horizons which allow the said to be spoken in the first place. In language-being where all meaning is interconnected, the task of hermeneutical questioning—to draw out what is in play within our philosophical and cultural concepts—is endless.[6]

The question with which we are primarily concerned—is the aesthetic approach to the work of art the appropriate one?—emerges from Gadamer's reflections on the subjectivization of aesthetics through Kantian critique,

Kant's doctrine of taste, and the implications of his account of genius. Gadamer's critique of these thematics clears the philosophical ground and enables his astonishing question to emerge. As gaining a consciousness of the history of concepts is, for Gadamer, a clear duty of critical thinking,[7] his approach to the experience of art needs to probe what informs Kant's aesthetics; not just to get beyond it, but rather to think through it in a way that does justice to our experience of art. This will entail Gadamer replacing Kant's aesthetic epistemology with his own aesthetic ontology. Although Gadamer has to distinguish his position from that of Kant, there is something informative about the term "critique" that both Kant and Gadamer share.

For Kant, the critique of (aesthetic) judgment concerns the *a priori* conditions under which such judgments become possible. "The judgment of taste, therefore, is not a cognitive judgment, and so not logical, but is aesthetic—which means that it is one whose determining ground cannot be other than subjective."[8] The referent of the judgment of taste "denotes nothing in the object [i.e., the artwork] but is a feeling which the subject has of itself and of the manner in which it is affected by the representation."[9] These passages underwrite Gadamer's accusation that Kant's aesthetics is barred from making knowledge claims about states of affairs in the world. For Kant, the formal (transcendental) conditions of aesthetic judgment lie in a "subjective condition" within all rational subjects—that is, in the possibility of synthesizing "the free play of the imagination and understanding" which is "valid for everyone."[10]

Gadamer's concern with philosophical critique is also evident. He declares that the leading question of *Truth and Method* "is (to put it in Kantian terms): how is understanding possible?" (*TM*, xxvii). It is immediately apparent that Gadamer's orientation toward the possibility of the experience of art shifts the debate from an epistemological ground to an ontological ground with significant consequences for the development of a hermeneutical aesthetics.

> How is understanding possible? . . . This is a question that *precedes any action of understanding on the part of subjectivity.* . . . Heidegger's temporal analytics of *Dasein* has, I think, shown convincingly that understanding is not just one of the various possible behaviors of the subject but the mode of Being of *Dasein* itself. . . . It denotes the basic being-in-motion of *Dasein* that constitutes finitude and historicity, and hence embraces the whole of its experience of the world. (*TM*, xxvii, emphasis added)

For Gadamer, the transcendental conditions of our experience of art are ontological: they concern our very mode of being among the communal cognate objectivities (traditions) that transcend singular individuals. For the most part, these concern the shared structures of our temporal being and the traditions of meaning that arise from our historicity. They do not concern principles of agreement within the subjective consciousness nor are they solely imposed on the artwork by epistemic consciousness. Gadamer reminds us that his broad aim is

> to discover what is common to all types of understanding and to show that *understanding is never a subjective relation to a given "object"* but to the history of its effect; in other words, understanding belongs to the being of that which is understood. (*TM*, xxvii, emphasis added)

In other words, in our experience of art, we confront the actuality of knowledge structures that transcend individual subjective consciousness. These arguments enable Gadamer to propose against Kant that our experience of art involves a great deal more than a commentary upon the condition of feeling within a spectator.

Gadamer's relation to Kant's *Critique of Judgment* is profoundly dialectical. Given his interests in Heidegger and phenomenology, it could be asked why he need bother with Kant's philosophical abstractions at all rather than embarking directly on a phenomenological analysis of what the experience of art entails. Gadamer is plainly respectful of Kant's enormous historical achievement. Though standing on the shoulders of Alexander Baumgarten, Kant made formal philosophical discourse about art and nature possible.[11] And yet by appropriating our experience of art to the formalities of his aesthetic categories, Kant's discourse appropriates to itself, covers over, and estranges us from the living content of such experience. *Kant presides over what is for Gadamer the disaster of an aesthetic alienation which renders us deaf to art's address.* His critique of Kant's position amounts to a form of Heideggerian *Destruktion*[12] which seeks a conceptual descaling of its formal idealism in order to re-cover what it has inappropriately displaced. The experience of art is reduced to a question of its sensible properties with all elements of significance suppressed. Here the full force of Gadamer's question becomes apparent: *is aesthetics in the formal Kantian sense actually appropriate to our experience of art at all?* Why is Gadamer intent on forcing this divorce? A partial answer to this lies in section I.1 of *Truth and Method*, "The Significance of the Humanist Tradition for the Human Sciences."

In the aforementioned section, Gadamer displays a fundamental historical orientation toward the application of concepts. The transmission and concrete application of philosophical categories within the long-established traditions of practical reason (*Bildung*) that belong to the humanities demonstrate their continued efficacy. They provide both narrative structure, sense, and direction to the complexities of collective human experience and thereby offer a basic orientation toward the world and our place within it. Though not grounded in confirmable certainties, they serve us well in organizing experience into intelligible structures. Gadamer remarks, "Is all this acquired and accumulated knowledge groundless? Does what has always supported us need to be grounded?" (*TM*, xxxiv). The problem is that once models of mathematical and scientific knowledge monopolize the question of truth, the status of inherited knowledge within the arts and humanities is diminished. Kant's veneration of mathematical certainties has the historical consequence of alienating us from the formative processes (*Bildung*) which give form and content to everyday experience. Here Gadamer and Kant collide. What Gadamer regards as objective (the shaping of experience by categories of understanding that are historically transmitted and communally shared) Kant judges to be subjective, that is, accidental historical formations without any formal necessity. And yet what Kant regards as objective—the subjection of sensible experience to universally shared *a priori* categories of understanding—Gadamer regards as the action of subjective consciousness. Whereas Kant seeks to guarantee the objectivity of subjective representations from *within* the subject's naturally endowed *a priori* forms of judgment, Gadamer upholds the objectivities of profound subjective experience by showing how they are rooted in linguistic and cultural categories characterizing a collective form of existence. The dialectical interplay of outer and inner, of objective and subjective, animates the hermeneutic drama of whole and part which is essential to Gadamer's claim that the individual subjectivities of our experience of art have real collective knowledge-content. Philosophical hermeneutics delves deep into subjective experience in order to discern the objectivities of history and language-being that shape it.

A signature argument in Kant's *Critique of Pure Reason* places in clear relief that which simultaneously attracts and repels Gadamer about Kant's subjectivist epistemology. Kant is a phenomenalist, whereas Gadamer is a phenomenological thinker. Kant argues,

> Without sensibility no object would be given to us, without understanding no object would be thought. Thoughts without content are empty, intuitions without concepts are blind. It is, therefore, just as necessary to make our concepts sensible, that is, to add the object to them in intuition, as to make our intuitions intelligible, that is, to bring them under concepts. These two powers or capacities cannot exchange their functions. The understanding can intuit nothing, the senses can think nothing.[13]

Kant's passage admirably demonstrates the translational task of the artist: to allow us to see our ideas in the world by rendering them perceptible in sensible particulars and to draw sensible particulars into frameworks of ideas whereby they acquire a sense and significance beyond the moment. However,

Gadamer disagrees with Kant's strict separation of cognitive powers (understanding and intuition). According to Kant, it is intuition that supplies understanding with its objects and understanding that subsequently applies its own norms and forms to those objects. The objects of intuition have no sense or meaning of their own. They are phenomena whose intelligible meaning and structure are extrinsically projected onto them. In themselves, they remain phenomenal, that is, something that makes sense only *after* the understanding has projected the appearance of form upon it. Gadamer is disturbed by the epistemological internalism of this argument: *our* bodily receptivity gives to *our* mind sensible representations which *our* mind then structures according to its own innate forms of understanding. This leads to Gadamer's riposte: what, "is there to be no knowledge in art?," is there no way in which an art object can challenge and disrupt our mind's "radical subjectivization" of its sensible world? (*TM*, 88). If not, the epistemological structure of Kant's theory of aesthetic judgment undermines the possibility of our experience of art and the transformation that it can induce. Gadamer's conception of hermeneutical experience is evidently dependent on a similar synthesis or "fusion" of idea and sense, but it strives to escape Kant's epistemological internalism by showing how a sensible artwork can convey to a receiving consciousness intellectual content about a subject matter that has not already been anticipated by that consciousness. How does an artwork initiate a change in how consciousness thinks about its world such that it is understood differently?

Gadamer's language-ontology is key. Unlike Kant's phenomenalism, in which the ideas and the sensible phenomena they overlay are logically separate, Gadamer conceives of phenomena phenomenologically: an ideational element is integral to the appearance of an object of experience. A physical gesture is immediately perceived as embodying lovingness rather than being seen first as a bodily movement and then subsequently interpreted as lovingness. Insofar as the objects of experience embody subject matters, such as caring or nobility, their phenomenological occurrence gives them a reach beyond themselves. Such objects are in effect constituted collectively, each historical instantiation touching and mediating upon other manifestations of a shared subject matter within a community. This partly linguistic constitution implies that the objects of phenomenological experience embody part-whole structures in continuous movement. The possibility of such experience is grounded in Gadamer's underpinning ontology of *Sprachlichkeit*.[14] This "linguistic constitution of the world"[15] is the most fundamental level of our existence. Universal "language being" is made up of the constant movement of parts and the wholes to which they belong. It embodies the continual transitioning of what is individual and what is collectively shared. The "linguistic constitution of the world" enables the artwork to operate transformatively. Such a conception of the phenomenological objects of experience not only assumes an integration of sense and meaning but also that the sensible and ideational aspects of experience can respectively mediate each other. It is this mediation that grounds Gadamer's claim that the experience of art does indeed disclose *new* knowledge.

Because phenomenological objects are partially constituted linguistically, artworks are able to transmit, via cultural tradition, aspects of a subject matter not anticipated by a receiving consciousness. This forces the spectator to think again about their limited conception of the subject matter with which an artwork is dealing. The linguistically constituted world, which is ontologically more than any individual consciousness can grasp, extends the limits of that consciousness. The artwork reveals how an individual consciousness belongs to and speaks to that which is more than itself. Such hermeneutical traffic is not one way. For significant ideas and abstract subject matters to find their place within the sensible world, they need to be visualized in particular concrete form. In this context, the artwork places in a public forum embodied ideas that would otherwise be imprisoned within the subjectivity of the artist or composer. Once in that forum, concretized subject matters can transform the thinking of those who engage with them. Ontologically speaking, this suggests that our experience of art is a *perpetuum mobile*, an unending dialectical conversation between those aspects of our being defined by our individual linguistic consciousness (the personal) and those shaped by our being within language-being (the cultural, the historical, the collective). Having mapped the terrain shaping Gadamer's approach to Kantian aesthetics, let us now turn to the specific philosophical maneuvers Gadamer deploys in his negotiation with Kant's heritage.

Gadamer's position is ambiguous from the start. The section title, "The Subjectivization of Aesthetics through the Kantian Critique," directly addresses Kant's claim that "the judgment of taste is not a cognitive judgment and so not logical but aesthetic—which means that its determining ground cannot be other than subjective."[16] This suggests that "aesthetics" concerns a field of experience that is *subjectivized* by Kant. Does this suggest that Kant has diminished a collective form of experience as subjective? For Gadamer, Kant is guilty of rendering our experience of an artwork a second-order experience that does not appertain to what it is saying but to its alleged primary properties. It is not what is experienced but the alleged properties of the experience that matters. For Kant, it is the qualities of the representation that matter and not what is represented. Gadamer reverses this epistemological ordering. Accordingly, Kant's phenomenalist account of "aesthetic experience" is replaced by an appeal to what Gadamer regards as phenomenologically primary—that is, the "experience of art" itself. Because he grounds knowledge in subjective consciousness, Kant effectively constrains aesthetic experience within the epistemological. Gadamer, however, wants to ground the experience of art in the ontological, in the structure of our being rather than in the structure of consciousness. He wants to present art not as the manifestation of individual being but as the disclosure of our historical and cultural being. So what does Gadamer mean by the pivotal term *the experience of art*?

Gadamer has no doubt that *art speaks to us* in the diversity and ambiguity of human experience. "The significance of art also depends on the fact that it speaks to us"—it speaks to us directly, in a significant direct way (*TM*, 51). Indeed, it is this ability to speak so directly that constitutes art's claim to truth.[17] Kant's aesthetics of perception gets in the way of discerning this truth. For Gadamer, aesthetic consciousness distorts our experience of art and, worse, it is indicative of an alienation from the phenomenological actuality of "art speaking to us."

> The consciousness of art—the aesthetic consciousness—is always secondary to *the immediate truth-claim* that proceeds from the work of art itself. To this extent, when we judge a work of art on the basis of its aesthetic quality, something that is really much more intimate and familiar to us is alienated. This alienation into aesthetic judgment always takes place when we have withdrawn ourselves and are no longer open to *the immediate claim of that which grasps us*.[18]

This is why Gadamer asks, "Is the aesthetic approach to a work of art the appropriate one?" and then suggests that "to do justice to art, aesthetics must go beyond itself and surrender the 'purity' of the aesthetic" (*TM*, 73, 84). In this lies the astonishing nature of Gadamer's claim. Kant's historic achievement of grounding the discipline of aesthetics actually serves to distort our experience of art such that aesthetics as Kant understands it alienates us from what is at play within art's experience. In effect, Gadamer is implying that the abstractions of aesthetic perception—that is, the formal aesthetic properties of an artwork (its form, color, texture, balance, etc.), actually obscure the hermeneutical address of a work.

The difference between Gadamer and Kant in this regard reveals that at least two meanings of the aesthetic are in play. Kant's usage is strictly classical. *Aisthesis* only concerns *sensible* objects. It does not involve their "meaning." This implies that for Kant questions concerning the "aesthetic" are logically separate from questions about what art is. As we have seen in his approach to the phenomenological, Gadamer's usage of the aesthetic is more contemporary: it fuses *both* the sensible *and* the ideational: "Pure seeing and pure hearing are dogmatic abstractions that artificially reduce phenomena. Perception always includes meaning" (*TM*, 84). In this, Gadamer appeals to the precedent of Aristotle, who contended that all *aisthesis* tends towards a universal, even if every sense has its own specific field and thus what is immediately given in it is not universal. But the specific sensory perception of something as such is an abstraction. The fact is that we see sensory particulars in relation to something universal. (*TM*, 82)

The "aesthetic" in Gadamer's phenomenological sense of the term embraces sensuously embodied ideas. Sensible particulars can convey, albeit partially, the subject matter (the universal) that informs them. Gadamer's implicit claim against Kant concerns his containment of our experience of art in the sensible alone. This has the consequence of emptying aesthetics of all significant content. We can only conclude that aesthetic consciousness, as Kant understands it, is an obstacle to the understanding of art. Does not Kant himself argue that "the senses can think nothing" and that "intuitions without concepts are blind"?[19] How is it that the question of aesthetics and our direct experience of art addressing us have become so divorced in Kant's thinking? The key lies in Kant's response to Alexander Baumgarten's aesthetics, where his rationalist tendencies betray him. In his *Critique of Pure Reason* Kant argues,

> The Germans are the only people who currently make use of the word "aesthetic" in order to signify what others call the critique of taste. This usage originated in the abortive attempt made by Baumgarten, that admirable analytical thinker, to bring the critical treatment of the beautiful under rational principles, and so to raise its rules to the rank of a science. But such endeavors are fruitless. The said rules or criteria are, as regards their chief sources, merely empirical, and consequently can never serve as determinate *a priori* laws by which our judgment of taste must be directed. On the contrary, our judgment is the proper test of the correctness of the rules.[20]

Whereas Kant insists that it is the free activity of judgment that gives structure to our sensible intuition, for Baumgarten sensible intuitions are already simply structured as "dark perceptions." Aesthetics springs from what Baumgarten calls a dark faculty of the soul giving expression to an *ars combinationis*, which instinctively fuses a sensuous manifold into a coherent whole, the perfection of which depends on the degree of its intensive and extensive clarity.[21] Kant's mechanist view of the empirical world is incompatible with the independent spontaneity he requires of aesthetic judgment: knowledge must be freely arrived at by judgment and not by the mechanisms of sensuous response. This strengthens Kant's claim that the determining ground of aesthetic judgment is epistemologically "subjective," since sensible intuitions have no order, pattern, or sense of their own. The latter is derived from being brought under the forms of judgment. This rigid opposition between the determinacy of reason and the indeterminacy of sense is not as prominent in Gadamer's aesthetics, which remains closer to Baumgarten's conception of the world considered as an intelligible totality constituted by relations of greater and lesser sensible and intellectual wholes.

The differences could not be starker, nor their philosophical outcomes more striking. If a Newtonian world picture governs Kant's account of the origin of sensible intuition, Heidegger's existential ontology informs Gadamer's rejection of Kant's position as an "alienated aesthetics" insensitive to the meaningful aspects of sensuous being. It is in between these two very different conceptual backgrounds that Gadamer's astonishing question emerges. *Is it not the case that in Kant's hands, aesthetics—the very discipline that his* Critique of Judgment *brings into the heart of philosophy—remains insensible to the claims of art?* The juxtaposition sustaining Gadamer's distinction between Kantian aesthetics and the "experience of art" is Heidegger's differentiation between the ontological and the ontic.

Whereas for Kant and his great advocate Arthur Schopenhauer sensuous being is a realm of estrangement in which subjective consciousness does not feel itself much at home, for Heidegger *Dasein* finds itself in an environment which speaks directly to it of its projects and history. This primary ontological realm is, in Gadamer's words, indicative of "the totality of our involvements" in which our singular being is immersed. Heidegger's ontological discourse is woven through with aesthetic terms but used in an ontological context. Being *manifests* itself, it *appears, discloses,* and *presents* itself. Terminology which in Kant's aesthetics is associated with the subjective internalities of how we represent phenomena to ourselves is in Gadamer's aesthetics bound up with the ontology of artworks themselves. As with Being, artworks are processes of emergence which exceed what consciousness can grasp of them. However, in stark contrast, the "ontic" realm is a secondary derivative of the ontological, an analytical simplification of it. It is not the world of immediate experience, but that world organized by *Dasein* so that it can be represented in thought. This realm concerns the distinguishing features of objects, their formal properties, characteristics, and attributes.

Gadamer's account of aesthetic alienation is decisively shaped by Heidegger's ontological/ontic distinction. The immediate truth-claim of art (its emerging out of and subsequent revelation of the totality of our worldly involvements) has the status of an ontological disclosure. It addresses us immediately. In contrast, the world of significant forms and aesthetic properties, which so animated early twentieth-century British aesthetics, is for Heidegger and Gadamer an utterly secondary, derivative world abstracted from the primary life-world of actual experience. Gadamer does not deny the utility of such terminology: it renders the communication of complex aspects of sensuous experience possible. Yet the philosophical mistake is to suppose that such interpretive constructs are the cause of sensuous experience rather than its effect—that is, there is no objective world of primary properties at the root of sensuous experience. Heidegger's example of the Greek temple is a case in point. Rather than dwelling on the what the building 'says' to us as the living heart of a historical community, we suppress these allegedly secondary 'subjective' qualities in favor of its supposedly primary architectural features.[22] This reversal of the primary and secondary aspects of sensuous experience has the consequence of rendering the voice of the artwork inconsequential if not indiscernible. This gives rise to Gadamer's claim that Kant's aesthetic is indicative of an alienated aesthetic, one which brackets if not anaesthetizes our response to what an artwork immediately says to us in favor of its formal "aesthetic" properties. The consequence is that we become alienated from, and condemn as secondary, the very features of art which give sense and meaning to our individual and collective existence. This is the basis of Gadamer's claim that "in order to do justice to art, aesthetics must go beyond itself and surrender the 'purity' of the aesthetic" (*TM*, 84). "Aesthetics has to be absorbed into hermeneutics," where the event of meaning retains ontological primacy (*TM*, 164). This would be a step toward rendering aesthetics hermeneutical.

Gadamer's central claim is that the aesthetic approach to art (aesthetic consciousness) is inappropriate because its philosophical foundations lie in the doctrine of *Erlebnisse*, and it is this above all that hinders the conditions necessary for the formation of hermeneutical knowledge. To put it more strongly, an *Erlebnis-Ästhetik* deprives art of its ability to address us and to function hermeneutically. By insisting on the phenomenological primacy of the experience of art, Gadamer endeavors to recover the hermeneutical element of meaningfulness that Kant's subjectivist aesthetic suppresses. "Aesthetics has to be absorbed into hermeneutics" because our experience of art is hermeneutical—that is, it concerns the disclosure of the meaningful. For Gadamer, it is an article of faith that the experience of art is hermeneutical. The philosophical question concerns what it is about the formal character of Kantian aesthetics that is incompatible with the development of such content. The concept of *Erlebnis* represents a significant obstacle to that development.

Erlebnisse relate to the intense sensations of the lived moment whilst *Erfahrungen* denote an unfolding over the long term, as, for example, when one speaks of one's long-term experience of music. *Erlebnisse* tend to the lived-moment of intense sensation whilst *Erfahrungen* incline toward the unfolding pattern of living.[23] *Erlebnisse* denote discrete moments in time, while *Erfahrungen* unfold within and establish their own temporality—that is, they unfold from within themselves. The two terms are not mutually exclusive. As with listening to a Mahler Symphony, long-term experiences (*Erfahrungen*) can include moments of stunning singularity, but in themselves the latter can distract from the whole of which they are a part. The question is how they contribute to the collective structure. The *Erlebnis/Erfahrung* distinction notably maps on to the differentiation between "aesthetic consciousness" (in the Kantian sense) and the "experience of art" as hermeneutically conceived. Gadamer's hostility toward Kantian aesthetics concerns its reduction of the experience of art to a series of fragmentary experiences that have no coherence of their own. For them to gain that coherence requires that they be placed in a larger part-whole structure (tradition), which cannot itself be an object of immediate experience. "Basing aesthetics on experience leads to an absolute series of points, which annihilates the unity of the work of art, the identity of the artist with himself, and the identity of the person understanding or enjoying the work of art" (*TM*, 86). The bluntness of these remarks exposes the underlying issue. Basing aesthetic knowledge on *Erlebnisse* alone is not only a contradiction in terms but threatens nihilism. To approach the artwork as the summation of discrete *Erlebnisse* renders knowledge of a continuous work impossible. Memory, comparison, and reappraisal are all sacrificed to the intensity of the living moment, a moment which, if not placed into the continuity of a wider sense-giving framework, will be rendered meaningless.

> The work of art is [reduced to] only an empty form, a mere nodal point in the possible variety of aesthetic experiences (*Erlebnisse*), and the aesthetic object exists in these experiences alone. As is evident, absolute discontinuity—i.e., the disintegration of the unity of the aesthetic object into the multiplicity of experiences—is the necessary consequence of an aesthetics of *Erlebnis*. (*TM*, 86)

Gadamer describes this philosophical predicament as an "untenable hermeneutic nihilism" (*TM*, 86). The arguments supporting this charge are as follows.

For Gadamer, if our experience of art is to count as genuine knowledge, it must include understanding something other than the self (*TM*, 87), whereas for Kant the axioms of knowledge and judgment depend entirely upon the self. If subjective consciousness imposes upon aesthetic sensations its own forms, how does it come to understand anything other than what it is always primed to know? Furthermore, if *Erlebnisse* are the ultimate data and basis for all knowledge, it follows that our immediate sensuous awareness is always episodic, lacking "inner coherence" and "permanent significance" (*TM*, 63). *In other words, Erlebnisse cannot of themselves produce the points of continuity which enable the points of non-identical repetition upon which knowledge of a subject matter can be based.* Furthermore, because Kant associates judgments of the beautiful with the operation of human understanding and its "natural" *a priori* endowments, the knowing subject does not change or become different to itself. In other words, if our understanding of art is based upon *Erlebnisse* alone, we never get beyond ourselves. The continuities beyond the moment that are necessary for the development of both self-understanding and an understanding of an artwork cannot be derived from discrete *Erlebnisse* alone. Precisely because it is dependent upon the intensities of the lived moment, an *Erlebnis-Ästhetik* disrupts the conditions which govern art's capacity for self-discovery and education. Kant's subjectivization of aesthetics has the consequence of rendering a hermeneutical approach to the experience of art impossible. It fragments the experience of art and in consequence disrupts the continuities and repetitions which are key to transforming our understanding of art and, hence, of ourselves.

It is easy to misread the appeal to continuity in Gadamer's argument. It is not the fact of continuity *per se* that matters, but what it enables. Gadamer refers to the "hermeneutic continuity of human existence" (*TM*, 87). "We recognize that even the phenomenon of art imposes an ineluctable task on existence, namely to achieve that continuity of self-understanding which can alone support human existence, despite the demands of the absorbing presence of the momentary aesthetic impression" (*TM*, 87). Gadamer, like Heidegger and Nietzsche before him, wants to show how subjective consciousness is far from self-contained; rather, it only comes to understand itself by engaging with the transmitted structures of our historical, cultural, and linguistic being that are external to it. These transmitted structures establish the circumstances against which change and movement in understanding can be assessed. Continuity is hermeneutically important not because of the sameness it establishes over time, but because of the differences it makes discernible within the temporality of existence. We should remember that the category of *Erfahrung* denotes a mode of being (*Dasein*) rather than an attribute of subjective consciousness. *Erfahrungen* constitute the basic being in motion of *Dasein* (*TM*, xxvii). It is by means of the continuities and differences within *Erfahrungen* that the temporality and historicity of *Dasein* becomes *apparent*. In the finite experiences of the artwork, *Dasein meets with the categories of its own being. It is this that enables the artwork to address us so intimately.* It is only when the expectations surrounding the historical and cultural continuities of our traditions are breeched that difference, learning, and change become possible. That an *Erlebnis-Äesthetik* undermines the continuities that enable the hermeneutic continuities of *Erfahrungen* to unfold is the ground of Gadamer's charge that such an aesthetic promotes hermeneutic nihilism. Though Kant seeks to ground aesthetics in the judgments of the cognitive subject, his *subjectification* of aesthetics actually serves to disrupt the very subjectivity upon which such experience depends. Gadamer's defense of an *Erfahrung-Ästhetik* implies that it is not so much subjective consciousness which is the ground of our experience of art but the historicity and temporality of our experience of art which *subjectivizes* our being. In revealing the finitude of our understanding, its temporality and its historicity, art reveals dispositions and inclinations of our being. The experience of art is one of self-implication. The type of knowledge that the experience invokes is hermeneutical. The power of an artwork to make us look again, to make us confront what we have overlooked or misjudged, reveals the limits and shortcomings of our understanding. The experience of art is hermeneutical because it brings us up short against the temporality of our own being. Such an experience *subjectivizes*. It makes us aware of the shortcomings of how we have understood both ourselves and a given subject matter. Gadamer's defense of hermeneutical awareness against Kant's subjectivization of aesthetics evolves into an aesthetics of subjectivization in its own right. It is the "experience of art" that subjectivizes us, giving us an ever-sharper sense of the limits and changing narrative of our understanding. This brings the notion of *Erfahrung* into a tighter conceptual relationship with the themes of polyphony and questioning mentioned above. The relationship becomes particularly evident when we consider the hermeneutical implications of adopting an *Erfahrung-Ästhetik*.

The argument that *Erfahrungen subjectivize* suggests that when viewed ontologically such experiences should not be considered just as predicates of a knowing consciousness but rather as situations that announce themselves to consciousness, take consciousness up, and in which that consciousness participates. In our experience of art, we encounter much more than a specific artwork. We encounter something marked by history, culture, language, and outlook. We encounter in the work and its subject matter dimensions of our own perspectives and narrative, such that when I experience a Ben Nicolson painting extensive passages in my history are brought into review. "There is no absolute progress and no final exhaustion of what lies in a work of art. The experience of art knows this of itself" (*TM*, 90). "*All encounter with the language of art is an encounter with an unfinished event and is itself part of this event*" (*TM*, 90). However, for a being that resides within the temporality of experience, this is no disadvantage. It is precisely because our knowledge of a work and its subject matter is finite that we can come to know more of it. Multidisciplinary and multi-perspectival approaches to a work serve as ways of drawing out more of what that experience holds. Similarly, questioning a work and its meaning is really a way of prompting us to think more carefully about our initial responses to it. No understanding of a work can be complete. The open-ended and unfinished nature of our experiences of art guarantees that participating in them remains hermeneutically transformative. Being brought to see something new about an artwork forces us to question the adequacy of what we thought we knew about it. It allows the work to become more itself—that is, to disclose the unfolding history of its effects. This is the basis of Gadamer's ontological reworking of the classical doctrine of *mimesis*. *Mimesis* is an anticipation of completion, of an artwork becoming ever more itself through the accumulations of its non-identical recurrences. This of course also suggests that in the temporality of conscious experience an artwork reveals something of the truth of Being itself. It forever shows and hides itself. Being brought to see a work in another perspective can force me to review, recalibrate, and question the adequacy of both my own and my tradition's understanding of that work's subject matter. This is why Gadamer is so suspicious of the *Erlebnis-Ästhetik*. By fixating on "the absorbing presence of the momentary aesthetic impression" (*TM*, 87), it dissolves the points of significance transmitted across a tradition which allow for comparison and appraisal. These are crucial to hermeneutical knowledge, for it is only against the relative stabilities of received tradition that deviations from the norm can be judged. How far off the mark is our perspective, and what does the emergence of that deviation tell us about changes within our own understanding? In this sense, the experience of art is genuinely hermeneutical: it forces us into a review of our understandings. It reveals not just the limitations of previous ways of thinking but also how far we have travelled since being in their thrall. The experience of art is hermeneutical in that through the medium of an artwork it reveals in a most intimate way the temporality and historicity of our own being. It is therefore quite erroneous to think that an *Erlebnis-Ästhetik* could ever do justice to our experience of art. On the contrary, it collapses art and the question of meaning into a nihilistic fetishization of the moment. To recover the transformative hermeneutic content of our experience that Kant's subjectivization of aesthetics surpasses, his aesthetics has to be replaced by an aesthetic that *subjectivizes*. This is the achievement of Gadamer's ontologization of aesthetic response, for it is in our experience of art (what it discloses of ourselves in relation to a given work) that the temporality and historicity of our being is reflected back to ourselves. What is experienced in our experience of art is, ontologically speaking, an experience of genuine truth (*TM*, 76). Art teaches us that we are part of an unfinished event. Privileging *Erlebnisse* as the ground of aesthetic understanding threatens to destroy art's capacity for self-discovery and education and to undermine the preconditions necessary to sustain a hermeneutical aesthetics. Establishing *Erfahrungen* as the basis of our experience of art guarantees that philosophy is always subordinate to the truth of art's address—that is, always seeking to unfold and to understand more of what that experience entails.

NOTES

1. Gadamer, Hans-Georg. *Truth and Method*, 2nd ed., trans. Joel Weinsheimer and Donald G. Marshall (New York: Bloomsbury Publishing, 2013), 77/90. Hereafter

cited in text as *TM*. Where the German is cited or the translation has been altered, the page number of the original is indicated after the slash. The latter refer to Hans-Georg Gadamer, *Wahrheit und Methode*, Gesammelte Werke I (Tübingen: Mohr Siebeck, 1990).

2. Such extensive deployments evidence the need for scholarly work to be done on the extensive conceptual histories that underpin Gadamer's somewhat 'easy' usage of the term 'aesthetic.'

3. See Hans-Georg Gadamer, "Autobiographical Reflections," in *The Gadamer Reader*, ed. and trans. by Richard E. Palmer (Evanston: Northwestern University Press, 2007), 24. This is the basis of the argument that our knowing is *mehr Sein als Bewusstsein*.

4. Gadamer, 37.

5. Gadamer, 28.

6. Gadamer, 33.

7. Gadamer, 21.

8. Immanuel Kant, *Critique of Judgment*, trans. J.C. Meredith (Oxford: Oxford University Press, 2007), 35.

9. Kant, 35.

10. Kant, 49.

11. See Alexander Gottlieb Baumgarten, *Texte zur Grundlegend der Ästhetik* (Hamburg: Felix Meiner Verlag, 1983).

12. *Destruktion* is Martin Heidegger's term for a philosophical de-scaling which aims to remove the unnecessary encrustations of accumulations of meaning which often obscure what a received term can communicate. Heidegger offers an outline of his account of Destruktion in *Being and Time*, trans. John Macquarrie and Edward Robinson (Oxford: Basil Blackwell, 1962), 41–49.

13. Immanuel Kant, *Critique of Pure Reason*, trans. Norman Kemp Smith (London: Macmillan-St Martin's Press, 1970), A 51/B 75.

14. Hans-Georg Gadamer, "The Artwork in Word and Image," in *The Gadamer Reader*, ed. and trans. by Richard E. Palmer (Evanston, IL: Northwestern University Press, 2007), 203.

15. Hans-Georg Gadamer, "On the Universality of the Hermeneutical Problem," in *The Gadamer Reader*, ed. and trans. by Richard E. Palmer (Evanston, IL: Northwestern University Press, 2007), 85.

16. Kant, *Critique of Judgment*, 35.

17. This should be understood as art truly making a claim upon our reflective awareness rather than art making a truth claim which has to be tested and verified in the manner of a proposition.

18. Hans-Georg Gadamer, "The Universality of the Hermeneutic Problem," in *Philosophical Hermeneutics*, ed. and trans. David E. Linge (Berkeley: University of California, 1976), 5, emphasis added.

19. Kant, *Critique of Pure Reason*, A 51/B 75.

20. Kant, A 21/B 36.

21. See Nicholas Davey, "Baumgarten," in *A Companion to Aesthetics*, ed. Stephen Davies, Kathleen Marie Higgins, Robert Hopkins, Robert Stecker, and David

E. Cooper (Oxford: Wiley-Blackwell, 2009), 162–63. Baumgarten's *ars combinationis* involves a principle of synthesis which re-appears in Kant's aesthetics as the synthesis of judgment and subsequently in Gadamer's aesthetics in the form of the hermeneutic imagination able to unify a manifold of elements as a coherent whole.

22. Martin Heidegger, *Poetry Language, Thought*, trans. and ed. Albert Hofstadter (New York: Harper Colophon, 1975), 42.

23. The term *Erfahrung* is connected to the notion of journeying and adventure. It has the sense of an ongoing process which maintains itself through its temporal thickening.

Chapter 3

TM I.1.3

Re-claiming Art's Claim to Truth

Daniel L. Tate

Gadamer describes the experience of art as one of "being struck" by the work. "The work of art that says something confronts us with ourselves [such that] what is said is like a discovery, a disclosure of something previously concealed."[1] Suddenly the artwork is "there"; it is, quoting Goethe, "'*So wahr, so seiend*,' 'So true, so full of being.'"[2] This characterizes the experience of truth we encounter in art. In the disclosure, one is struck by the very presence of what presents itself there. This highlights the phenomenological dimension of truth as presence. But we are also struck by the unfamiliarity of what confronts us in the work. This features the hermeneutical dimension of the experience of truth that requires integrating what the other says into our self-understanding. Furthermore, the Goethe quote underscores the ontological aspect of the experience of truth in art as an event in which being presents itself. All three belong to the encounter with art as "*experience* in a real sense."[3] In such experience lies the claim to truth that Gadamer seeks to vindicate for art. Rather than attempt to rationalize this claim, however, he admits it and seeks to understand it.[4] His effort to retrieve art's truth-claim thus issues in an ontology of the work of art. But the tacit measure of that effort is whether the being of the work so understood remains true to the truth we experience in the experience of art.

I pursue Gadamer's recovery of art's claim to truth in three sections. The first treats his retrieval of the question of truth in art through the analyses of play and transformation into structure. The second section elucidates art's truth-claim as an event of being by considering the coming-to-presence of being in the work, the spectator's being-present-to this event, and truth itself as a revealing-concealing event of being. The third examines art's truth within the movement of historical spirit understood as dialogical, mediational, and temporal.

1. RETRIEVING THE QUESTION OF ART'S TRUTH

For Gadamer, our encounter with art attests to an experience of truth. However, he defends art's claim to truth not by demonstrating it but by attending to that attestation. From the outset, he rejects the concept of art as a purely aesthetic phenomenon. This conception requires submitting the work to a process of abstraction that removes everything extrinsic to its "aesthetic quality" to attain the "pure" artwork. Experiencing art aesthetically thus entails differentiating the work from its purpose, function, and even the significance of its content. Produced by the "aesthetic consciousness," such "aesthetic differentiation" separates art from those relations to the world that supports its truth-claim.[5] Moreover, by conceiving art as a matter of pleasure rather than knowledge, aesthetics subjectivizes the experience of art, thereby invalidating any such claim. To overcome the alienation of art from truth that results from the subjectivization by aesthetic theory and the abstraction of aesthetic consciousness, Gadamer proposes the phenomenon of play as an appropriate model by which to understand what art is, in truth. The "transformation into structure" that follows provides the basic features of his ontology of the work of art.

1.1 Art as Play

To retrieve the question of truth in art, Gadamer seeks to lay aside the aesthetic (mis)conceptions that distort and conceal the authentic experience of art. This retrieval, however, requires an approach to the experience of art that will reveal its true being as an experience of truth. The aim, in other words, is let the work of art be the being that it is. To this end, Gadamer turns to the phenomenon of play. First and foremost, play is a phenomenon of motion, a to-and-fro movement. "The movement of playing has no goal that brings it to an end; rather it renews itself in constant repetition." It is decisive, however, that play has no "subject" that performs the movement. "It is the game that is played—it is irrelevant whether or not there is a subject who plays it" (*TM*, 108). Gadamer insists on this point. Play is not properly conceived as the activity of something or someone who plays; it is not the activity of a subject. On the contrary, play consists in the occurrence of the movement itself. In short, play plays. But in the course of its movement, play also presents itself. As Gadamer observes, "Play appears as a self-movement that does not pursue any particular end or purpose so much as movement as movement, exhibiting, so to speak, a phenomenon of excess, of the self-presentation of living-being (*der Selbstdarstellung des Lebendigseins*)."[6] Play thus consists in the ever-renewing self-movement that presents itself.

Human play characteristically plays something. By playing the game we shape the play-movement, thereby fulfilling our assigned tasks as players. Here too Gadamer insists on "the *primacy of the play over the consciousness of the player*" (*TM*, 109). So even in human play the players are not its subject; "instead play merely reaches presentation (*Darstellung*) through the players" (*TM*, 107). By introducing rules and boundaries, human play sets off the playing field as a separate domain that marks out its own space and time. It thereby opens a place, a *Da*, within which the game is played and wherein the play-movement presents itself. But "all presentation is potentially a representation for someone" (*TM*, 113). Where the self-presentation of play is intended for someone we cross into the sphere of art. Here the closed world of play lets down one of its walls, becoming open to an audience. In the play of art, the work is presented to, and properly experienced by, the spectator. Just as much as the performer, the spectator is a player who must participate in the movement in order for the play to present itself as it is intended. Indeed, "the genuine reception and experience of the work of art can only exist for one who 'plays along,' that is, one who performs in an active way himself."[7] Insofar as both are players who enable the work to 'come out,' the distinction between performer and spectator is elided. Yet Gadamer accords a certain privilege to the spectator, to whom the work is presented as a meaningful whole and in whom it achieves its full significance. Participating in the play, the spectator belongs to the performance of the work by which it presents itself. The audience therefore only completes what the play is.

Refusing any subjectivizing account, Gadamer adopts the "medial sense" of *play* as a constantly self-renewing movement (*TM*, 108–9). But, as noted, the self-movement of play also discloses itself as a movement of self-presentation characteristic of all living-being (*Lebewesen*). The being of the artwork finds its proper place within this movement. Yet the import of play bears not only on art but on being as well. A guide word reminiscent of Heidegger suggests itself—being of play: play of being. Being, like play, *is* this movement, a pure *energeia* that has no purpose other than to present itself and no external *telos* in which it ends. Instead, being constantly renews itself as a movement of self-presentation. However, this movement cannot become present without a 'dative' of presentation, someone who receives and recognizes it *as* present. For this to happen, a stabilizing factor is needed, something in which this motion comes to rest. The energeia of being therefore finds its counterpart in the *ergon* of the work (*TM*, 117). Paradoxically, only where the self-presenting movement of being is held fast in the work and beheld by the spectator does being become present. It is in the work of art that being appears *as such*. But motion also belongs to the being of the work (inclusive of the spectator as participant) as a coming-to-presence. Being comes to presence where the work comes to stand. Truth thereby occurs in the work of art as an event of being. Although arrested by the work, the movement of being arrives at no final rest. Instead, the work is taken back up into the self-presenting movement of being where, received anew, it spawns yet further events of truth.

1.2 Art as Transformation

Gadamer conceives the change whereby play becomes art as the *"transformation into structure (Verwandlung ins Gebilde)"* (*TM*, 115/116). This is no gradual transition from one mode of being to another; instead, what is transformed acquires—"suddenly and as a whole"—a new ontological status (*TM*, 115). What now exists is an ideal structure or configuration, a *Gebilde*. "The work of art transforms our fleeting experience into a stable and lasting form of an independent and internally coherent creation (*Gebilde*)."[8] In the work, something "stands" before us. At the same time, this change receives its full meaning as a transformation into truth (*Verwandlung ins Wahre*) which accomplishes a presentation of being. Indeed, Gadamer asserts, "we must recognize that 'presentation' (*Darstellung*) is the mode of being of the work" (*TM*, 119–20/118). As complementary concepts, configuration and presentation belong inseparably together. The presentation of true being only occurs within the work as an ideal configuration, yet the purpose of every configuration is just to offer such a presentation. Here Gadamer's account appeals to the mimetic concept of art where "the mimetic is and remains a primordial phenomenon in which it is not so much an imitation that occurs as a transformation."[9] He thus conceives the mimetic as a "transformed reality in which the transformation points back to what has been transformed in and through it."[10] As I argue below, his account of transformation is simultaneously a retrieval of mimesis that takes Aristotle's *Poetics* as its reference point.[11]

If "all true imitation is transformation," then "true imitation" is no mere copy of reality.[12] It is rather a presentation of being that occurs in the artwork through its transformation into configuration. The *Poetics* conveys this in the concept of *mythos* or plot. In tragic poetry, the plot configures the discrete events into an ordered and coherent narrative that offers the dramatic unfolding of a single action. So configured, the drama comprises a meaningful whole that is about something, its *Sache(n)*, in this case, the tragic action it presents. Therefore, *mythos* and *mimesis* are strictly correlated. As Paul Ricoeur argues, this is a "quasi-identification" where the imitation of action (*mimesis*) takes place via the structuring of events (*mythos*) provided by the poetic composition.[13] By virtue of its narrative configuration, the *mythos* unifies the course of events which facilitates *mimesis* by enabling the presentation of an action that is "single and a whole." The unity of action is thus a function of plot. The aspects of wholeness, completeness, and magnitude that Aristotle attributes to the *mythos* likewise determine the *mimesis* of the action it presents.[14] By unifying the action it presents, the narrative transforms it into a meaningful whole that acquires the ideality and permanence of a *Gebilde*. The imitated action is stripped of its accidental aspects so that its essential features become more clearly discernable. What is imitated is thereby "raised . . . into its own validity and truth" (*TM,* 124). Thomas Prufer offers confirmation: "The imitated action is heightened and sharpened by the imitation into being more truly itself than it would be if it were not imitated and thus made available to contemplation through the transforming imitation."[15] The imitation illumines what is obscure, reveals what is hidden, and intensifies unseen possibilities. This means that "imitation enables us to see more than so-called reality."[16] From this perspective, "'reality' is defined as what is untransformed and art as the raising up (*Aufhebung*) of this reality into its truth." Once transformed, the action of a drama no longer permits any direct comparison with reality. "It is raised above all such comparisons because a superior truth speaks from it" (*TM,* 116–17).

Imitation, then, is no mere copying but a "bringing-forth." This retrieves the original meaning of *mimesis* as transformation. So conceived, *mimesis* is a presentation where what is presented is made manifest in its truth. For Gadamer, though, this presentation does not take place apart from its recognition by the spectator. If the imitation renders what is imitated intelligible, as Aristotle holds, then its meaning is only fulfilled when what is presented is received and recognized as such. In the imitation, the spectator recognizes the imitated for what it is. For this reason, recognition is a mode of knowing, but not one where we simply know again what was already familiar to us. Presented through imitation, what is imitated emerges from the variable and accidental circumstances in which we ordinarily encounter it so that it can be grasped in its essential features. Thus recognition, Gadamer says, is "the joy of knowing *more* than is already familiar." Accordingly, "the 'known' enters into its true being and manifests itself as what it is only when it is recognized" (*TM,* 118). In hermeneutic terms, recognizing something means cognizing it *as* something. The *as* here means that something has become present to the spectator in its true being. Recognition is an act of identification, not of distinction. In it, one identifies the imitated *as* present in the imitation that presents it. "Thus the situation basic to imitation . . . implies that what is presented is there [*das Dargestellte da ist*], but also that it has come into the There more authentically" (*TM,* 119/120, translation altered).

2. THE HAPPENING OF TRUTH IN THE ARTWORK

Gadamer holds that the work-being of the artwork consists in presentation; in the work of art something becomes present. Furthermore, we have seen that presentation requires both configuration and recognition. Something only becomes present in the configuration of the work and even then only for someone who, receiving the presentation, recognizes what becomes present *as* present in its being. By virtue of this *as*, Gadamer says, "it comes forth."[17] Where the being of something comes forth in the work, there is an event of truth. This is the experience of truth that takes place in the encounter with the work of art. To understand this event, however, it is necessary to elucidate the coming-to-presence that occurs in the artwork. I propose to do so by elaborating the three constituent elements of Gadamer's account of the ontological event that takes place in the work of art as a happening of truth—presentation, participation, and event.

2.1 Art as Presentation

To assert that the being of the artwork consists in presentation is to claim that what is presented comes to presence there. Such coming-to-presence is the event of being that occurs in the work of art. Therein lies art's claim to truth. Though perhaps initially perplexing, in *Truth and Method* Gadamer clarifies this claim to truth by invoking the mimetic relation of image and original. However, he rejects the Platonic view that places art at three removes from truth (*TM*, 119). He argues that the distance this implies between image and original is inappropriate to the real ontological meaning of *mimesis* as presentation. He insists that, with art, "it is precisely not the ontological distinction between the presentation and the presented, but the total identification with what is presented that constitutes the nature of the presentation."[18] The act of recognition, in turn, completes the identification of the presented in the presentation, the original in the image. Gadamer therefore maintains that *mimesis* has nothing essentially to do with being a copy (*Abbild*) that effaces itself in pointing to the original it strives to resemble. Instead, properly understood, *mimesis* does not point to something but rather makes something present; it is the coming to presence of the original (*Urbild*) in its image (*Bild*). Artworks in general exhibit this same ontological structure where the original cannot be separated from its presentation in the image. What is presented there, the being of the original, is only to be found in the image. "Paradoxical as it may sound," Gadamer writes, "the original acquires an image only by being imaged, and yet the image is nothing but the appearance of the original" (*TM*, 142).

Gadamer develops this identification of image and original in his concept of the picture (*Bild*).[19] Analysis of pictorial being, he argues, confirms that the identity (non-differentiation) of picture and pictured is essential to the experience of pictures (*TM*, 140). But pictorial intentionality is complex. On the one hand, the picture intends an original which it is not; the original is distinct from its picture. On the other hand, the primary intention of the picture is not to differentiate between the original presented in the picture and its pictorial presentation; in the picture, the original becomes present. As Robert Sokolowski observes, "The peculiarity of pictorial presencing . . . is that pictures do not merely refer to something, but make that something present."[20] Actually, Sokolowski's term *picturing* better conveys the ontological process of coming-to-presence that Gadamer is discussing. For the picture is a part of the process of pictorial presencing that also involves an original and a viewer. Through the picture, the viewer recognizes the original *as* present in some essential respect. In picturing, then, something comes to presence in the picture such that the depicted original appears in its being. Since the being of the original only appears *as* depicted, it is found only in the picture; the original *is* as it becomes present there. This entails an ontological dependence of the original on how it presents itself in the picture. Thus, the picture presents something which, without it, would not present itself in this way. But because the picture has its own independent reality, the appearance of the original does not require this or that particular picture. Nonetheless, picturing has the ontological structure of an image where the original it presents cannot be separated from its presentation. How the original comes to presence in this picture now belongs to its being. Gadamer concludes: "Every such presentation is an ontological event" (*TM*, 141). Picturing is thus a process wherein being appears; it is an event of truth.

So only by being pictured does an original come into (its) being. Portraiture is illustrative. The portrait depicts an individual but does not merely reproduce the sitter; it is not a copy. Instead, it is a picture that presents the person; it is an image. By drawing on their distinctive features and personal characteristics the portrait forms—and transforms—the individual into "the concrete living presence of the person."[21] These features and characteristics are aspects by which their personality emerges in the continuity of experience built up over time. Gathering these aspects into a unified image that heightens and condenses them, the portrait completes this process such that the person thereby acquires greater coherence and presence.[22] Where this happens the person portrayed comes alive; as Gadamer says, they are "suddenly there" in the picture.[23] Presenting the person in the heightened truth of their being, the portrait depicts who they essentially are.[24] Accordingly, the picture allows what it presents "to be for the first time fully what it is" (*TM*, 143). So it matters *how* the person appears in *this* picture. Consequently, the individual is not diminished by their depiction, rather their being is enhanced. Ontologically, the original becomes more due to its pictorial presentation. "Every such presentation is an ontological event. . . . By being presented, it experiences, as it were, an increase of being (*Zuwachs an Sein*)" (*TM*, 141/145). Homer's Achilles, he says, is "more" than the "real" Achilles. The image is thus an ontological event; "in it being appears, meaningfully and visibly" (*TM*, 144). As presentation, the artwork is not reproductive, but productive; it is an emanation of being. Through the work something comes to presence that was hitherto absent, hidden, or withdrawn. In it, "something new comes forth as true."[25] On this event of coming-to-presence hinges the truth-claim of art.

2.2 Art as Participation

The spectator is no mere onlooker but a genuine participant in the work, that is, one who participates by letting being appear there. This is an activity of disclosure without which it would not come forth. A dialectical tension surfaces here between the openness and the closedness of the work. As a meaningful whole, it has the structure of a completed work that presents a closed world. Yet the work is essentially incomplete, in that it remains open toward the spectator for whom it is intended. Thus "openness toward the spectator is part of the closedness of the play" precisely because "the audience only completes what the play as such is" (*TM*, 113). By taking part, the spectator belongs to the dynamic of the work's self-presentation. Decisive for Gadamer's participatory account of the experience of art is the *presence of the spectator* to the presentation that takes place in the work. He declines the posture of critical distance that defines aesthetic consciousness, regarding it as an abstraction from the immediacy of the experience of art. Such distance "is always secondary to the immediate truth-claim that proceeds from the work of art itself."[26] Instead, Gadamer maintains, the spectator's engagement with the work consists in their "being there present" (*Dabeisein*). As "true participation," being present means "being totally involved in and carried away by what one sees" (*TM*, 127/129). This involves a self-forgetfulness wherein one gives themselves over to the work. Viewed subjectively, this is a mode of being outside oneself by which one is wholly with something else. The being-present proper to the experience of art is thus the ecstatic condition of being immersed in the work. Such participation describes the disclosive comportment proper to the spectator as one who lets the work present itself by being-present to it.

Being-present lends the spectator's participation a contemplative quality that is active as well as passive. It is passive, in that our experience with art is prompted by the work itself. Arrested by our encounter with the work of art, we experience ourselves as addressed by what it says. In *Truth and Method*, Gadamer construes this address as a claim (*Anspruch*) that the work makes upon us (*TM*, 128/131). Addressed by the work, we are called to respond to it as if bound by a claim. Claimed by the work, our responsibility is to let it come to presence, thereby completing the work and fulfilling its claim to truth. Yet there is no claim apart from being addressed; it is in being claimed by the work that we find ourselves responsible to its claim to truth. Here the claiming, the claim, and the claimed coalesce. At the heart of this claim, then, is a dialogical relation between address and response. The one addressed is properly receptive insofar as they are fundamentally open to what the work offers. Such receptivity is not merely passive but is an active holding-oneself-open. As a configuration, the artwork *draws together* aspects of what it presents into a meaningful whole. One's response is receptive when, absorbed in the work and open to what it says, it *draws us in*. The response is active where, engaging the work, one *draws out* what the work offers, letting it come to presence.

Regarding the active response, Gadamer's descriptions of reading poetry are the richest. Reading requires patient listening to the language of the poem in order to let it speak. More than an open receptivity, this involves pursuing those directions of meaning opened up through its linguistic configuration. To let the poem speak is to listen toward the "completion of meaning" at which it aims.[27] Such listening consists in a "tarrying" that attends to the rhythm of the poem, seeking a balance between its interlaced movements of sound and sense. A thickened network of meaning builds up through successive readings by which the poem acquires resonance, thereby gaining density and clarity, depth and coherence. When interpretation succeeds, Gadamer avers, "everything in the text tightens up, the degree of coherence is unmistakably increased as well as the overall cohesion of the interpretation."[28] What emerges is the poem's "tone," which binds its aspects together into a distinctive whole by which the poem achieves its unique saying.[29] One's response is genuinely responsible where it attends to the poem, following the movement of language. By letting it speak in this way, the participant fulfills their responsibility to the work. Where this happens, it comes forth and its interpretation recedes into the presence of the poem. In this ontological event of language lies the truth of the poetic word.

2.3 Art as Event

Through the participation of the spectator, the work of art achieves a presentation of being. The event of truth that takes place in art consists of this reciprocal relation. This reaffirms Gadamer's assertion that presentation is the mode of being of the work of art. It also reaffirms his contention that the artwork is only "there" in the event of its appearing. This is borne out by the experience of art. In our encounter with the work, he says, "we have the experience of something emerging—and this one can call truth!"[30] Immersed in the work, we witness something come to presence there such that it appears in its being. Moreover, what is presented becomes more truly itself by virtue of its presentation in the work. For "in presentation, the presence of what is presented reaches its consummation" (*TM*, 138). The presentation that takes place in art is no mere appearance that must be distinguished from reality. Rather, what appears in the artwork is elicited from the flux of manifold reality where it is held—and beheld—in its being. What appears in the appearance is being itself. Presentation thus has an ontological significance, in it an event of being occurs. This is the genuine experience of art; in the presence of the work we experience a disclosure of being so evident and illuminating that it compels and binds us as an experience of truth. Gadamer is therefore adamant that the artwork is not simply the laying bare of an existing truth but the coming-to-presence (of being) as an event of truth.

In "The Relevance of the Beautiful," Gadamer approaches the truth of art through the concept of the symbol since both rest on "an intricate interplay of showing and concealing."[31] Like art, what the symbol refers to is present in the symbol. This marks the irreducible indeterminacy of the artwork that accounts for its fecundity. Citing Heidegger, Gadamer affirms that the "ontological plentitude or truth that addresses us in art [occurs] through the twofold movement of revealing, unconcealing, and manifesting, on the one hand, and concealing and sheltering on the other." In this interplay lies the complex presence of the work of art as an event of truth. It is decisive that what presents itself "is secured and sheltered in the ordered composure of the creation (*Gebilde*)."[32] The presentation that occurs in the work is embedded in its sensuous configuration. Here the corporeality of the work is not used as a sign that can be set aside; rather, like the symbol, it has its being within itself. What comes to presence there cannot be abstracted from its embodiment. "Rather, the meaning of the work lies in the fact that it is there."[33] It is this "facticity" that renders the work of art a unique and unsurpassable event of truth that resists the full recovery of its meaning. Herein lies the enigmatic quality of art that holds back as much as it reveals. Even in picturing, where the being of the original depends on how it is pictured, what comes forth in the picture is also drawn back into the arrangement of shapes, colors, and textures from which it emerges. Thus, the truth we experience in art is only encountered in *this* work.

Gadamer also considers the symbolic a mode of presentation where what is symbolized exceeds the symbol that presents it. Against the aesthetic concept of symbol as "the coincidence of sensible appearance and supersensible meaning," he argues that symbols retain "a disproportion between form and essence" (*TM*, 70–71). While symbol and symbolized belong together, a tension remains. In the symbolic, Gadamer observes, "the particular represents itself as a fragment of being that promises to make whole whatever corresponds to it."[34] Here the symbol-symbolized relation is recast as a part-whole relation such that art is likewise a part that presents the whole to which it belongs, although always in a partial way. "Amidst the variety of art," he writes, "the same message of the whole addresses us over and over again."[35] The whole which Gadamer invokes, however, is the world which is co-present with what becomes present in the work of art. For ultimately it is the world as a whole that is disclosed in the work. In art, "[it is] the totality of the experienceable world, our ontological place in it, and above all [our] finitude before that which transcends [us], that is brought to experience."[36] But the world disclosed in art is itself a dynamic interplay of emergence and hiddenness. Indeed, as Nicholas Davey observes, "what a work is capable of presenting depends on the nexus of cultural relationships in and through which it shows itself. What is accordingly disclosed and withheld will be relative to the horizons in which the work is received."[37] The world-disclosure of art thus engages the cultural-historical horizons that comprise the communal history to which we belong, but which are only given in a further interplay of revealing and concealing.[38] We now turn to the historical dimension of art's truth.

3. THE HISTORICITY OF ART'S TRUTH-CLAIM

It belongs to the historicity of human Dasein, Gadamer asserts, "to mediate itself to itself understandingly" and so "to the whole of its own experience of the world" which includes "all tradition."[39] Thus the truth-claim of art belongs within the context of hermeneutical experience and the task of integration that falls to our historical being. As the enveloping horizon of our lives that never becomes present as a whole, the world also opens onto past and future as temporal horizons that surpass our immediate experience but are co-present with it. Furthermore, the world disclosed in the work of art is always the historical world to which it belongs. An artwork thus invariably interprets the world it discloses. Likewise, every interpretation of a work is bound up with its historical world. But since it is available to worlds other than its own, the same work appears differently in other cultural and historical contexts. Thus, the artwork is both the interpretation of the world and is interpreted by one.[40] Such considerations introduce another dimension of art's truth as historically bound and yet contemporaneous with each present in which it is understood. Here Gadamer invokes a concept of historical being as the living spirit of tradition that exists in an ongoing movement of departure and return. To discuss this conception and its bearing on art's truth-claim, I consider art as dialogical, mediational, and temporal.

3.1 Art as Dialogical

Art is enigmatic not only because it is embodied but because it belongs to a historical world. This irreducible opacity in art indicates that the work, like its audience, lacks self-presence. Since art is not immediately intelligible or timelessly present, it requires interpretation. By interpreting the work of art, we interpret ourselves and our world. As a mode of our historical being, hermeneutic self-understanding "always occurs through understanding something other than the self and includes the unity and integrity of the other" (*TM*, 87). Without the immediacy of self-presence, we need something other by which to understand ourselves; "[art] provides the alterity necessary for self-understanding."[41] Interpretation must therefore preserve the otherness of the work necessary for self-understanding. And yet for such understanding to occur, the world of the work cannot remain utterly alien to our own world. As Joel Weinsheimer explains, "Without reflection, without a mirror in which I can see myself immediately, . . . the dark glass of art is a source of knowledge and of truth—the truth of self-knowledge."[42] Art confronts us with another way of seeing, as if through a different lens that brings into view something hitherto hidden that compels us to look at ourselves and our world anew. For Gadamer, "The work of art has its true being in the fact that it becomes an experience that changes the person who experiences it" (*TM*, 107). In such experience, the alterity of art alters our understanding.

The experience of art thus involves an encounter with otherness. This marks a limit to hermeneutical experience which harbors "a potentiality for being-other (*Andersseins*) that goes beyond every coming to agreement about what we have in common."[43] Yet, Gadamer insists, hermeneutical experience seeks a shared meaning even as it seeks the other. Hence the question, "how do the communality of meaning (*die Gemeinsamkeit des Sinnes*) built up in conversation and the impenetrable otherness of the other mediate each other?"[44] Thus at the heart of dialogue lies an injunction to listen to "the voice of the other."[45] The other, however, is not to be mastered or anticipated. Instead, it withdraws into the sheltering strangeness of its being-other. But strangeness does not preclude a relation with the other; rather it sustains that relation. Thus a genuinely dialogical encounter neither reduces nor sublates its being-other but rather preserves and respects it. This requires an openness to the artwork as (an) other that dialogically affirms it as a *you*. Regarding the other as a you is confirmed by the hermeneutic concept of experience (*Erfahrung*) that Gadamer analyzes in *Truth and Method*. There he develops the dialectical nature of experience, emphasizing its negative aspect as an experience of disappointment (*TM*, 355–70).[46] The disruption of one's horizon of anticipation is integral to such an experience. This element of surprise in our experience of the other underscores the vulnerability and risk involved in hermeneutical experience.[47] Exposed before the other, we are confronted by something unanticipated that requires our being-open. For Gadamer, "the important thing is . . . to experience the Thou truly as a Thou—i.e., not to overlook his claim but to really let him say something to us. Here is where openness belongs" (*TM*, 369).

In such openness, the dialogical dimension of the experience of art becomes evident. Faced with the alterity of art we find ourselves addressed by the work. Where the work refuses our anticipation of completeness, we are challenged not just to understand the work aright but also to understand ourselves and our world in view of it. Dispossessed by the work, our self-understanding is at stake. "In the experience of art we see a genuine experience (*Erfahrung*) induced by the work, which does not leave him who has it unchanged" (*TM*, 91/106). Responsive to what it says, we are responsible to its claim even before we fully understand it. "Suddenly," Gerald Bruns observes, "I find myself defined by this claim, as if it now mirrored a part of me that I may hardly know how to recognize but which I cannot renounce."[48] Tarrying with the work and entering into its claim, we let it inhabit our world and allow its truth to transform us. George Steiner describes our encounter with art as "the most 'ingressive' and transformative summons available to human experiencing."[49] In this "transformative summons" lies the truth-claim that seizes us in art. Responding to that summons, we engage in a reciprocal I-you relation with the work. The experience of art thus exhibits the dynamic of dialogue as the very medium by which truth occurs. Here dialogue culminates in a moment of rest when something comes to presence in the work only to be taken up again into its to-and-fro movement. This interplay of motion and rest pervades the hermeneutical experience of the artwork as an unfinished event of truth. The experience of art, like all genuinely hermeneutical experience, remains open to further experience. In contrast to Hegel's appropriative dialectic which would bring the movement of historical spirit to an end, Gadamer proposes non-appropriative dialogue as an unending movement of excursion and return that imbues the hermeneutic concept of mediation.

3.2 Art as Mediational

Aesthetic consciousness differentiates the work from its interpretations or performances. For Gadamer, however, this is an abstraction that removes us from the experience of art whenever we reflect on the interpretive approach or an actor's proficiency. But aesthetic differentiation is secondary; what is primary is the non-differentiation of the artwork and its performance. Through the interpretation, the work enacts its self-presentation. This means that various interpretations belong to the being of the work itself. How the work is presented in its performance is essential to it, not incidental. Hence, interpretations are not a subjective variety of conceptions but rather "the work's own possibilities of being that emerge as the work explicates itself

... in the variety of its aspects" (*TM*, 122). To consider interpretations as free or arbitrary fails to appreciate what is binding about the work. "In fact," Gadamer writes, "they are all subject to the supreme criterion of the 'right' presentation" (*TM*, 122). Even if this criterion is flexible and relative, he still insists that striving for the right presentation is an obligation that the work imposes on every interpretation. Furthermore, the fact that each interpretation strives to be right "serves only to confirm that the non-differentiation of the mediation (*Vermittlung*) from itself is the actual experience of the work" (*TM*, 123). Gadamer therefore asserts that the mediation communicating the work is, in principle, total. "Total mediation means that the medium as such is superseded (*aufhebt*). In other words, the performance . . . does not become as such thematic, but . . . the work presents itself through it and in it" (*TM*, 123–24/125). The task of interpretation is: to mediate the work so that it comes to presence.

The work of art stands within a world, its original life-world that the work discloses. Yet each work also presents "a world of its own in miniature."[50] While Gadamer never clarifies this relation, it is through its own world that the work discloses the life-world in which it stands. Here we find another level of mediation: a mediation between the closed world of the work and the open world to which it belongs.[51] As an autonomous configuration, the artwork presents a world of its own that offers "a closed circle of meaning" that is "lifted out of the ongoing course of events" and "resists all penetration and interference" (*TM*, 131). However, the work does not transpose us into another world; instead, it discloses the world common to the artwork and its audience. Immersed in our lived world, the distance enforced by the closed world of the work allows that common world to become present to us in some hitherto unnoticed but illuminating way. Thus, "it is the truth of our own world—the religious and moral world in which we live—that is presented before us and in which we recognize ourselves" (*TM*, 130). This disclosure occurs where the work mediates its closed world with the open world it shares with the spectator. Through this mediation, art becomes a *Weltanschauung*, an "intuition of the world that every work of art presents."[52] This entails that the relation of the work to its original life-world is not external but rather internal to it. The work of art therefore belongs to its original world.

There is a further mediation "without which a work of art has no real 'presence'" (*TM*, 156). Each work has an effective history comprised of its interpretative self-presentations over the course of its reception in diverse cultural and historical worlds (*TM*, 311–18). The temporal discontinuity that separates us from the past estranges us from works whose historical world has passed. Torn from their original world, artworks handed down by tradition suffer a loss of meaning and presence. Yet this loss does not entail that they only survive in alienated aesthetic consciousness. Instead "past and present are brought together in a work of art" (*TM*, 157). Thus, art poses the hermeneutic task of reestablishing continuity by mediating the past world of the work with the present world in which it stands. Although the work belongs to its original world, "it remains irrefutable that art is never simply past but is able to overcome temporal distance by virtue of its own meaningful presence" (*TM*, 165). This involves a "fusion of horizons" by which the work becomes present anew and a binding truth emerges (*TM*, 317). Since the work is truly there only in the interpretations where it presents itself, each presentation belongs to the work. So we find again, now in a historical register, the augmentation of the work that does not become "less" by dissolving into its interpretations but rather becomes "more" by being present in each of them. The circuit of reciprocity that joins the work and its audiences into communities of meaning formed by the work is drawn into the broader historical process of meaning-formation by which cultural communities are formed and re-formed. Art is thus taken up into the happening of tradition whereby the present world comes to understand itself differently by encountering other voices that address us in such works. Through this encounter we recognize hidden commonalities that bind us together, even if they exhibit more conflict than consensus. Here the work (and its interpretations) participates in the ongoing dialogue of cultural formation (*Bildung*) from which it arises and to which it contributes. In doing this work of finite historical spirit, works of art provide a locus of transmission in which the truths of tradition find new life.

3.3 Art as Temporal

The historical mediation of the artwork as a finite event of truth exhibits a temporal dimension. The three-fold mediation of the work sketched above calls for a temporal interpretation of its identity, repeatability, and contemporaneity. The mediation of work and performance prompts a temporal reading of its identity as manifest through its presentations. Defining the work of art as presentation means that "its actual being cannot be detached from its presentation and that in this presentation the unity and identity of a structure (*die Einheit und Selbigkeit eines Gebildes*) emerge" (*TM*, 125/127). Yet Gadamer conceives the unity proper to the work as its "hermeneutic identity."[53] Even in music, dance, or poetry, the work "compose[s] itself into the compact unity of a creation (*Gebilde*)—one that always remains the same."[54] This identity is "hermeneutic" because it is not contained in the work apart from the spectator's participation. Not only is a work's identity intended by each presentation of it, it cannot be identified apart from some interpretation of the work. Hence, in the experience of art, "we do not distinguish between the particular way in which the work is realized and the identity of the work itself."[55] While the work presents itself in one interpretation, it still holds in reserve other ways of presenting itself in different interpretations. The hermeneutic identity of the artwork thus consists in an interplay of sameness and difference. As Gadamer says, "the work as such still speaks to us as the same work, even in repeated and different encounters with it."[56] It remains the same work only by presenting itself differently through other interpretations that present it anew. The temporality of the work resides within this fold in its identity; it exists as the same by always being different.

The fold within the artwork's hermeneutic identity exhibits a dual condition. On the one hand, the interpretation of a work cannot be separated from its being as a work. For it is only in the presentation that we encounter the work itself. On the other hand, the work is essentially open to other interpretations of it. The work is never completely presented in any of its interpretations but withdraws from each. This belongs to the work-being of the work as a revealing-concealing event of truth. The artwork has an inner depth or "self-sufficiency" that cannot be exhausted. But the inexhaustibility of the work is just another way of describing its fecundity as a font of truth-events. The work is essentially open to other cultural-historical contexts and unforeseen audiences. Open to ever different presentations, the ideality of the work bears the possibility of repetition within itself. Indeed, repetition belongs to the being of the work of art because it only comes to presence when it is presented. So despite its formal character as a finished piece, the work has the open structure of an event that must be continually repeated. The repeatability of the artwork points to another aspect of its temporality. It has the temporal being of that which only exists in repetition. Like the festival, the artwork is an essentially recurrent phenomenon that "has its being only in becoming and return." But it is not literally repeated. Instead, "every repetition is as original as the work itself" (*TM*, 126). Moreover, as something to-be-repeated, the artwork is generative of further presentations; it is productive of new events of truth.

The hermeneutic task of mediating past and present calls us to hold onto the work so that all mediation is sublated in the work's presence. Totally mediated by its presentation, the work comes to presence; totally absorbed in its presence, the spectator is claimed by the work. For Gadamer, the directness and immediacy of this mutual presence is key to the encounter with art as an experience of truth. "It possesses a mysterious intimacy that grips our entire being, as if there were no distance at all between us and the work and as if every encounter with it were an encounter with ourselves."[57] Despite the heightened historical consciousness of our age, Gadamer maintains that an "absolute contemporaneousness" exists between the work and its beholder regardless of its cultural or historical origin. The fact that the artwork can take such hold of us demonstrates "the absolute presentness" of art to all times and places. He thus finds the paradoxical temporality of art "marked by an immediate presentness in time" and yet "by a rising above time."[58] Unrestricted to the horizon of its original world, the work of art is open to new mediations in which it can come to the presence in another present. In Gadamer's view, "the work of art is the absolute present for each particular present, and at the same time it holds its word in readiness for every future."[59] Wherever the work comes to presence, there it makes its truth-claim anew. Thus "it is the vivid presentness and contemporaneousness (*Gegenwärtigkeit und Gleichzeitigkeit*) of art that constitute and maintain its power."[60] In this contemporaneity of the work of art, Gadamer finds the temporal being of its absolute presentness (*TM*, 129).

Movement is vital to Gadamer's ontology of the work of art and the claim to truth it supports. But several related modes of movement are relevant here. As previously mentioned, Gadamer models being itself on play as a back-and-forth movement that has no other purpose than its self-presentation. Play likewise serves as the model for art. However, the play of art is distinguished by the presence of someone to whom it is presented—that is, the spectator whose participation is required. The play of art also requires a work—that is, a configuration which provides an integral whole with its own meaning-intention. The back-and-forth movement distinctive to the play of art thus consists in the reciprocal relation between work and spectator, configuration and participation. Their interplay achieves the presentation that defines the being of the work of art. In the self-presentation, we find a further movement proper to the being of the work of art—that is, the movement of coming-to-presence. It is this movement that constitutes the revealing-concealing event of being that takes place in the work. There, in such coming-to-presence, we encounter the ontological event that vindicates art's claim to truth. As an event where something new emerges into being, what presents itself in the work of art becomes more truly what it is where its being-more is its being-true.

Gadamer's ontological analysis of the artwork remains phenomenological in its inspiration, where truth is understood as coming-to-presence. But where he submits art's truth-claim to the historical and temporal condition of our finite being, the hermeneutic dimension that pervades Gadamer's account strides to the forefront. Historical being too is a matter of movement, but this to-and-fro moves across the temporal distance that opens between past and present, setting the quintessentially hermeneutic task of integration. Initially experienced as disruption, temporal distance introduces difference and discontinuity where the work is encountered as something other. Gadamer characterizes this encounter as a dialogue between the work and its interpreter which, if successful, mediates past and present in an event where the work comes to presence anew, reclaims the truth of art, and revitalizes our bond with tradition. But this means the artwork only remains the same by always differing from itself in an ongoing repetition that yields further events of meaning, being, and truth. As our historical being unfolds within this temporal movement of departure and return, Gadamer's philosophical hermeneutics affirms the truth of art as an unfinished event in which we are continually being taken up. Art's claim to truth is thus reclaimed in a movement of homecoming that describes the being of historical spirit.

NOTES

1. Hans-Georg Gadamer, "Aesthetics and Hermeneutics," in *The Gadamer Reader: A Bouquet of Later Writings*, ed. and trans. Richard E. Palmer (Evanston: Northwestern University Press, 2007), 129. This volume is hereafter abbreviated as *GR*.
2. Gadamer, "The Artwork in Word and Image," in *GR*, 213–14.
3. Gadamer, "Aesthetics and Hermeneutics," 129.
4. Joel Weinsheimer, *Gadamer's Hermeneutics: A Reading of* Truth and Method (New Haven: Yale University Press, 1985), 64.
5. Hans-Georg Gadamer, *Truth and Method*, 2nd ed., trans. Joel Weinsheimer and Donald G. Marshall (New York: Bloomsbury Publishing, 2013), 77–78. Hereafter cited in text as *TM*. Where the German is cited or the translation has been altered, the page number of the original is indicated after the slash. The latter refer to Hans-Georg Gadamer, *Wahrheit und Methode*, Gesammelte Werke I (Tübingen: Mohr Siebeck, 1990).
6. Hans-Georg Gadamer, "The Relevance of the Beautiful," in *The Relevance of the Beautiful and Other Essays*, ed. Robert Bernasconi (Cambridge: Cambridge University Press, 1986), 23/114, translation altered. This volume is hereafter abbreviated as *RB*. Where the German is cited or the translation has been altered, the page number of the original is indicated after the slash. The latter refer to Hans-Georg Gadamer, *Ästhetik und Poetik I Kunst als Aussage, Gesammelte Werke*, vol. 8 (Tübingen: Mohr Siebeck, 1993).
7. Gadamer, 25–26.
8. Gadamer, 53/142
9. Gadamer, "Poetry and Mimesis," in *RB*, 121/85
10. Gadamer, "The Festive Character of Theater," in *RB*, 64.
11. See also Daniel L. Tate, "Transforming *Mimesis*: Gadamer's Retrieval of Aristotle's *Poetics*," *Epoché* 13, no. 1 (Fall, 2008): 185–208.
12. Gadamer, "The Festive Character of Theater," 64.
13. Paul Ricoeur, *Time and Narrative*, Volume 1, trans. Kathleen McLaughlin and David Pellauer (Chicago: University of Chicago Press, 1984), 34.
14. See Gerald F. Else, *Plato and Aristotle on Poetry*, ed. Peter Burian (Chapel Hill: University of North Carolina Press, 1986), 106.
15. Thomas Prufer, "Providence and Imitation: Sophocles' *Oedipus Rex* and Aristotle's *Poetics*," in *Recapitulations: Essays in Philosophy* (Washington, DC: The Catholic University of America Press, 1993), 19.

16. Gadamer, "The Play of Art," in *RB*, 129.
17. Gadamer, "The Artwork in Word and Image," 217.
18. Gadamer, "Poetry and Mimesis," 121.
19. See Cynthia Nielsen's chapter in this volume.
20. Robert Sokolowski, "Picturing," *Review of Metaphysics* 31, no. 1 (1977): 21.
21. Gadamer, "Plato as Portraitist," in *GR*, 317.
22. James Elkins contends there is a deep correlation between the unity and coherence of the portrait and the personality it portrays. See *The Object Stares Back: On the Nature of Seeing* (New York: Harcourt, Inc., 1996), 102.
23. Gadamer, "Plato as Portraitist," 319.
24. Nicholas Davey's discussion of likeness brings this out. See *Unfinished Worlds: Hermeneutics, Aesthetics and Gadamer* (Edinburgh: Edinburgh University Press, 2012), 120–25.
25. Hans-Georg Gadamer, "The Truth of the Work of Art," in *Heidegger's Ways*, trans. John W. Stanley (Albany: State University of New York Press, 1994), 108.
26. Hans-Georg Gadamer, "The Universality of the Hermeneutic Problem," in *Philosophical Hermeneutics*, trans. and ed. David E. Linge (Berkeley: University of California Press, 1976), 5.
27. Hans-Georg Gadamer, "Who Am I and Who Are You?," in *Gadamer on Celan: "Who am I and Who Are You?" and Other Essays*, trans. and ed. Richard Heinemann and Bruce Krajewski (Albany: State University of New York Press, 1997), 72.
28. Gadamer, 144–45.
29. Gadamer, "On the Truth of the Word," in *GR*, 150.
30. Gadamer, "The Artwork in Word and Image," 207.
31. Gadamer, "Relevance of the Beautiful," 33.
32. Gadamer, 34/125.
33. Gadamer, 33.
34. Gadamer, 32.
35. Gadamer, 32.
36. Gadamer, 33.
37. Davey, *Unfinished Worlds*, 118.
38. Davey, 79.
39. Gadamer, "Aesthetics and Hermeneutics," 124–25.
40. See Weinsheimer, *Gadamer's Hermeneutics*, 125.
41. Weinsheimer, 98.
42. Weinsheimer, 98.
43. Gadamer, "Text and Interpretation," in *GR*, 163–64.
44. Gadamer, 164.
45. See James Risser, *Hermeneutics and the Voice of the Other: Re-reading Gadamer's Philosophical Hermeneutics* (Albany: State University of New York, 1997), 83–116.
46. See chapter 10 of this volume.
47. Gadamer, "Text and Interpretation," 163.
48. Gerald Bruns, "The Remembrance of Language: An Introduction to Gadamer's Hermeneutics" in Hans-Georg Gadamer, *Gadamer on Celan: "Who am I and Who*

Are You?" and Other Essays, trans. and ed. Richard Heinemann and Bruce Krajewski (Albany: State University of New York Press, 1997), 28.

49. George Steiner, *Real Presences* (Chicago: University of Chicago Press, 1989), 143.

50. Gadamer, "Art and Imitation," in *RB,* 103.

51. John Arthos, *Gadamer's Poetics: A Critique of Modern Aesthetics* (New York: Bloomsbury, 2013), 53–54.

52. Gadamer, "Intuition and Vividness," in *RB*, 166.

53. Gadamer, "Relevance of the Beautiful," 25.

54. Gadamer, "The Play of Art," 126.

55. Gadamer, "Relevance of the Beautiful," 29.

56. Gadamer, 29.

57. Gadamer, "Aesthetics and Hermeneutics," 124.

58. Gadamer, "The Artwork in Word and Image," 196.

59. Gadamer, "Aesthetics and Hermeneutics," 131.

60. Gadamer, "The Artwork in Word and Image," 200/377.

Chapter 4

TM I.2.1

Gadamer on Play as Ontological Explanation

Jessica Frazier

The discussion of "play as the clue to ontological explanation" in section I.2.1 of *Truth and Method* offers a striking change of tone from the surrounding passages of historical exegesis. It presents an evocative series of images that include

> the play of light, the play of the waves, the play of gears or parts of machinery, the interplay of limbs, the play of forces, the play of gnats, even a play on words . . . dance . . . the play of colors.[1]

These lyrical illustrations serve as the foundation on which to build an ontological model that would subsequently pervade Gadamer's thought. The significance of this section can appear restricted to problems of aesthetics, but late in the chapter he indicates that his goal extends further than this: "The intention of the present conceptual analysis . . . has to do not with theory of art but with ontology. Its first task, the criticism of traditional aesthetics, is only a stage on the way to acquiring a horizon that embraces both art and history" (*TM*, 138). As we will see, Gadamer's model of play as the taking up of individuals into a constantly transforming medial structure is meant to encapsulate the nature of all structured activity (any form of *Spiel*) and ultimately the mode of existence of humans themselves. He hints at this through the wide latitude of his conception of play, treating it not only as something people do, or as games, but as any kind of patterned but open-ended formation. His list encompasses board games and ball games, organic forms and mechanical processes, physical forces and poetic allusions, dance, drama, spatial design, and even religious rituals and seasonal festivals. Through these many examples the master metaphor of play emerges as a heuristic tool with which to unfold his historical exegesis of the West's approach to truth and improve on the dominant conception of truth as correspondence to an external reality.

Hence, the play metaphor is not merely a digression along the way. It bookends the whole of *Truth and Method*, making its first appearance in the epigraph from a poem by Rainer Maria Rilke that opens the book. The poet observes and exhorts:

When you're suddenly the catcher of a ball
thrown by an eternal partner
... in an arch
from the great bridgebuilding of God:
why catching then becomes a power—
not yours, a world's.

Here we already get a hint of the key theme of participating in something larger that connects with the structures of reality itself and adopting a view that empowers us while requiring that we rethink our very nature as individual subjects. The play metaphor returns in the final pages of the book where he turns from "the ontology of the work of art" to "the ontological shift of hermeneutics guided by language." Here at the end, he uses it to reveal the widest implications of his thought—what he calls "the universal aspect of hermeneutics" (*TM*, 490)—and clarifies that the concept of play is meant to determine "what we mean by truth" (*TM*, 505). In 1962, two years after the publication of *Truth and Method*, he tried to explain his core ideas in the essay "On the Problem of Self-Understanding," and here he revived the play/game analogy as a way to show how hermeneutics alters conventional notions of truth.[2] As we will see, despite allusions to playing and gaming by previous thinkers, his use of the idea has a speculative, poetic tone that is all his own. It seems that Gadamer was digging deep into his conceptual imagination to find a metaphor that would express *directly* the universal generative structure that he felt he had discovered through his hermeneutic reflection.

The significance of this extended play analogy has been much debated in the secondary literature. It has been interpreted by those interested primarily in hermeneutic theory as a way of showing that all meaning-making contains a hermeneutic circle which leads to new, creative elements,[3] or as the revelation of art's speculative yet ultimately contemporaneous way of revealing "the totality of our being-in-the-world."[4] Those interested in Gadamer's place in the history of philosophy have seen it as an extended reflection on Plato's dialogues,[5] a plagiarising of Herder in order to advance beyond Heidegger,[6] or a way of merging Platonic, Hegelian, and Heideggerian elements into a unified "hermeneutic ontology."[7] Some concerned with the development of phenomenology have taken play as Gadamer's way of contributing to the phenomenological project by conceptualizing the "pure appearance" of things—an idea that might foreshadow "Derridean disruptive play"[8]—or conversely as his affirmation of the value of structuring principles of constraint that differentiates him from both Derrida and Heidegger,[9] or even as a phenomenological critique of all standard substance ontology.[10] For those interested in its religious and ethical implications, it may be a device that helps us counter subjectivism, understand human being-in-the-world, and learn how to listen properly to theological language,[11] a way of explaining the sacred,[12] a metaphor bridging Gadamer's dialectical ontology and the ethos of playful and creative exploration that he derives from it,[13] or a way of modeling the life-giving, dynamic, "divine" characteristics of nature and our aspiration to become "ecstatically" united with it.[14] Yet despite such interpretations of this chapter's role within the wider agenda of Gadamer's thought, it can seem to sit oddly within the book, wedged awkwardly between discussions of Kant's aesthetics and the methodological goals of the human sciences. Its apparent digression into the ontology of art makes most sense when it is seen in terms of the larger historical narrative within which it features.

In the following sections, I will situate this curious play chapter within the overarching narrative of *Truth and Method*, follow the trajectory of its argument, identify the structural features that make it such an apt model for the ontological nature of meaning and experience, and finally touch on its application to individual and communal well-being in Gadamer's later work. Along the way, we will see how Gadamer's structural analysis of play was meant to improve on the phenomenological models of his predecessors. Gadamer was mindful of how Heidegger had struggled through awkwardly experimental means of expressing the radical change of perspective his philosophy required—speaking of there-being (*Dasein*) or dwelling (*wohnen*) to express our world-embedded-existence, replacing the old realism of things and substances with a new ontology of language. In places, Heidegger had tried to create a new grammar that excised the subjectivist, objectifying view of the world by emphasizing verbs over nouns, for instance. But these methods as often obscured his real meaning as revealed it. His pupil was eager to seek a new method, and as Walter Lammi notes, "his straightforward discursive prose stands in marked contrast to the later Heidegger's 'oracular' or quasi-poetic ruminations."[15] Metaphor suggested itself as a valuable explanatory tool. Gadamer said of the concept of play that

> here as always the metaphorical usage has methodological priority. If a word is applied to a sphere to which it did not originally belong, the actual "original" meaning emerges quite clearly. Language has performed in advance the

abstraction that is, as such, the task of conceptual analysis. Now thinking need only make use of this advance achievement. (*TM*, 108)

With this in mind, in the play chapter, Gadamer essayed an alternative approach: a poetic trope meant to express the nature of Being.

1. *PLAY* IN THE NARRATIVE OF *TRUTH AND METHOD*: A SOLUTION TO SUBJECTIVISM

In many ways, *Truth and Method* is a Fall-and-Redemption narrative with the idea of truth in the West as its protagonist and play as the saving touchstone. Part I deals with our prelapsarian experience of truth in which we dwelt in what he calls a natural *sensus communis*: we organically negotiated meanings according to each occasion or community and felt no Cartesian doubt, no distance from the world. But an increasingly subjectivist outlook came to predominate, exemplified in Kant's aesthetics; this led to a diminution of our sensitivity to meaning, anxiety about correctness, and a retreat into the idea that we only have access to private experience and individual taste. But in the second section of Part I Gadamer uses his play ontology to revive and reveal the actual nature of truth. We discover that it is not so much part of us as something of which we ourselves are a part. Armed with this new insight, Part II then goes on to look at the modern discourses concerning truth found in the fields of history and phenomenology. Here again we see confusions creeping into those fields, but Gadamer offers a further clarification diving back into Aristotle and Plato to pull up the problem at its roots. Finally, in Part III, he takes up the direction pointed out in the later essays of Heidegger and explains his idea in terms of language, ending in the last pages of the whole book with a return to the ontology of play, now used as a model of all our "understanding of the world" and any "event through which meaning asserts itself" (*TM*, 506).

Amidst all this, this section stands out because of its distinctive style within the text as a whole. Throughout most of *Truth and Method* (and in most other writings), Gadamer prefers to employ critical exposition of past views as his main way of developing an argument. It helps to contextualize every idea and allows him to show what is good and what needs correcting in each previous philosophy. Thus, he uses thinkers like Kant and Hegel to reject subjectivism or Dilthey and Heidegger to point the way forward. This tendency is particularly clear in the volumes of essays on Aristotle and Plato, Hegel, Heidegger, Husserl, Heraclitus, Parmenides, and others.[16] This exegetical approach was an expression of his philosophical advice to situate oneself in relation to tradition and engage with it critically yet constructively.

But this 'historical' style could be just as obfuscating as the language-play of Heidegger. He was aware that his point often got lost in his own tendency toward historical explanations, and those around him sometimes referred to these digressions as *Gads*: they were his own unique methodological failing. Even as a lecturer, his students were unclear about whether he was doing philosophy or just intellectual history.[17] But instead of "creating a special language" he wanted to make "the language which we normally use say what Heidegger speaks about."[18] Against this backdrop, we can see the play chapter as an attempt to grasp hold of a clear metaphor that would anchor his account and do the difficult work of the finer ontological points of his radical new view of truth.

2. THE ARGUMENT FROM PLAY: STRUCTURE, PARTICIPATION, CREATIVITY

Gadamer's argument unfolds through a slow analysis of everyday language about the term *play* in which his core observations gradually build into an account of a distinctive *kind of being* to which we habitually pay all-too-little attention. In the first section, Gadamer justifies his ontologization of the image of the metaphor of play and games (which by then had become familiar in its uses by Schiller, Wittgenstein, and Huizinga, all of which Gadamer acknowledges) by arguing that the real subject of art-experiences is not the person but the "work itself" (*TM*, 107). He begins with an ontological twist on Schiller's earlier use of the play analogy: as an aesthetic concept, it usually refers to the playing subjectivity of the artist or the audience, whereas in part A on "The Concept of Play" he immediately announces his intention to use it for analyzing "the mode of being of the work of art itself" (*TM*, 91). This is supported with the observation that play only exists as such when "the player loses himself in play" in such a way that the game or activity proves itself to be the more fundamental reality (*TM*, 107).

He then goes on to explain the characteristics of play from this player-encompassing perspective. Across the range of different aesthetic, natural, and recreational phenomena that he describes, what defines them is an open-ended repetition of a "to-and-fro movement" in which it is not the substrate—the player or material—that matters but the occurrence of the actual form. Thus he insists that "the movement of play as such has, as it were, no substrate . . . The play is the occurrence of the movement as such" (*TM*, 108). From the perspective of subjective persons, our immersion within such formations is absorptive so that there is no strain but rather a kind of naturalness to it, as when we are caught up in the refrain of a song (*TM*, 109). It may be that he has in mind Heidegger's similar point about the absorptive character of ready-to-hand experiences.

At this point, Gadamer pauses to highlight the generalized nature of the movement that he has identified. He argues that human play is a "natural process" like the play of water or light precisely because man "is part of nature." More than this, artworks too "are only remote imitations of the infinite play of the world, the eternally self-creating work of art" (*TM*, 109–110). The participation of the player in that whole entails a being in some structuring relation with something, whether a ball with its movements, a jigsaw puzzle with its shape constraints, or one person with another. Play happens "in between" these different constraints expressing itself as movement between them (*TM*, 113), as when chess players calculate the allowed movements of the pieces on the board or the spectators speculate on how the situation in a drama may develop. A further insight arises from the realization that different games gain their distinct identities by their differing patterns, "rules and regulations," or "structure that determines the movement of the game from within" (*TM*, 111).

Part B on "Transformation into Structure and Total Mediation" builds on this focus on patterned relations, honing in on the underlying analysis of structure (*Gebilde*) that the play analogy facilitates. Gadamer explains this phenomenon as a transformation of the actual human person into part of a structure. But more than merely incorporating the person into a certain formal interaction, this new structure genuinely redefines its parts, in that "something is suddenly and as a whole something else, [and] that this other transformed thing that it has become is its true being, in comparison with which its earlier being is nil" (*TM*, 115). Here we begin to see the life-illuminating implications of this idea *as an ontology of human being*. Such immersion in structure reveals to us our immersive participation as a component within larger patterns. Gadamer tries to explain this in a key passage that is worth citing at length:

> This gives what we called transformation into structure its full meaning. The transformation is a transformation into the true . . . it is itself redemption and transformation back into true being. In being presented in play, what is emerges. It produces and brings to light what is otherwise constantly hidden and withdrawn. Someone who can perceive the comedy and tragedy of life can resist the temptation to think in terms of purposes, which conceals the game that is played with us . . . someone who can see the whole of reality as a closed circle of meaning in which everything is fulfilled will speak of the comedy and tragedy of life. . . . The being of all play is always self-realization, sheer fulfilment, energeia which has its telos within itself. (*TM*, 116–17)

At this stage in the argument, he points to the purely formal, structural insight to which the analysis of play has led, stating that "the concept of transformation characterizes the independent and superior mode of being of what we called structure" (*TM*, 117).

The immediately following discussion of recognition and *mimesis* in Plato and Aristotle is meant partly to refute the usual interpretation of art as imitation of reality—as in a still-life or a historical play. In the same way that Gadamer tried to move away from correspondence theories of truth, here he tries to overturn the mimetic account of art. He replaces it with an account that emphasizes the way every part of the whole event of interpretive experience is taken up into a higher or authentic (*eigentlich*) overall structure. So, in his example, the Achilles that Homer creates when imitating reality in the *Illiad* is never just a copy of the real Achilles; it is always richer in symbols, connotations, and interpretations than any original (*TM*, 118–19).

This is a crucial step toward *Truth and Method*'s revisionist conception of what any phenomenon really is; phenomena are not merely experiences subjective consciousness has. They are always one fragment of an overarching medial structure that transcends the subject/object divide. The contrast with old imitative ideas of truth allows Gadamer to highlight his recuperated conception of art. Focusing not on the template created by the rules of a game or text of a play but on the hermeneutic event of playing/performing/spectating, he sees each occasion as the arising of a fresh, encompassing structure that is uniquely created in each instance and includes the subject who experiences it. The metaphors demonstrate this aptly—each game of football is different, as is each performance of *Romeo and Juliet*. Yet Gadamer is eager that we not misinterpret his claim in either of two metaphysical wrong directions: we must not revert back to a subject-object metaphysics and think that the presentation of a work is what some *subjectivity*—usually assumed to be the purportedly *real* entity—experiences. Each work is not "enclosed in the subjectivity of what they [the players] think, but it is embodied there. Thus it is not at all a question of a mere subjective variety of conception" (*TM*, 122). The work should not be counterposed to the "lifeworld," he says (using the terminology of the wider phenomenological tradition) (*TM*, 124). It should instead be seen as continuous with it. Nor is it a version of some more basic and more real pure *Form*; that would be to revert back to some Platonic Formalism that sees the *Gebilde*—the shape, pattern, or structure that creates the consistency of things—as the alleged really real part.

What kind of thing is left that play-like things might be? Borrowing the Hegelian language of *sublation* or being taken up into some higher encompassing reality, Gadamer says that in play things are superseded by their new collective identity. Each undergoes a "transformation into structure" (*TM*, 115) that is constantly "contemporaneous" yet does not "disintegrate into the changing aspects of itself so that it would lose all identity, but it is there in them all. They all belong to it" (*TM*, 124).

The rest of Gadamer's long discussion of drama expands on this central idea. Subjectivism, which focuses on the experience of isolated individuals, is wrong-headed: artworks do not exist "in" the physical objects or the subjectivity of the players, but are really events into which all those things are taken up as a complex relationship that shapes the meaning. The need for a dynamic model rather than a fixed, atemporal view of things is demonstrated by the performing arts, which remind us that works are always coming into being anew through free creation. This helps replace the old notion of truth as "mimetic representation" or *Darstellung* with an improved idea of art as a structure that only exists through each case of "mediation" or *Vermittlung* (*TM*, 121–22). The discussion of festivals brings out the idea that we often live in just such a themed yet constantly-made-anew time (every Christmas, Eid, Diwali, Independence Day, etc.) and cultures often celebrate it as "sacred" (*TM*, 124).

Gadamer uses this idea of truth as a phenomenon of dynamic participation to build on Heidegger's thought, suggesting we are not merely *Dasein*—existing there—but actually *Dabei-sein*—existing there included along with something more that determines us. Thus "to be present means to participate" (*TM*, 127) rather than to be a Cartesian spectator onto our surroundings. Even Greek metaphysics, *theoria*, and presence-to-hand in Heideggerian terms can be rehabilitated as present, non-subjectivistic, participatory phenomena when seen in this light (*TM*, 127). He also uses it to connect his thought to Kierkegaard and the Lutheran idea of faith as a claim ever-renewed in life and through the unfolding work of revelation (*TM*, 128).

The final discussion in this chapter allows Gadamer to connect all of this with the artform to which German culture most clearly attributed wider metaphysical implications: tragedy. Looking back to Aristotle's analysis, we see that tragedy effects a kind of *ekstasis* that takes us into a situation beyond our own immediate concerns and brings us to a "tragic pensiveness" in which we see the whole "metaphysical order of being that is true for all" (*TM*, 133). Tragedy brings the consciousness of the spectator into "continuity with himself" (*TM*, 130). In a sense, it is art, play, and other kinds of participation that perform the *real* phenomenological reduction—by allowing us to be what we already are without its being obscured by specific goals and interpretations. Aristotle is a guide on this point; in a later essay exploring the philosophical value of literature Gadamer writes, "Aristotle made the convincing statement that poetry is more philosophical than history . . . how does everything that shines forth in the poetic word share in this transfiguration into the essential?"[19] Part of this illumination is the way a play or game analogy helps our consciousness see clearly what it is doing from the medial perspective rather than our habitually limited, subjectivist, literally *self*-centered viewpoint. His subsequent accounts of pictorial arts, portraiture, sacred arts, and architecture all show how communications that may seem mimetic can in fact be a representation of what we already know as something genuinely new, the being of which necessarily makes reference to the original yet adds something new and utterly unique by which it is defined.

3. PLAY AND BEING: FROM SUBSTANCE METAPHYSICS TO ONTOLOGICAL STRUCTURE

So what insight was Gadamer trying to express through the idea of play? His painstaking analysis of the various examples works to show that all play is really a process by which many parts undergo "transformation into structure," and defining the nature of that structure became an important task in Gadamer's work. His writings on the semantics of poetry in the work of Rainer Maria Rilke and Paul Celan,[20] on the nature of number and concepts in Plato,[21] on dialectic in Hegel,[22] on art and beauty,[23] on language in Heidegger's later thought,[24] and even on health as a form of balanced harmonic proportion,[25] are all areas in which he sees similar insights at work. Each develops the central notion of play as an encompassing, dynamic, relational structure.

Boiled down, this play-structure is characterized by three essential defining features of (a) structure, (b) participation, and (c) dynamism:

(a) *Structural relationships are the defining medium of experience*, giving shape to Being (which in phenomenology is always Being-for-us, insofar as we can encounter it). Structures are determined by proportions of similarity and dissimilarity, contrast and entailment. It is the proportions of relationship between parts that constitute any structure, making it what it is. Even distortions and departures from a given structure can only be known in relation to that structure; so, for instance, the jazz musician Keith Jarrett's gradual deconstruction of a classic melody into something unrecognizably new only makes sense in relation to the structure from which it departs. The most raw example of structure is perhaps mathematics; the number 6 really has a nature that consists in a formal position defined by relative degrees of differentiation and entailment to 1, 3, 12, 0.6, 6000, and so on. One of the richest examples of this is musical form: a piece of music is what it is despite transposition and change because of the proportion of its notes and durations. Play is Gadamer's way of bringing the purely formal element of structure to the fore. It captures what he means when he speaks of being tied to and enabled by tradition. Tradition is like the musical melody that a song inherits at each moment and builds on even when it breaks into something radically new.

(b) *Play incorporates all its parts into a new uniting, encompassing, medial identity*—and so do art and all understanding. From the overview vantage point of the larger play or game that we are part of, our individual identity is sublated into a more relevant and powerful shared identity. Among other things, this is Gadamer's way of taking up the phenomenological theme of overcoming subject-object distinctions.
(c) *These structures always (and necessarily) have a dynamic, processual mode of existence.* Contrary to the kinds of timeless and unchanging structures associated with Platonism, in the world's real structures, it is impossible for things to stay the same because they are constantly being newly instantiated. The analogy shows this: there could be no game without changes and developments, and an artwork that was never looked at and interpreted anew would just be an object. This point builds on Heidegger's account of temporality; he reminds us that our sense of "care and the movement towards death" constantly drives forward the nature of understanding. (*TM*, 125)

To what extent is this specifically an account of aesthetic experiences and to what extent is it a universal account of experience itself? This chapter incorporates many instances of the structure in question, including games, artworks, natural phenomena, living in faith, applying law, and interpreting history. In his discussion of the tragic, he makes clear that what he is discussing should not be seen merely as an aesthetic matter but as "a fundamental phenomenon, a structure of meaning that does not exist only in tragedy . . . Indeed, it is not even a specifically artistic phenomenon, for it is also found in life" (*TM*, 130). This universality is why Hamann and Scheler treat tragedy as "something extra-aesthetic, an ethical and metaphysical phenomenon that enters into the sphere of aesthetic problems only from outside" (*TM*, 130).

Admittedly, Gadamer does focus on aesthetic experiences in this chapter in explicit contrast to quite different kinds of "practical or goal-oriented participation" (*TM*, 129). He seems to assume that our focus on goals is allied with a subjectivistic self-centeredness that veils the true nature of the world by imposing our own concerns upon it. In this respect, he replicates Heidegger's present-to-hand and ready-to-hand (*vorhanden* and *zuhanden*) distinction and similarly prefers the one that lets us lose ourselves in the reality that we thereby encounter. Yet Gadamer makes it clear that he focuses on art precisely because it is more authentic to our fundamental mode of being, and analyzing it reveals what is always true of our experiences as opposed to the simpler but distorting way that we conceptualize experience to ourselves—seeing it as something that approximates a separate, fixed reality. Aesthetic experience is epistemologically superior in that it brings us into the right phenomenological attitude for seeing Being as it is in itself. It cultivates in us the distance necessary for seeing, and thus makes possible a genuine and comprehensive participation in what is presented before us. A spectator's ecstatic self-forgetfulness corresponds to his continuity with himself . . . it is the truth of our own world—the religious and moral world in which we live—that is presented before us and in which we recognize ourselves . . . What rends [the spectator] from himself at the same time gives him back the whole of his being. (*TM*, 130)

With this new model in hand, his hope is that we can now let the old correspondence model of truth be superseded by the new dynamic structure model. For Gadamer, this is already implicit in Kant, urged by Nietzsche, and central to Heidegger: we must stop thinking of art (which is the focus of the chapter) and truth more generally (which is the topic of *Truth and Method*) in terms of isolated subjects experiencing external objects and forming limited mimetic pictures. He declares that "there is something absurd about the whole idea of a unique, correct interpretation" (*TM*, 123). Its promise to secure reliable reference points for our purposes and calculations can be helpful, but what is gained from the new understanding of truth on the model of play is of much greater value. Play, which this chapter shows to be one instance of the wider phenomenon of transformation into structure, "is itself redemption and transformation back into true being" bringing to light what is hidden and revealing "the game that is played with us" (*TM*, 117).

Art and play are "the coming-to-presentation of Being" (*TM*, 159), and at the end of the sequence of discussion on play and aesthetic presentations of all kinds, it is Hegel who foreshadowed the ever-living, ever-new character of our understanding consciousness and the truths it helps to construct. His own analogy in the prologue to *The Phenomenology of Spirit* imagines a girl plucking fruit in an orchard then realizing that she too is an outgrowth and, as it were, a fruit of nature. This analogy is similarly meant to help us see that we are part of a larger, encompassing, structured but ever-growing phenomenon; in this case, we are "spirit conscious of itself as spirit" (*TM*, 168). Here Gadamer finally returns from his excursion into aesthetics back full-circle to philosophy: "For Hegel, then, it is philosophy, the historical self-penetration of spirit, that carries out the hermeneutical task" and play serves just such a self-penetrating purpose by revealing "the truth that manifests itself in art and history" (*TM*, 168).

Gadamer's investigation thus works on three levels: it illuminates the nature of art, it reveals the character of all interpretation, and—since all experience is for him a form of interpretive encounter and creative understanding—it presents a phenomenology of human Being in the fullest sense. It is with respect to this last dimension that the play chapter of *Truth and Method* represents the core of Gadamer's attempt to move beyond realist substance-metaphysics and its accompanying conception of truth as correspondence. This dimension of his thought is relatively little discussed, almost as if he had at some point exited the phenomenological tradition in which he began under the tutelage of Husserl, Heidegger, Scheler, and others. Yet we can interpret this chapter as the beginnings of what he hoped would be a path forward toward a new ontology, much in the way that Heidegger had sought in his later essays for new schemes for understanding Being in terms of language, of *aletheia* or unveiling, and of dwelling understood as "the manner in which mortals are on the earth."[26] As had Heidegger with his focus on *language*, so in this chapter Gadamer is trying to strike out a new course with *play*.

A number of scholars have acknowledged this aspect. As Georgia Warnke puts it, the play account of interpretation "indicates how little Gadamer's view depends on a substantialist metaphysics."[27] The conceptual essences revealed in interpretation do not derive their truth from correspondence to a real reality beyond thought. Similarly, Donatella di Cesare interprets play as one of "the concepts that fundamentally undermine, unhinge, and call metaphysics of subjectivity into question,"[28] such that

> it is play that, traversing hermeneutics, puts metaphysics into play. Even more so: the phenomenology of play presents itself as an alternative to all ontology or to any discourse on Being that claims to be final and fundamental.[29]

Jean Grondin describes the ever-contemporary speculative structural nature of meaning as a "metaphysics of finitude,"[30] and Lammi has similarly described play as Gadamer's expression of the "temporal ontology" of language.[31]

It is perhaps Brice Wachterhauser who has most explicitly treated Gadamer's account of conceptual understanding as a "post-Platonic hermeneutic ontology" that formulates a phenomenological analysis of the structural prerequisites of our life-world, in order to go "beyond Being" and overcome the problems of "onto-theology."[32] He reads the play-example against the backdrop of Gadamer's rehabilitation of Plato, showing how it describes the world not as an objective, mind-independent reality grounded in a substrate of hylomorphic substance but as a field of structural formations that shape the themes, patterns, or "games" that define each object, idea, action, and person as what it is. In this sense, it expresses the kind of relational formation of (constantly varying) similarity and difference that Plato tried to capture in his discussion of participation (*methexis*) and difference (*chorismos*) in the *Parmenides*. In Gadamer's Plato studies, number appears as another play-like structure that can serve as an "ontological model": "What *is* revealed [by Plato] is that the number of the unity of many is the ontological paradigm."[33] In his major essay on art, "The Relevance of the Beautiful," Gadamer argued that Greek thought revealed how *symmetria* or proportion and *harmonia* or fitting relation are both factors that describe the kind of structure in which a given relational proportion exists in sufficient continuity that it is able to anchor identity despite change—as when musical intervals define a certain chord or melody even when the notes become transposed into a new pitch or tempo. This idea that the relative proportion of connection and difference defines structures as what they are despite continual development and change was an important precursor of Gadamer's idea of play as defined by rules that give shape to each new instantiation.

4. LIFE AS CREATIVE PARTICIPATION: PLAY FROM SCHILLER TO HUIZINGA

Gadamer's use of the metaphor of *Spiel* (play or game) and *spielen* (to play)—took a powerful cue from its use by Friedrich Schiller and Johann Huizinga, although it also built on the notion of dialectic that Gadamer inherited from Plato and Hegel, two thinkers with whom he saw himself in continuity as much as with Heidegger. In taking up these influences and repurposing them, Gadamer aimed to express the way that art incorporates the thinking subject into an overall, constantly evolving phenomenon of meaning-making. Schiller had captured an important part of Gadamer's idea—the way that all our interpretation, thought, and indeed experience of reality consists in a constantly renegotiated balance between the structure of what we receive from the world and the openness through which it takes new form in the present moment as inflected by language, mood, memory, environment, etc. In *Truth and Method,* Gadamer interpreted Schiller's relegation of art to an "ideal kingdom" alienated from "practical reality" (*TM,* 75) as one step in our journey away from a correct grasp on truth. Yet, nevertheless, he saw much to affirm in Schiller, approving of the way he and Goethe opened up the "symbolic" form of discourse as one in which everything "points towards everything else" (*TM,* 70), of his efforts to build on Kant's association of beauty with morality (*TM,* 69), and his work toward reviving a Greek model of life in which morality gives "shape to the whole . . . so allowing men to recognize themselves in their own world."[34]

Above all, Schiller was a champion of the importance of play in human life, understood in the sense of a dynamic, engaged, contributory, creative approach to the world. In his *Letters on the Aesthetic Education of Man,* Schiller argued that art allows a free play of the human faculties and used this to affirm the importance of liberty, spontaneity, and originality over against the "blind force" of brute senses, on the one hand, and social conventions, on the other.[35] Schiller set the scene for Gadamer by establishing an axis of "passive force" versus "active force," "material impulsion" versus "formal impulsion," and "receptive" versus "determining" modes of engagement.[36] These two directions of force need "tempering" in "a free act, an activity of the person," and it is as a solution to this need that Schiller points to the natural human impulse found in "the instinct of play" that "unites the double action of the two other instincts."[37] An important part of being fully human is the use of this harmonizing, creative instinct to synthesize the world into ever-new creative contributions, and Gadamer aligns this idea with Friedrich Schleiermacher's emphasis on living feeling, Hegel's historicist idea of human nature as "finite-infinite," and the later skepticism toward the idea of a fixed reality that Friedrich Nietzsche, Henri Bergson, Stefan George, Georg Simmel, and Wilhelm Dilthey all expressed in their different ways (*TM*, 58). Yet here we also come to one of the ways in which Gadamer aimed to improve on Schiller's model by expanding it. Schiller limits the play instinct to art, but for Gadamer, as we have seen, this aesthetic application is only one illuminating instance of the more general way that experience works.

Another important source of the play metaphor was Johann Huizinga's book *Homo Ludens*, in which play was even more central to human nature—as the title suggests. Huizinga used it as a key with which to decode various aspects of culture, including law, war, ritual, and philosophy. Playfulness is an element in our most basic practices of thinking, speaking, and acting, so that "in the making of speech and language the spirit is continually "sparking" between matter and mind, as it were, playing with this wondrous nominative faculty." In this respect, play seemed to be "one of the main bases of civilisation."[38] Huizinga's style of reasoning across disciplines and apparent dichotomies, in such a way that the concept could be seen to dialectically synthesize and rise above "the domain of the great categorical antitheses,"[39] may also have been an inspiration to Gadamer. He uses Huizinga to emphasize at least two things: one is the *medial* character of play in which all parts, including subject and object, are united, and another is the *fundamental relationality* of play that is exemplified in the tense "to-and-fro movement" that underpins both games and the attention of any spectator to an artwork (*TM*, 108). Medial unities and dynamic relations are ways in which play captures something universal in human activity. Finally, for Gadamer, Huizinga's account also highlights something that separates play from quotidian activity: its character as something that is a self-contained "closed world, one without transition and mediation to the world of aims" (*TM*, 112). It is because of this aspect, Gadamer argues, that play appears as both verb and noun in the common German sentence *man spielt ein Spiel*, or *one plays a game*, and it is also perhaps in this connection that play is linked to what is "holy," "sacred," goal-less, and timeless when one is caught up in it—as Huizinga notes (*TM*, 108, n. 6, 110, 112).

Beyond its obvious sources in Schiller and Huizinga, the metaphor of play also evoked other figures in Gadamer's philosophical history, both recuperating earlier conceptions of dialectic and highlighting their mistakes. Plato's dialectic was too determinate and static: it failed to stay true to the way that ideas actually happen in constantly evolving moments of mental encounter. Furthermore, it failed to acknowledge the porous borders and inter-relationality of forms: only through hints in middle period texts, such as the *Phaedo*,[40] and more fully developed in later texts, such as the *Parmenides*,[41] did Plato begin to mine the implications of Zeno's paradox and Heraclitus' notion of change.

The metaphor also offered to solve some of the limitations Gadamer saw in Hegel's dialectic by affirming the open, infinitely generative character of structure (as demonstrated by the way each game's rules facilitate infinite new iterations). Hegelian elements pervade Gadamer's work,[42] but where Hegel seemed to see completely open and unending development as a "bad infinite," for Gadamer the whole point of a game is that the rules can be applied in such a way that it can be played repeatedly with ever new possibilities. No final form is possible or even desirable since its fundamental being is creative. Thus, the play metaphor seems to be a valuable advance upon existing conceptions of dialectic; it redeems that notion from the features Nietzsche had criticized in the *Twilight of the Idols* as conceptually mummifying and Heidegger had similarly overruled in *Being and Time* as a part of the old, bad notion of metaphysics. But, above all, it offered an image meant to make us feel at home in the world as part of the natural play of history and to empower us as part of the dynamic, creative process of reality's unfolding.

5. IMPLICATIONS AND APPLICATIONS: THE PLAY STRUCTURE IN GADAMER'S LATER WORK

Echoes and applications of the play idea can be found throughout Gadamer's later works. Play becomes not only a hermeneutic model of meaning but also an ethical template for the vibrant, continuing, functioning existence of almost anything. On the small scale, it defines our own human health: in his later essays on health, this emerges clearly with reference to the "interplay" of the body's parts with each other and their surroundings:

> We are ourselves part of nature and it is this nature within us, together with the self-sustaining organic defence system of our bodies, which is capable of sustaining our "inner" equilibrium. This is the unique interplay of functions which constitutes life.[43]

Musical harmony serves as the form of art that illuminates good mental and physical functioning: "Good health requires a harmonious relationship consonant with both our social and our natural environment. It is this harmony which first enables us to move in accord with the natural rhythms which govern our bodily life."[44] The Greeks had already intuited the connection between complex yet balanced structured activity that immerses itself collaboratively in its environment in their conception of the good life. Thus "What Plato seeks . . . as 'the good life' is not the pure exactness of a mathematical type, but the measured proportionality of a well-mixed drink of life," composed in the measure (*metrion*) of what is "the appropriate, the fitting, and the needful at the favorable moment."[45] This, still, is the structure of a game well-played, and this 1960 chapter remains relevant to Gadamer's 1996 statement that he is addressing "each and every one of us who must take care of our own health through the way in which we lead our lives" and accept that this "expands into a much broader dimension of responsibility in our highly complex civilisation."[46]

On a larger scale, this structural relation of harmonious dynamic interplay also defined the constructive, collaborative, and diverse solidarity that characterized good community for Gadamer. Like Heidegger, he saw technological progress as a popular ideal that put private profit above development through fruitful engagement with other cultures and the cultivation of the environment's own life. It threatened modernity with an

> immense increase in weapons technology and the destructive potential it harbours . . . the arms trade, which is as difficult to control as the drugs trade; and not least of the deluge of information which threatens to engulf our human faculty of judgement.[47]

By contrast, organic models of community replicate the play structure at the interpersonal level and thereby achieve "a sustaining solidarity which alone makes possible the organised structure of human coexistence."[48] A small example of this creative, collaborative human play—familiar to Gadamer himself—was the university community which "still remains one of the few precursors of the grand universe of humanity, of all human beings, who must learn to create with one another new solidarities."[49] A larger-scale example of this was global culture and its increasing multiculturalism, of which he was an early advocate, priding himself on his early liberal upbringing among female and Jewish intellectual friends in the culture of Breslau. Late in life he would describe cultural diversity as kind of game and a "training ground" where "otherness . . . contributes to the encountering of one's own self" in such a way that "the coexistence of different cultures and languages, religions and confessions supports us."[50]

The principles of structure that shape play thus work *microcosmically* as an account of art, *macrocosmically* as a template for healthy communal life, and *universally* as an analysis of the phenomenological structure of Being itself. Although, arguably, Gadamer did not convey the wide scope of his metaphor very clearly in this long, elusive section of his *magnum opus*, elsewhere he did express the change that he hoped it would spark in his audience: "Every act, as an element of life, remains connected with the infinity of life that manifests itself in it. Everything finite is an expression, a representation of the infinite" (*TM*, 58). Once assimilated into our perspective, this insight was intended to bring us to a kind of self-awareness that "will lead us towards a new equilibrium in the respective spheres of the body, the soul, and the harmony of the world as a whole."[51] By understanding the sublation of the self into play, we may learn to sublate personal identity into what Rilke, in the epigraph of *Truth and Method*, calls the world's own power, an extension of "the great bridgebuilding of God."

NOTES

1. Hans-Georg Gadamer, *Truth and Method*, 2nd ed., trans. Joel Weinsheimer and Donald G. Marshall (New York: Bloomsbury, 2013), 104. Hereafter cited in text as *TM*. Where the German is cited or the translation has been altered, the page number of the original is indicated after the slash. The latter refer to Hans-Georg Gadamer, *Wahrheit und Methode*, Gesammelte Werke I (Tübingen: Mohr Siebeck, 1990).

2. Hans-Georg Gadamer, "On the Problem of Self-Understanding," in *Philosophical Hermeneutics*, ed. and trans. David E. Linge (Berkeley: University of California, 1976), 44–45.

3. Georgia Warnke, *Gadamer: Hermeneutics, Tradition and Reason* (Stanford: Stanford University, 1987), 48–62.

4. Jean Grondin, *The Philosophy of Gadamer*, trans. Kathryn Plant (Montreal: McGill-Queen's, 2002), 43, cf. 40–46.

5. Rod Coltman, *The Language of Hermeneutics: Gadamer and Heidegger in Dialogue* (Albany: SUNY, 1998), 52–53.

6. Frederick Burwick, "The Plagiarism of Play: The Unacknowledged Source of Gadamer's Ontological Argument in 'Truth and Method,'" *Pacific Coast Philology* 25, no. 1/2 (November 1990).

7. Brice Wachterhauser, *Beyond Being: Gadamer's Post-Platonic Hermeneutic Ontology* (Evanston: Northwestern University, 1999).

8. James Risser, *Hermeneutics and the Voice of the Other: Re-reading Gadamer's Philosophical Hermeneutics* (Albany: SUNY, 1997), 171, cf. 140–47.

9. James Risser, "The Remembrance of Truth, the Truth of Remembrance," in *Hermeneutics and Truth*, ed. Brice Wachterhauser (Evanston: Northwestern University, 1994), 131, cf. 131–34.

10. Donatella Di Cesare, *Gadamer: A Philosophical Portrait*, trans. Niall Keane (Bloomington: Indiana University, 2013), 48–61, 170–72.

11. Philippe Eberhard, *The Middle Voice in Gadamer's Hermeneutics: A Basic Interpretation with Some Theological Implications* (Tübingen: Mohr Siebeck, 2004), 65–76.

12. Muharrem Hafiz, "The Place of the Sacred with Regard to Gadamer's Ontology of Art," *M.Ü. İlâhiyat Fakültesi Dergisi* 39 (2010): 97–116.

13. Jessica Frazier, *Reality, Religion and Passion: Indian and Western Approaches in Gadamer and Rupa Gosvāmī* (Lanham: Rowman and Littlefield, 2009), 49–122.

14. Walter Lammi, *Gadamer and the Question of the Divine* (London: Continuum, 2008).

15. Walter Lammi, "Hans-Georg Gadamer's 'Correction' of Heidegger," *Journal of the History of Ideas* 52, no. 3 (July–September 1991): 487.

16. Many of Gadamer's essays on Aristotle and Plato can be found in: *Dialogue and Dialectic*, trans. P. Christopher Smith (New Haven: Yale University, 1980); *The Idea of the Good in Platonic-Aristotelian Philosophy*, trans. P. Christopher Smith (New Haven: Yale University, 1988); *The Beginning of Philosophy*, trans. Rod Coltman (New York: Continuum, 2001); *The Beginning of Knowledge*, trans. Rod Coltman (New York: Continuum, 2002); on Hegel: *Hegel's Dialectic*, trans. P. Christopher Smith (New Haven: Yale University, 1976); on Heidegger: *Heidegger's Ways*, trans. John W. Stanley (Albany: SUNY, 1994). Numerous essays on Heraclitus, Parmenides, Husserl, and others, and even the biographical sketches of his colleagues are collected in *Philosophical Apprenticeships* (Cambridge: MIT, 1987).

17. Jean Grondin, *Hans-Georg Gadamer: A Biography*, trans. Joel Weinsheimer (New Haven: Yale University, 2003), 275.

18. Hans-Georg Gadamer, "Interview: Historicism and Romanticism," in *Hans-Georg Gadamer on Education, Poetry, and History: Applied Hermeneutics*, ed. Dieter Misgeld and Graeme Nicholson, trans. Lawrence Schmidt and Monica Reuss (Albany: SUNY, 1992), 128.

19. Hans-Georg Gadamer, "On the Truth of the Word," trans. Richard E. Palmer, in *The Gadamer Reader: A Bouquet of the Later Writings*, ed. Richard E. Palmer (Evanston: Northwestern University, 2007), 148.

20. Hans-Georg Gadamer, *Gadamer on Celan: "Who Am I and Who Are You?" and Other Essays*, ed. trans. Richard Heinemann and Bruce Krajewski (Albany: SUNY).

21. Gadamer, *Dialogue and Dialectic*; *The Idea of the Good in Platonic-Aristotelian Philosophy*.

22. Gadamer, *Hegel's Dialectic*; cf. *Reason in the Age of Science*, trans. Frederick G. Lawrence (Cambridge: MIT, 1981).

23. Hans-Georg Gadamer, *The Relevance of the Beautiful and Other Essays*, ed. Robert Bernasconi, trans. Nicholas Walker (Cambridge: Cambridge University, 1986).

24. See, for example, *Heidegger's Ways* and relevant essays in *Philosophical Hermeneutics*.

25. Hans-Georg Gadamer, *The Enigma of Health: The Art of Healing in a Scientific Age*, trans. Jason Gaiger and Nicholas Walker (Stanford: Stanford University, 1996).

26. Martin Heidegger, "Building Dwelling Thinking," in *Poetry, Language, and Thought*, trans. Albert Hofstadter (New York: Harper & Row, 1971), 147.

27. Warnke, *Gadamer*, 66.

28. Di Cesare, *Gadamer: A Philosophical Portrait*, 66.

29. Di Cesare, 183.

30. Grondin, *The Philosophy of Gadamer*, 150.

31. Lammi, *Gadamer and the Question of the Divine*, 66.

32. Wachterhauser, *Beyond Being*.

33. Hans-Georg Gadamer, "*Amicus Plato Magis Amica Veritas*," in *Dialogue and Dialectic*, 203.

34. Gadamer, *The Relevance of the Beautiful and Other Essays*, 14.

35. Friedrich Schiller, "Letters Upon the Aesthetic Education of Man," in *Literary and Philosophical Essays: French, German and Italian*, ed. Charles W. Eliot (New York: Collier, 1910), Letter VII.

36. Schiller, Letter XIII.

37. Schiller, Letter XIV. In Letter XIX Schiller alludes to his own kind of dialectic, minus the name, giving a description of space and time that resonates in Gadamer's analysis of the way that games function: "Before we determine a place in space, there is no space for us; but without absolute space we could never determine a place. The same is the case with time. Before we have an instant, there is no time to us; but without infinite time—eternity—we should never have a representation of the instant. Thus, therefore, we can only arrive at the whole by the part, to the unlimited through limitation; but reciprocally we only arrive at the part through the whole, at limitation through the unlimited."

38. Johann Huizinga, *Homo Ludens: A Study of the Play Element in Culture*, trans. R.F.C. Hull (London: Routledge & Kegan Paul, 1949), 4–5.

39. Huizinga, 6.

40. Plato, *Phaedo*, 102b.

41. Plato, *Parmenides*, 129c.

42. See Jeff Mitscherling, "The Hegelian Element in Gadamer's Notions of Application and Play," *Man and World* 25, no. 1 (1992).

43. Hans-Georg Gadamer, "On the Enigmatic Character of Health," in trans. Jason Gaiger and Nicholas Walker (Stanford: Stanford University Press, 1996), 116.

44. Hans-Georg Gadamer, "Treatment and Dialogue," in *The Enigma of Health*, 132.

45. Hans-Georg Gadamer, "The Artwork in Word and Image: 'So True, So Full of Being!,'" trans. Richard E. Palmer, in *The Gadamer Reader: A Bouquet of the Later Writings*, ed. Richard E. Palmer (Evanston: Northwestern University, 2007), 204, 205.

46. Gadamer, *The Enigma of Health*, viii.

47. Gadamer, viii.

48. Hans-Georg Gadamer, "Citizens of Two Worlds," in *Hans-Georg Gadamer on Education, Poetry, and History: Applied Hermeneutics*, ed. Dieter Misgeld and

Graeme Nicholson, trans. Lawrence Schmidt and Monica Reuss (Albany: SUNY, 1992), 219.

49. Hans-Georg Gadamer, "The Idea of the University: Yesterday, Today, and Tomorrow," in *Hans-Georg Gadamer on Education, Poetry, and History: Applied Hermeneutics*, ed. Dieter Misgeld and Graeme Nicholson, trans. Lawrence Schmidt and Monica Reuss (Albany: SUNY, 1992), 59.

50. Hans-Georg Gadamer, "The Diversity of Europe: Inheritance and Future," in *Hans-Georg Gadamer on Education, Poetry, and History: Applied Hermeneutics*, ed. Dieter Misgeld and Graeme Nicholson, trans. Lawrence Schmidt and Monica Reuss (Albany: SUNY, 1992), 234.

51. Hans-Georg Gadamer, "Between Nature and Art," in *The Enigma of Health*, 85.

Chapter 5

TM I.2.2

Gadamer and the Plastic Arts

Cynthia R. Nielsen

This chapter examines Gadamer's account of the plastic arts (*bildende Künste*) and how his claim regarding the performative nature of art applies *mutatis mutandis* to the plastic arts. Gadamer's discussion of the picture (*Bild*) is the central focus of the chapter; however, his insights regarding architecture will also be briefly considered. In the sections leading up to I.2.2 of *Truth and Method*, Gadamer's investigation of art's ontology draws primarily on the performing arts such as drama and music. He emphasizes repeatedly that music and dramatic plays *are* their performances or enactments. That is, when it comes to our phenomenologico-hermeneutic experience of music and theatrical plays, apart from their various and diverse performances over time, they have no being. Their presentations emerge in their varied interpretative performances. However, the question naturally arises: how do Gadamer's claims about the "variability of presentation" apply to the plastic arts, which include painting, sculpture, and architecture?[1] That is, could a case for aesthetic differentiation not be made when it comes to these seemingly more static forms of art? As his account unfolds, it becomes clear that Gadamer rejects a Platonic understanding of *mimesis*, wherein the artwork as "copy" is understood as ontologically inferior to an "original" (*Urbild*).[2] In contrast, for Gadamer, a picture is not a self-effacing copy (*Abbild*); rather, a picture directs attention to itself, has its own significant, ontological "weight," and remains essentially connected to the "original." It involves, as Gadamer puts it, an "ontological sharing" (*ontologische Teilhabe*) or participation in the original (*TM*, 153/158). Moreover, the picture (*Bild*) discloses something about the original that we would not see apart from the picture's coming into being. Instead of a diminution of being, the picture is what Gadamer describes as an "increase in being" (*TM*, 141). Such an understanding opposes a Platonic view since Gadamer's account of the relation of a picture and an original is one of reciprocity and mutual dependence. In addition to the implications of Gadamer's ontological elevation of the picture, other relevant topics such as occasionality, decoration, institution (*Stiftung*), and the ongoing hermeneutical tasks of integration and mediation will likewise be discussed.

1. GADAMER'S ONTOLOGICAL ELEVATION OF THE PICTURE (*BILD*)

When one turns to the plastic arts—for example, painting, sculpture, and architecture—to speak of different presentations or performances seems counterintuitive. As Gadamer puts it in the opening paragraph of the section entitled "The Ontological Valence of the Picture":

> In the plastic arts it first seems as if the work has such a clear identity that there is no variability of presentation. What varies does not seem to belong to the side of the work itself and so seems to be subjective. Thus one might say that certain subjective limitations prevent one's experiencing the work fully, but these subjective limitations can ultimately be overcome. We can experience every work of plastic art "immediately" as itself—i.e., without its needing further mediating to us. (*TM*, 135)

In his discussion of play in the previous section (I.2.1), Gadamer argues against various abstracting tendencies in modern aesthetics and its concomitant aesthetic consciousness.[3] Aesthetic consciousness engages in acts of aesthetic differentiation, one of which is to separate the so-called artwork itself from its various interpretations, performances, and presentations. In his analysis of the performing arts, Gadamer shows that this alleged separation does not hold. A musical piece, for example, is not separate from its performances; rather, the musical piece *is* its various performances. The same applies with dramatic plays. Aesthetics, drawing upon insights from Plato, posits another differentiation—namely, it claims that a sharp distinction exists between the artwork (copy) and what it represents (original). It is to this distinction or differentiation that Gadamer turns his attention in his investigation of the picture (*Bild*).

2. A PICTURE (*BILD*) IS NOT A COPY (*ABBILD*)

In Gadamer's discussion of the picture (*Bild*), we see not only how his view differs from a Platonic account, but we also come to understand how he is able to answer the objections of modern aesthetics—in particular, its emphasis on aesthetic differentiation vis-à-vis the plastic arts. We recall that in the

Republic Socrates offers a critique of artistic *mimesis*, which aligns with his placement of images at the lowest level of his divided line. In this account, the ideal bed is the "original" and is ontologically superior to the carpenter's bed (first imitation) and even more so to the painter's painting of a bed (second imitation), which is considered three steps removed from the truth.[4] In contrast with this Platonic understanding of the relationship between image and original, Gadamer offers his account of art's aesthetic *non-differentiation*, which rejects the sharp distinction between artwork and performance, as well as image and original.

Before discussing his own view of the relationship between image and original, Gadamer reiterates some of the challenges of modern aesthetic consciousness in relation to the plastic arts and his own claims regarding the performative character of all types of art. Modern aesthetic consciousness conceives of paintings and sculptures displayed in a modern museum as self-contained, autonomous, and free-floating. On this view, a painting in a museum is

> not tied to a particular place but offers itself entirely by itself by virtue of the frame that encloses it. This makes it possible for such pictures to be put side by side in any order, as we see in modern galleries. Such pictures apparently have nothing about them of the objective dependence on mediation that we emphasized in the case of drama and music. (*TM*, 136)

Unlike music and dramatic plays, which require musicians and actors to mediate and make present their subject matters, paintings and sculptures seem to present themselves to us immediately. Gadamer, however, stresses that even though paintings and sculptural works can be and are detached from their original life worlds, they, nonetheless, carry a "trace" of their world with them (*TM*, 155). Moreover, paintings and other works of the plastic arts must be performed or enacted through spectatorial engagement in order to come to presentation. One must "read" and tarry with a painting, synthesizing its various aspects, allowing it to "come forth," and returning to it on different occasions to see what else it might disclose.[5] Similarly, one must inhabit a work of architecture, walking around its exterior and interior spaces in order to grasp its internal intelligibility and beauty, as well as its fittingness with its environment.

Having laid out potential challenges to his hermeneutical aesthetics, Gadamer turns to discuss his own view of the "mode of being of the picture" (*TM*, 136). A picture (*Bild*), although related to an original (*Urbild*), should *not* be understood as a copy (*Abbild*). Stated otherwise, the relationship between picture and original is not one of an ontologically inferior copy to a superior original. Gadamer's analytic focus at this point is to clarify how a picture differs from a copy and to clarify how, in light of this difference, we are to understand "the picture's relation to its *world*" (*TM*, 138). As we will see, his account emphasizes the reciprocal—rather than one-sided—relationship between picture and original. He begins by reiterating that "the mode of being of the work of art is *presentation* (Darstellung)" (*TM,* 139). This claim was argued for in a previous section in the analysis of play and the performing arts. Now the task is to clarify how the claim applies to the plastic arts. Thus, he turns to investigate how a picture's mode of being is likewise presentation and involves enactment. When it comes to a picture, presentation or presenting is not to be understood as copying. A copy, according to Gadamer, has "no other task but to resemble the original. The measure of its success is that one recognizes the original in the copy. This means that its nature is to lose its own independent existence and serve entirely to mediate what is copied" (*TM*, 139). A copy is, thus, self-effacing; it does not point *to* itself but rather *away* from itself.[6] Although this might suggest that a reflected image in a mirror would be the ideal copy, Gadamer denies that the mirror image qualifies as a copy, since, as a mere reflected image, it has no independent existence. In contrast, both a picture and a copy have their own independent existence. A copy, for example, can exist on its own, apart from the original, and as such can be utilized for various practical purposes. As Joel Weinsheimer observes, "[i]t would not do to improve the accuracy of passport photos by replacing them with mirrors. A copy necessarily exists in its own right, and yet that existence best serves its function by canceling itself out and ceding its rights to the original."[7] The self-effacing, self-concealing function of the copy is characteristic of its being; as such, a copy is always a means to something else and not an end.

In contrast, a picture points to itself and discloses something about its subject matter that would not be disclosed otherwise. The picture, in other words, is what is important because it shows us "how the thing represented is presented in it. This means first of all that one is not simply directed away from the picture to what is represented. Rather, the presentation remains essentially connected with what is represented—indeed, belongs to it" (*TM,* 140). Although the picture offers a unique disclosure or way of seeing of the original, it remains connected to or in communion with the original. The picture, as it were, is a particular presentation or enactment of the original and cannot be completely detached or separated from it because what it presents is the original, albeit in a new aspect. Unlike aesthetic differentiation's emphasis on a sharp distinction between a picture *qua* inferior, representational copy and the original, Gadamer's account lays stress on the picture's elevated ontology and essential connection to the original. The picture's being allows the original to be presented in just *this* way, and without the picture, the original "would not present itself in this way" (*TM*, 141). The picture opens up a space for play between the original subject matter and the picture's unique presentation of the subject matter. Gadamer goes on to say that the picture's elevated ontology means that the relationship between it and the original is no longer one-sided, since the original is dependent on the picture's presentation of itself to be seen in just that way. "*It is no longer a one-sided relationship.* That the picture has its own reality means the reverse for what is pictured, namely that it comes to presentation in the representation. It presents itself there" (*TM*, 141).[8] The painting presents the original or subject matter in a new light—that is, it reconfigures the subject matter and in doing so puts it in play. Gadamer's elevation of the ontological status of the picture reconceives the picture as an "ontological event," which brings about an "*increase in being*" (*Zuwachs am Sein*) (*TM*, 141/145, emphasis in original). As Dennis Schmidt observes, this increase should be understood in a qualitative rather than a quantitative sense.[9] In other words, the increase in being that the picture generates puts our understanding of the subject matter in play; it expands, enriches, and perhaps challenges our previous understanding. Commenting further, Schmidt writes:

> One might say that the image has the capacity to *change* what is imaged and what is seen, and thus it changes the world out of which the image has emerged. This is the force of the artwork: that we no longer see the world independently of the images by which the world has been interpreted.[10]

On Gadamer's account, not only is the ontological status of the picture or image exalted, but we also find an emphasis on the image's formative role in keeping subject matters in play. Art's increase of being, so to speak, gives birth to new ways of seeing the world. As Schmidt puts it,

> [I]mages, above all images in the work of art, educate our seeing and understanding of the world. They are not copies of a world, but, in some sense, they come to be coterminous with the disclosure of a world at all. In this sense, one must say that the work of art is at the origin of our understanding of a world.[11]

Gadamer's understanding of the formative interplay between image and original, image and world, thus serves as a critique of aesthetic consciousness and its model of the framed picture separated from the world and doubly contained within its frame and the walls of the museum. The frame and museum as figures of separation contrast sharply with Gadamer's view of art's intimate connection with and role in our self- and world-understanding. The artwork's working—its ongoing play and movement—brings forth and makes possible the reconfiguring of new possibilities, new ways of seeing.

To illustrate his point, Gadamer turns to discuss portraits such as those of famous rulers or statesmen to further highlight the interplay between image and original. A governmental leader, such as a president or chancellor, by virtue of his or her representative position, must present himself or herself both to those whom he or she represents and to other heads of state. Such public showings occur through national ceremonies, speeches, interviews, and public interactions with other leaders. The idiosyncrasies and "style" of a leader are on display in these public activities. Whether a leader is bombastic and impulsive or thoughtful and serious-minded can be interpreted from his or her actions, and painters can likewise disclose these traits (and much more) through portraiture. For example, George Peter Alexander Healy's 1869 portrait of Abraham Lincoln depicts the president seated in a chair in a contemplative pose that captures the *gravitas* that characterized his approach to and understanding of his position.[12] Along these lines, Gadamer states "The way the ruler, the statesman, the hero shows and presents himself—this is brought to presentation in the picture" (*TM*, 142). However, the portrait is neither a mere copy that points away from itself nor a mirror image that reflects only what is already known. The painting, having its own reality and mode of being, presents the leader with his or her self-showing, which, of course, can provoke a range of reactions from inspiration to disorientation and despair. One may not like the likeness of oneself portrayed by the artist. The portrait may, for example, show us what others have been telling us for years but which we have failed or refused to see. In addition, because we are immersed in our daily tasks and projects, we are, as Nicholas Davey describes,

> to a degree absent from ourselves, passing from task to task without catching sight of ourselves. Rooted in actuality, we bear the marks of its untransformed nature: everything about us is undecided, incomplete and fragmented. There are, of course, implicit patterns and open lines of continuity in all that we do, but . . . rarely do we see ourselves, albeit provisionally, as coherent wholes.[13]

When an artist presents me with my likeness, she gives me a "visual summation" (Davey's term) of myself that I would not see otherwise, owing to my immersion in everyday activities and my dispersed and fragmented mode of being. My being is increased, in that I am presented with a particular, intensified, unified summation of myself that brings together my multiple self-fragments and can provoke self-reflection and perhaps even self-transformation. Returning to the portrait of Abraham Lincoln, perhaps upon gazing at his likeness it discloses exhaustion and strain of which at that point in his life he was only vaguely aware. Portraits, of course, can also inspire by depicting the sitter as courageous or compassionate. Here again the painting draws from the various fragmented, dispersed presentations of the sitter—perhaps through observing his actions over a period time, reading his speeches, or interviewing him and those close to him—and creates a poignant and moving presentation of his likeness, to which he must now, as it were, strive to live up. The likeness, thus, comes back to shape the sitter, as it impacts not only how he sees himself but also how others see him. Thus, the successful portrait presents the statesman or leader with a likeness of himself that creates the conditions for his own and others' critical and constructive reflection on his self-showing. Since the statesman's "being necessarily and essentially includes showing himself, he no longer belongs to himself" (*TM*, 142).

Gadamer concludes this section by returning to his notion of play and offering a brief summary of how play is valuable to a hermeneutico-aesthetic understanding of the picture as an "event of being" (*TM*, 144). In other words, *contra* a representational account of pictorial art, Gadamer articulates a presentational view of painting, in which the painting is not understood as an ontologically inferior copy of an original but rather as having its own being which is then put in play with the original or subject matter it presents. What is distinctive about art's *presentational* being—and what characterizes important aspects of its work and play—is its ability to gather into a unified whole what in our daily experience of ourselves and the world is multiple, dispersed, fragmented, and in the process of becoming. It presents the subject matter in a unique, arresting, and unified manner that we would otherwise miss owing to our immersion in the flux of everyday life. In contrast to Socrates' account of the picture's ontology in the *Republic* as deflated, Gadamer gives us an account of its being as elevated. What is characteristic of all art is not its representational character but its *presentational* character. Gadamer's elevated ontology of the picture not only contrasts with Socrates' view, but it is also at odds with the abstracting and separating tendencies of modern aesthetics. That is, in emphasizing that the picture is "an event of being" in which the subject matter itself is presented and put into play, Gadamer's account of the picture's being and working offers a critique of aesthetic consciousness and its activity of aesthetic differentiation. For Gadamer, the picture's presentational play necessitates its communion with the subject matter presented. "The picture contains an indissoluble connection with its world" (*TM*, 144).

3. OCCASIONALITY AND THE DECORATIVE

Gadamer turns next to discuss occasionality in reference to portraits, dedicated poems, and allusions to events in ancient Greek comedy (*TM*, 144). He describes the occasionality of a portrait or dedicated poem as follows:

Occasionality means that their meaning and contents are determined by the occasion for which they are intended, so that they contain more than they would without this occasion. Hence the portrait is related to the man represented, a relation that is not just dragged in but is expressly intended in the representation itself and indeed makes it a portrait. The important thing is that this occasionality belongs to the work's own claim and is not something forced on it by its interpreter. (*TM*, 144)

On the one hand, in a portrait of a statesman, monarch, or other leader, a trace of the original world is given with the presentation of the subject matter. Although pointing to itself, the portrait also refers to the sitter and the events, challenges, and circumstances of his or her day. On the other, while one can, of course, benefit from studying the historical context and events in which a portrait, poem, or other artwork was created, Gadamer argues against a historicizing position that overemphasizes the need to reconstruct all the historical details of an artwork in order to truly understand it. One need not, as Donatella Di Cesare states, "know all the references to understand a satire by Horace."[14] A point that Gadamer elaborates in his discussion of architecture and in the final paragraphs of I.2.2 is that the occasional meaning of the artwork applies not only to the artwork's content and the world that it presents, it also applies to our world, and, as Di Cesare puts it, "to the meaning that [the artwork] gathers for us in the course of its effective history. Hence this occasional meaning constantly determines itself anew."[15]

Continuing his discussion of occasionality, Gadamer considers the differences in a painter's approach to the sitter of a portrait and a model employed for a genre painting. When an artist paints a portrait, she aims to depict the individuality of the person. In contrast, when she uses a model to paint a genre picture, the goal is not to capture the model's individuality. The model is used rather to assist the painter in capturing certain poses and gestures or to represent a type. Models, in other words, have an instrumental role—they wear hats, uniforms, and other attire and sit for specific poses—but their *individuality* should not come through in the painting. Unlike the person portrayed, a model is self-effacing and is not meant to be recognized for who he or she is as an individual person. Gadamer describes a model as "a disappearing schema" whose "relation to the original that served the painter must be effaced in the picture" (*TM*, 145). For Gadamer, the differences between a model and a portrait offer insights into the meaning of occasionality. "Occasionality in the sense intended clearly lies in what the work itself claims to mean, in contradistinction from whatever is discovered in it or can be deduced from it that goes against this claim. A portrait asks to be understood as a portrait" (*TM*, 145). For example, a historian might examine a portrait of nineteenth-century Russian Czar Alexander II in order to see whether the portrait properly depicts a specific kind of uniform worn during that period. In doing so, he misses the point of the portrait—namely, to present us with the individuality of Alexander II and the meaning of this particular presentation. Even so, that what we see is understood *as* a portrait is not dependent upon whether or not we know the identity of the person portrayed. As Gadamer explains,

> Although the relation to the original resides in the work itself, it is still right to call it occasional. For the portrait does not say who the person portrayed is, but only that it is a particular individual (and not a type). We can "recognize" who it is only when the person portrayed is known to us, and be sure only when there is a title or some other information to go on. At any rate there resides in the picture an undetermined but still fundamentally determinable reference to something, which constitutes its significance. This occasionality belongs essentially to the import of the "picture," regardless of whether one knows what it refers to. (*TM*, 146)

An artwork's meaning is not reducible to its original occasion, but rather its meanings are always conditioned by its various occasionings over time. If the meaning of the artwork is determined in part by each occasion of interpretation, then we can speak of a kind of "universal occasionality" (*TM*, 148). As Weinsheimer observes, "[u]niversal occasionality implies that occasions, not just intentional acts, determine meanings. These meanings, moreover, are the working of the work and inseparable from it."[16] Here, as Gadamer himself does, one must connect occasionality and the artwork's performative nature. As noted at the beginning of this chapter, his concern in this section to show how the plastic arts, as is the case with the performing arts, also involve different "performances" and "presentations." Emphasizing the performative character of the plastic arts, he states:

> It is, therefore, in keeping with the essence of dramatic or musical works that their performance at different times and on different occasions is, and must be, different. Now it is crucial to see that this applies, *mutatis mutandis*, also to the plastic arts. Here, as well, it is not that the work is "in itself" and only the effect is different—the work of art itself is what presents itself differently under ever-changing conditions. Today's observer not only sees differently, he also sees different aspects. (*WM*, 153, my translation)[17]

By stating that the work does not exist *an sich*, Gadamer rejects any view of an artwork as an atemporal, de-worlded essence. Rather, an artwork itself exists only in its various enactments and presentations. Each *different* enactment presents the work differently because each is informed by horizons or hermeneutical fields of meaning which themselves change over time. Since these hermeneutical fields of meaning are dynamic, new meanings and new aspects of the work are disclosed in light of the ever-changing contexts, occasions, and horizons which shape how the artwork appears. Although there are differences between the performing and plastic arts, both musical works and portraits present themselves through enactment and, for the reasons just outlined, likewise disclose new aspects. By examining occasioned artforms such as portraits, we come to understand the "universal occasionality characteristic of the work of art inasmuch as it determines itself anew from occasion to occasion" (*TM*, 148). Gadamer's emphasis on the artwork's performative and occasional being highlights his understanding of the artwork's dynamic ontology. The artwork is both determinable, in that it presents us with a subject matter, and yet indeterminate, in that its occasionality and performative character make possible the disclosure of new aspects and meanings of the same subject matter. Using the portrait as his example, Gadamer comments on the inter-*play* between the determinable subject matter and its indeterminability owing, in part, to its occasionality:

> The work's unique relation to the occasion can never be finally determined, but though indeterminable this relation remains present and effective in the work itself. In this sense the portrait too is independent of its unique relation to the original, and contains the latter even in transcending it. (*TM*, 148)[18]

4. A PICTURE AS A MEAN BETWEEN *VERWEISUNG* AND *VERTRETEN*

Gadamer engages in a brief discussion of the nature of indicating, which he contends will help us to better understand the nature of a picture. A picture's essence is best understood as a kind of mean between two extremes of representation. Gadamer describes these extremes as

> *pure indication* (Verweisung: also, reference), which is the essence of the sign, and *pure substitution* (Vertreten), which is the essence of the symbol. There is something of both in a picture. Its representing includes indicating what is represented in it. (*TM*, 151–52)

As we saw with his earlier analysis, a portrait points to an original and remains in "ontological communion" with it. However, a portrait or picture is not a sign; it does not point away but rather to itself. The successful portrait arrests us, draws us in, and compels us to linger or tarry with it. In contrast, if a sign draws attention to itself in this way, it fails. The sign's purpose is to make present something that is absent and to do so in such a way that the absent thing, and that alone, comes to mind. . . . There is something schematic and abstract about [signs], because they point not to themselves but to what is not present—e.g., to the curve ahead [as with traffic signs]. (*TM*, 152)

So neither signs nor copies help us to understand the essence of a picture. In the following passage, Gadamer provides a helpful summary of what characterizes a sign and likewise introduces his understanding of a symbol.[19]

> The difference between a picture and a sign has an ontological basis. The picture does not disappear in pointing to something else but, in its own being, shares in what it represents. This ontological sharing (*ontologische Teilhabe*) pertains not only to a picture but to what we call a *symbol*. Neither symbol nor picture indicates anything that is not at the same time present in them themselves. Hence, the problem arises of differentiating between the mode of being of pictures and the mode of being of symbols. (*TM*, 153/158)

So, ontologically speaking, a picture is more like a symbol and less like a sign, which raises the question of how to understand the difference between the mode of being of a picture and that of a symbol. Before answering this question, Gadamer clarifies a symbol's essence and function. A symbol does not simply point to that which is absent; rather, a symbol makes present what it symbolizes. In other words, a symbol in some sense comes to stand for what it points to by taking its place. Hence his earlier description, which describes the essence of the symbol as "pure substitution" (*Vertreten*). Both a sign and a symbol indicate, but *how* they do so differs. A symbol indicates or points to something by substituting itself for what it indicates. However, as Gadamer explains, "to take the place of something means to make something present that is not present." A symbol, in other words,

> makes something immediately present. Only because it thus presents the presence of what it represents is the symbol itself treated with the reverence due to the symbolized. Such symbols as a crucifix, a flag, a uniform have so fully taken the place of what is revered that the latter is present in them. (*TM*, 153)

Whereas most people tend not to treat a highway construction sign with respect, they often treat a country's flag or a religious symbol with respect because such items stand for entities and institutions about which communities care deeply and to which they have devoted much thought and praxis.

Although pictures are more like symbols than signs, pictures are not merely symbols because they are not merely substitutes. That is, a picture presents its subject matter and through this presentation an "increase in being" occurs;

new aspects of the subject matter are disclosed, which are both ontologically connected to the original and put it in play. A symbol-qua-substitute does *not* bring about an increase in being of what it symbolizes; rather, it simply takes the place of what it points to. A picture makes the original or subject matter present "through itself, through the increment of meaning that it brings" (*TM*, 154). In sum, a picture is neither a sign construed as "a pure pointing-to-something" nor a symbol construed as "a pure taking-the-place-of-something" (*TM*, 154). Rather, a picture is a mean between *Verweisung* (indication or reference) and *Vertreten* (substitution), and "it is this intermediate position that raises it to a unique ontological status" (*TM*, 154).[20]

5. INSTITUTION

Gadamer next introduces what he calls "institution" (*Stiftung*) and describes how it relates to signs and symbols. Whereas the picture obtains its signifying function from its own content, artificial signs and symbols

> must be taken as signs or as symbols .... In determining the ontological valence of a picture (which is what we are concerned with), it is decisive that in regard to a picture there is no such thing as "institution" in the same sense. By "institution" we mean the origin of something's being taken as a sign or functioning symbolically. (*TM*, 154)

What Gadamer says shares certain similarities with Ferdinand de Saussure's insights about language. Saussure argues that the relation between the sign (sound-image) and the signified (concept) is arbitrary, by which he means that the connection between the two is based on social convention. For example, in English, the link between the sign "tree" and the signified—the concept of an entity with bark, branches, and leaves—is arbitrary and was established by a particular linguistic community. For a German speaker, the sign *Baum* is linked to the concept of an entity with bark, branches, and leaves. The connection between the sign and signified in English, German, or any other human language is not natural but rather conventional. Similarly, Gadamer says that signs are "taken as signs only because the linkage between the sign and the signified has previously been established. This is true of all artificial signs. Here the sign is established by convention, and the originating act by which it is established is called its 'institution'" (*TM*, 154–55). Gadamer's example of an artificial sign is a traffic sign, whose significance is conferred by the Ministry of Transport. Not only signs but also symbols require this originary act of institution in order to be associated with a certain meaning. For example, a white dove does not in itself signify peace, nor does an owl signify wisdom. A symbol must be instituted, Gadamer states, "for only this gives it its representational character. For what gives it its significance is not its own ontological content but an act of institution" (*TM*, 155).

In contrast, a work of art, Gadamer claims "does not owe its real meaning to such an act of institution, even if it is a religious picture or a secular memorial" (*TM*, 155). Take, for example, a portrait unveiled at a ceremony to honor a political or religious figure. The purpose of the ceremonial unveiling—to honor and commemorate a particular individual—does not give the portrait its meaning. Rather, the portrait itself "is already a structure with a signifying function of its own" (*TM*, 155). A series of commissioned portraits to honor a monarch, which, if removed from their prominent place in the palace and displayed in a foreign museum, still present us with a subject matter. As Gadamer puts it, "the trace of their original purpose cannot be effaced. It is part of their being because their being is presentation" (*TM*, 155). Although it may seem at first that what Gadamer says here about artworks "themselves lay[ing] claim to their place, . . . even if they are displaced" opposes his emphasis on the occasionality of artworks, his claims can be understood as describing different aspects of the dynamic ontology of artworks. That is, in the context of denying that artworks owe their meaning to an originary instituting act, Gadamer lays stress on the artwork's presentation of a subject-matter—whether representational or abstract. Something "stands" before us and invites interpretation. A *determinate* yet not fully determinable, identifiable subject-matter is presented and invites us to linger with it. The artwork's occasionality, in contrast, draws attention more specifically to the *indeterminability* and openness of the artwork. That is, through its various historical enactments, situated in and informed by the interplay of ever-changing hermeneutical fields of meaning and historical contexts, an artwork discloses new aspects and meanings.

6. ARCHITECTURE AND THE DECORATIVE

Although Gadamer's comments on architecture are brief, they complete his discussion of the plastic arts and disclose important truths about the ongoing hermeneutical task of integrating past and present. Gadamer begins with an explanation of how an architectural work is an *impure* work of art because it serves a specific, practical function. In addition, it must be integrated with the historical world into which it is placed and at the same time enhance it. Commenting on this "dual ordering," Gadamer states,

> Every architect has to consider both these things. His plan is determined by the fact that the building has to serve a particular way of life and adapt itself to

particular architectural circumstances. We call a successful building a "happy solution," and mean by this both that it perfectly fulfills its purpose and that its construction has added something new to the spatial dimensions of a town or landscape. Through this dual ordering the building presents a true increase of being: it is a work of art. (*TM*, 155–56)

An architectural structure must draw us in, for example, owing to its beauty, complexity, or elegance; yet it must also be designed such that it accomplishes its intended practical function in an artistic and fitting manner. A place of worship that looks like a shopping mall may provide a space for people to gather; yet it is in no way esteemed as a work of art because it does not achieve the fittingness one would expect given its subject matter and purpose. Conversely, an aesthetically beautiful concert hall that produces poor acoustics fails to achieve the practical purpose for which the building was designed. Furthermore, the building must also harmonize with its surroundings; it must creatively integrate the community's past history and present way of life. If it succeeds, it will necessarily change the world into which it has been placed and will itself be seen in a new light. Architectural works, as Gadamer attests, do not exist

> motionless on the shore of the stream of history, but are borne along by it. Even if historically-minded ages try to reconstruct the architecture of an earlier age, they cannot turn back the wheel of history, but must mediate in a new and better way between the past and the present. (*TM*, 156)

Thus, the work of architecture, like the other forms of art analyzed, is also dynamic; it necessarily changes with time, as its context changes and as it itself is renovated and repaired due to age or use. As *impure* works of art, buildings can be radically transformed and come to have both a new purpose and a new look while retaining vestiges of their former appearance. Take, for example, the transformation of old warehouses into modern lofts whose chic, interior spaces feature exposed brick walls and exposed wooden ceilings and supporting beams. Works of architecture, like all works of art, are characterized by occasionality; they are, as Jean-Claude Gens explains, "contingent and changing, but no less essential[ly] connected to a world."[21] Along similar lines, Weinsheimer describes the architectural work as a

> locus of mediation between past and present. It gives people a history that is not simply bygone; it is their own history, for they are still living in it, adding to it, and changing it. . . . Architecture too is occasional. It exists and persists in renovation and reproduction.[22]

Not only does the architectural work bring traces of its world and historicity with it but it also shapes space and houses multiple other art forms.

> Architecture gives shape to space. Space is what surrounds everything that exists in space. That is why architecture embraces all the other forms of representation: all works of plastic art, all ornament. Moreover, it gives a place to the representational arts of poetry, music, acting, and dancing. By embracing all the arts, it asserts its own perspective everywhere. That perspective is *decoration*. (*TM*, 157)

On the one hand, paintings and sculptural works are housed in museum buildings and, as it were, ornament or decorate it. On the other, the museum building itself is a commissioned work of art; its structure draws attention to itself—as is the case with all artworks—and it must integrate with and enhance the world in which it is situated. In this sense, the museum building itself can be understood as decorative. Yet, in order for its function of housing paintings and sculptural works to be successful, it must partially conceal itself. That is, if a museum building's interior design, while intricate and aesthetically arresting, creates lighting or spatial difficulties for the proper display of the artworks it houses, or if it draws too much attention to itself and eclipses the artworks, the building fails. The proper balance must be found between function and artistry and likewise between enhancing and integrating. Similarly, in music a good piano accompanist tastefully and artfully provides a harmonic structure that enhances the piece and at the same time allows the soloist to shine. If the accompanist plays overly repetitive harmonic or rhythmic patterns, the accompaniment falls flat; it is neither in dynamic interplay with the soloist nor does it enrich the piece as a whole. If the pianist ornaments excessively and draws attention to her musical contribution, she has foregrounded and thematized what was supposed to function as a background enhancement, yet one whose tasteful artistry is essential to what makes the piece remarkable and unique. Similarly, an architectural work must strike the proper balance—neither overdoing repetition and becoming "unbearably monotonous," nor foregrounding itself such that it fails to harmonize with its surroundings or to achieve the practical goals for which it was designed. Architecture, Gadamer states,

> involves a twofold mediation. As the art which creates space it both shapes it and leaves it free. It not only embraces all decorative shaping of space, including ornament, but is itself decorative in nature. The nature of decoration consists in performing that two-fold mediation: namely to draw the viewer's attention to itself, to satisfy his taste, and then to redirect it away from itself to the greater whole of the life context which it accompanies. (*TM*, 157)

With his use of the terms *decoration* and the *decorative*, it should be clear that Gadamer does not have in mind a superficial aesthetic quality but rather a work's fittingness, which, as Paul Kidder notes, has etymological roots in the Latin term *decōrum*. In his book *Gadamer for Architects*, Kidder explains that for Gadamer *decoration* means

> that which unifies a work of architecture and thus serves as the means of resisting aesthetic superficiality. He draws, here, on Vitruvius' sense of *"decorum,"* which refers to the fittingness of a work's form to its meaning and function, exemplified, according to Vitruvius, in the way a temple's structures—and particularly its columns—must be suited to the divinity that the temple is meant to honor.[23]

Rather than a superficial, external imposition, the decorative speaks of the suitability or fittingness of the building's form to its meaning and purpose. Kidder then highlights a connection with Gadamer's use of the decorative and Heidegger's essay, "Building, Dwelling, Thinking."[24] In Heidegger's reflections on a bridge, he emphasizes how it gathers a world—that is, it connects two riverbanks, thus creating a path that facilitates various human activities, whether journeying, connecting with others, or accomplishing daily tasks. Both Gadamer and Heidegger lay stress on how artifacts and architectural works exist and belong to a larger complex of relations and meanings. Commenting on Heidegger's essay, Kidder writes,

> As a thing [a bridge] is always caught up in a web of natural and cultural involvements; as an architectural thing it is especially dedicated to the gathering of a landscape . . . The bridge orients one within the landscape and complements that landscape by virtue of what it adds. It serves its purpose; it draws significance from its mediation of an environment; yet within the fulfillment of these purposes it realizes its unique artistry.[25]

Along similar lines, Gadamer speaks of how an architectural work must be fittingly integrated with its external and internal environments and their respective purposes. In addition, when the architectural work succeeds, a fittingness is achieved concerning the work's ability both to reveal its artistry and to conceal itself in accord with its function. In short, the decorative is not set in opposition to or separable from the "real work of art." Rather, it belongs to the artwork's presentational ontological structure, which means that it belongs to the artwork's mode of being. Toward the end of his discussion of architecture and the decorative, Gadamer reminds us that "the ornamental and the decorative originally meant the beautiful as such," to which he adds, it is necessary to recover this ancient insight. . . . Ornament is not primarily something by itself that is then applied to something else but belongs to the self-presentation of its wearer. Ornament too belongs to presentation. But presentation is an event of being. (*TM*, 158–59)

Architecture makes clear that artworks are *not* self-contained objects whose essence exists outside time and space; they are instead historical, spatial, occasioned and occasioning dynamic events; they invite us to linger with them so that their "increase in being" might facilitate a transformation in how we see ourselves and engage the world. Given their practical ends and the need to integrate with their environment, architectural works cannot be properly conceived as mere works of inspiration in accord with a (romanticized) model of a creative genius. Gadamer emphasizes this point in his 1985 essay "The End of Art." Regarding works of architecture, he writes,

There is a given place and a specific purpose, as well as a predefined environment, urban or rural, and quite certainly it is only in this that the architect's art is fulfilled: to blend into (*fügen sich*) the spatial conditions and to create new spatial arrangements. Buildings are never utopias.[26]

Since architectural works are always constrained by practical ends, they, as Gens puts it, "compel us to reiterate the question of what truly defines a work of art."[27] Not only are architectural works *impure* works of art, but their character as decorative and the two-fold mediation that they perform bring to the fore two seemingly competing ideas that must be held together. On the one hand, we have the artwork's autonomy and internal integrity, which exudes a fittingness—that is, "nothing may be removed or added to it."[28] On the other, we have the artwork's relation to "a world of practical purposes" in which it is situated, integrated, and which puts its self-closure in play. Architecture makes evident that "the closure of a work of art . . . does not imply a separation or isolation from its environment."[29]

7. THE HERMENEUTICAL TASKS OF INTEGRATING AND RE-INTEGRATING

In the final section of I.2.2, Gadamer states that philosophical hermeneutics is no longer a supplementary discipline focused on the interpretation of religious or literary texts. Rather, it must be understood in a more comprehensive sense. Provocatively put, "*Aesthetics has to be absorbed into hermeneutics*" (*TM*, 164). Gadamer's claim should not be understood as a downgrading or destruction of aesthetic experience, but instead, as Davey explains, it "initiates a phenomenological re-description of aesthetic experience so that the discipline can be established as a cognitively significant mode of a subject's being-in-the-world. Aesthetic experience is redeemed as a form of hermeneutical engagement with the world, that is, it gives expression to not a subject's feeling but a subject's being."[30] Our engagement with works of art, like our engagement with texts, is not merely a private, subjective experience but rather is a dialogical event of understanding in which we linger with a subject-matter and allow it to speak to us. The hermeneutical experience (*Erfahrung*) of art is centered on a subject-matter presented in the artwork and is an experience which, while not reducible to verbal language, can nonetheless be expressed in language. Moreover, just as the written text presents us with a hermeneutical task of integration and reintegration, so too does the work of art. Although occasioned and occasioning, the artwork is not rigidly constrained or measured by its original occasion. An artwork's internal intelligibility or "meaningful presence" allows it to "overcome temporal distance," yet "understanding art always includes historical mediation" (*TM*, 165). For Gadamer, the proper hermeneutical approach to historical mediation is not reconstruction but rather integration. Gadamer claims that Schleiermacher's hermeneutics represents the path of reconstruction. That is, for Schleiermacher, an artwork's full significance is found only in its original world; when it is taken out of its original world, it becomes alienated and suffers a loss of intelligibility. In order to overcome this alienation, one must then restore the work and its world in all their historical details. Although Gadamer agrees that studying the historical context of a text or work of art is important to understanding it, he holds that Schleiermacher's position implies that one must "reproduce the writer's original process of production" (*TM*, 166).[31] For Gadamer, this is an impossible task that denies our historicity. Whatever one might reconstruct, no matter how careful and meticulous, it will not produce the original.

Hegel, in contrast, rejects a hermeneutics of restoration and argues instead for a hermeneutics of integration. While Hegel, too, sees value in studying art from a historical perspective, he considers such an approach to be an "external activity." Artworks allegedly restored to their original conditions are likened to "fruit torn from the tree. Putting them back in their historical context does not give us a living relationship with them but rather a merely ideative representation (*Vorstellung*)" (*TM*, 167).[32] Of course, Gadamer does not go the full way with Hegel.[33] For example, while he rejects Hegel's view that art is surpassed by philosophy, which is revealed as the highest expression of absolute *Geist*, he nonetheless judges Hegel's emphasis on historical mediation and criticism of historical restoration as the proper hermeneutical orientation. The key point that Gadamer affirms is Hegel's claim that the essential nature of the historical spirit consists not in the restoration of the past but in *thoughtful mediation with contemporary life*. Hegel is right when he does not conceive of such thoughtful mediation as an external relationship established after the fact but places it on the same level as the truth of art itself. (*TM*, 168)

Given Gadamer's interest in the question of art's truth, his hermeneutics and hermeneutical aesthetics demand a critical interrogation of the assumptions and claims of both aesthetic consciousness and historical consciousness. Such an interrogation gives rise to an understanding of artworks as occasioned and occasioning, decorated and decorating, mediated and mediating; artworks ever open and fecund with meaning; artworks not dead and frozen in the past but alive and in play.

NOTES

1. Gadamer, Hans-Georg. *Truth and Method*, 2nd ed., trans. Joel Weinsheimer and Donald G. Marshall (New York: Bloomsbury Publishing, 2013), 135. Hereafter cited in text as *TM*. Where the German is cited or the translation has been altered, the page number of the original is indicated after the slash. The latter refer to Hans-Georg Gadamer, *Wahrheit und Methode*, Gesammelte Werke I (Tübingen: Mohr Siebeck, 1990). For the sake of clarity, in two instances I have cited the German text independently as *WM*, #.

2. Although I am aware and take as significant that the view of *mimesis* presented as Plato's is presented by Plato's character Socrates, I retain the term "Platonic" in order to avoid the cumbersome and inelegant phrase "Plato's Socrates' view."

3. For a detailed examination of Gadamer's notion of play in relation to artworks, see Cynthia R. Nielsen, "Play and the Play of Art," in *The Gadamerian Mind*, eds. Theodore George and Gert-Jan van der Heiden (New York: Routledge, 2022), 139–54.

4. Plato, *Republic*, 596a–598c.

5. For additional discussion on Gadamer's notion of "tarrying" with an artwork, see Gadamer's 1992 essay, "The Artwork in Word and Image: 'So True, So Full of Being!'" in *The Gadamer Reader*, ed. and trans. by Richard E. Palmer (Evanston: Northwestern University Press, 2007), 192–224, esp. 211–12. In this same essay, Gadamer further develops his ideas of an artwork's being as performative, thematizing the concept of *Vollzug*. For example, he writes: "Art has its 'being' in the *Vollzug*—the vital, living event of its appearing or its performance" (215).

6. See also, Dennis J. Schmidt, *Between Word and Image. Heidegger, Klee, and Gadamer on Gesture and Genesis* (Bloomington: Indiana University Press, 2013), esp. chapter 3. Schmidt makes the same point about the self-effacing character of the copy but also highlights how Gadamer's understanding of the nature of a picture encompasses abstract art. For example, Schmidt writes: "This is the case with all painting—namely, that in painting we look at the image itself, not through it to

something else—but abstract art, which calls attention to itself and not to an object, makes this especially clear. Abstract, non-representational works remove all pretense that something other than the image itself defines the painting. The abstract work reminds us that the image *is* the work" (115).

7. Joel C. Weinsheimer, *Gadamer's Hermeneutics: A Reading of Truth and Method* (New Haven: Yale University Press, 1985), 120.

8. A few paragraphs later, Gadamer adds: "The picture then has an autonomy that also affects the original. For strictly speaking, it is only through the picture (*Bild*) that the original (*Urbild*) becomes original (Ur-bild: also, ur-picture)—e.g., it is only by being pictured that a landscape becomes picturesque" (*TM*, 142).

9. See also Gaetano Chiurazzi, "Truth Is More Than Reality. Gadamer's Transformational Concept of Truth," *Research in Phenomenology* 41 (2011): 60–71. Along similar lines, Chiurazzi states: "It is a question not of an 'extensive' but of an intensive difference in reality, an increase, a different *modality* of being. The picture is not something added to the original, but shows the original in another form, literally in another *mode* of its existence. The different reality—the difference in *reality*—that the picture or the representation confers to the original is thus what Gadamer calls 'increase in being'" (66).

10. Schmidt, *Between Word and Image,* 116. Of course, the interplay between images and the world can generate both fruitful and problematic ways of seeing. Consider, for example, the various ways in which womens' bodies have been depicted in Western art, film, and photography and how these images have shaped notions of beauty, desirability, and "femininity."

11. Schmidt, 117.

12. In an early painting of Lincoln in 1868 entitled "The Peacemakers," Healy painted Lincoln in a similar leaning, contemplative pose; however, here Lincoln is surrounded by three counselors, including General Sherman, in whose direction he is leaning and to which appears to be attentively listening. In Healy's 1869 portrait he decided to paint Lincoln alone, yet he retained the "listening, absorbed pose." "Abraham Lincoln," *White House Historical Association*, accessed December 5, 2020, https://web.archive.org/web/20100626051004/https://www.whitehousehistory.org/whha_about/whitehouse_collection/whitehouse_collection-art-05.html.

13. Nicholas Davey, *Unfinished Worlds: Hermeneutics, Aesthetics, and Gadamer* (Edinburgh: Edinburgh University Press, 2013), 125.

14. Donatella Di Casare, *Gadamer: A Philosophical Portrait*, trans. Niall Keane (Bloomington: Indiana University Press, 2007), 58.

15. Di Cesare, 58.

16. Weinsheimer, *Gadamer's Hermeneutics*, 125.

17. Granted, I take some interpretative liberty toward the end of the passage, when I translate: "er sieht auch anderes" as "he also sees different aspects." However, the other English translations, which render the German "he sees different things," give the impression that in each enactment the artwork becomes a *new* artwork—a position that Gadamer rejects. By translating "anderes" as "different aspects," Gadamer's concern for the unity of the artwork is upheld, while, nonetheless, acknowledging that new and different aspects of the *same* artwork are disclosed in each enactment.

The full German passage reads: Es liegt also im Wesen dramatischer oder musikalischer Werke, daß ihre Aufführung in verschiedenen Zeiten und bei verschiedenen Gelegenheiten eine veränderte ist und sein muß. Nun gilt es, einzusehen, daß das mutatis mutandis auch für die statutarischen Künste zutrifft. Auch da ist nicht so, daß das Werk ‚an sich' wäre und nur die Wirkung eine je andere ist—das Kunstwerk selbst ist es, was sich unter je veränderten Bedingungen anders darbietet. Der Betrachter von heute sieht nicht nur anders, er sieht auch anderes (*WM*, 153).

18. Gadamer makes a similar point a few paragraphs earlier when he states that the artwork's being "experiences a continued determination of its meaning from the 'occasion' of its coming-to-presentation." While this is true of the plastic arts, he goes on to say that "this is seen most clearly in the performing arts, especially in theater and music, which wait for the occasion in order to exist and define themselves only through that occasion" (*TM*, 147).

19. Compare Gadamer's discussion of a symbol in his later essay, "The Relevance of the Beautiful: Art as Play, Symbol, and Festival," in *The Relevance of the Beautiful and Other Essays,* ed. Robert Bernasconi and trans. Nicholas Walker (Cambridge: Cambridge University Press, 1986), 3–53; see esp. 31–39.

20. Although Gadamer's discussion of the picture focuses primarily on portraiture and thus representational painting, his emphasis on the performative, eventual, and presentational character of art applies also to abstract art. Abstract painting makes evident that the artwork is not a sign pointing to some original; rather, it points to itself and the subject matter it presents, however abstract that subject matter might be. See also Schmidt, *Between Word and Image,* 120. For Gadamer's discussion of abstract painting, see "The Speechless Image," in *The Relevance of the Beautiful and Other Essays,* ed. Robert Bernasconi, trans. Nicholas Walker (Cambridge: Cambridge University Press, 1986), 83–91. See also, Daniel Tate, "The Speechless Image: Gadamer and the Claim of Modern Painting," *Philosophy Today* 45 (2001): 56–68.

21. Jean-Claude Gens, "The Configuration of Space Through Architecture in the Thinking of Gadamer," in *Place, Space, and Hermeneutics,* ed. Bruce B. Janz (Cham, Switzerland: Springer International Publishing, 2017), 160.

22. Weinsheimer, *Gadamer's Hermeneutics,* 126.

23. Paul Kidder, *Gadamer for Architects* (London: Routledge, 2013), 29.

24. See Martin Heidegger, "Building, Dwelling, Thinking," in *Basic Writings,* rev. ed., ed. David Farrell Krell (New York: Harper Collins, 1993), 343–63.

25. Kidder, *Gadamer for Architects,* 29.

26. Hans-Georg Gadamer, "Ende der Kunst? Von Hegels Lehre vom Vergangenheitscharakter der Kunst bis zur Anti-Kunst von heute," in *Kunst als Aussage,* Bd. 8, *Gesammelte Werke* (Tübingen: Mohr Siebeck, 1993), 216, translation mine. The German reads: "da ist ein gegebener Platz und ein bestimmter Zweck und eine vorgegebene Umgebung, städtische oder ländliche, und ganz gewiß ist es erst das, worin sich die Kunst des Architekten erfüllt: sich in die Raumgegebenheiten fügen und neue Raumordnung stiften. Bauten sind niemals Utopien."

27. Gens, "The Configuration of Space Through Architecture in the Thinking of Gadamer," in *Place, Space, and Hermeneutics,* ed. Bruce B. Janz (Dordrecht: Springer, 2017), 159.

28. Gens, 159.
29. Gens, 159–60.
30. Davey, *Unfinished Worlds*, 169.
31. For a critique of Gadamer's reading of Schleiermacher, see Kristin Gjesdal, "Hermeneutics and Philology: A Reconsideration of Gadamer's Critique of Schleiermacher," *British Journal for the History of Philosophy* 14, no. 1 (2006): 133–56. See also Kevin Vander Schel's chapter in the present volume, which focuses on Gadamer's interpretation of Schleiermacher in *TM* II.1.1 and reexamines Schleiermacher's own approach to hermeneutics in light of more recent scholarship on his work.
32. See, Hegel, *Phenomenology of Spirit*, §753.
33. For an extended examination of Hegel's influence on Gadamer, see Gjesdal, "The Hermeneutical Impact of Hegel's Phenomenology," *Hegel-Studien* 43 (2008): 103–24.

Part II

TRADITION, HISTORY, AND THE HUMAN SCIENCES

Chapter 6

TM II.1.1

Schleiermacher's Hermeneutics and Historical Meaning

Kevin M. Vander Schel

Gadamer's influential consideration of Friedrich Schleiermacher's hermeneutics in *Truth and Method* is accompanied by a pair of ironies. The first of these concerns the scope and aim of hermeneutics overall. Schleiermacher's contributions to the question of understanding lie at the intersection of post-Enlightenment trajectories in philological and theological hermeneutics, and Gadamer, following Wilhelm Dilthey, credits his work with effecting a decisive transition to a universal hermeneutic method, which seeks no longer to apply hermeneutics as an occasional technique but as a method aimed at overcoming misunderstanding as such. Yet, as Gadamer also recognized, Schleiermacher himself envisioned the field of hermeneutics as having a notably limited and modest focus. It centered not on the question of understanding itself but on the more specific tasks of correctly interpreting another's speech or discourse and of addressing the need for a critical method for uncovering the distinctive meaning preserved in written texts. Indeed, while the reception of his work has focused on his "general hermeneutics," the bulk of his own writings focused on the challenges of "special hermeneutics," particularly in the area of New Testament exegesis.[1] And although Schleiermacher continued to develop and refine his thinking on the discipline of hermeneutics throughout his life, it did not occupy a central place in his philosophical writings but was one of a number of "mixed" critical and technical disciplines that mediate between speculative concepts and the specific data of historical and empirical research. Thus while Dilthey credited Schleiermacher with recognizing hermeneutics and the universality of understanding as foundational to the study of the humanities overall, and Paul Ricoeur found in his works the beginnings of the deregionalization of the problem of understanding as such, Schleiermacher himself conceived his hermeneutics with a more restricted scope. Its aim was to contour the practical skill, "technique" (in the sense of *techne*), or "art" of successful text interpretation and to outline a broader framework for analyzing meaningful communication.[2]

The second irony relates to the "psychological" dimension of Schleiermacher's thought. While recognizing that Schleiermacher also examines historical dimensions of interpretation, Gadamer presents his hermeneutics as offering a quintessentially Romantic theory of interpretation, typifying a predominantly psychological approach to hermeneutics that focuses not on the subject matter of a text but on the subjective individuality of the author. Gadamer identifies this dimension of psychological interpretation as Schleiermacher's "most characteristic contribution" to hermeneutics, and one which became the dominant focus of his mature thought.[3] Yet as more recent critiques of Gadamer's treatment have convincingly shown, this characterization of Schleiermacher's hermeneutics itself rests on a misinterpretation of central features of his approach.[4] Some of Schleiermacher's most pronounced statements on hermeneutic understanding emphasize the communal nature of human rationality, the thoroughgoing linguisticality of thinking, and the provisional and uncertain character of human knowing. While Schleiermacher's hermeneutics indeed describe a "psychological," or "technical" (as it is more often labeled) moment of reconstructing the distinctive thought of the individual author, this is always coordinated with a "grammatical" moment which views each text as arising within a determinate historical and linguistic context. Thus, while Schleiermacher's contributions to hermeneutics are best known for their influence on Romantic hermeneutics and their treatments of individuality, they also present fruitful if often overlooked insights into the collective dimension of rationality, the inseparability of thought and language, and the unsettled and unfinished character of meaning-making.

Such ironies create significant difficulties for reconsidering Schleiermacher's thought in relation to Gadamer's analysis of the nineteenth-century development of hermeneutics and historical understanding. Yet beyond them lies a further set of textual-critical challenges. Though he wrote and lectured widely in philosophy, few of Schleiermacher's mature philosophical writings were published in his own lifetime, and the majority of writings that have been preserved consist of a combination of his own compact and aphoristic lecture notes together with student lecture transcripts (*Nachschriften*). Furthermore, these manuscripts have only relatively recently become available through the ongoing work toward a complete critical edition of his writings.[5]

The task of reconsidering Schleiermacher's distinctive contribution to hermeneutics in light of the larger question of understanding pursued in *Truth and Method*, then, involves both navigating a variety of stubborn interpretative challenges and grappling with more recent scholarship on Schleiermacher's wider philosophical works, particularly in those areas treating the interplay of thought and language and the study of history. This chapter aims to outline a preliminary response to this task, and its treatment proceeds in three parts. It begins with a brief rehearsal of the main lines of Gadamer's critique of Schleiermacher's Romantic hermeneutics and its influence on the methodology of the German historical school. It then examines the reception and the growing criticisms of Gadamer's treatment in later reappraisals of Schleiermacher's work. Finally, it sets Schleiermacher's hermeneutical writings within the context of his own broader treatments of thought and language and historical study, as found in his foundational treatments of dialectic and ethics. Set within these broader philosophical investigations, it argues that Schleiermacher's critical theory of textual interpretation does not center on a naïvely psychological or empathetic approach but describes a careful and historically-minded practice of discerning the characteristic meaning of an author's text, a methodological approach that at once reflects and resists the Romantic hermeneutics taken up by Dilthey, Droysen, and Ranke.

1. SCHLEIERMACHER AND ROMANTIC HERMENEUTICS

"We will pass over Schleiermacher's brilliant comments on grammatical interpretation."

(*TM*, 193)

1.1 Schleiermacher and Psychological Interpretation

Though Schleiermacher's thought is engaged throughout *Truth and Method*, Gadamer's analysis of Schleiermacher's theory of hermeneutics falls under the historical indications and preparations of the volume's second part, in describing the development of modern hermeneutical method and the rise of historical consciousness. Gadamer accords Schleiermacher an important place in the development of philosophical hermeneutics. Though his own contributions remained incomplete and limited, Schleiermacher outlines a set of insights that allowed a significant step toward a method of universal hermeneutics, an approach freed from the prevailing concerns of responding to normative claims of the theological or classical tradition.

Schleiermacher in this regard is a central transitional figure in the movement from the earlier positions of figures such as Chladenius and Ernesti, which centered on the practical difficulties of interpreting obscure texts, to a more disciplined and systematic hermeneutical method that focused on the problem of understanding itself. Through this universal hermeneutics, Gadamer describes Schleiermacher as opening a horizon for hermeneutic reflection: "But now understanding as such becomes a problem. The universality of this problem shows that understanding has become a task in a new sense, and hence theoretical reflection requires a new significance" (*TM*, 185).

Schleiermacher's own method, as Gadamer notes, is oriented around the two poles of the "grammatical" and "psychological" dimensions of interpretation. The former involves recognizing each utterance as located within and deriving from a given language.[6] It calls for a thoroughgoing acquaintance with the developing "language area" (*Sprachgebiet*) in which a text or discourse is situated, examining the linguistic and cultural resources of a language in its grammatical rules and structures, terms and representations, and semantic potential.[7] The latter focuses on the distinctive "manner of thought" of individual authors.[8] And it seeks to reconstruct the "specific sequence of thoughts" determining each discourse and to characterize the author's individual "style."[9] Schleiermacher insists that each of these operations presuppose and condition the other and that genuine understanding of a text requires navigating the fundamental tension between the individuality of the author and the linguistic tradition in which they stand: "Speech is the mediation of the communal nature of thought . . . Speech is admittedly also the mediation of thought for the individual."[10]

Significantly, however, Gadamer sets aside the grammatical aspects of interpretation and centers his analysis on the psychological dimension of Schleiermacher's thought. Such a move is warranted, he argues, as it is this psychological element that would prove Schleiermacher's most influential contribution to later hermeneutics. Furthermore, drawing on the work of his student Hans Kimmerle, who developed a new edition of Schleiermacher's manuscripts on hermeneutics, Gadamer maintained that the psychological dimension of interpretation came to greater prominence in Schleiermacher's later outlines of hermeneutics and "gradually came to dominate the development of his thought" (*TM*, 193).[11] For Schleiermacher, Gadamer writes,

> Hermeneutics includes grammatical and psychological interpretation. But Schleiermacher's particular contribution is psychological interpretation. It is ultimately a divinatory process, a placing of oneself within the whole framework of the author, an apprehension of the "inner origin" of the composition of a work, a re-creation of the creative act. (*TM*, 193)

Gadamer notes that, on one hand, then, Schleiermacher recognizes the central linguistic tensions inherent in the work of interpretation, and like his contemporaries, he describes understanding as having a circular character, which grasps the part only in relation to the whole, which in turn is properly understood only in light of its parts. Yet he maintains that for Schleiermacher the difficulties of this oscillating movement between whole and part are resolved suddenly and almost completely by the "immediate solution" of an act of "divination" (*TM*, 195). The "barrier to reason and understanding" is thus "to be overcome by *feeling*, by an immediate, sympathetic, and congenial understanding" (*TM*, 196–97, emphasis original).

This view holds important implications for understanding the assertion that Gadamer regards as Schleiermacher's formula for hermeneutics overall: the maxim to "understand a writer better than he understood himself" (*TM*, 198). The aim of interpretative understanding is the creative reproduction of an author's thought through identifying with their intended meaning.

1.2 Schleiermacher and the German Historical School

Through this analysis, Gadamer also discerns Schleiermacher's connection to broader trends in the nineteenth-century study of history. Though Gadamer notes that Schleiermacher's hermeneutics, with its narrower focus on textual interpretation, could not itself form a basis for the study of universal history, still this developing historical worldview was rooted in a Romantic theory of individuality and its corresponding hermeneutics. In studying the history of humanity as a whole, it retained the basic "schema of whole and part" (*TM*, 202). And crucially, subsequent historians would follow the Romantic impulse to emphasize the individuality of the author's thought rather than the subject matter (*Sache*) of the text, thereby expelling "critique based on understanding the subject matter from the sphere of scholarly interpretation" (*TM*, 201).

Gadamer finds this perspective present and operative in Leopold von Ranke and J.G. Droysen but argues that it becomes a conscious and deliberate method first with Dilthey, who expands Romantic hermeneutics into "an epistemology of the human sciences." In "transposing hermeneutics to the study of history," Gadamer writes, Dilthey "is formulating what Ranke and Droysen really think" (*TM*, 203).

In this manner, Schleiermacher's "concept of individuality" provides an important contrast to Hegel's "philosophy of world history" and establishes an influential methodological orientation that directs the historical sciences "toward research" (*TM*, 203). At issue in this contrast are two competing conceptions of historical study, one which focuses on the progress of knowing and the developing unity of historical reality and another which emphasizes the particularity and the uniqueness of individual developments. It is Ranke, as Gadamer notes, who proved especially influential for this second view. Ranke's scholarship, and his notoriously influential research seminars, elevated the disciplinary standards of history and exerted an enormous influence over the development of the study of history as an autonomous university discipline in nineteenth-century Germany.[12] He championed a disciplined approach to research based not on *a priori* principles or philosophical speculation but on careful first-hand study and rigorous historical archival research conducted in original languages.

Through Ranke's influence, the historical school that emerged at the University of Berlin in the mid-nineteenth century—which also included figures such as F.C. Savigny and August Boeckh—stood apart from the philosophy of history expressed by Hegel and his followers and emphasized not the unity and developing synthesis of history but historical particularity, prizing specialized, methodical, and empirical research. Here the providential working of God in the universal history of humanity is not evinced in the progressive becoming of the whole but in the plenitude and variety of its individual forms, a view reflected in Ranke's famous dictum that "every epoch is immediate to God."[13]

Ranke's approach was further developed by Droysen, an "acute methodologist" who sought to articulate the "conceptual presuppositions" of this methodological orientation (*TM*, 203, 216). Moving beyond a focus on particular individuals, his work centered on the investigation of "moral powers" that constituted the common work of humanity. Again, however, as with Rilke, the labor of the historian is not to speculate on the final goal or trajectory of history but to cultivate "understanding through research" and to patiently engage in the sober task of reconstructing "the great text of history from the fragments of tradition" (*TM*, 219, 221).

In its central respects, then, Gadamer argues that this methodological orientation toward ceaseless research into historical particulars and away from the considerations of universal history continues to reflect Schleiermacher's notion of individuality and has introduced longstanding implications for the development of the human sciences (*TM*, 206).

2. RE-CONSIDERING SCHLEIERMACHER'S PLACE IN ROMANTIC HERMENEUTICS

"The human soul thinks with *words*."[14]

Since the 1960 publication of *Truth and Method*, Gadamer's characterization of Schleiermacher's hermeneutics and its connection to historical understanding has exercised an enduring influence, with the reading of Schleiermacher as pioneering a Romantic and psychologistic tradition of textual interpretation achieving nearly canonical status through much of the twentieth century. Yet Gadamer's analysis has also been the target of frequent criticism, giving rise to a series of close and thorough studies of Schleiermacher's philosophical manuscripts which move beyond the emphasis on the psychological dimensions of this thought to highlight his hermeneutics as a discerning and critical theory of interpretation.

Shortly after the appearance of *Truth and Method*, in a pivotal 1966 essay, Hermann Patsch demonstrated that it was Friedrich Schlegel rather than Schleiermacher who initiated the Romantic turn in hermeneutics, a claim subsequently reinforced and supported by later scholarship.[15] Indeed, several key elements of the description of Romantic hermeneutics in *Truth and Method*, such as the role of divination, hermeneutics as an art and not merely a science, and the admonition to understand the author better than they understood themselves, were emphases introduced by Schlegel and modified by Schleiermacher.[16]

This deepened engagement with Schleiermacher's hermeneutics continued in the 1970s, particularly in the works of Peter Szondi and Manfred Frank. Szondi found in Schleiermacher's subtle method important resources for fresh explorations in the fields of literary criticism and literary hermeneutics. Frank, who in 1977 edited a new edition of Schleiermacher's outlines of hermeneutics, argued that Schleiermacher's approach discloses an agile and original theory of language that holds important insights into the at-once universal and irreducibly individualized activities of discourse and interpretation, insights that he maintained are especially relevant for addressing the aporias of continental philosophy after the linguistic turn.[17]

These works have been followed in subsequent decades by detailed studies from scholars in Germany, Italy, and France, which have promoted more nuanced readings of Schleiermacher's hermeneutics as a sophisticated method that displays rich connections with the philosophical writings of his contemporaries and with his own broader philosophical contributions in ethics, aesthetics, education, political theory.[18] These more comprehensive studies have furthermore been spurred on by the 2012 publication of a complete critical edition of Schleiermacher's writings on hermeneutics.[19]

If this more multifaceted character of Schleiermacher's hermeneutics has elsewhere been recognized, Anglophone scholarship has tended to a less balanced appraisal. Schleiermacher's hermeneutics in this context have often been read as exemplifying a Romantic emphasis on authorial intent, foregoing all difficulties of historical consciousness in favor of an immediate intuitive grasp of authorial intention—one which reaches through the linguistic and historical complexities of the text to divine the shape of the author's individual mind. Though frequently receiving honorary mention as a classic figure in the development of philosophical hermeneutics, then, here

Schleiermacher's specific philosophical contributions have only infrequently been the focus of sustained scholarly critique.

In recent decades, however, an increasing number of careful English-language studies have sought to correct these lingering misconceptions. In 1998, Andrew Bowie, drawing upon Frank's edition of Schleiermacher's manuscripts, published an English translation of Schleiermacher's outlines of hermeneutics, together with portions of his dialectic, under the title *Hermeneutics and Criticism*. With this work, he pushed back against the continuing dismissive portrayals of Schleiermacher's thought to highlight the complex discussions of language and cognition in his philosophical writings, as well as Schleiermacher's underappreciated insights into the persistent challenges of modern textual criticism. When viewed with a fresh and more balanced perspective, Bowie suggests that Schleiermacher's theory of interpretation emerges as "surprisingly relevant to contemporary philosophical accounts of language and epistemology."[20] His edition further makes clear that the focus on "technical" or "psychological" interpretation did not become more prominent in Schleiermacher's later hermeneutics, as Gadamer's student Kimmerle had maintained; rather, the "grammatical" and linguistic aspects of interpretation received equal emphasis throughout Schleiermacher's outlines.[21]

Kristin Gjesdal offers a more forceful and pointed criticism of Gadamer's position. Gadamer's analysis in *Truth and Method*, she maintains, "never enters into a fair discussion" of Schleiermacher's approach. In leaving aside considerations of the grammatical and semantic dimensions of interpretation to emphasize the subjective intention of the author, his treatment leaves readers with a "systematically distorted" account of both Schleiermacher's conception of individuality and his critical method of interpretation.[22] Consequently, his analysis privileges "existentially challenging rather than historically accurate interpretations" and fails to extend to Schleiermacher's writings the interpretative generosity called for by his own hermeneutic vision.[23] Such an approach, Gjesdal argues, overlooks Schleiermacher's considerable achievement, which consists in framing a complex set of critical and philological reflections on the practical challenge of understanding others in order to allow "a context-sensitive and detailed reading" of texts.[24] Such a position does not aim to "appeal to the inner, psychological state of mind of a given artist or individual," as Gadamer regularly emphasizes, but "to do justice to the uniqueness of a given individual work" and to strive against one's own interpretative prejudices through cultivating critical skills, hard work, and active and imaginative reading (*TM*, 192–96).[25]

For his own part, Gadamer began to address the emerging criticisms of his analysis of Schleiermacher in the late 1960s and early 1970s and to somewhat modify his reading of Schleiermacher's position. In the wake of the studies by

Kimmerle, Patsch, and Frank, Gadamer recognized that "for Schleiermacher the problem of language is completely central" and that his own treatment had displayed "a certain one-sidedness" regarding Schleiermacher's reflections on the "connection between thought and speaking."[26] Considered more closely, he granted that Schleiermacher's theory focuses not on the psychological cast of the author's mind but on understanding expressions in the balance between individual and grammatical aspects, and that these two modes of interpretation "belong inextricably together."[27] Nonetheless, while acknowledging this more adequate account of Schleiermacher's position, Gadamer continued to maintain that Schleiermacher's hermeneutics yet has its "metaphysical ground in the concept of individuality" and that within the ongoing tension between the grammatical and psychological poles of Schleiermacher's hermeneutics, psychological interpretation emerges as more prominent.[28] He furthermore held that if his account was mistaken in the particulars it still aligns with the central lines of Schleiermacher's influence within later philosophical hermeneutics: "Perhaps I overemphasized Schleiermacher's tendency towards psychological (technical) interpretation rather than grammatical-linguistic interpretation. Nevertheless, that is his peculiar contribution, and so his school was based on psychological interpretation."[29]

3. THE CRITICAL TASK OF TEXTUAL INTERPRETATION

"Das Anfangen aus der Mitte ist unvermeidlich."[30]

As these more recent lines of study indicate, a proper understanding of the shape of Schleiermacher's theory of interpretation requires moving beyond one-sided or reductive treatments of his thought and situating his more specialized writings on hermeneutics within the context of his wider philosophical studies. More fully relating Schleiermacher's own approach to the deepened and enlarged scope of hermeneutic understanding and historical consciousness discussed in *Truth and Method*, then, calls for a broadened reading of his specific contributions to hermeneutics against the backdrop his broader investigations into thought and language and the study of history.

When set within this context of Schleiermacher's larger philosophical inquiries, his work on hermeneutics occupies a curiously limited role. Hermeneutics takes up the vital task of understanding the spoken or written word, grasping the meaning of meaningful conversation.[31] As such, it outlines an endeavor that in practice touches virtually every field of inquiry in the humanities. Yet under Schleiermacher's arrangement both the shape of hermeneutics and its connection to questions of historical meaning derive from its relation to his inquiries in two more fundamental areas of study: ethics and dialectic.

3.1 The "Science of History": Schleiermacher's Lectures on Philosophical Ethics

Though the strong tendency of twentieth-century scholarship has been to emphasize Schleiermacher's hermeneutics as his most noteworthy philosophical contribution, in his own philosophical studies, it was the study of ethics that seized the central position. He began developing his ethics already as a student at the University of Halle and in his subsequent years as a tutor, developing a series of essays inquiring into classical Greek thought, Kantian moral philosophy, and Spinoza's "deterministic" ethical system. He established the framework for his own distinctive conception of ethics in his 1803 work *Outlines of a Critique of Previous Ethical Theories*, a dense and unforgiving systematic critique of ethical systems from Plato to Fichte that served as his first academic publication. Schleiermacher continued to incrementally develop his investigations of ethics throughout his academic career. Though he devoted much of his time to developing the innovative theological system of his *Christian Faith*, or *Glaubenslehre*, he did not neglect his "first love" of philosophy and maintained a vigorous and enduring concern for the "resolution of the 'ethical task.'"[32] Throughout the nineteenth century, it was for this contribution to ethical theory, and not his theory of hermeneutics, that Schleiermacher's philosophical writings gained recognition. Only later with Dilthey, who closely engaged Schleiermacher's lectures on ethics and dialectic but was particularly captivated by the theory of understanding outlined in his hermeneutics, did the focus began to shift away from this ethical orientation.[33]

In its mature form, Schleiermacher's conception of ethics differed notably from the descriptions of moral life prevailing among his contemporaries. Reflecting an Aristotelian emphasis on practical reason and the cultivation (*Bildung*) of human action,[34] he envisioned the study of ethics as focused not on abstract descriptions of moral duties or virtues but on the diverse forms of human *Sittlichkeit*, the moral expressions of reason embedded in the institutions, cultural practices, and mores (*Sitte*) of historical communities. In this fashion, he described ethics not as narrowly oriented toward the prescriptive aim of identifying moral imperatives but as a comprehensive field of inquiry that critically depicts and compares the developing forms and structures of historical human action.[35] Accordingly, he characterizes the scope of ethics in broad and comprehensive terms. Its subject matter is the "life of reason," considered as the "science of history."[36]

In place of the Kantian emphasis on duty and rational obligation, then, Schleiermacher's more descriptive ethics gave priority of place to an innovative account of a doctrine of goods (*Güterlehre*), emphasizing the differentiation and integration of the products of human action in four interrelated domains of human living: free sociality, nation, religion, and science (*Wissenschaft*).[37] In this way, the structure of Schleiermacher's ethics does not neatly align with conventional moral theories but rather with what one might call a "theory of culture," an overarching theory of the diverse tasks and practices underlying human communities.[38] His explorations in ethics provided a flexible and adaptable framework for understanding human historical living, which identified the continuing expressions of rational human action not as ascending stages within a larger overarching philosophical system but as abiding and interrelated dimensions of human living that remain open to further development.

Here, alongside the significant contrasts between Schleiermacher's philosophical orientation and Gadamer's presentation of hermeneutic consciousness, one finds several surprising points of connection between their approaches. Gadamer too resisted abstract and dogmatic conceptions of moral and social principles and highlighted the central importance of *Bildung*, a concept "intimately associated with the idea of culture" that indicates "the properly human way of developing one's natural talents and capacities" (*TM*, 9–10). Furthermore, with Aristotle he emphasizes the constitutive role of *phronesis*, or practical "moral knowledge" (*TM*, 324), in understanding historical human action. In this vein, for example, he points to the cultivation of "good taste," which "operates in a community" (*TM*, 35) and serves to discern the value and significance of individual objects and developments in their relation to a larger whole (*TM*, 33–39). And following Hegel, Gadamer likewise shifts focus away from the pure and timeless principles of *Moralität* favored by Kant toward an emphasis on *Sittlichkeit*, the concrete embodiment of communal ethical living in historical practices, cultural customs, and social institutions.[39]

Significantly, for Schleiermacher, it is this ethical inquiry into historical human action, and not his reflections on hermeneutics, that provides a basis for conceiving the organization of the human sciences and the arrangement of disciplines in the university.[40] He outlines the various fields of human knowing through a threefold arrangement hearkening back to classical Greek thought: dialectic, physics, ethics. The first area of dialectic signals a speculative foundational discipline (*Grundwissenschaft*), conceived as an alternative to Fichte's *Wissenschaftslehre*, which presents a formal investigation into the structure and operations of human thought and knowing itself. The remaining fields of physics and ethics correspond by contrast to the "real" disciplines (*Realwissenschaften*), those fields of human knowing oriented respectively toward apprehending the development of finite reality in nature and its transformation through human action.[41]

The various further areas of historical and scholarly inquiry find their place within a group of mixed "critical" (*kritisch*) and "technical" (*technisch*) disciplines, which mediate between the speculative concepts of ethics and ongoing empirical and historical research. The first class of critical disciplines, which includes philosophy of religion, philosophy of right, grammar, and aesthetics, inquires into the distinctive "essence" of individual and concrete historical phenomena.[42] The second class of technical disciplines, a group including fields such as pedagogy, statesmanship, and hermeneutics, concerns the "production of a given phenomenon" and the art of bringing forth specific forms of moral production amid varying conditions and circumstances.[43]

Instead of providing a basis for study in the humanities, then, Schleiermacher's teaching on the art of understanding has its place at this point, as the discipline treating the production of meaning through the interpretation of the spoken or written word. And insofar as Schleiermacher's philosophical writings can rightly be said to encompass a broader "hermeneutics of culture" or history, a claim maintained by a number of recent interpreters,[44] such an approach is anchored not primarily in his hermeneutics but in the comprehensive inquiry into human action outlined in his philosophical ethics.

3.2 The Structure of Human Knowing: Lectures on Dialectic

While Schleiermacher's ethics provides a basis for locating and identifying particular disciplines within the realm of human knowledge, his lectures on dialectic present a foundational inquiry into the structure and operations that govern human knowing itself. Inspired by his studies of Plato, Schleiermacher conceived the study of dialectic as a wholly formal enterprise. Unlike the study of ethics, it is concerned not with particular historical forms or expressions but with a rigorous analysis of the movement of thought through human consciousness, as this movement results in knowing.[45] It unfolds as an inquiry into "the inner connection (*Zusammenhang*) of all knowing," both in the transcendental relation of thought to being and in the operations of human knowing as it emerges through perception, apprehension, concepts, and judgment and finds expression in language.[46] As such, it offers an investigation into the genesis and possibility of the rigorously scientific form of thinking presupposed in all fields of human inquiry.

Despite the formal character of his dialectic, however, Schleiermacher also highlights throughout the thoroughgoing historical contingency of human knowing and the intimate connection of thought and language. He acknowledges that knowing, even considered in its most transcendental aspect, is a communal enterprise that proceeds not in isolated expressions of individual cognition but through ongoing communication and conversation, as the individual stands within a "community of recognition."[47] In its historical development, then, human thinking is bounded by language on every side, fixed within a determinate historical context and a particular "linguistic circle" (*Sprachkreis*).[48] By consequence, the advance of reason in history, as described in Schleiermacher's ethics, experiences stubborn limitations. While he makes clear that the ceaseless activity of reason is the same in all and can be communicated across linguistic barriers, still he insists that in its actual manifestation, "no knowing can be considered entirely the same in two languages, not even 'thing' or 'A=A.'"[49] Thus, although his teaching on dialectic is comprehensive in scope, Schleiermacher at the same time is aware that the actual progress of human knowledge is ever modest, a slow and gradual progression that remains situated within particular historical contexts and advances incrementally through dialogue and dispute.

This brief overview of Schleiermacher's investigations in ethics and dialectics underscores the complexity and variety of his philosophical studies. Yet it also serves to clarify the central task Schleiermacher assigns to his hermeneutics and the abiding tension between thought and language that animates the discipline. In contrast to the comprehensive scope of these more foundational philosophical areas, Schleiermacher's theory of hermeneutics has a more targeted aim, taking up concepts and distinctions furnished by his ethics and dialectic in order to examine the historically contingent expressions of thought in language, the rational utterances of the mind fixed in speech or text. Where dialectic treats the structures of thinking as pure and unconditioned, then, the practice of hermeneutics enters in where the workings of reason become manifest in language. As human reason is nowhere accessible simply in itself but emerges only through the medium of language, meaningful communication is conditioned at every point by a particular historical and linguistic context, and hermeneutic interpretation has this historically contextualized thinking as its proper object. In this respect, hermeneutics is based "on the fact of the non-understanding of discourse" and begins from the recognized need for a critically reflective approach to understanding the unfamiliarity or foreignness of another's speech or writing.[50]

Lying at the center of Schleiermacher's reflections on this hermeneutic task is a tension between reason and language. Each human being, Schleiermacher notes in his lectures on philosophical ethics, occupies a privileged position in the natural world, as a distinctive "unity of consciousness" in whom the activity of reason becomes luminous and articulate.[51] This activity of reason is—in its general terms—the same in all, present in each as a plastic and generative agility that gives rise to "moments of cognition" in consciousness and results in real instances of knowing.[52] Yet Schleiermacher is clear that for these acts of cognition to be complete, these internal operations of consciousness must be fleshed out through language, without which it is impossible to express and signify these conscious acts.[53] The capacity of cognition itself, as Schleiermacher notes in his outlines of hermeneutics, is inextricably bound to the linguistic mold within which consciousness develops: "The innateness of language modifies the mind."[54]

This emphasis on the inextricability of language and the operations of knowing echoes and develops the restriction on communication Schleiermacher articulates in his dialectic. Languages differ from one another "not only in tone but also in meaning."[55] They thematize individual differences within human living, as caused by outward circumstances of time, history, and social location, into a self-enclosed system of signification, and thereby introduce a permanent element of unstranslatable relativity into rational discourse. Yet precisely because language is intrinsic to the performance of cognition, each language also carries within itself a kind of deposit of communal rationality, an accumulation of the symbols, concepts, and schemas that inform the distinctive manner of thought of particular communities. Thus, a language emerges "wherever human beings are to be found in a true community of cognition," and each distinct language "becomes the repository of a particular system of concepts and ways of combining."[56] The organic systems of language, then, do not serve as tools for translating inner thought into outward speech but inform and shape each human being within a wider tradition of rationality, anchoring an individual's own thinking in relation to a wider "community of knowledge."[57]

Accordingly, the focus of the interpretative task falls not upon the author as an isolated individual but on their work as it stands in a determinate relation to a larger community of thought. Each author's thought is, on the one hand, a reflection of a larger communal manner of thinking; on the other, it is a unique expression of human knowing capable of freely expanding and reshaping the inherited meaning of their tradition. And here the relation between the two moments of Schleiermacher's hermeneutics comes into sharper focus. The first moment, the grammatical, treats the individual as "determined in his thought by the (common) language."[58] In this respect, the thought of each "appears only as an organ of the language."[59] The goal of the interpretative task in this aspect is to arrive at a full knowledge of the structure, rules, and forms of a language in a given historical context. The second moment, the technical or "psychological," considers the individual author as a free and creative mind that develops beyond the bounds set by language, and in this respect "language with its determining power disappears and reappears only as the organ of the person."[60] Within this technical aspect, the interpreter aims to characterize the text's characteristic style, the irreducibly distinct way in which an individual author's thought is expressed, which follows from the intellectual principle that moves the writer. Each of these moments, Schleiermacher further notes, has dimensions of both "comparison" and "divination."[61] The skill of "divination," which Herder had emphasized as an active and animated form of reading that draws upon the imaginative creativity of the interpreter,[62] has a place in the interpretative process in providing more immediate and intuitive hypotheses about a text's meaning, but Schleiermacher cautions that this hypothetical reconstruction of a text's meaning must always be checked and revised through the comparative dimensions of interpretation so that it does not become uncertain or fantastic. Divination is not reducible, then, to mere empathetic identification with the mind of an author but always occurs in conjunction with the careful philological work of comparison.[63]

In this way, each author's thought stands in a dual relationship to the language in which it is expressed, as stamped and shaped by one's language while also freely contributing to its further formation and development. Thus, in the context of his ongoing efforts in translating Plato's dialogues, Schleiermacher locates one of the distinguishing characteristics of Plato's genius in his facility for forming new expressions, manifesting "a new aspect of language (*etwas neues Sprachliches*)" in bringing forth genuinely new ideas, distinctions, and connections.[64] Similarly, in his exegetical studies, he notes that while the language of the New Testament had "camped on" and appropriated earlier Jewish linguistic formulations, in the writings of Paul, the familiar terms of *sacrifice*, *piety*, and—especially—*righteousness* are refashioned into new concepts that are incommensurate with previous understandings.[65] And indeed even Christ spoke in an inherited language while communicating a new and decisive revelation irreducible to what came before.[66] In each case, the author's distinctive thought is inseparably bound to the linguistic tradition they inhabit, and adequately understanding the proper meaning of the text requires strict attention to both of these aspects and the abiding tension between them.

Schleiermacher readily acknowledged the immense difficulty of this interpretative task. There exists no simple recipe or fixed set of rules for uncovering a text's specific sense. All endeavors in this direction involve considerable effort and exertion and ultimately rely upon the skill and judgment of the interpreter. Far from envisioning a direct and intuitive process that slips beyond the historical complexity of the text to glimpse the individual genius of the author, he presents the work of interpretation as a painstakingly demanding undertaking, a continual and repeated grappling with the text to discern its particular meaning. Such labor neither offers a secure point of entry nor promises a satisfying or certain resolution. Unavoidably, one begins and remains "in the middle;" and interpretative understanding moves always in this oscillation between the author's given historical-linguistic context and the unique progression of their own thought. While genuine understanding always remains possible, still the concrete results of this interpretative labor remain an ever-greater approximation of the text's distinctive meaning. The maxim to understand an author's discourse better than the author thus does not signal a naïve interpretative method that seeks an empathetic identity with an author but holds a more modest and regulative function. It is a call to the important if unglamorous task of understanding a text or discourse well in its own right, inviting the interpreter to strive for a fuller and more genuine apprehension of the text's meaning even while recognizing that this task remains unending and reached only "by approximation."[67]

Viewed in this light, what is perhaps most striking about Schleiermacher's approach is not its focus on the intention and subjective interiority of the author but on situating their distinctive manner of thinking within a developing linguistic community. The emphasis of interpretative understanding indeed falls for Schleiermacher upon understanding the individual author, but it does so in a manner differing from the one-sidedly psychological portrayals of his work. The significance of each author's linguistic utterance consists in characterizing its distinctive meaning in relation to a particular historical and linguistic context. On the one hand, this relation allows the potential for recognizing significant creativity and inventiveness in the author. Each author's capacity to think outside the strict bounds of linguistic convention enables the expression of new meaning, which can broaden, challenge, or reform accepted opinion.[68] Yet, on the other hand, and precisely because of the ability to move beyond the determinate linguistic context, an individual author represents not only the potential for ingenuity but also for irrationality. Each is capable not only of creative innovations but of faulty reasoning, myopia, oversight, and misunderstanding, and for Schleiermacher, this dimension of idiosyncratic and erroneous reasoning belongs equally to the interpretative task. It is the goal of the interpreter to understand the distinctiveness of the author's thought in its peculiar shortcomings, as well as its characteristic strengths.

This accent upon grasping the distinctive character of the author's thought highlights a subtle but important dimension of Schleiermacher's reflections on hermeneutics. The specific understanding sought after in the interpretation of texts is not principally the grasp of the correctness of the author's position. Nor indeed, as Gadamer correctly recognized (*TM*, 193, 201), is the primary aim an understanding of the subject matter (*Sache*) under consideration. Its first aim is critical: apprehending the particular meaning of the author's specific position through characterizing its unique difference. Such an interpretative approach enables recognition not only of agreement but also of dissent and dispute, making possible a critical awareness of the substantial and dialectical differences between authors' standpoints. And this acknowledgement of disagreement is not incidental to the continuing progress of the human and cultural sciences. It underlines what is for Schleiermacher the dialogical character of human rationality in the historical world, as human knowing becomes manifest not in uniform fashion, nor by the assumption of elements into a total or absolute system, but through the patient explication and articulation of competing viewpoints. Where the progress of reason in history exists, it consists in such modest but real gains in knowing, through the meaning that emerges amidst concrete dialogue and conversation.

Once again, in this carefully restrained portrayal of the development of human knowing, Schleiermacher's approach displays a curious likeness with Gadamer's later descriptions of the finite character of hermeneutic understanding. Setting aside the nineteenth-century "ideal of perfect enlightenment" (*TM*, 351, 368) or the attempt to arrive at a final and limitless horizon of absolute knowing, Gadamer models hermeneutic consciousness on the openness of Platonic dialectic, which seeks after truth through ongoing dialogue and conversation and the unassuming "art of questioning" (*TM*, 375) and inquiring.[69] The attempt to gain full clarity into one's own historical or hermeneutic situation is "a task that is never entirely finished" (*TM*, 312).

Taken in this more modest sense, Schleiermacher's treatment of interpretative understanding points to a continuingly vital practice for ongoing scholarship, if perhaps one that will appear unextraordinary when compared to later hermeneutic explorations of self-understanding, ontology, and the nature of language. His own hermeneutics does not provide a theory of historical consciousness or historical understanding as such. Nor does it establish a framework for organizing the human sciences or university disciplines. It outlines the detailed and difficult work of textual understanding, whose chief aim is not to relate authors to a larger narrative or movement in history but to understand each text and work as far as possible on its own terms. Only through this patient study at the feet of an author, as it were, cultivating the modest and elusive talent of listening to the text, does one come to grasp—or be grasped—by the work's particular meaning.

5. CONCLUSION

This chapter began by noting two ironies in Gadamer's treatment of Schleiermacher. To these may be added a third: it was Gadamer's analysis of Schleiermacher's hermeneutics in *Truth and Method* that established Schleiermacher as a central figure in the development of philosophical hermeneutics and which spurred on more comprehensive and detailed studies of his own hermeneutical theory. Gadamer's penetrating study succeeded in placing Schleiermacher's thought within foundational discussions of the nature of historical understanding and historical consciousness, debates that extended well beyond the narrower interpretative aims of his own work but which remain crucial for ongoing studies in the human and cultural sciences, particularly in a time when the operations of understanding are reduced to a narrowly conceived notion of scientific method or dismissed in favor of technological utility.

Yet Schleiermacher's hermeneutics sits uneasily within this broader tradition. While not numbered among the major philosophers of his period, Schleiermacher was nonetheless a sophisticated and original thinker, one who articulated a philosophical posture toward historical meaning that follows neither Kant's critical idealism nor Hegel's speculative philosophy, and thus stands in a uniquely critical position to the two dominant classical influences of contemporary hermeneutical thought.[70] Schleiermacher's own "historicism" fits none of the dominant molds of nineteenth-century historical understanding so emphatically rejected by twentieth-century philosophers and theologians. His approach was neither a "naïve historicism" nor the "historicism of Droysen and Dilthey" (*TM*, xxxi, xxxii), but a meticulous method that reflected an acute awareness of the historically contingent character of all expressions of meaning, and which centered on the critical task of articulating the distinguishing character of historically situated texts, developments, and thought-forms.

While Schleiermacher's philosophical writings reflect the broader trends of the developing *Historismus* of his age, then, his work also exemplifies an important if often overlooked feature of this tradition: "historicism" was never a stable and established concept but a contested one admitting of a variety of sharply competing methodological orientations. Here, then, the relationship between Schleiermacher's innovative theory of interpretation and the rise of historical consciousness proves more intriguing and complex than the narrative Gadamer offers in *Truth and Method*, and one deserving of further exploration.

NOTES

1. For this reason, the first edition of Schleiermacher's hermeneutical writings, published posthumously in 1838 by Friedrich Lücke, located hermeneutics among Schleiermacher's theological rather than his philosophical works. See "Introduction" in Friedrich Schleiermacher, *Hermeneutics and Criticism and Other Writings*, trans. and ed. Andrew Bowie (New York: Cambridge University Press, 1998), vii–viii.

2. See Paul Ricoeur, "Schleiermacher's Hermeneutics," *The Monist* 60, no. 2 (April 1977): 181; Schleiermacher, *Hermeneutics and Criticism*, 5, 11–12.

3. Hans-Georg Gadamer, *Truth and Method*, 2nd ed., trans. Joel Weinsheimer and Donald G. Marshall (New York: Bloomsbury, 2013), 192–93, cf. 543–44. Hereafter cited in text as *TM*. Where the German is cited or the translation has been

altered, the page number of the original is indicated after the slash. The latter refer to Hans-Georg Gadamer, *Wahrheit und Methode*, Gesammelte Werke I (Tübingen: Mohr Siebeck, 1990).

4. See, for example, Kristin Gjesdal, *Gadamer and the Legacy of German Idealism* (New York: Cambridge Univ. Press, 2009), 155–84; Manfred Frank, *Das Individuelle-Allgemeine: Textstrukturierung und -interpretation nach Schleiermacher* (Frankfurt am Main: Suhrkamp, 1977).

5. See Friedrich Schleiermacher, *Kritische Gesamtausgabe* (KGA), eds. Lutz Käppel et al. (Berlin: De Gruyter, 1980). The critical edition of Schleiermacher's writings on hermeneutics is published as Schleiermacher, *Vorlesungen zur Hermeneutik und Kritik*, KGA II.4, ed. Wolfgang Virmond, in collaboration with Hermann Patsch (Berlin: De Gruyter, 2013).

6. Schleiermacher, *Hermeneutics and Criticism*, 8.

7. Schleiermacher, 30.

8. Schleiermacher, 229.

9. Schleiermacher, 254, 255.

10. Schleiermacher, 7.

11. See also Friedrich Schleiermacher, *Hermeneutik: Nach den Handschriften*, ed. Heinz Kimmerle (Heidelberg: Carl Winter, 1974).

12. Thomas Howard notes that in the latter nineteenth century, Ranke's students would come to occupy virtually every important university chair in history throughout Germany. Howard, *Protestant Theology and the Making of the Modern University* (New York: Oxford Univ. Press, 2006), 276.

13. Leopold von Ranke, *Über die Epochen der neueren Geschichte: Historisch-kritische Ausgabe*. Werk und Nachlass II (Munich: Oldenbourg, 1971), 59–60.

14. Johann Gottfried Herder, *Eine Metakritik zur Kritik der reinen Vernunft*, in *Sprachphilosophie. Ausgewählte Schriften* (Hamburg: Meiner, 2005), 184.

15. See Hermann Patsch, "Friedrich Schlegels 'Philosophie der Philologie' und Schleiermachers frühe Entwürfe zur Hermeneutik," *Zeitschrift für Theologie und Kirche* 63, no. 4 (1966): 434–72.

16. See Michael N. Forster, "Friedrich Schlegel's Hermeneutics," in *German Philosophy of Language: From Schlegel to Hegel and Beyond* (New York: Oxford University Press, 2011), 45–82. On Schleiermacher's close collaboration with Schlegel, see Andreas Arndt, "Schleiermacher and Friedrich Schlegel," in *The Oxford Handbook of Friedrich Schleiermacher*, eds. A. Dole, S. Poe, and K.M. Vander Schel (New York: Oxford Univ. Press, forthcoming 2022), ch. 8. See also Gunther Scholtz, "Ast and Schleiermacher: Hermeneutics and Critical Philosophy," in *The Routledge Companion to Hermeneutics* (Abingdon: Routledge, 2014), 62–73.

17. See Manfred Frank, *Hermeneutik und Kritik* (Frankfurt am Main: Suhrkamp Verlag, 1993); Frank, *Das Individuelle-Allgemeine*.

18. See, for example, Gunther Scholtz, *Ethik und Hermeneutik: Schleiermachers Grundlegung der Geisteswissenschaften* (Frankfurt am Main: Suhrkamp, 1995); and Christian Berner, *La philosophie de Schleiermacher* (Paris: Editions du Cerf, 1995).

19. See, for example, Julia Lamm, *Schleiermacher's Plato* (Berlin: De Gruyter, 2021); Fred Rush, "Hermeneutics and Romanticism," in *The Cambridge Companion*

to *Hermeneutics*, ed. Michael N. Forster and Kristin Gjesdal (Cambridge: Cambridge University Press, 2019); and the essays in *Friedrich Schleiermachers Hermeneutik: Interpretationen und Perspektiven*, ed. Andreas Arndt and J. Dierken (Berlin: De Gruyter, 2016).

20. Andrew Bowie, "Introduction," in Schleiermacher, *Hermeneutics and Criticism*, vii.

21. As Wolfgang Virmond discovered, one of the prominent texts on "technical" or psychological interpretation, which Kimmerle had assigned to Schleiermacher's late work, actually dates to 1805. See Virmond, "Neue Textgrundlagen zu Schleiermachers früher Hermeneutik," *Schleiermacher-Archiv*, vol. 1 (Berlin: De Gruyter, 1985), 575–90.

22. Gjesdal, "Schleiermacher's Critical Theory of Interpretation," 155.

23. Gjesdal, 156.

24. Gjesdal, 168.

25. Kristin Gjesdal, "Aesthetic and Political Humanism: Gadamer on Herder, Schleiermacher, and the Origins of Modern Hermeneutics," *History of Philosophy Quarterly* 24, no. 3 (July 2007): 281.

26. Hans-Georg Gadamer, "The Problem of Language in Schleiermacher's Hermeneutic," trans. David E. Linge, in Robert W. Funk, ed., *Schleiermacher as Contemporary: Journal for Theology and the Church*, vol. 7 (New York: Herder & Herder, 1970), 68; Gadamer, "Afterword," in *TM*, 589.

27. Gadamer, "The Problem of Language in Schleiermacher's Hermeneutic," 73.

28. Gadamer, 73.

29. Gadamer, "Afterword," in *TM*, 590.

30. Friedrich Schleiermacher, *Dialektik (1814/15) / Einleitung zur Dialektik (1833)*, ed. Andreas Arndt (Hamburg: Felix Meiner, 1988), 104.

31. On the logic and organization of Schleiermacher's hermeneutic method, see Christian Berner, "Hermeneutics," in eds. A. Dole, S. Poe, and K.M. Vander Schel, *The Oxford Handbook of Friedrich Schleiermacher*, (New York: Oxford Univ. Press, forthcoming 2022) ch. 12.

32. Kurt Nowak, *Schleiermacher: Leben, Werk und Wirkung* (Göttingen: Vandenhoeck & Ruprecht, 2001), 281–83, 293.

33. Gunther Scholtz notes that while before Dilthey one rarely finds mention of Schleiermacher's hermeneutics in the nineteenth century, afterwards one rarely finds mention of any other aspect of his philosophy. Scholtz, "Einleitung," *Ethik und Hermeneutik*, 12.

34. In this respect, Schleiermacher's ethical theory is well-described as a "*Bildungsethik*." See Brent Sockness, "Schleiermacher and the Ethics of Authenticity: the 'Monologen' of 1800," *The Journal of Religious Ethics* 32, no. 3 (2004): 278.

35. For a clear overview of Schleiermacher's innovative system of philosophical ethics, see Brent Sockness, "The Forgotten Moralist: Friedrich Schleiermacher and the Science of Spirit," *Harvard Theological Review* 96, no. 3 (2003): 317–48; and Moxter, "Philosophical Ethics," in eds. A. Dole, S. Poe, and K.M. Vander Schel *The Oxford Handbook of Friedrich Schleiermacher*, (New York: Oxford Univ. Press, forthcoming 2022) ch. 10.

36. Friedrich Schleiermacher, *Lectures on Philosophical Ethics*, ed. Robert B. Louden, trans. Louise Adey Huish (New York: Cambridge University Press, 2002), 8.
37. Schleiermacher, 60–99, 168–74.
38. Scholtz, *Ethik und Hermeneutik*, 35.
39. See, for example, Gadamer's discussions of the "moral being of man" (*von dem sittlichen Sein des Menschen*), "moral consciousness" (*sittliches Bewußtsein*), and "moral knowledge" (*sittliches Wissen*) in his description of Aristotle's ethics (*TM*, 323–24/318–20).
40. See Hans-Joachim Birkner, *Schleiermachers Christliche Sittenlehre. Im Zusammenhang seines philosophisch-theologischen Systems* (Berlin: Töpelmann, 1964), 30–35.
41. Schleiermacher, *Lectures on Philosophical Ethics*, 5.
42. Schleiermacher, 8; cf. Birkner, *Schleiermachers Christliche Sittenlehre*, 35.
43. Schleiermacher, *Lectures on Philosophical Ethics*, 8-9.
44. See, for example, Scholtz, "Ethik als Theorie der modernen Kultur. Mit vergleichendem Blick auf Hegel," in *Ethik und Hermeneutik*, 36–40.
45. Birkner, *Schleiermachers Christliche Sittenlehre*, 31–33.
46. Schleiermacher, *Dialektik* (1814/15) / *Einleitung zur Dialektik* (1833), 149–50.
47. Schleiermacher,105.
48. Schleiermacher,126.
49. Schleiermacher, 24–25.
50. Schleiermacher, *Hermeneutics and Criticism*, 227.
51. Schleiermacher, *Lectures on Philosophical Ethics*, 48.
52. Schleiermacher, 48–49.
53. Schleiermacher, 48–50.
54. Schleiermacher, *Hermeneutics and Criticism*, 9.
55. Schleiermacher, *Lectures on Philosophical Ethics*, 82.
56. Schleiermacher, 50, 82.
57. Schleiermacher, 81.
58. Schleiermacher, *Hermeneutics and Criticism*, 9.
59. Schleiermacher, 94.
60. Schleiermacher, 94.
61. Schleiermacher, *Vorlesungen zur Hermeneutik und Kritik*, KGA II.4, 156–58.
62. See Scholtz, "Ast and Schleiermacher," 64.
63. See Schleiermacher, *Vorlesungen zur Hermeneutik und Kritik*, KGA II.4, 158.
64. See Schleiermacher, 32–33; and Lamm, *Schleiermacher's Plato*, ch. 3.
65. Schleiermacher, *Hermeneutics and Criticism*, 81–87.
66. See Schleiermacher, 52–53.
67. Schleiermacher, 96.
68. Schleiermacher, 32, 82.
69. On the centrality of conversation in Gadamer's thought and the heightened awareness that emerges through the "logic of question and answer" (*TM*, 378–87) see also Frederick G. Lawrence, *The Fragility of Consciousness: Faith, Reason, and the Human Good*, eds. Randall S. Rosenberg and K.M. Vander Schel (Toronto: University of Toronto Press, 2017), chs. 2, 3, and 5.

70. On Schleiermacher's disagreements with Hegel's conception of the absolute, identity, and historical knowledge, see Andreas Arndt, "Schleiermacher: Dialectical and Transcendental Philosophy, Relationship to Hegel," in *Schleiermacher, the Study of Religion, and the Future of Theology*, eds. B. Sockness and W. Gräb (Berlin: De Gruyter, 2010), 349–60.

Chapter 7

TM II.1.2-3

Phenomenology's Essential Role in the Hermeneutic Tradition

David Vessey

Some magicians surprise you with their trick; some announce beforehand what they are going to do. For the latter, the tension is whether they will actually pull it off. Sometimes they actually do what they promise—"I will guess your card!" Sometimes they don't—"I will saw a woman in half!" The sleight of hand gives the impression they have done it. Hans-Georg Gadamer promises us upfront that he will be "overcoming the epistemological problem of historicism through phenomenological research,"[1] but has he done this? Or has he merely given the impression he has done it? As Martin Heidegger asserts about his own attempt to address this issue, we "need explicit assurance that the following inquiry does not believe that the problem of history can be solved by a sleight of hand."[2]

What is the epistemological problem of historicism? Historicists were a loosely connected group of philosophers spanning the nineteenth and early twentieth centuries who argued that, first, actions are only explicable by appeal to the historical context in which they took place. This has three parts. All actions have a sufficient cause that explains why the agent took that action and not another action; actions are understandable by understanding the sufficient cause of the action; all agents, no matter how free, are in part responding to their current historical environment through their actions. Thus, to grasp the sufficient cause of the action, we must understand how it is a response to the agent's particular historical situation.

The historicists argued that, second, history needs to become rigorous—a *Wissenschaft*, a scientific discipline—in order that we may have a proper understanding of historical situations. There need to be rigorous standards for what counts as reliable historical evidence, and there needs to be a core understanding about what a historical claim looks like. Included among those actions that must be understood as responses to historical situations are thoughts and written and spoken ideas. A text, no matter how much it claims ahistorical validity, is always in part a reflection of its time and can only be properly understood in its historical context. The implications for hermeneutics are clear: we can only interpret a text if we understand the historical context to which the text is a response.

Historicism raises two epistemological *aporias*. First, there is the status of its own key claim—if all actions can only be understood as responses to their time, how can that claim speak to all actions at all times? Isn't that key historicist claim subject to the same criticism it raises toward any other claim that pretends to be transhistorical? Or, put differently, if the key historicist claim is true, then the claim itself seems only historically valid. If it is transhistorically valid, then it seems not to be true. This parallels the famous argument against the relativist claim that all claims are only true or false relative to their times. What then is the truth status of *that* claim, which seems to be claiming to be true across all times?

The second epistemological aporia that plagues historicism is different. Given the necessity of understanding the historical context for understanding actions, we need a more scientific, rigorous approach to acquiring historical understanding. We need to acquire an objective understanding of the historical context in order to understand the action within that context. The problem is that if the views of historians are always historically conditioned, they would seem to be incapable of arriving at an objective understanding of another historical period. Their understanding would always be distorted by contemporary historical interests.

When Gadamer talks about the aporia of historicism, he is focused on the first aporia more than the second one. How can a historicist justify the seemingly universal claim that all claims can only be understood in light of their historical context? His argument will be a transcendental one. Transcendental arguments begin with what is inescapably the case and then argue to what must be a condition for the possibility for that being the case. They are especially valuable when there is a threat of skepticism or relativism. The most famous is Descartes' *cogito* argument: I think, therefore I am. It is impossible to doubt one is thinking; a condition for the possibility of thinking is existing; therefore, it must also be the case that one exists. Immanuel Kant also provided a transcendental argument. If we take as a starting point that certain, scientific knowledge of the natural world exists, then as a condition for the possibility of that knowledge transcendental idealism must be true, where transcendental idealism is the position that space and time are transcendentally ideal and empirically real. This kind of argument inspired Dilthey to attempt to justify the first historicist claim. At the core of Gadamer's view in sections II.1.2–3 of *Truth and Method* is that Dilthey's attempt to solve the aporias of historicism fails and that only a phenomenological approach can succeed.

Looking ahead, Dilthey's approach failed for three reasons. First, his account of life shows how we are essentially historical but not in a way that makes historicity an ontological trait of human beings. He treats historical understanding as something we engage in, not something we are. Second, Dilthey posited a kind of experience—an *Erlebnis*, a lived experience— which grounds the possibility of historical understanding but is plagued by Cartesianism and the idea that we only have understanding if we have subjective immediacy. Third, Dilthey retained the distinction between a scientific *explanation* and a humanistic *understanding*. He based the success of humanistic understanding on the application of scientific explanation to history. By doing so, Dilthey tried to split the difference between positivist and romantic theories of history, but, according to Gadamer, he failed to appreciate how historical explanation is itself a mode of humanistic understanding. According to Gadamer, Heidegger's phenomenological hermeneutics of facticity makes none of these mistakes. A phenomenological account of temporality and historicity provide the resources for escaping the aporias of historicism and for revealing historical truths to be as legitimate as the truths of the natural sciences.

The overall structure of Gadamer's argument follows three transcendental arguments, one by Dilthey, one by Edmund Husserl, and one by Heidegger. Gadamer thinks the first two move us forward but fail in important ways, which only Heidegger's fundamental ontology reveals and avoids. Gadamer's actual discussion and critique of Dilthey plays out as a reading of Dilthey in conversation with Hegel, however. Thus, first, I will lay out Dilthey's transcendental argument that life is essentially historical and his argument for the possibility of objective historical consciousness. In order to see the failure of Dilthey's position, I will present Husserl's transcendental argument that time-consciousness is the most basic level of constitution and his account of the life-world. Then I will explain how Gadamer sees Johann Yorck, Count von Wartenburg's account of life as showing the limitations of Husserl's and Dilthey's theories of life. At that point, it will be clear how important Hegel is to Gadamer and how Hegel functions as an interlocutor through Gadamer's discussions of Dilthey and Yorck. Finally, I will give Heidegger's transcendental argument for Dasein's essential historicity. Only then, Gadamer argues, can we escape the aporias of historicism by understanding how the fact that we are essentially historical can be transhistorically, transcendentally, true.

1. DILTHEY: LIFE AND *ERLEBNIS*

Gadamer has two sections on Dilthey; we can treat each as addressing one of the two aporias of historicism. The first, II.1.2.A, "From the Epistemological Problem of History to the Hermeneutic Foundation of the Human Sciences," considers Dilthey's justification of the transhistorical principle that all actions are historically conditioned; the second, II.1.2.B "The Conflict between Science and Life-philosophy in Dilthey's Analysis of Historical Consciousness," considers Dilthey's argument for the ideally objective, scientific character of historical investigation.

Kant's critical legitimation of the natural sciences is Dilthey's model for his legitimation of the humanities and especially the first principle of historicism. Kant argues that a condition for the possibility of knowledge is that the world is informed by our minds in lawlike ways; Dilthey says about Kant's view of the transcendental subject that "no real blood flows in the veins of the knowing subject constructed by Locke, Hume, and Kant, but only the attenuated sap of reason as a mere activity of thought."[3] This directs us to Dilthey's starting point, life. A condition for the possibility of historical knowledge is that it is achieved by someone alive. "Life is the fundamental fact that must form the starting point of philosophy."[4] What we need is an understanding of what it means to be alive; "what we seek to show is life itself . . . to show life as it is—that is what we strive for. To describe life—that is our goal . . . We also want to make life visible in its unfathomable depths, and in its unfathomable nexus."[5] Naturally, Dilthey argues that this is something we have immediate access to. "Being alive is something with which we are acquainted from within and behind which we cannot go."[6] Essential for our insights about life is a kind of experience—an *Erlebnis*, a life-experience—which is subjective, certain, and revelatory about life.

> Lived experience (*Erlebnis*) is always certain of itself. And since lived experience constitutes the justifying ground for the entire system of my knowledge about psychic objects, I must analyze lived experience with regard to the certainty contained in it . . . No matter how this is accounted for psychologically, the certainty of lived experience requires no further mediation. It can accordingly be called immediate.[7]

Gadamer had already discussed the concept of *Erlebnis* in Part I of *Truth and Method* in the context of discussing the aesthetics of genius. There he wrote,

> If something is called or considered *Erlebnis*, that means it is rounded into the unity of a significant whole. An experience is as much distinguished from other experiences—in which other things are experienced—as it is from the rest of life

in which "nothing" is experienced. An experience is no longer just something that flows past quickly in the stream of conscious life; it is meant as a unity and thus attains a new mode of being. (*TM*, 60–61)

The whole, according to Dilthey, is both a temporal whole and a conceptual whole. What he means by it being temporal is that it belongs to the nature of a lived-experience that it stands out from the flow of time in a way that shows its significance. The lived-experience also brings the past into the present givenness in a way that points toward its significance for the future. "The principle of a lived-experience is that everything that is there for us is so only as a given in the present. Even when a lived experience is past, it is only there for us as a given in a present experience."[8] The temporal structure of lived-experiences reveals the essentially temporal structure of life. Dilthey writes,

> Temporality is contained in life as its first categorical determination and the one that is fundamental for all others. The expression "passage of life" already points to the temporality. Time is there for us by means of the gathering unity of our consciousness. Life, and the external objects encompassed by it, share the relationships of simultaneity, succession, time interval, duration, and change.[9]

A few pages later he adds, "Life is intimately related to temporal fulfillment. Its whole character, both in its inherent corruptibility and its capacity to form a nexus in which it has a unity or a self, is determined by time."[10] Because life is essentially temporal, unfolding in a historical context shaped by our projects, self-understanding also only occurs through recognizing ourselves as located in history. So, at least for our own self-understanding, there is no understanding of an action which is not understanding it as a response to a historical situation. The first principle of historicism is not just one principle among others; it is a necessary condition for all self-understanding given what it means to be alive.

> The initial tasks involved in apprehending and explicating a historical nexus are already half solved by life itself. The constituents of this nexus can be found in conceptions of lived experience in which present and past events are held together by a common meaning. Among these lived experiences, those that have special worth, both for themselves and for the overall life-nexus, have been preserved by memory and raised from the endless stream of forgotten events. A coherence is formed within life itself, albeit from different standpoints with constant shifts. The work of historical narrative is already half done by life itself. . . . Here we approach the roots of all historical comprehension. . . . The power and scope of our own lives and the energy with which we reflect on them provide the basis of historical vision.[11]

As Gadamer will say, for Dilthey "the historical sciences only advance and broaden the thought already implicit in the experience of life" (*TM*, 225).

The unity of a lived-experience is not only temporal; it is conceptual. What I mean by that is that Dilthey argues that we always understand things as parts of wholes. We recognize that experiences are shared by others and that they reflect shared social values and institutions, what Dilthey calls (following Hegel) "objective spirit."

> Understanding is a rediscovery of the I in the Thou; spirit rediscovers itself at ever higher levels of connectedness; this selfsameness of spirit in the I and the Thou, in each subject of a community, in each cultural system, and finally in the totality of spirit and universal history, makes possible the cooperation of the various functions of the human sciences.[12]

So, again, the work of history is the work of locating actions as expressions in wider historical contexts—"milieu is indispensable for understanding"[13]—and this work is a necessary consequence of what it means to be alive and engage in the act of understanding. Gadamer writes, "Life interprets itself. Life itself has a hermeneutical structure. Thus, life constitutes the real ground of the human sciences. Hermeneutics is not a romantic heritage in Dilthey's thinking, but follows from the fact that philosophy is grounded in 'life'" (*TM*, 229). To be alive is to be historically conditioned. This is an inescapable truth, and thus transhistorically true, even if only ever realized by someone historically conditioned.

2. DILTHEY: HISTORICAL CONSCIOUSNESS

So much for the first principle of historicism, but what about the second? Dilthey recognizes that the process of understanding is the central goal of the humanities and its strength. "Understanding is the domain of all who are actively involved in human affairs, and differs from explanation (*Erklären*) by participating in life, which is possible only on the basis of life. Life is the great object as well as the organon of those who are concerned with human affairs."[14] The natural sciences aim at explanation, however, and if history is going to be scientific, it has to adopt that standard for research into the historical context of actions. To do that requires a kind of objectivity where the historical investigations are not themselves shaped by one's historical context. According to Gadamer, Dilthey's account of historical consciousness makes that possible.

> It is clear that Dilthey did not regard the fact that finite, historical man is tied to a particular time and place as any fundamental impairment of the possibility

of knowledge in the human sciences. Historical consciousness was supposed to rise above its own relativity in a way that made objectivity in the human sciences possible. We may ask how this claim can be justified without implying a concept of absolute, philosophical knowledge beyond all historical consciousness. What is the special virtue of historical consciousness—by contrast to all other forms of consciousness in history—that its own relativity does not endanger the fundamental claim to objective knowledge? (*TM*, 236)

According to Dilthey, historians only developed a fully historical consciousness in the nineteenth century. Previously there were "chroniclers"—whose interest was to tell an epic story—and "pragmatic historians"—whose interest was to make a political point. In the nineteenth century, there emerged "universal historians" who embraced "the task of reconstructing the whole of inner life."[15] A historical consciousness is one that raises "itself above the procedure of a particular epoch . . . [and] finally comprehends all these historical tendencies within a purposive system as a series of possibilities contained within it."[16] Gadamer is skeptical that this rising above is possible or desirable. It seems to go against Dilthey's very idea of life as essentially historical, which was required for him to escape the first aporia of historicism. As a way of criticizing Dilthey, Gadamer asks,

But if life is the inexhaustible, creative reality that Dilthey thinks it, then must not the constant alteration of historical context preclude any knowledge from attaining to objectivity? Is it not the case, then, that historical consciousness is ultimately a utopian ideal, containing an internal contradiction? (*TM*, 233)

Gadamer's criticism that Dilthey relies too much on a natural scientific account of explanation for historical understanding is well known. The same criticism is made by Heidegger, as is the criticism that Dilthey is too Cartesian in his account of *Erlebnis* and the attempt to ground all understanding in its self-certainty. To fully appreciate the problems with Dilthey's view, however, Gadamer turns to Husserl, for, as Gadamer wants to argue, only phenomenology can enable us to escape historicism's aporias.

3. HUSSERL: TIME-CONSCIOUSNESS AND GENETIC PHENOMENOLOGY

In the first decade of the twentieth century, Dilthey read Husserl's *Logical Investigations* and was inspired to revisit his earlier defense of the humanities in light of Husserl's phenomenology. He reached out to Husserl, inspiring Husserl to read Dilthey and culminating in an exchange of mutually appreciative letters in 1911, the year Dilthey died. 1911 is also the year in which Husserl came upon his mature account of time-consciousness. Husserl argued that for anything to appear to perception we must be aware of more than what is immediately given. We are aware of objects as being three dimensional, so that we are not surprised when we walk around them and find they have a backside to them. We are aware of them persisting in time, perhaps even changing in time as in the case of musical pieces, specifically as having a past and a future. Of course, we are not directly aware of the object's past or future, but nonetheless for something to appear to us as an object it must appear to us as something with a past and a future. These temporal organizations of our perceptions are essential to any perception. We also recognize the perception of the object as standing in temporal relations to other perceptions. These investigations into the constituting acts of consciousness, which are necessary conditions for the appearances of objects, Husserl will call "extremely important matters, perhaps the most important in all phenomenology."[17] About them Gadamer writes,

> There is such a thing as givenness that is not itself the object of intentional acts. Every experience has implicit horizons of before and after, and finally fuses with the continuum of the experiences present in the before and after to form a unified flow of experience. Husserl's investigations of the constitution of time consciousness come from the need to grasp the mode of being of this flow and hence to draw subjectivity into research on intentional correlation. (*TM*, 246)

And Gadamer will immediately draw the critical consequence for Dilthey's approach to grounding the humanities in life. "This shows that the discreteness of experience (*Erlebnis*)—however much it may retain its methodological significance as the intentional correlate of a constituted meaning value—is not an ultimate phenomenological datum" (*TM*, 246).

Husserl's argument that temporalizing occurs at the root of all conscious awareness places the temporal character of the subject on a deeper footing than Dilthey's account of the temporal structure of life. But his view is not without its paradoxes. For the constituting acts of time-consciousness seem themselves to be occurring in time, so they too must require a more fundamental form of time-consciousness which temporally organizes them. To avoid an infinite regress that would undermine the possibility of perceptual awareness Husserl argues for an "absolute" level of constituting temporal consciousness which is not itself in time.

> We have no alternative here but to say: the flow is something we speak of *in conformity with what is constituted*, but it is not "something in objective time."

> It . . . has the absolute properties of something to be designated *metaphorically* as "flow." . . . For all of this we have no names.[18]

Since we are aware of this, there must also be *an absolute Ego* who is able to grasp the flow through repeated uses of the phenomenological reduction.

These are not the end of Husserl's reflections on the temporal structure of the constituting acts of consciousness; in the second decade of the twentieth century, he will take more seriously the idea that the Ego is not constituting from nowhere but is shaped by a history of sedimented constitutions, passed on through history, culture, and tradition, which guide and explain the acts of constitution. In the 1917–1918 Bernau Manuscripts, Husserl first develops his account of genetic phenomenology, recognizing the "life-processes"—instincts, drives, and habituations—that operate pre-theoretically to shape the constituting acts of consciousness.[19] In the *Cartesian Meditations* he writes,

> Each man understands first of all . . . *his* concrete surrounding world or *his* culture; and he does so precisely as a man who belongs to the community fashioning it historically. A deeper understanding, one that opens up the horizon of the past (which is co-determinant for an understanding of the present itself), is essentially possible to all members of that community.[20]

These can only be understood through genetic phenomenology, through a tracing of the historical situation of the subject. That requires the postulation of a shared, lived world which operates on us through our culture, the life-world, and in the C-Manuscripts Husserl will refer to the most primordial level of time constitution as the "streaming *living* present." Thus, for Husserl's phenomenology, as a necessary condition of making sense of the possibility of the givenness of objects, we must engage in historically informed phenomenological inquiry recognizing the operations of life across the pre-thematic acts of constituting consciousness.

On the one hand, Gadamer gives Husserl credit:

> He is trying to penetrate behind the actuality of the sense-giving consciousness, and even behind the potentiality of shared meaning, to the universality of an achievement that is alone able to measure the universality of what is achieved—i.e., constituted in its validity. The all-embracing world horizon is constituted by a fundamentally anonymous intentionality—i.e., not achieved by anyone by name. (*TM*, 248)

On the other hand, he points out that "'life' is not just the unreflective living characteristic of the natural attitude. 'Life' is also, and no less, the transcendentally reduced subjectivity that is the source of all objectification"

(*TM*, 249). Husserl never gives up the view that we only arrive at an epistemologically satisfactory position when we have reduced the phenomena to their presentation to consciousness. Gadamer argues that Husserl, like Dilthey, remains Cartesian in the end. He misses the way that life points us away from self-certainty and toward the other, toward the future, and toward speculative understanding.

> The speculative import of the concept of life remained undeveloped in both men. Dilthey simply tries to play off the viewpoint of life polemically against metaphysical thinking, and Husserl has absolutely no idea of the connection between this concept and the metaphysical tradition in general and speculative idealism in particular. (*TM*, 251)

How does this connect to the aporias of historicism? Husserl, like Dilthey, makes a transcendental argument for the necessity of understanding all actions as shaped by their historical context; this means, it can be a transhistorical principle even though it applies to itself.

> The conceptual pre-suppositions for the problem of overcoming historicism ... were lacking. Here the work of the phenomenological school has proved fruitful. Today, now that the various stages in the development of Husserl's phenomenology can be seen, it seems clear to me that Husserl was the first to take the radical step in this direction, by showing the mode of being of subjectivity as absolute historicity—i.e., as temporality. (*TM*, 548)

The problem arises with the second principle, where again the standards for what counts as a historical explanation move away from the idea that we are essentially historical beings in the hopes of obtaining certain insights. The advantage phenomenology has over Dilthey's philosophy of life is that it treats the positivist position of the natural sciences as a special case of validity, arising historically and requiring a more fundamental phenomenological legitimation. Husserl's philosophy does not begin from a split between the epistemic expectations of the natural sciences and the humanities but finds an underlying phenomenological validity which grounds both of them.

4. COUNT YORCK: LIFE AS SELF-ASSERTION

Count Yorck engaged in a twenty-year correspondence with Dilthey. Their correspondence was published in 1923, and it inspired Heidegger to quote him at length both in his 1924 "The Concept of Time" and in *Being and Time*. Heidegger says that Yorck gets his clear insight into the fundamental character of history . . . from his knowledge of the characteristics of being of human existence itself, thus precisely not in a theoretical and scientific way oriented to the object of historical observation [as Dilthey had].[21]

Only Yorck understood the ontological character of historicity and its inescapability for historical investigation. Between the publication of *Being and Time* and the publication of *Truth and Method*, Yorck's philosophical fragments, *Stances of Consciousness and History*, were published. With the advantage of reading those writings, Gadamer still comes to the same conclusion as Heidegger.

> Dilthey's epistemological reflections went wrong in that he derived the objectivity of science too easily from life comportment and its drive toward something fixed. Husserl entirely lacked any more exact definition of what life is, although the central core of phenomenology—correlation research—in fact follows the structural model of life comportment. Yorck, however, is the missing link between Hegel's *Phenomenology of Mind* and Husserl's *Phenomenology of Transcendental Subjectivity*. (*TM*, 254)

What does Yorck understand about life that Dilthey and Husserl missed? It's only sketched out, but according to Gadamer, it is the essentially historical and essentially speculative character of life. "Life is self-assertion" (*TM* 252). As self-assertion, it becomes aware of itself through differentiating itself from what is around it. Self-consciousness belongs to life, not as the root of consciousness, but as a development beginning from consciousness of what is alien.

> From the correspondence between life and self-awareness [Yorck's work] derives a methodological standard by means of which it defines the nature and task of philosophy. Its leading concepts are projection and abstraction. Projection and abstraction constitute the primary life comportment; but they apply equally to recapitulatory historical comportment. (*TM*, 254)

Although incomplete, Gadamer sees in Yorck's writing an account of life that argues for our essential historicity and for a speculative moment as essential to life such that only because of our historicity can we have historical understanding. What Gadamer says about Heidegger's argument applies as well to Yorck (though about life, not Dasein).

> The mode of being of Dasein is defined in an ontologically positive way. It is not presence-at-hand but futurity. There are no eternal truths. Truth is the disclosure

of being that is given with the historicity of Dasein. Here, then, were the foundations from which the critique of historical objectivism occurring in the sciences themselves could receive its ontological justification. It is, as it were, a second-degree historicism which not only opposes the historical relativity of all knowledge to the absolute claim of truth but works out its ground—namely the historicity of the knowing subject—and hence can no longer see historical relativity as a limitation of the truth. (*TM*, 548–49)

What Yorck understands is that the second aporia of historicism does not need to be overcome by escaping our essential historicity.

5. ECHOES OF HEGEL

Gadamer's discussion of Dilthey is haunted by Hegel. Dilthey calls for a return to the critical approaches of Kant and Hegel but seeks to avoid the universal and speculative history Hegel defends. Yet, as Gadamer speculates, "it is still not clear whether Dilthey's grounding of hermeneutics in 'life' really avoided the implicit consequences of idealistic metaphysics" (*TM*, 229). Dilthey has to accept something like Hegel's objective spirit—social institutions, practices, and ideas which provide the historical and cultural context for the development of individuality. "He speaks of the 'thought-forming work of life.' It is not easy to say how this phrase differs from Hegel. . . . He is simply repeating a conceptual development that Hegel himself underwent" (*TM*, 231). In the end, Gadamer claims that Dilthey "differs from Hegel ultimately on one thing only, that according to Hegel the homecoming of the spirit takes place in the philosophical concept whereas, for Dilthey, the philosophical concept is significant not as knowledge but as expression" (*TM*, 231–32). This conclusion, that Dilthey is not as far from Hegel as Dilthey thinks, is presented as a strength of Dilthey's position and is the key transition point to the discussion of historical consciousness as Dilthey's equally problematic analogue to Hegel's absolute spirit.

> Is not the fact that consciousness is historically conditioned inevitably an insuperable barrier to its reaching perfect fulfillment in historical knowledge? Hegel could regard this barrier as overcome by virtue of history's being superseded by absolute knowledge. But if life is the inexhaustible, creative reality that Dilthey thinks it, then must not the constant alteration of historical context preclude any knowledge from attaining to objectivity? Is it not the case, then, that historical consciousness is ultimately a utopian ideal, containing an internal contradiction? (*TM*, 233)

It is against the background of Hegel that Gadamer reads Dilthey; it is also the background against which he reads Yorck.

When Gadamer approvingly mentions Yorck's criticisms of the comparative approach to history, he immediately notes that "before [Yorck] Hegel brilliantly criticized the comparative method" (*TM*, 236). About Yorck's central insight—"the correlation between life and self-consciousness"—Gadamer points out that it was "already developed in Hegel's *Phenomenology*" (*TM*, 253). For "As Hegel had already shown and Yorck continues to hold, this structure of being alive has its correlative in the nature of self-consciousness" and "Hegel quite rightly derives self-consciousness dialectically from life" (*TM*, 253). By holding this Hegelian view, Yorck "is superior to both Dilthey and Husserl" and, remarkably, Yorck, "is the missing link between Hegel's *Phenomenology of Mind* and Husserl's *Phenomenology of Transcendental Subjectivity*" (*TM*, 254). Yorck gets life right because he echoes Hegel, and Hegel gets it right. The only question is whether he can avoid Hegel's problems, "the dialectical metaphysicizing of life" (*TM*, 255). This question is Gadamer's transition to Heidegger, and it provides us with the insight that, for Gadamer, Hegel had the answer all along. Romantic hermeneutics makes the mistake of dividing the aesthetic from the scientific, a division that persists in Dilthey's writing. What we need is not to divide romanticism and positivism, as Dilthey tries to do, but to divide Hegel and Husserl, as Yorck could be seen as doing, though he lacked the proper background in phenomenology and could not complete the job. That falls to Heidegger. This historical background section of *Truth and Method* functions to set up Heidegger's phenomenological hermeneutics of facticity and his account of Dasein's essential temporality as providing the solution to the aporias of historicism. As Heidegger himself says in *Being and Time*, "If historicity itself is to be illuminated in terms of temporality . . . then it is essential to this task that it can only be carried out by way of a phenomenological construction."[22] The only questions left are: What is Heidegger's position? How does it solve the aporias? And does Gadamer's view differ at all from Heidegger's?

6: HEIDEGGER: THE HISTORICITY OF DISCLOSEDNESS

The last subsection, 2.1.3.B, "Heidegger's Project of a Hermeneutic Phenomenology," is both the culmination of Gadamer's "Historical Preparation" and a transition to the next section, "The Elevation of the Historicity of Understanding to the Status of a Hermeneutic Principle." Gadamer is clear at the start that the mistake made by both Dilthey and Husserl is the Cartesian mistake of thinking that all grounding must "be based methodologically on the self-givenness of experience" (*TM*, 255). It is only by breaking with the identification of temporality and consciousness that we can legitimate the humanities in a way that avoids the aporias of historicism. One part of the argument follows Husserl's account of the lifeworld as a level of validity prior to the distinction between the natural sciences and the humanities. Both are forms of understanding rooted in a deeper, more basic form of understanding which is ontological—which is a defining feature of Dasein's being-in-the-world, something Dasein *is* rather than something Dasein *does*. Heidegger writes, "'Understanding' in the sense of one possible kind of cognition among others, let us say distinguished from 'explanation,' must be interpreted along with that as an existential derivative of the primary understanding which constitutes the being of the there [of Dasein] in general."[23] Gadamer writes, "Before any differentiation of understanding into the various directions of pragmatic or theoretical interest, understanding is Dasein's mode of being, insofar as it is potentiality-for-being and 'possibility'" (*TM*, 260). But what is Heidegger's argument for this position?

Heidegger opens *Being and Time* by arguing that as part of the process for understanding Being, we need to investigate Dasein, the being for whom Being is a question, to understand the way that Being does or does not appear to Dasein. Since we need to start with *a* being in our search for Being, we may as well focus on Dasein itself. This is a kind of transcendental argument: What do we know about Dasein? Dasein is the being for whom Being is a question. What does that say about Dasein's being? Here Heidegger launches into Dasein as being-in-the-world. But Heidegger's reply to Dilthey preceded *Being and Time,* and the kind of transcendental argument Heidegger is making also preceded the argument about Dasein. Gadamer writes,

> The fact that being is an issue for Dasein, that it is distinguished from all other beings by its understanding of being, does not constitute the ultimate basis from which a transcendental approach has to start, as seems to be the case in *Being and Time*. Rather, there is a quite different reason why the understanding of being is possible at all, namely that there is a "there," a clearing in being—i.e., a distinction between being and beings. (*TM*, 258).

Heidegger made a similar point against Dilthey in 1925:

> What is important is to work out the being of the historical, i.e., historicity rather than the historical, being rather than beings, reality rather than the real . . . Dilthey penetrated into that reality, namely, human Dasein—which, in its authentic sense is the meaning of historical being. He succeeded in bringing this reality to givenness, defining it as living, free, and historical. But he did not pose

the question of historicity itself, the question of the meaning of being, i.e., the question of the being of beings.[24]

We already have from Husserl that one condition for the awareness of things is that they are disclosed to us in ways that go beyond their immediate givenness. They are given with temporal horizons, for example, and also in a horizon of other possible disclosures. Heidegger turns to ask about Dasein as that being for whom beings appear. Better put, Heidegger asks about Dasein as the occasion for the disclosure of beings. Disclosiveness must belong essentially to Dasein—it "is its disclosure."[25] What does this disclosiveness look like? Heidegger says it takes two forms, and they are not independent of each other. First, there is an emotional disclosiveness. Heidegger calls this *attunement* and we might recognize it as moods. Things are disclosed to us through feelings of fear, shame, or joy, for example. Second, there is also cognitive disclosiveness. Heidegger calls this *understanding* and says that it is the disclosivenesss of the possibilities of a situation for Dasein. "*Understanding is the existential being of the ownmost potentiality of being of Da-sein in such a way that this being discloses in itself what its very being is about.*"[26] For something to be disclosed in its possibilities, however, requires that it be disclosed temporally and in light of the possible future actions of Dasein. Understanding, then, as an essential feature of Dasein's disclosiveness has the character of a temporal projection. Importantly for Gadamer's hermeneutics, understanding also has an essentially interpretive character, though for the argument in front of us, it is enough to point out that there is a kind of ontological understanding which grounds the possibility of the kind of explanation one finds in the sciences and the kinds of understanding one finds in the humanities. This understanding is a necessary condition for them and is an ontological feature of Dasein not dependent on Dasein's conscious awareness.

Furthermore, according to Heidegger, understanding has an essentially temporal structure. Gadamer confirms that "Heidegger's radical ontological reflection . . . revealed the projective character of all understanding and conceived the act of understanding itself as the movement of transcendence, of moving beyond the existent" (*TM*, 260). This means that understanding is revealed as opening up the ontological difference between beings and being. The essentially temporal character of Dasein is the condition for disclosure, not a hurdle to disclosure. It is also the root of Dasein's historicity, for Dasein "*is not 'temporal,' because it 'is in history,' but, on the contrary, it exists and can exist historically because it is temporal in its ground of being.*"[27] The essential historicity of Dasein is what makes being historical essential to Dasein; it is not, as Dilthey argued, rooted ontically in the fact Dasein is alive but rooted ontologically in the fact Dasein is disclosive. As

Gadamer explains, "That we study history only insofar as we are ourselves 'historical' means that the historicity of human Dasein is its expectancy and its forgetting is the condition of our being able to re-present the past" (*TM*, 262). Through this transcendental argument, the first principle of historicism can be shown to be inescapably grounded in our nature as understanding beings. Given the nature of understanding, we can recognize that being historical is not an impetus to understanding but a condition of understanding, and we can recognize that there is a more fundamental goal of phenomenological disclosure that is not about scientific objectivity. "Truth is the disclosure of being that is given with the historicity of Dasein" (*TM*, 548). In this way, even though it wasn't Heidegger's goal in *Being and Time*, Gadamer argues that Heidegger's fundamental ontology avoids the aporias of historicism. It is accomplished through a kind of argumentation—a transcendental argument—that is designed to help us see what must be the case especially when skepticism and relativism are threatening. Gadamer sums it up at the end of the section: "'Historicity' is a transcendental concept" (*TM*, 549).

Gadamer gives Heidegger the last word, as he planned all along. The historical background of hermeneutics goes astray with Romantic hermeneutics and only returns when phenomenology recovers the anti-subjectivist insights of Hegel without absolute spirit or the conceptual account of universal history. Gadamer hints, however, at one point of divergence from Heidegger. Much of Gadamer's argument has been based around the position that neither Dilthey nor Husserl had a proper understanding of *life*. Yorck got it right when he claimed life was self-assertion and recaptured Hegel's insight that there is a connection between life and self-consciousness. Heidegger had little interest in the concept of life; he thought it failed to capture the ontological character of Dasein and interfered with our understanding of the existential character of death. Gadamer, however, keeps the term. He writes that "Heidegger's own transcendental grounding of fundamental ontology in the analytic of Dasein did not yet permit a positive account of the mode of being of life" (*TM*, 263). The positive, Hegelian account of life as self-assertion is a reoccurring theme across Gadamer's writings after *Truth and Method*.

NOTES

1. Hans-Georg Gadamer, *Truth and Method*, 2nd ed., trans. Joel Weinsheimer and Donald G. Marshall (New York: Bloomsbury, 2013), 244. Hereafter cited in text as *TM*.

2. Martin Heidegger, *Being and Time*, trans. Joan Stambaugh (Albany: SUNY Press, 1996), 360.

3. Wilhelm Dilthey, *Selected Works, Volume I: Introduction to the Human Sciences*, ed. Rudolf A. Makkreel and Frithjof Rodi (Princeton: Princeton University Press, 1991), 50.

4. Wilhelm Dilthey, *Selected Works, Volume III: The Formation of the Historical World in the Human Sciences*, ed. Rudolf A. Makkreel and Frithjof Rodi (Princeton: Princeton University Press, 2010), 280.

5. Dilthey, *Selected Works* I, 490–91.
6. Dilthey, *Selected Works* III, 280.
7. Dilthey, 47–48.
8. Dilthey, 250.
9. Dilthey, 214–15.
10. Dilthey, 249.
11. Dilthey, 222.
12. Dilthey, 193.

13. Wilhelm Dilthey, *Selected Works IV, Hermeneutics and the Study of History*, ed. Rudolf A. Makkreel and Frithjof Rodi (Princeton: Princeton University Press, 1996), 253.

14. Dilthey, *Selected Works* I, 439.
15. Dilthey, *Selected Works* IV, 234.
16. Dilthey, 258.

17. Edmund Husserl, *On the Phenomenology of the Consciousness of Internal Time*, trans. John Barnett Brough (Dordrecht: Kluwer, 1991), 346.

18. Husserl, 382.

19. Edmund Husserl, *Die Bernauer Manuskripte Über das Zeitbewusstsein (1917/18)*, ed. Rudolf Bernet and Dieter Lohmar (Dordrecht: Springer, 2001)

20. Edmund Husserl, *Cartesian Meditations: An Introduction to Phenomenology*, trans. Dorion Cairns (The Hague: Martinus Nijhoff, 1960), 133.

21. Heidegger, *Being and Time*, 366.
22. Heidegger, 344.
23. Heidegger, 134.

24. Martin Heidegger, "Wilhelm Dilthey's Research and The Struggle for a Historical Worldview," trans. Charles Bambach, in *Supplements: From the Earliest Essays to Being and Time and Beyond*, ed. John Van Buren (Albany: SUNY Press, 2002), 159.

25. Heidegger, *Being and Time*, 125.
26. Heidegger, 135, emphasis in original.
27. Heidegger, 345, emphasis in original.

Chapter 8

TM II.2.1

The Historical Situation of Thought as a Hermeneutic Principle

Carolyn Culbertson

There are two attitudes regarding the historical situation of understanding commonly held today. On the one hand, we believe that we only achieve a real, worthwhile understanding of a topic when our thinking manages to break free from the dogmas of the past. We believe that this transcendence of the historical situation of thought is both possible and desirable. We applaud those whose thought appears to us to proceed unfettered by traditional dogmas, whether those dogmas be old habits of scientific thought or traditional ideas about social life. We celebrate as epistemic heroes those who discover their own way of thinking. On the other hand, many are quick to accept as a general rule that one's understanding is inevitably bound to one's particular historical and cultural situation. Nobody understands things in a historical vacuum. Accordingly, we believe that there is no transcending the historicity of the understanding, and thus no epistemic heroes to applaud. Despite the tension between these two positions, most people find each compelling enough to invoke with some frequency today.

Gadamer's *Truth and Method* makes the case that both of these common positions on the historicity of understanding—which we may call the *transcendence argument* and the *immanence argument*—are mistaken. According to Gadamer's account, understanding does not require that one simply abandon the prejudices of tradition at the start. Inquiry always begins in a situation where prejudices are operative. This is inevitable. However, contrary to what the immanence argument suggests, inquiry is not locked into these prejudices in a way that would exhaustively determine what can emerge from it. The historical situation of thought is not an impediment to understanding but a precondition for the process of understanding to occur. The core of this argument is presented in the section of *Truth and Method* entitled "The Elevation of the Historicity of Understanding to the Status of a Hermeneutic Principle" (hereafter referred to as "The Elevation of the Historicity of Understanding").

In what follows, I will explain how Gadamer challenges these two common attitudes toward the historical situation of thought in "The Elevation of the Historicity of Understanding." I will explain Gadamer's argument that the preconceptions that emerge from our historical situation are an inevitable part of the process of understanding and are indeed part of the hermeneutic constitution of the object itself, grounded as it is in historical consciousness. I go on to explain how the transcendence argument and the immanence argument are historically rooted in the Enlightenment and Romanticism, as Gadamer presents them in this section, and how both of these historical models of understanding misconstrue the way that understanding is grounded in historical consciousness. Along the way, I will highlight some of the problems we face in the contemporary social world that put into relief the continuing relevance of Gadamer's account of understanding in this section.

1. THE NECESSITY OF PRECONCEPTIONS

Gadamer begins "The Elevation of the Historicity of Understanding" by reflecting on Heidegger's concept of the "fore-structure of the understanding" (*die Vorstruktur des Verstehens*).[1] According to Heidegger in *Being and Time*, understanding is not a matter of simply passively absorbing new information. When one goes to understand something, one inevitably brings with them preconceptions of what they are going to understand. Heidegger speaks here of a differentiated structure of "fore-having, fore-sight, and fore-conception"—all ways in which one anticipates and prepares for what they will discover.[2] Gadamer follows Heidegger in arguing that the fore-structure of the understanding is operative all of the time—that is, whenever understanding is at work.

Consider the process of reading a text. To read a text, one must anticipate each step of the way. We anticipate what comes next—whether it is the next step in the plot of a story or in a theoretical argument. As Gadamer puts it, "One projects meaning for the text as a whole as soon as some initial meaning emerges in the text" (*TM*, 279). When we read a historical text, we inevitably bring with us a preliminary sense for the historical context and historical significance of the work. Finally, we inevitably read by anticipating the meaning of the terms used in the text. This entails taking for granted a preliminary, operative understanding of the terms based on their conventional meaning in the genre of the text. The contextual meaning of some of these terms may indeed change under the pressure of the meaning of the text as a whole;

however, we must inevitably grasp some meaning of the terms in advance of the whole in order for our reading to get underway. Hence, a fore-structure of understanding is inevitably at work in the process of reading.

Now, it is our instinct today to understand this process as one that unfolds when an individual subject encounters some immediate object that is ontologically separate from them and relies upon their own particular experiences and associations to guide them. If we conceive of the activity this way, however, we make an important assumption that will then shape what we think we can legitimately expect to happen in reading. When we assume that what the reader seeks to understand is independent from the reader's preconceptions, then the understanding developed through reading will appear to have no bearing on the self-knowledge of the reader. Moreover, the understanding developed will appear to at best approximate the object of inquiry, disclosing very little about subject matter itself. This assumption, then, opens the door to skepticism about what can really be accomplished through reading and, by extension, by any inquiry that engages its object through historical preconceptions.

The preconceptions operative in reading a text, however, are not as a whole simply the product of a reader's individual proclivities or personal experiences. Many of them are effects of being historically situated and are thus preconceptions that we have in common with others who are similarly situated. Gadamer refers to this as the condition of being situated in "a web of historical effects (*wirkungsgeschichtliche Verflechtung*)" (*TM*, 311/306). So, for example, it is by virtue of being situated within the effects of history that a text would first appear to the one who picks it up within a particular context as having this or that potential significance, and so on. Educators have an intimate knowledge of this point, as they must anticipate the preconceptions that their students as a whole will bring with them in reading a particular text. Students may, for example, bring with them the expectation that a text assigned from antiquity is either an artifact of an outdated worldview or a source of secret wisdom that conveys possibilities of authenticity lost to modern society today. Such preconceptions are the effects of history possessed by subjects who are historically situated in a similar way.

When the object of our inquiry is mediated by the effects of history in such ways, Gadamer argues that it is imperative to reflect on the web of historical effects that condition it and, in fact, to treat these effects as inseparable from the object itself. If the mediating web of historical effects is set aside without comment, Gadamer argues, one can only attain partial knowledge of the object.[3] As Gadamer explains,

> If we are trying to understand a historical phenomenon from the historical distance that is characteristic of our hermeneutical situation, we are always

already affected by history. It determines in advance both what seems to us worth inquiring about and what will appear as an object of investigation, and we more or less forget half of what is really there—in fact, we miss the whole truth of the phenomenon—when we take its immediate appearance as the whole truth. (*TM*, 311)

This is why, for Gadamer, it is wrong to imagine the process of understanding such an object as the encounter between two completely independent horizons (*TM*, 314–15).

We can now grasp how Gadamer challenges one of the attitudes toward the historical situation of the understanding with which we began. According to the transcendence argument, one achieves real understanding by setting aside any effect of history that would mediate between the knower and the object. For Gadamer, though, this commits the error of taking the immediate appearance of the object as its truth and ignoring what mediates this appearance. When this happens, Gadamer argues, there is an actual "deformation of knowledge (*Deformation der Erkenntnis*)" (*TM*, 312/306). This deformation takes place, for example, when one presents knowledge of some historical subject without recognizing or analyzing the mediating, pre-theoretical effects of history that have imbued the subject with a particular significance and positioned it within a particular context. Something similar happens, Gadamer explains, when one professes to 'let the "facts" (or the "data") speak for themselves.' Whether it is some historical fact or some data point, Gadamer argues, the danger lies in "simulat[ing] an objectivity that in reality depends on the legitimacy of the questions asked" (*TM*, 312). For Gadamer, genuine understanding (and, indeed, truthful speaking) does not require that one set aside their "consciousness of being affected by history (*wirkungsgeschichtliches Bewusstsein*)" (*TM*, 312/307) but that they, in fact, recognize this as consciousness of their hermeneutical situation.

We can now understand part of what Gadamer means when he says that prejudices have a productive role in the process of understanding. Contrary to the view that holds that genuine inquiry requires that one set aside all prejudices and approach the object as a blank slate, Gadamer argues that these preconceptions are a necessary part of inquiry—and, indeed, are constitutive of the hermeneutic object itself. Neither the inquiry nor the object can be adequately approached without some consciousness of this fore-structure and, in particular, without a consciousness of being affected by history. This is an inevitable part of inquiry and a *necessary* aspect of the appearance of the hermeneutic object. Does this mean, however, that it is *sufficient* for understanding the matter at hand? And if it is not sufficient, what else is involved in understanding?

2. THE PROBLEMATIZATION AND TESTING OF PRECONCEPTIONS

Gadamer emphasizes the necessary role that preconceptions play in the process of understanding. He does not, however, argue that the process of understanding is complete when these preconceptions are operative or when one becomes aware of their operation. Becoming aware of them is only the first step. It is necessary but not sufficient for the process of understanding. The next and crucial step in the process is, as Heidegger put it, "working out" these preconceptions "in terms of the things themselves (*in deren Ausarbeitung aus den Sachen selbst)*" (*TM*, 279/271).[4] Gadamer returns to the example of reading to clarify this point. While, as we have seen, one needs to work with a particular set of preconceptions for any meaning to emerge as one reads, actually *understanding* what one is reading requires another step. It requires that one critically evaluate these preconceptions in light of what emerges as one reads. Only by engaging in this additional step can one determine if their operative preconceptions are legitimate or illegitimate—justified or unjustified. Gadamer describes this process and characterizes the understanding that arises from it as follows:

> A person who is trying to understand is exposed to distraction from fore-meanings that are not borne out by the things themselves. Working out appropriate projections, anticipatory in nature, to be confirmed "by the things" themselves, is the constant task of understanding. The only "objectivity" ("*Objektivität*") here is the confirmation of a fore-meaning in its being worked out. Indeed, what characterizes the arbitrariness of inappropriate fore-meanings if not that they come to nothing in being worked out? (*TM*, 280/272)

Our preconceptions, then, while not as a whole arbitrary, are nevertheless not sufficient for understanding the hermeneutic object. One must check to see whether they are confirmed by the things themselves. When reading a text, for example, one may begin by taking for granted the meaning of a certain term, and this projection will allow an initial meaning to emerge. For genuine understanding to occur, though, one must put this meaning at stake. One must be open to the way that the more cumulative meaning that unfolds through the rest of the text will either confirm or problematize this projection. Indeed, Gadamer even claims that understanding, properly speaking, only begins at this moment where we put at stake our preconceptions to be confirmed or problematized, that is, when we engage in a "suspension of our own prejudices" (*TM*, 310).

To engage in the process of understanding, then, one must find some of one's own preconceptions put into question, and this means that understanding necessarily involves a self-interrogative component. In reading through a text, for example, one must find oneself pulled up short—an initial projection of meaning or a set of operative beliefs must be put into question. Moreover, because, at a certain level, one's self-understanding is bound up with the fore-meanings (especially the historical fore-meanings) that they carry around with them, this development can often involve not only a problematization of one's beliefs but also of one's self-understanding. In this sense, it is appropriate to speak about this problematization as a moment at which one is oneself personally put into question by what they encounter. It is for this reason that Gadamer speaks about this development as a moment "when something addresses us" (*TM*, 310).[5]

With the role of problematization in understanding now in view, we can now appreciate one of the distinctive characteristics of Gadamer's hermeneutic theory of understanding. For Gadamer, *understanding is not something that we execute at will*. One does not, after all, oneself conduct the process of being addressed. Nor does one will for oneself the possession of historical consciousness. In this sense, the title of Gadamer's book, *Truth and Method*, can be misleading, as Gadamer's book does not present a formal method for arriving at truth.[6] As Gadamer makes clear in the Introduction, he intends *Truth and Method* to be descriptive rather than prescriptive (*TM*, xxii). His intention is to describe the process of understanding as it takes place. That being said, as we will see shortly, Gadamer does not refrain from identifying what we may formally exposit and prescribe as hermeneutic virtues—habits of mind that, when possessed, make one generally more likely to participate fully in the process of understanding.

First, though, let us consider another step in the process of understanding as Gadamer describes it. For understanding of the hermeneutic object to occur, according to Gadamer, it is not enough for preconceptions to be in operation or even to be put into question during our engagement with the object. Those preconceptions that are put into question must then be tested to determine their adequacy for understanding the matter at hand. In reading a text, for example, when the meaning that one assumes of a certain term is called into question by an occurrence of that term in the text, one must then look to see whether, as the text's broader meaning develops, the initial projected meaning must be revised. Likewise, in conversation, when one's interlocutor says something that problematizes one's projection of the subject matter to be addressed, one must then look to see whether, as the conversation develops, one's projection must be revised. According to Gadamer, this is the part of the process of understanding where one tests which of one's preconceptions are arbitrary and which are "to be confirmed 'by the things' themselves (*die sich ‚an den Sachen' erst bestätigen sollen*)" (*TM*, 280/272). This is, then, how one determines if a particular preconception is arbitrary or justified. A justified, non-arbitrary preconception is one that, when applied, proves productive in bringing forth the meaning and truth of what is said.

What is most striking about Gadamer's conception of this way of arriving at justified beliefs is the alternative that it provides to the common view that holds that honest inquiry requires that we put aside all preconceptions. For Gadamer, one does not need to set aside preconceptions at the beginning. This is, after all, not possible. Instead, understanding requires that we put our preconceptions to the test. Conceiving of the process of arriving at justified beliefs in this way has a notable advantage over the alternative view. Since it is not possible to set aside all preconceptions when one goes to understand an object, there is a clear problem with the conception of inquiry that makes this a requirement. It not only misdescribes what takes place in the process of understanding but perpetuates a myth of epistemic heroism that discourages people from reflecting on the constitutive role that their preconceptions play in shaping how and what they understand. This, according to Gadamer, is the problem with what he calls historicism—that approach to history that attempts to know historical objects by setting aside from the start any meaning that comes from the interpreter's present situation. By discouraging any reflection on one's hermeneutical situation, it sets aside any chance at knowing the historical object.

> The naivete of so-called historicism consists in the fact that it does not undertake this reflection, and in trusting to the fact that its procedure is methodical, it forgets its own historicity. We must here appeal from a badly understood historical thinking to one that can better perform the task of understanding. Real historical thinking must take account of its own historicity. Only then will it cease to chase the phantom of a historical object that is the object of progressive research, and learn to view the object as the counterpart of itself and hence understand both. (*TM*, 310)

So, as we can see, the preconceptions that come from historical consciousness cannot be regarded from the start as arbitrary. Nor should they be regarded as equally harmonious with the object from the start. *The only way to determine if specific preconceptions are arbitrary is to put them at risk and to see whether they are or are not confirmed by the object as it unfolds in the interpretive interaction.* Those that are confirmed by the object in this way are justified.[7] Those that are challenged by it, however, are not without epistemic value, as such challenges ultimately allow one to bring their preconceptions into greater harmony with the object.

Now, this part of the process of understanding as Gadamer describes it will sound familiar and unproblematic to those accustomed to thinking about truth as the correspondence between a belief or a proposition and an independent object. As Gadamer conceives of it, though, what is involved in this process of testing is not a matter of seeing whether some preconception corresponds with the independent, *immediate* object that one comes upon at the beginning of the inquiry. This is because the things themselves (*die Sachen*) by which one tests one's preconceptions are not independent objects that can be known immediately but, on Gadamer's view, come into relief only through the interpretive, self-interrogative interaction. Hence, when it comes to humanistic inquiry, Gadamer explains, "such an 'object in itself' clearly does not exist at all (*Ein solcher ›Gegenstand‹ an sich existiert offenbar überhaupt nicht*)" (*TM*, 296/289).[8]

3. HERMENEUTIC VIRTUES AND THEIR ROLE IN UNDERSTANDING

With Gadamer's theory of the process of understanding and the role of historical preconceptions in this process now in view, let us turn our attention to those habits of mind that facilitate or hinder this process from taking place. For as much as Gadamer himself claims to be only describing rather than prescribing the process of understanding in *Truth and Method*, one of the things that is likely to stand out most to readers of "The Elevation of the Historicity of Understanding" is *the creative redescription of epistemic responsibility that it offers according to which habits of mind like openness, courage, and self-awareness are necessary for epistemic responsibility*. Though Gadamer does not speak to these habits of mind all together at any point or develop a general concept for them, it is not surprising to find recent theorists interested in just this. After all, contemporary society suffers in various ways from that idea, reinforced by the transcendence argument, that success in knowing has nothing to do with such virtues or even virtue at all.[9] In response to this tendency, theorists in the developing field of epistemic justice studies have argued that virtues like self-awareness and open-mindedness are essential to epistemic responsibility, while opposite conditions like meta-blindness and epistemic arrogance are hindrances to it.[10] In this way, epistemic justice theorists help put into relief the historical-cultural horizon with which Gadamer's argument in *Truth and Method* addresses us today. What, then, are the specific hermeneutic virtues that can be implied from Gadamer's description of the process of understanding in "The Elevation of the Historicity of Understanding"?

One crucial hermeneutic virtue is that habit of mind that makes one aware that they are being addressed by a truth claim in the way described above. Gadamer describes the role such a habit of mind plays in reading, explaining that "a person trying to understand a text is prepared for it to tell him something" and that "that is why a hermeneutically trained consciousness must be, from the start, sensitive to the text's alterity" (*TM*, 282). The description is helpful in clarifying why, despite Gadamer's claim to be offering only a descriptive and not prescriptive account of understanding, there is need for some account of hermeneutic virtues. The ready availability of historical phenomena that challenge one's preconceptions is no guarantee that one will seek out such opportunities for self-interrogation. Only those with a certain habit of mind will be receptive to such opportunities—being open to them when they arise and even actively seeking them out. Some are highly defensive of and largely unwilling to suspend their preconceptions. One may be defensive in this way, for example, if they perceive at some level that their sense of self-worth and social authority may be jeopardized if one or more of their preconceptions are rationally undermined. This happens when people with certain forms of social and economic privilege, for example, are resistant to opportunities to learn about the forms of exploitation that have historically contributed to their privilege.[11] In other cases, the issue may be less that one is actively defensive against self-interrogation and more that one lacks any education in the art of questioning that opens up a hermeneutic object. Being able to ask a good question is itself, after all, a valuable reflexive skill that many people are not taught (including many who pass through the current education system). In either case, one is caught up in what Gadamer describes as the "tyranny of prejudices"—unable or unwilling to subject one's preconceptions to critical interrogation.

While we may want to conceive of the virtue just described as the virtue of "openness," this description only works if we add an important caveat. *To be open in a way that is hermeneutically virtuous is not the same as possessing no beliefs*. The goal is not to be so open that one never comes to settle on any beliefs at all and one is without any anticipatory understanding. After all, one must hold beliefs and meanings to some degree in order for them to be called into question. Otherwise, one cannot possibly be putting oneself at risk in the way Gadamer describes. Similarly, to be seriously open to the truth claim of another in the way that Gadamer describes requires that one be willing to adopt new beliefs in light of what emerges in the hermeneutic encounter. This in turn requires that one become, not more open to, but in fact more closed off to other contradictory beliefs. For example, having a conversation that convinces you to take the continuing history of racism more seriously should make you more closed off to arguments that underplay this history. To wager one's preconception in this situation (e.g., to wager one's understanding of the role of racism in American history up to the present) means nothing if the end result is that one is in a state of indecision regarding different claims about this history. To engage fully and honestly in the hermeneutic process of understanding, one needs to stand firmly by the beliefs that come from these hermeneutic encounters until there is compelling reason to put those beliefs into question.

Although it can be helpful to talk about hermeneutic virtues in the abstract, this last point helps us to see clearly why Gadamer resists presenting these virtues as part of a formal method for understanding which, if followed, would be sufficient for arriving at knowledge. While we should certainly be cautious to avoid the "tyranny of prejudices," it is not the case that every conception, meaning, and belief should—by virtue of operating as a prejudice—be cast into doubt. Rather, they should be cast into doubt only when a legitimate challenge arises in the course of a hermeneutic encounter—when, in relying upon them, we are pulled up short by the *Sache* itself. The doctrine of hermeneutic virtue clarifies what it means to respond appropriately to this challenge, and it may even shed some light on what it means to regularly seek out the conditions where such challenges are likely to arise. It does not, however, constitute a formal method for determining what constitutes a legitimate or illegitimate challenge. As familiar as the search for such a method would be to us moderns today, Gadamer's account is not intended to provide such a method, as this would mean that understanding is no longer grounded in historical consciousness. This point is made clear in Gadamer's critique of the Enlightenment model of understanding. It is to this section of "The Elevation of the Historicity of Understanding" that we turn next.

4. THE TWOFOLD CRITIQUE OF THE ENLIGHTENMENT AND ROMANTICISM

Recall the two common ways of thinking about the historical situation of our understanding described at the beginning of this chapter: the transcendence argument and the immanence argument. The conclusions of these two arguments seem obvious to us today. They seem so obvious today, in fact, that it is hard to believe that philosophers once had to argue for them and that they initially struck most of their original audience as untenable. Yet, these two conclusions are the offspring of the approach to knowing once rigorously argued and advocated for by the thinkers of the Enlightenment. To think clearly about the historicity of the understanding, then, it would be helpful to bring to light the fundamental maxims of the age of the Enlightenment so as *to put the beliefs inherited from this age at risk* in the sense described above. This is indeed what Gadamer does in "The Elevation of the Historicity of Understanding"—particularly in two sections entitled "The Discrediting of Prejudice by the Enlightenment" and "The Rehabilitation of Authority and Tradition."

It is hard to overstate the influence of the Enlightenment on our conceptions of thinking today. Indeed, we celebrate the accomplishment of the Enlightenment on grounds that we have inherited from the Enlightenment itself. We applaud the figures of the Enlightenment for being courageous in their thought and, specifically, for breaking away from the stronghold of the prejudices that they would inevitably be bound to if their thought remained rooted in tradition. We find perfectly understandable Francis Bacon's desire to recognize and cast away the various "idols" that tend to beset human thinking, and we immediately agree with him when he writes in 1620 that "it is pointless to expect any great advancements in science from grafting new things onto old" and that, for this reason, "we must make a fresh start with deep foundations."[12] We find quite natural René Descartes' desire for a method of arriving at beliefs that he can be absolutely certain of and find intuitive his argument—again, once considered wildly counter-intuitive—that, for this reason, we cannot rely entirely upon either the senses or common custom. We thus easily appreciate the praise expressed by Jean Le Rond d'Alembert in the *Encyclopédie* (1760) where he attributes to Descartes "a strong imagination, a most logical mind, knowledge drawn from himself more than from books, great courage in battling the most generally accepted prejudices, and no form of dependence which forced him to spare them."[13] Indeed, the Enlightenment ideal of thinking in a way that breaks free from the prejudices of tradition is so intuitive that we are taken aback when we come across indications that these Enlightenment figures were invariably observant of religious and cultural norms and working within a particular historical consciousness in some way.

What we have inherited, in short, is a presupposition handed down to us from the Enlightenment: a "prejudice against prejudice itself" (*TM*, 283). Essential to Enlightenment thought was the belief that real progress in knowledge requires freeing thought from the guardrails of tradition. In the eyes of Bacon, what we inherit from tradition and custom can be summed up as the "idols of the tribe"—beliefs and practices that we adhere to because of tenacity alone and which thus have no real justification.[14] Enlightenment thought, by contrast, proceeds under the banner of the motto articulated in 1784 by Kant: "*Sapere aude!* Have the courage to use your own intelligence!"[15] It is with this opposition between reason and tradition in mind that D'Alembert praises Descartes for courageously combatting widely held prejudices and for not deriving knowledge from books. Texts in particular were seen as carrying the dead weight of tradition—of passing ideas down from generation to generation in a way that did not require one to think for oneself. As such, written tradition was often presented by Enlightenment figures as a source of error. If they were not subjected to a rationalizing interpretation, such texts were nothing more than "idols of the tribe." Such a conception is still present today when people operate under the assumption that they can either think for themselves or spend their time reading old books.[16] This assumption—that tradition is opposed to reason and to thinking for oneself—is, ironically, an assumption born out of the historical tradition of the Enlightenment.

The Enlightenment understood itself as freeing thought and human society specifically from tradition and, by extension, viewed tradition as a powerful force from which thought and human society must be freed. According to the Enlightenment, thinking that proceeds from tradition or from any other preconception is, as a whole, illegitimate. As Gadamer puts it,

> In general, the Enlightenment tends to accept no authority and to decide everything before the judgment seat of reason. Thus, the written tradition of Scripture, like any other historical document, can claim no absolute validity; the possible truth of the tradition depends on the credibility that reason accords it. It is not tradition but reason that constitutes the ultimate source of all authority. What is written down is not necessarily true. We can know better: this is the maxim with which the modern Enlightenment approaches tradition and which ultimately leads it to undertake historical research. It takes tradition as an object of critique, just as the natural sciences do with the evidence of the senses. (*TM*, 285)

It should now be clear that this aspect of the Enlightenment is the historical basis for the first of the common positions on the historical situation of thought that we referred to as the transcendence argument. It is quite common today for people to believe that honest inquiry into a subject matter requires that one bracket any beliefs one has about it by virtue of the transmission of tradition, which is to say, by virtue of one's particular historical horizon. What differentiates most people today from the Enlightenment thinkers, however, is the degree of difficulty each perceives in this task. While thinkers like Descartes, Bacon, and Kant devised elaborate formal methods for determining when and to what extent a belief was rationally justified, the mass popularization of the ideal has made it so that we strain today to imagine how anyone at all could fall short of the benchmark. With the popularization of the Enlightenment, we begin to simply take for granted that, with few exceptions aside, we are all thinking for ourselves. Ironically, then, in the current wake of the Enlightenment, there is comparatively little commitment to searching out, critically assessing, and revising the beliefs one has inherited from one's historical-cultural situation.

For Gadamer, though, this problem plagued the Enlightenment from the beginning. While it is true that the reception of ideas transmitted through tradition is not sufficient for knowledge, the Enlightenment, on Gadamer's view, went too far in categorizing all thought situated within a tradition as epistemically illegitimate and insisting that tradition function only as an object of critique. To understand Gadamer's assessment of this problem, let us consider, first, the argument presented above regarding the productive role of preconceptions in the process of understanding. Recall that, for Gadamer, genuine inquiry into a subject matter puts those preconceptions relevant to that subject matter into play. It requires both that one actively rely upon them and that one puts them at risk when they become problematized. In this way, Gadamer argues that, contrary to the Enlightenment model, preconceptions are not only inevitable but that they play a productive role in the process of understanding—by either bearing themselves out in terms of the subject matter or by becoming problematized in a way that changes the way the subject matter comes to appear.

Gadamer has no dispute, then, with the Enlightenment thinkers' concern about our tendency to take traditional beliefs for granted and to assume that these beliefs are, without any criticism or reflection, sufficient for understanding any subject matter. As we know, Gadamer himself is concerned with the "tyranny of prejudices," that is, with what transpires when one lacks the virtue required to put traditional beliefs and meanings that have become problematized to the test. Gadamer differs from the Enlightenment thinkers, however, in insisting that it is possible to relate to prejudices in a different way. A subject with a "hermeneutically trained consciousness" will not treat the traditions to which they belong as having a validity and a significance that are beyond any question or revision. Tradition will appear to them to be equally something relied upon and something thought through and put to the test. Indeed, for them, beliefs and meanings inherited from tradition are only really epistemically relevant when they are put genuinely into play—facilitating a hermeneutic encounter that may very well fundamentally transform them. In this way, Gadamer argues that Enlightenment thinkers are wrong to treat tradition as the abstract opposite of reason. One can certainly relate to tradition in a way that hinders critical reflection and self-interrogation, but this is not the only way of relating to tradition possible.

Gadamer's critique of the Enlightenment, though, is not simply a methodological correction. It is not only about how we ought to seek knowledge but also about how to properly conceive of the object of inquiry. According to the Enlightenment model, the process of understanding renders irrelevant any particular features of the inquiring subject's situation, including their historical-cultural situation. It is this model that is operative today when we as a society feel no need to inquire into the historical-cultural situation of our collective thinking on certain topics (e.g., race in America). On the Enlightenment model, no such self-reflection is required for understanding the subject matter, and the inquiry will have no bearing on the self-understanding of the inquirer. The object is, after all, ontologically separate from the historical horizon in which it comes to appear. As we have seen, though,

Gadamer challenges the assumption of this ontological separation on the grounds that knowledge of objects in the human sciences requires knowledge of the historical horizon within which a given object appears. As he puts it, "What appears to be a limiting prejudice from the viewpoint of the absolute self-construction of reason in fact belongs to historical reality itself" (*TM*, 289).[17] This is why an attempt to inquire that does not make conspicuous and put at risk relevant aspects of its historical-cultural horizon can achieve only partial results.

In the face of this criticism of the Enlightenment ideal, it may be tempting to set up an alternative model of understanding that embraces tradition and the guardrails it offers to the understanding. Rather than conceiving of understanding as something that takes place sporadically through feats of individual epistemic heroism, we might insist that understanding is always bound to definite forms of social life. This option aligns with the second common position on the historical situation of the understanding described above, namely, that of the immanence argument. Here again this attitude has historical roots that are generally unacknowledged by those who take it today to be common sense. It first emerged as a critical reaction to the Enlightenment ideal. Embraced in different ways by a number of writers in modernity, we find this reaction articulated, for example, by the Romantic Novalis (Friedrich von Hardenberg), in his infamous "Christianity or Europe" (1799), where he laments the social transformations brought about by the Enlightenment and, in particular, the transfer of authority from Christian traditions and institutions to the ideas and institutions associated with the Enlightenment. Novalis describes the waning relevance of Christianity in the age of the Enlightenment as follows:

> One saw in faith the source of universal stagnation; and through a more penetrating knowledge one hoped to destroy it. Everywhere the sense for the sacred suffered from various persecutions of its past nature, its temporal personality. The result of the modern manner of thinking one called "philosophy," and regarded it as anything opposed to the old order, especially therefore as any whim contrary to religion. . . . Every trace of the sacred was to be destroyed, all memory of noble events and people was to be spoiled by satire, and the world stripped of colorful ornament. Their favorite theme, on account of its mathematical obedience and impudence, was light. They were pleased that it refracted rather than played with its colors and so they called their great enterprise 'Enlightenment.'[18]

Now, both Novalis and Gadamer are critical of the Enlightenment ideal insofar as both take issue with the claim that all beliefs and meanings that emerge from out of a particular cultural-historical worldview are epistemically irrelevant. Gadamer finds value in the insights of Romanticism up to this point. His treatment of Romanticism in "The Elevation of the Historicity of Understanding," however, is primarily critical. Where does he find the Enlightenment model of understanding misguided then? For Gadamer, Romanticism, no less than the Enlightenment, achieves only partial knowledge of its object, because it accepts the Enlightenment's basic premise that tradition is "the abstract opposite of self-determination" (*TM*, 293). For Gadamer, this is a faulty premise, and its acceptance by both Enlightenment thinkers and those reacting in defense of tradition against the Enlightenment must be seen as problematic. As Gadamer explains it,

> What determines the romantic understanding of tradition is its abstract opposition (*abstrakte Gegensatz*) to the principle of enlightenment. Romanticism conceives of tradition as an antithesis to the freedom of reason and regards it as something historically given, like nature. And whether one wants to be revolutionary and oppose it or preserve it, tradition is still viewed as the abstract opposite of free self-determination, since its validity does not require any reasons but conditions us without our questioning it. (*TM*, 293/278)

Romanticism, for Gadamer, longs for tradition understood in a distorted way. What it longs for is not the possession of tentative beliefs and meanings that must be renegotiated in hermeneutic encounters—a process which involves ongoing self-interrogation. Instead, it professes its devotion to "the idols of the tribe," in other words, to tradition as construed by Enlightenment thinkers. Here again we find Gadamer's account illuminating for understanding the present. After all, Gadamer's description of the Romantic misconception of tradition applies to sizable portions of the human population today who embrace as "tradition" doctrines and practices that arose only as a reaction to developments in modernity. One can find neo-traditionalists within all major religions and forms of modern nationalism today. These neo-traditionalists see themselves—as Novalis did—in conflict not only with the tenets of modern liberal society but also with those in their own tradition for whom inhabiting that tradition means contributing to its ongoing critical and rational transformation.[19] Of course, even the neo-traditionalists are innovators. This is why their conception of their own self-activity (e.g., as "fundamentalists") is false. As much as they want to view their tradition (e.g., their religious doctrine, their national identity and history) as something that never changes, their interpretations of the tradition are inevitably the result of a historical consciousness that is very much ongoing.[20] This is why such neo-traditionalists, in Gadamer's words, "lag behind their true historical being" (*TM*, 293). He writes,

> In tradition there is always an element of freedom and of history itself. Even the most genuine and pure tradition does not persist because of the inertia of what

once existed. It needs to be affirmed, embraced, cultivated. It is, essentially, preservation, and it is active in all historical change. But preservation is an act of reason, though an inconspicuous one. For this reason, only innovation and planning appear to be the result of reason. But this is an illusion. . . . Preservation is as much a freely chosen action as are revolution and renewal. This is why both the Enlightenment's critique of tradition and the romantic rehabilitation of it lag behind their true historical being. (*TM*, 293)

What both the Enlightenment and Romanticism have in common, then, is a denial of historical consciousness and its relevance for the process of understanding. Understanding is no more able to simply break free from the past than it is absolutely bound within the past. Both of these misconstrue not just the nature of understanding but the nature of our historicity. Yet it is common to imagine the meaning of past cultures as frozen in time. Indeed, for this form of historicism, which develops out of the same abstract opposition between reason and tradition introduced by the Enlightenment, traditions of the past should not be interpreted through a reasoning that is informed by present historical consciousness. They should be understood as curiosities of a time no longer present. For Gadamer, though, this denies the intrinsic unity between our past and present. It misconstrues the past as something that we happen upon without any anticipatory understanding. Gadamer disputes this sort of historicism on this point though. For him, "The closed horizon that is supposed to enclose a culture is an abstraction. The historical movement of human life consists in the fact that it is never absolutely bound to any one standpoint, and hence can never have a truly closed horizon. The horizon is, rather, something into which we move and that moves with us" (*TM*, 315).[21] Thus, just as the abstract opposition between reason and tradition can prevent us from embracing the hermeneutic process of understanding described above, so too can the abstract opposition—taken for granted for the most part today—between present historical consciousness and the past.

Now, to be clear, the claim that there is an intrinsic unity between present historical consciousness and the past should not be taken to imply that every aspect of a past culture that we might possibly encounter is equally significant for present consciousness. Likewise, the claim that there is a similar unity between tradition and reason should not be taken to imply that every aspect of a tradition will turn out to be rational. If this were Gadamer's argument, after all, one would never experience the problematization of one's preconceptions in a hermeneutic encounter and the historical phenomena that we encounter would in no sense be unfamiliar. One would not have to grapple, when reading about American history, for example, with what elements of it are attempting to speak to us today and what they are attempting to disclose about the present. There would be no problematization of beliefs and no need for interpretation in this sense. These are vital to Gadamer's conception of the process of understanding though.[22] Hence, when he proposes that reason and tradition, present and past, are unities, Gadamer is simply arguing that, for a self-aware historical consciousness, these cannot be regarded as abstract oppositions. A person that has self-aware, historical consciousness is one that has the requisite hermeneutic virtues to engage critically and reflectively with tradition—for example, by allowing themselves to be addressed by truth claims issuing from traditions, to put to the test those beliefs that are legitimately problematized by these claims, and to critically revise traditional beliefs and practices in light of the commitments that emerge through this ongoing process of understanding. Such a person would not, like the Enlightenment thinkers, disregard tradition as a whole as epistemically irrelevant. Nor would they operate under the Romantic thinker's assumption that tradition contains truth that is inaccessible to reason. Finally, to operate in this way would be to inhabit historical consciousness as dynamic in the way that Gadamer describes it above—"as something which we move and that moves with us."

We can now see how Gadamer's argument in "The Elevation of the Historicity of Understanding" challenges the two common positions on the historical situation of understanding described earlier. The transcendence argument, which claims that real understanding requires that we step outside of our historical situations and the particular traditions by which we find ourselves addressed, is familiar to us today in the wake of the Enlightenment. It is so familiar, in fact, that it is very difficult for us to understand these arguments as innovative proposals. Their suggestion that real understanding takes the form of a thinking that has achieved independence from traditional ideas appears obvious and unquestionable to us today. Yet, as Gadamer argues, this claim rests upon a problematic premise, namely, that thinking that is historically conscious in any way is irrational. This claim is betrayed, for one, by any acknowledgement of the historical-cultural situation of Enlightenment thought. It is problematized as well by any consideration of the productive role that historical preconceptions play in the process of understanding. As we have seen, preconceptions in general provide an interpretation in advance. In some cases, these preconceptions are confirmed by the object, and we are justified in holding to them—even in using them as a basis for critiquing other beliefs—until they undergo a legitimate challenge. In other cases, when we go to apply a preconception to an object, it is problematized by it and must be revised accordingly. In either case, preconceptions play a productive role in the process of understanding. Indeed, when they are preconceptions grounded in our historical consciousness, even those that are problematized cannot be regarded as arbitrary, since they belong to the dynamic development of historical consciousness itself.

The immanence argument is often presented today in reaction to and in opposition to the transcendence argument. Here too Gadamer's account in "The Elevation of the Historicity of Understanding" sheds light by allowing us to recognize the roots of the immanence argument in Romanticism. The ground of Romanticism's opposition to the Enlightenment is recognizable to us today as the rationale of neo-traditionalism. Although these developments emerge in response to the Enlightenment, Gadamer argues, they accept from the Enlightenment its problematic opposition between tradition and reason. For Romantics and neo-traditionalists, tradition is that which the light of reason cannot penetrate. To find ourselves as part of a historical-cultural tradition, moreover, is to reach the limit of our self-determination. Romantics and neo-traditionalists attempt to reduce historical consciousness to this moment of finding oneself bound to a particular historical-cultural situation. Historicists, in turn, inherit this conception of tradition by conceiving of the past not as something that we actively preserve in the present, and thus not as something grounded in human freedom, but as something that can be understood without reason and reflection on the contemporary age.

In sum, both the Enlightenment and Romanticism make the mistake of attempting to arrest the dynamic movement of historical consciousness and to ground understanding in one moment of this movement taken in abstraction from the rest of it. The Enlightenment thinker denies the historical-cultural situation of their thought. They reduce the ground of their understanding to the moment of transcendence. The Romantic and the neo-traditionalist deny the reason and freedom at work in the way that their historical-cultural situation appears to them. They reduce the ground of their understanding to the moment of immanence. In place of these two dominant models of understanding, Gadamer offers instead a description of understanding as historically dynamic and irreducible to any formal method. In this, he offers a relevant alternative to ways of thinking about understanding that, while epistemologically, ontologically, and socially problematic, are widely accepted today.

NOTES

1. Hans-Georg Gadamer, *Truth and Method*, 2nd ed., trans. Joel Weinsheimer and Donald G. Marshall (New York: Bloomsbury Publishing, 2013), 278/274. Hereafter cited in text as *TM*. As is the case here, where the German is cited or the translation has been altered, the page number of the original is indicated after the slash. These refer to Hans-Georg Gadamer, *Wahrheit und Methode*, Gesammelte Werke I (Tübingen: Mohr Siebeck, 1990).

2. Heidegger does not put much weight on the distinction he introduces between *Vorhabe, Vorsicht*, and *Vorbegriff*. On my reading, his articulation of these three

different modalities of the fore-structure of the understanding functions primarily to give a sense for some of the different ways in which interpretation is grounded by something apprehended in advance. Gadamer tends to use the related term *Vorurteil* rather than *Vorhabe, Vorsicht,* or *Vorbegriff*. Nevertheless, it is clear that he intends by *Vorurteil* what Heidegger captured in his articulation of these three modalities. To avoid the possible confusion caused by switching among these terms, I will follow Gadamer's lead and use primarily the term "preconception" (one translation of *Vorurteil*) to refer to the general set of things that are apprehended in advance in interpretation. Martin Heidegger, *Being and Time*, trans. John Macquarrie and Edward Robinson. (New York: Harper Collins, 1962), 190–91.

3. To be precise, Gadamer argues that this reflection is requisite in the human sciences (*Geisteswissenschaften*) and intrinsic to all objects taken up in these fields, but not requisite for making certain discoveries in the natural sciences (*Naturwissenschaften*) (*TM*, 295/288). This does not mean that, for Gadamer, it is never appropriate or important to reflect on the historical situation of scientific inquiry but that there is an epistemic value of inquiry in the natural sciences that is distinct from the epistemic value of inquiry in the human sciences. While Gadamer prefers to treat these two domains separately, it should be noted that there is no formal method for determining when an object of inquiry belongs to the domain of the natural sciences or the human sciences, and Gadamer does not shy away from bringing humanistic inquiry to bear on matters where competency is thought to lie exclusively with the natural sciences. This is the case, for example, in his interpretation of the phenomenon of health throughout *The Enigma of Health: The Art of Healing in a Scientific Age*, trans. Jason Gaiger and Nicholas Walker (Stanford, CA: Stanford University Press, 1996).

4. Gadamer takes these formulations directly from Heidegger's description of the hermeneutic circle in *Being and Time*. Heidegger writes, "In the circle is hidden a positive possibility of the most primordial kind of knowing. To be sure, we genuinely take hold of this possibility only when, in our interpretation, we have understood that our first, last, and constant task is never to allow our for-having, fore-sight, and fore-conception to be presented to us by fancies and popular conceptions, but rather to make the scientific theme secure by working out these fore-structures in terms of the things themselves." Heidegger, *Being and Time*, 195.

5. For an excellent treatment of the interpersonal and ethical character of this address, see James Risser, *Hermeneutics and the Voice of the Other: Re-reading Gadamer's Philosophical Hermeneutics* (Albany, NY: State University of New York Press, 1997).

6. Gadamer explains, "The circle, then, is not formal in nature. It is neither subjective nor objective, but describes understanding as the interplay of the movement of tradition and the movement of the interpreter" (*TM,* 305).

7. This form of justification will be unsatisfactory to one whose standard of justification is certainty. For a helpful explanation of why this form of justification is nevertheless epistemically valuable and even more valuable than the measure of certainty invoked by skeptics, see Brice Wachterhauser, "Getting it Right: Relativism, Realism, and Truth," in *The Cambridge Companion to Gadamer*, ed. Robert J. Dostal (Cambridge: Cambridge University Press, 2006).

8. This claim should not be taken to mean that, for Gadamer, there is no sense in which objectivity is a measure for justified belief, as Emilio Betti suggests. For Gadamer, it is just that the *Sache* by which one tests one's preconceptions is not independent of interpretive interaction. For Betti's argument that "a loss of objectivity" results from Gadamer's account in "The Elevation of the Historicity of Understanding," see Emilio Betti, "Hermeneutics as the General Method of the *Geisteswissenschaften*," in *Contemporary Hermeneutics: Hermeneutics as Method, Philosophy, and Critique*, ed. Josef Bleicher (London: Routledge and Kegan Paul, 1980), 76–80.

9. The assumption that the pursuit of knowledge is entirely separate from the pursuit of virtue and self-knowledge makes it difficult to recognize and combat epistemic injustice. For an account of the harms—epistemological and distributive—that result from forms of epistemic injustice, see Miranda Fricker, *Epistemic Injustice: Power and the Ethics of Knowing* (Oxford: Oxford University Press, 2007), 43–59 and 161–69.

10. Central to the field of epistemic justice studies is the insight that, although one's cultural-historical situation can encourage one to engage in epistemic injustice (e.g., by denying epistemic relevance to the testimony of hermeneutically marginalized people), it is possible to correct this deficiency through the development of certain habits of mind referred to as "epistemic virtues" and "hermeneutic virtues." For an especially illuminating discussion of these virtues and what can encourage their cultivation, see José Medina, *The Epistemology of Resistance: Gender and Racial Oppression, Epistemic Injustice, and Resistant Imaginations* (Oxford: Oxford University Press, 2013).

11. Medina argues that color-blindness and gender-blindness are forms of epistemic vice for this reason. For Medina, these attitudes, common in our contemporary social world, involve a failure in self-knowledge. José Medina, *The Epistemology of Resistance*, 37.

12. Francis Bacon, *The New Organon*, ed. Lisa Jardine and Michael Silverthorne (Cambridge: Cambridge University Press, 2000), 39.

13. Jean Le Rond d'Alembert, *Preliminary Discourse to the Encyclopedia of Diderot*, trans. Richard Schwab (Evanston, IL: University of Chicago, 1995), 77.

14. Bacon, *The New Organon*, 40.

15. Immanuel Kant, "What is Enlightenment?," in *Kant: Basic Writings*, ed. Allen Wood (New York: Modern Library, 2001), 135.

16. For a compelling description of how the current devaluation of the history of philosophy reflects this Enlightenment ideal, see Charles Taylor, "Philosophy and Its History," in *Philosophy in History: Essays on the Historiography of Philosophy*, ed. Richard Rorty, J.B. Schneewind, and Quentin Skinner (Cambridge: Cambridge University Press, 1984).

17. Gadamer's critique of the Enlightenment on this point echoes the critique that G.W.F. Hegel gives in the *Phenomenology of Spirit* in the section on "The Struggle of the Enlightenment with Superstition." See G. W. F. Hegel, *Phenomenology of Spirit*, trans. A.V. Miller (Oxford: Oxford University Press, 1977), 329–49.

18. Novalis, "Christianity or Europe: A Fragment," in *Early German Romantic Political Writings*, ed. and trans. Frederick Beiser (Cambridge: Cambridge University Press, 1996), 70.

19. Novalis had as much contempt for those who advocated for a rational interpretation of the Bible as he had for those who advocated for secularization. Similarly, fundamentalists today often hold special contempt for those practitioners of their own religion who embrace its historical aspect and advocate for changes on this basis.

20. This is one way of understanding the error in the rationale behind efforts by Republicans in several states within the United States in recent years to eradicate critical race theory from school curricula. Those behind these efforts insist that the story of American history has already been told and that attempts to tell this story in a new way are innovations that undermine the knowledge of this history implied by nationalist traditions. Gadamer's argument helps us to see, though, that there is no way of preserving the memory of the past except through a rational reflection that determines the meaning of the past and present in conjunction with one another.

21. Gadamer offers an extended example of this point in his discussion of the category of the "classical" (*TM*, 296–302). Classical works are not something, according to Gadamer, that can be properly understood by reconstructing the classic world as a closed horizon in the past, since "our understanding will always retain the consciousness that we too belong to that world, and correlatively, that the work too belongs to our world" (*TM*, 301). Catherine Zuckert offers the following helpful gloss of Gadamer's critique: "Insofar as it treats the past as simply past, as the product of a set of circumstances and expressing an understanding of the world that cannot possibly be duplicated in the present, an exclusively historical or scholarly reading of a past text precludes the text from challenging the truth of our current conceptions, including the historical insight itself. We do not learn anything new, which is to say that we do not really learn anything at all, about ourselves or the part of the tradition that shaped us contained in the particular text. To expand our horizon, we must not only identify the way in which things from the past are different; we also have to ask how they can be combined with or otherwise affect our current understanding." Catherine H. Zuckert, "Hermeneutics in Practice: Gadamer on Ancient Philosophy," in *The Cambridge Companion to Gadamer*, ed. Robert J. Dostal (Cambridge: Cambridge University Press, 2002), 205–6.

22. Gadamer makes this especially clear in his discussion of the hermeneutic significance of temporal distance. The hermeneutic object is familiar in one sense, belonging within the horizon of historical consciousness, but it is unfamiliar in another sense, being part of that consciousness that is not yet appropriated. In the hermeneutic object, one finds a "play between the traditionary text's strangeness and familiarity to us, between being a historically intended, distanced object and belonging to a tradition" (*TM*, 306).

Chapter 9

TM II.2.2

"The Recovery of the Fundamental Hermeneutic Problem": Application and Normativity

David Liakos

A reader traversing *Truth and Method* for the first time may be surprised to discover that the chapter entitled "The Recovery of the Fundamental Hermeneutic Problem" does not outline the book's most celebrated ideas.[1] The chapter does not introduce the authority of tradition, conversation or dialogue, the fusion of horizons, historically effective consciousness, linguisticality, play, prejudice, or the speculative character of language. Rather, the chapter's main topic is application (*Anwendung*), which refers to the way an interpreter involves herself with the item of her understanding and allows the text's meaning to be intimately relevant and, in that sense, *applied* to her own situation. Application is fundamental to recovering the genuine phenomenon of hermeneutical experience from its modern alienation, which discourages this form of involvement and instead objectifies and distances the interpreter from what she attempts to understand. Gadamer thus places application at the heart of his conception of understanding. And yet, despite its avowedly fundamental status, application has not been as prominent in the reception and influence of Gadamerian hermeneutics as more famous ideas from *Truth and Method* like those just mentioned.

The present chapter provides an interpretation of Gadamer's idea of application that clarifies the relationship between the *first and third persons* in application. By emphasizing this sense of application, we will appreciate why Gadamer considers application fundamental to the hermeneutic problem. We will also be in a better position to assess a significant objection to Gadamer's project. Beginning with Emilio Betti's discussion of this chapter in *Truth and Method*, Gadamer has often been criticized for his alleged neglect of normativity. This *normative critique* of Gadamer, which especially targets his idea of application, has been rejuvenated and reformulated by scholars of hermeneutics in recent years. I will argue that this objection suffers from a failure adequately to come to terms with Gadamer's attention to the first person in addition to the third person, both of which are integrated into application in a complex combination. The normative critique betrays a misunderstanding of the role of the first person in Gadamer's account and an overemphasis on third-person factors of understanding. My commentary will respond to the normative critics by showing how the relation between the first and third persons in application contains a viable conception of the normativity of understanding.

My argument will proceed as follows. I will first explain the normative critique by reconstructing Betti's early criticism of *Truth and Method* as well as similar arguments in the contemporary literature to frame my reading. These critics suggest that Gadamer's conception of application abandons normative criteria for humanistic research. Next, I will present my reading of "The Recovery of the Fundamental Hermeneutic Problem" by clarifying the role of normativity there. Application includes a measure for understanding. The thing that is to be understood must be allowed to address me, and such involvement responds to the text's meaning. While this measure is not expressible in principled rules, application is normatively accountable both to the text's third-person claim to meaning and to my first-person involvement with the text. The participation of the interpreter with the item of her understanding forms a normative standard. To conclude my response to the normative critique, I will illustrate Gadamer's account with a phenomenological example of application.

1. THE NORMATIVE CRITIQUE OF GADAMER

The effective history of *Truth and Method* has been shaped by the diverse and often critical responses the book has elicited. For several decades, deconstruction and critical theory articulated the most prominent of these objections within Continental European philosophy.[2]

But much recent hermeneutical research bears the influence not so much of Jacques Derrida or Jürgen Habermas but of another early critic of Gadamer, namely, Emilio Betti. As I will show, Betti's response to *Truth and Method* forms the unsurpassed horizon for several recent criticisms of Gadamerian hermeneutics. This fact is of interest for us not only because this normative critique is influential in the contemporary scholarly literature. Furthermore, and even more importantly, Betti's critique precisely takes its provocation from "The Recovery of the Fundamental Hermeneutic Problem" in particular.

For this reason, this chapter in *Truth and Method* is the ideal place to look for resources for defending Gadamerian hermeneutics from its contemporary critics who are inspired by Betti. The purpose of this section of this chapter is to explore this background from *Truth and Method*'s reception in order to frame my reading of Gadamer's idea of application, which will respond to this critical horizon.

A distinguished and erudite historian and theorist of law, Betti draws upon the rich historical legacy of hermeneutics to formulate what he calls, as per the title of one of his treatises, "a general method of the humanities (*allgemeine Methode der Geisteswissenschaften*)." Of course, Gadamer subjects to criticism much of the Romantic inheritance from which Betti draws inspiration. One area where Gadamer develops his critique of Romanticism is legal hermeneutics, which he discusses in "The Recovery of the Fundamental Hermeneutic Problem." Here, Gadamer generously acknowledges Betti's important scholarship on this subject (*TM*, 334–35). Gadamer's account of legal hermeneutics, which I will say more about later, undoubtedly raised Betti's ire. Only a few years before the publication of *Truth and Method*, Betti had systematically laid out his own philosophy of interpretation, taking the technical practice of legal interpretation and other procedures in the humanities as his point of departure.[3] Based on this disagreement, Gadamer goes so far as to refer to Betti's discussion of Gadamer's hermeneutics as an "almost angry polemic" (*TM*, 276 n.172). Indeed, Betti places Gadamer's idea of application at the center of his critique. For Betti, acts of application "open the door to subjective arbitrariness and threaten to cover up or misrepresent historical truth and to distort it, even if only unconsciously."[4] When I allow a text to apply to my own situation, Betti suggests, I risk ignoring the text's independent meaning by imposing my own subjective experiences and ideas onto the object during my act of putative understanding. Applying the text to myself prevents me from grasping the real meaning of what I am trying to understand by allowing my subjective consciousness to filter and distort my hermeneutical engagement.

Undoubtedly, the conflation of my personal experience with the meaning of a text is a danger in any hermeneutical intervention. As Friedrich Schleiermacher warns, "One should not unconsciously or indirectly think possible for him [the author] what is only possible for us [the interpreters] . . . one should not attribute our material to his."[5] Betti argues that this risk of subjective distortion is particularly acute for Gadamer, however, because he "does not provide a reliable criterion for the correctness of understanding"; in other words, Gadamerian hermeneutics suffers from "the loss of objectivity."[6] By not formulating *normative criteria* for research in the humanities, Gadamer cannot prevent the subjective imposition of my experience onto a target of interpretation which his idea of application encourages. Betti concedes that Gadamerian application can be appropriate in restricted contexts, including in "the fields of practical co-existence" in which engagement with the past serves the present needs and purposes of a community.[7] But even in such cases, application should occur only after objective knowledge of history has already been established. If it is to be justified, historical knowledge demands the structure of rules. To guard against subjectivism, hermeneutics requires canons of interpretation that attend to the author's original intentions, the historical distance between the text and the present, and other factors. On Betti's view, such discursively formulated guidelines and parameters will permit the reliable discovery of meaning in a rigorously structured manner of which Gadamerian application is incapable.

Betti's normative critique seemed to have lost the day in debates in hermeneutics for several decades. As Donatella Di Cesare puts it, "In light of the history of effects, however, it must be admitted that today very little remains in the humanities of the search for a method, undertaken by . . . Betti, that could ascertain objective textual meaning."[8] In the confrontation between philosophical hermeneutics and deconstruction, for example, objectivity and discursive rules were not even on the table as ideals toward which interpretation should strive. Betti's normative critique, which focuses on norms for humanistic research, also largely overlooks political ideology, unlike critical theory, whose responses to Gadamer continue to prove influential. And yet, although this fact has not always been explicitly acknowledged, Betti's position has been revitalized in the recent scholarly reception of Gadamerian hermeneutics.[9]

Three contemporary philosophers deserve our consideration for following in Betti's wake and, hence, also responding to "The Recovery of the Fundamental Hermeneutic Problem." Like Betti, these critics advocate a revival of the methodological focus of nineteenth-century hermeneutics against Gadamer's phenomenological and ontological approach. By regaining normative criteria for humanistic research, they contend, hermeneutics can properly ground and legitimate research in the humanities and social sciences. These philosophers also echo Betti's discussion in another way. In their reformulation of hermeneutics, these contemporary scholars focus their critical attention on Gadamer's idea of application.

In her important study of Gadamer and German Idealism, Kristin Gjesdal argues that Gadamer's

> collapse of the distinction between understanding and application . . . makes it possible for the interpreter freely to project upon the text his or her own pre-reflected or reflected prejudices, thereby breathing, as it were, the interpreter's own meaning into the texts of a past long gone or a culture distant from his or her own.[10]

Although Gjesdal does not cite him, Betti developed more or less the same objection to Gadamerian application more than four decades earlier, as we have seen. Gjesdal's omission of Betti is even more surprising given that, exactly like Betti, her critique of Gadamer is motivated by the overarching conviction that Gadamer is unable to provide "an adequate notion of normative issues in hermeneutics."[11] For Gjesdal and Betti, Gadamerian application is excessively subjective, that is, it *exaggerates first-person features of understanding* and discourages objective knowledge structured by normative rules.

As Gjesdal goes on to argue, Gadamerian hermeneutics is unable to provide normative guidelines because of its assumption of a radical asymmetry between the interpreter and tradition:

> The proper hermeneutic experience allows the interpreter to encounter a totality that is stronger than him- or herself, a totality that he or she cannot reflectively master or objectify, but only deal with to the extent that he or she participates in and subjects him- or herself to the truth of tradition.[12]

Application, which merely relates an item of understanding to my condition and situation, is unable, according to Gjesdal, actively to guard me against the overwhelming power of tradition. Instead, tradition's horizon of significance threatens to swallow me whole, leaving me unable to establish a cognitive distance between me and the past that would permit objective knowledge of the original meaning at issue. Here we see another crucial feature of the normative critique—namely, its claim that Gadamerian application *overemphasizes third-person aspects of understanding*, such as tradition.

In his own recent critique of Gadamerian application, Rudolf A. Makkreel echoes Gjesdal's objection when he argues that, for Gadamer, "everything may dissolve into an overarching universal perspective."[13] According to Makkreel, Gadamer does not permit the interpreter to arrive at an individuated and distinctive response to an item of understanding. Instead, the Gadamerian interpreter fuses with the horizon of tradition in general. The past subsumes the present interpreter, prohibiting cognitively legitimate scholarly knowledge. For this reason, Gadamer's "approach leaves little room for the initiative of individual judging subjects."[14] To correct Gadamer's distorted focus on potent third-person factors such as historical tradition, Makkreel develops a dynamic and innovative theory of judgment inspired by Kant and Dilthey. This method would permit the interpreter to produce a normatively structured judgment about the item of her understanding without allowing formidable third-person factors like tradition to prevent her from arriving at her own objectively constructed response.

Another contemporary proponent of nineteenth-century hermeneutics also objects to Gadamerian application. In his vigorous defense of

Herder's philosophy of language and theory of interpretation, Michael N. Forster concurs with Gjesdal and anticipates Makkreel when he argues that "Gadamer conceives meaning as something that only arises in the interaction between texts and an indefinitely expanding and changing interpretive tradition."[15] In other words, Gadamer obscures the first person in interpretation and locates significance only in the fusion between past and present horizons. Gadamer's neglect of normative criteria allows the historical past unduly to influence interpretive validity. Furthermore, Forster makes a similar point to Betti and Gjesdal in his characterization of Gadamer's idea of application: "[Gadamer] holds that [interpretation] must and should incorporate an orientation to distinctive features of the interpreter's own outlook and to the distinctive application that he envisages making of the text in question."[16] Application illegitimately permits subjective considerations to contaminate interpretive research. For Forster, it would seem, Gadamer's notion of application involves a simultaneous and unstable orientation toward *both* the first person (that is, my subjective situation), *as well as* the third person (in other words, historical tradition which conditions meaning). By emphasizing both these registers, Forster's account of Gadamerian application synthesizes the insights of the normative critique as an overall theoretical movement.

The normative critique takes Gadamerian application to task for two reasons. First, these thinkers suggest that the application of the target of my understanding to my own situation allows subjective considerations to distort my reception of the text's meaning. This danger signals the excessively *first-person* character of application. Next, according to the normative critics, Gadamer does not provide any mechanism for distinguishing and protecting the interpreter from the overwhelming power of historical tradition, which threatens to subsume both the interpreter as well as the item of understanding into tradition's expansive horizon of meaning. That is, Gadamerian application overstates *third-person* features of understanding. These twin dangers, these philosophers argue, would be obviated by normative criteria for humanistic research that will provide rules against subjective impositions and, further, would preserve the independence of the interpreter by ensuring objective distance from the past. Interpretation, as practiced in this rigorously objectified fashion, would produce historical knowledge proper for academic disciplines.

These arguments by Betti, Gjesdal, Makkreel, and Forster are reminiscent of, and draw upon, those made by Herder, Schleiermacher, and Dilthey, the Romantic founders of modern hermeneutics whom Gadamer criticizes in his development of a phenomenology of understanding. The normative critics remain loyal to and deepen this Romantic heritage. Their advancement of debates in hermeneutics is impressive, and their commitment to the dignity of the humanities is laudable. But their account of Gadamer's idea of application, which is central to their departure from his hermeneutics, is incoherent.

2. GADAMER'S NORMATIVE ACCOUNT OF APPLICATION

My gambit is that the key to defending Gadamer from the normative critique is found in clarifying the relationship between the third and first persons in his theory of application. The dynamic interplay between these aspects will reveal a conception of normativity, which of course is precisely what these critics claim Gadamerian application lacks. To make headway on this issue, we can begin with the fact that in this chapter Gadamer employs the term "normative" when objecting to Betti's theory: "To distinguish between a normative function and a cognitive one is to separate what clearly belong together" (*TM*, 321). To explain this important criticism, I will now contrast two models of application, which will thereby reveal the relevant sense of normativity that Gadamer advocates.

The first approach is best illustrated by an admittedly crude and even vulgar formulation of what is (significantly) called "applied ethics." On this view, application takes place by means of the following procedure. One begins with an explicitly formulated rule that has been fixed in advance. In the context of ethical reasoning, such rules include inflexible principles like Kant's Categorical Imperative or Mill's Greatest Happiness Principle, which admit of discursive expression and provide guidelines and demands for action. In other words, such moral principles provide the source of normativity for subsequently resolving moral dilemmas or decisions. These rules get *applied* to an instance or example that falls under the rubric of situations or dilemmas that these principles are meant to govern. The specific content of the instance is insignificant on its own; what matters above all is that the rule genuinely applies to the case. When this fit obtains, the instance receives its normative shape from the rule that gets applied to it. We shall call this model *objectifying application*.

Objectifying application is familiar in moral philosophy today in examples like Peter Singer's animal ethics.[17] Singer's view proceeds from the assumption of the basic correctness of Mill's Greatest Happiness Principle, which suggests that the rightness of an action is assessed in terms of the extent to which it maximizes pleasure and minimizes pain for as many beings as possible, given the extent and reach of the action at issue. Singer's celebrated contribution to utilitarian ethics is to have grasped how this absolute principle applies to our treatment of sentient animals (that is, animals capable of suffering). Understood in this way, Singer's argument extends the applicability of the already formulated principle of Mill's moral theory. Singer shows that, if one accepts the Greatest Happiness Principle, then there are clear and unambiguous implications for how we should treat animals. The relationship between humans and animals, in other words, is an instance of utilitarian ethics to which the relevant moral rules apply. Notice that the first person is erased in this formulation.[18] Insofar as I am a member of human society who comes into contact with animals, I am bound by the results of Singer's argument. My personal stance toward these norms, such as whether I authentically identify with them, is irrelevant. The normative consequences of Singer's view follow only from the relationship between a binding norm that is formulated in advance and an instance of that rule which must, in turn, abide by the norm.

Singer's objectifying approach to ethical reasoning is significant for us not because of any conclusions of his animal ethics. Indeed, we are not challenging Singer's moral prescriptions, the arguments for which I have not fully reconstructed. Rather, the general structure of Singer's argument is an illustrative exemplification of a form of rationality that defines application in terms of a discursive norm applied to instances of the rule. Put another way, Singer provides a mechanistic decision procedure. Gadamer departs from and rejects this form of application: "Application does not mean first understanding a given universal in itself and then afterward applying it to a concrete case" (*TM*, 350). To understand how, let me explain why I call this model "objectifying." The notion of a norm that stands over and against instances of that rule is basically characteristic of the subject/object ontological scheme of the modern age: "It is clearly an incorrect description of this [hermeneutical] understanding to speak of an object [*Gegenstand*] existing in itself and of the subject's approach to it" (*TM*, 337–38/334). The rules of utilitarian ethics, returning to our example, belong to subjective consciousness. Outside that consciousness lies an objective reality consisting of situations to which the rules apply. Just as the Kantian categories inhere within transcendental subjectivity and constitute experience, so too do explicit rules originate in conscious subjects. In turn, these rules provide the normative structure that governs scenarios encountered throughout objective reality. Following from the subject/object dichotomy, objectifying application recurs throughout our scientific and technological culture and fits so naturally within our dominant form of intelligibility that we scarcely notice its eminent questionability.

Indeed, the ontology behind applied ethics in this mechanistic and procedural vein also provides the background for the hermeneutical theory of the normative critics. Betti is once again exemplary in this regard. As mentioned, Betti's philosophy of interpretation aims to provide, as per a section heading from his treatise, "Guidelines for interpretation: the canon of the hermeneutical autonomy of the object."[19] Such canons or guidelines provide discursively explicit rules in advance of interpretation. Specifically, these norms apply to what Betti does not hesitate to call hermeneutical *objects* whose historical distance from the present must be kept in mind. Proper methodological regulations, such as this awareness of historical distance, will ensure the necessary separation between the interpreter and the autonomous object of her attention in order to produce historical knowledge. This form of knowledge, further, will have no direct bearing on the interpreter herself. Since its "task is purely contemplative," Betti's theory pursues scholarly knowledge of the hermeneutical object in its historical context.[20]

Betti's hermeneutics, which remains indebted to the subject/object dichotomy, includes a distinction between normativity and cognition that Gadamer rejects. Consider here again Singer's ethics. On the one hand, there is a normative structure provided by the assumed principle; on the other, there is the application of the Greatest Happiness Principle to the case at issue, which will in turn produce a moral decision. Betti's hermeneutics mirrors this procedural structure that separates normativity from the interpretive act. According to Betti, canons provide the normative framework for interpretation in advance; the correct judgment about the hermeneutical object is subsequently arrived at by applying the rule to the object. Importantly, this process is entirely impersonal and contains no regard or role for the interpreting self. The identity and attitude of the agent or interpreter do not matter either to Singer or Betti; what matters is that the rules are properly applied. The objectification involved in a mechanistic decision procedure, whether in ethics or hermeneutics, erases the first person in the name of arriving at a correct judgment.

Gadamer challenges the assumptions behind this form of rationality by employing Aristotle as his guide:

> The alienation [*Überfremdung*] of the interpreter from the interpreted by the objectifying methods of modern science, characteristic of the hermeneutics and historiography of the nineteenth century, appeared as the consequence of a false objectification. My purpose in returning to the example of Aristotelian ethics is to help us realize and avoid this. (*TM*, 324/319)

Now we can grasp why moral approaches like Singer's provide an ideal foil for Gadamer's Aristotelian critique of Betti's hermeneutical method. There are many ways to illustrate why Gadamer insists upon "The Hermeneutic Relevance of Aristotle" (*TM*, 322).[21] But given our foregoing discussion, the following well-known passage from the *Nicomachean Ethics* provides a point of departure:

> But let it be agreed to in advance that every argument concerned with what ought to be done is bound to be stated in outline only and not precisely—just

as we said at the beginning as well, that the demands made of given arguments should accord with the subject matter in question. Matters of action and those pertaining to what is advantageous have nothing stationary about them, just as matters of health do not either.[22]

Here Aristotle sketches a form of application that differs from the objectifying version we have considered so far. That mechanistic and procedural model of application, we will recall, begins with a norm that remains external to the instance to which it is applied. The rule then imprints the normative shape upon the situation, producing a judgment or decision. By contrast, Aristotle claims that such inflexible or "stationary" norms are categorically inappropriate for human ethical life. To achieve the goal of flourishing (*eudaimonia*)—living well and doing well—no absolute or precise rule formulated in advance can genuinely guide us. As any spiritually hungry person who has yearned for enlightenment and inner peace can tell you, there is no single path to the good life. To achieve excellence at becoming who we are, we need sufficiently sensitive and dynamic norms, not precise but reductive ones. To that end, we actualize the best qualities within ourselves by cultivating our talents and passions in cooperation with social and communal forms of life as expressed in the virtues. We respond, in other words, to an inchoate and imprecisely expressed goal or "outline" that cannot be stated in advance of the process of flourishing. In turn, the accomplishing of that goal responds to the particularities of our unique position and situation.

On Gadamer's reading, Aristotle's ethics unfolds a dynamic interplay between the goal of flourishing and that goal's responsiveness to and effect upon the first-person character of the ethical agent: "What interests us here is precisely that [Aristotle] is concerned with reason and with knowing, not detached from a being that is becoming, but determined by and determinative of it" (*TM*, 322/317). As an ethically sensitive and thoughtful human being, I submit myself to fulfilling my function to live well. But the norm of flourishing does not provide me with specific rules for how, exactly, to actualize myself. Like vainly trying to find a single measure for physical health, such absolute rules for living well are not forthcoming. Instead, as I open myself to wanting to live and do well, flourishing gradually shows up for me as latent within my own special talents. I see what could become better within myself. When I try to become a better friend, for example, I work on and develop my proclivities toward sociality and intimacy. I am cultivating my distinctive tendencies in the direction of excellence. In doing so, I am genuinely responding to the call to flourish but without that norm objectively imposing itself on me and dictating any absolute recommendations. Indeed, it is my own particular way of being human that allows the norm of flourishing to take shape in my life in the way it does. But in pushing myself to flourish, I am also in turn responding to and allowing myself to be shaped by the goal of *eudaimonia*.

Departing from the procedural model of objectifying application, Gadamer's positive conception, which I shall refer to as *hermeneutical application*, follows this Aristotelian lead. Interpretation, Gadamer thinks, possesses the same structure as Aristotle's ethics. Gadamer explains in particularly clear terms the movement from the objectifying to hermeneutical forms of application in the following programmatic passage:

> We also determined that application is neither a subsequent nor merely an occasional part of the phenomenon of understanding, but codetermines it from the start and as a whole. Here too application did not consist in relating some pregiven universal to the particular situation. The interpreter dealing with tradition tries to apply it to himself. But this does not mean that the traditionary text is given for him as something universal, that he first understands it, and then afterward uses it for particular applications. Rather, the interpreter seeks no more than to understand this universal, this text—i.e., to understand what tradition says, what constitutes the text's meaning and significance. In order to understand that, he must not try to disregard himself and his concrete hermeneutical situation. He must relate the text to this situation if he wants to understand at all. (*TM*, 333/329)

Coming at the very end of the section on Aristotle, this passage clarifies how Aristotelian ethics prepares the roadmap outside of objectifying application. No rule formulated prior to interpretation can genuinely determine the hermeneutical process. Understanding, like living a good life, cannot be reduced to discursive principles. Betti's theory and its contemporary analogues locate normativity outside of or prior to interpretation, so to speak. In other words, rules formulated in advance provide the normative shape of the interpretive process. Crucially, however, the absence of expressed rules in Gadamer's account does not mean he thinks that understanding lacks normative criteria. Instead of having the prescriptive rule given previously by an objective and third-person authority, *hermeneutical application is normative from the very outset of interpretation*. The irreducible normativity of application includes two poles that govern the interpretive process, as this passage indicates. One pole of normativity comes from the first person, which means I apply the text to myself and my situation when I interpret. The second comes from the third person, referring now to interpretive faithfulness to the text's meaning and how that mode of significance has been shaped by tradition. These two poles shape and codetermine each other.

Gadamer explains both these aspects of normativity throughout "The Recovery of the Fundamental Hermeneutic Problem." Let us begin with the *first-person* valence of this form of normativity. Hermeneutical application means involving myself with the text and allowing it to speak directly to me. I must give the item of my understanding permission to show itself as relevant and, hence, applicable to my situation. Gadamer provides a particularly effective and even beautiful description of the first-person character of application through a phenomenological account of giving advice:

> Both the person asking for advice and the person giving it assume that they are bound together in friendship. Only friends can advise each other or, to put it another way, only a piece of advice that is meant in a friendly way has meaning for the person advised. Once again we discover that the person who is understanding does not know and judge as one who stands apart and unaffected but rather he thinks along with the other and from the perspective of a specific bond of belonging, as if he too were affected. (*TM*, 332–33)

Advice is positioned within a normative structure related to and shaped by my first-person stance toward the person who speaks to me. If I hear counsel from my boss, my father, or a stranger, I will receive and interpret their utterances differently than if I received them from my friend. The words of the friend are received *as advice* in this special sense when they are contextualized within a particular history and set of practices that establish that my friend has my best interests at heart and that I trust him. No discursive rule can exhaustively express this dynamic context of intimacy in advance of my interpretation of the utterances. As I interpret the words and allow them to address me as advice, my understanding is shaped by the norms of our relationship and the current context in which the words were spoken. Advice applies to me or counts for me as advice to the extent that I am engaged in friendship with the person offering advice. If I find out that my friend has betrayed my trust or that he offered me his advice with a sinister agenda, then I will now understand his words in an entirely new light. The success conditions for advice—namely, the norms structuring it as intelligible for me as advice—are related to my identity and situation.[23] Far from objective factors that have no intrinsic connection to who I am, these conditions matter profoundly to me.

Another paradigmatic example of hermeneutical application Gadamer discusses at length in this chapter is theological hermeneutics. According to Gadamer, theological hermeneutics includes an irreducibly first-person element: "The word of Scripture addresses us and . . . only the person who allows himself to be addressed—whether he believes or doubts—understands. Hence the primary thing is application" (*TM*, 341). Certainly, some forms of scholarly knowledge of biblical and ecclesiastical texts will require objectifying methods, such as acquaintance with facts about the text's historical context or philological techniques. But I can also understand the Passion of Christ, for example, as a deeply moving illustration of Christ's divine sacrifice on behalf of humanity and not merely as some historical artifact. My first-person attitude toward the text shapes how its significance shows up to me. I have to adopt a particular stance toward the Passion to receive its meaning in a distinctively spiritual fashion. Understanding the religious significance of the Passion of Christ requires giving the text permission to address me in an affective and moral register. The text will resonate with me most profoundly when I connect its message with, for example, my sense of nobility and loss. Any good teacher of the humanities knows how readers need to be open to hearing what a text has to say to genuinely understand it. The cultivation of this openness to the text's meaning cannot be stated in precise rules. Indeed, in the case of theological hermeneutics, I do not need to be a religious believer or adopt any creed to appreciate the beauty of the Passion of Christ. I only need to allow myself to be moved by the story as if it were the word of God. Then the text will address my situation in any number of surprising and unexpected ways, encouraging the text's meaning to show up for me in dynamic dialogue with my attitudes and experiences.

My first-person comportment toward a target of interpretation is a necessary condition of understanding for Gadamer. But it is not sufficient. *Third-person* normative factors contribute to hermeneutical application as well. Gadamer's account of third-person conditions for understanding, including language and tradition, count among his best-known philosophical contributions.[24] Indeed, the preeminence of such celebrated ideas as the fusion of horizons and historically effective consciousness in the reception of *Truth and Method* has perhaps occluded application because of the first-person elements the latter idea encompasses. But Gadamer's account of application also incorporates the statement of meaning that a text from the past makes that gets heard in the present. By the third-person pole of normativity in hermeneutical application, I mean all such claims to meaning as mediated in the present. Here again, we may illustrate Gadamer's insight with an example. In addition to virtue ethics and theological interpretation, legal hermeneutics provides Gadamer with a model for application:

> The judge who adapts the traditional law to the needs of the present is undoubtedly seeking to perform a practical task, but his interpretation of the law is by no means merely for that reason an arbitrary revision. Here again, to understand and to interpret means to discover and recognize a valid meaning. The judge seeks to be in accord with the "legal idea [*Rechtsgedanken*]" in mediating it with the present. (*TM*, 337/333)

Gadamer's discussion here anticipates politically charged debates in contemporary American jurisprudence concerning the possibility of accessing the original intentions behind the U.S. Constitution. But, regardless of such currently simmering controversies, his thesis should be clear enough. Certainly, when a judge interprets a law written in the past, he must be attuned to the present context in which the law is enacted, both in the case at hand and in society at large. Here we recall the first-person factors discussed earlier: The judge is attuned to his situation. But in addition, the judge is responsive to the "valid meaning" of the law itself. He cannot invent the law's meaning to suit his own purposes, such as his preferred political outcome or social arrangement. Rather, he must relate the real sense of the law, as it has been historically transmitted, to the present. Gadamer calls this process mediating between past and present.

Interpretation requires the sensitive disclosure of the law's statements of meaning. This thesis exemplifies Gadamer's attention to third-person conditions of hermeneutical application. The interpreter's first-person situation is not enough to understand. We also need to factor in the meaning from the past that we receive: "Is this not true of every text, that it must be understood *in terms of what it says*? Does this not mean that it always needs to be restated? And does not this restatement always take place through its being related to the present?" (*TM*, 337, emphasis mine/334). The meaning of an item of interpretation from the past is related to the present. But this mediation must always respond to and draw upon the actual content of the target of understanding. To be sure, these statements cannot be divorced from their historical effects. But the item of interpretation nevertheless stands over and against us and issues its claim to meaning.[25] We must hear these statements in their genuine challenge to us.

Gadamer goes so far as to call interpretation "not a form of domination but of service [*Dienstformen*]": "We have the ability to open ourselves to the superior claim the text makes and to respond to what it has to tell us" (*TM*, 322/316). Interpretation brings the meaning of, say, a law or theological text to bear upon the interpreter's situation. But this integration of the past into the present context must always responsively serve and subordinate itself to whatever meaning is being brought to life. Meaningful statements belonging to items of interpretation provide an essential input for the interpretive process. To serve or perform a duty on behalf of textual meaning may sound disturbingly reminiscent of religious fundamentalism or conservative traditionalism.[26] But this reaction would be misleading. Gadamer is clear that *third-person* textual meaning, while it demands our attention, always remains in dynamic dialogue with the interpreter's *first-person* present situation. Together these twin valences form a normative standard:

> We participate in the essential expressions of human experience that have been developed in our artistic, religious, and historical tradition—and not only in ours

but in all cultures; this possible participation is the *true criterion* for the wealth or the poverty of what we produce in our humanities and social sciences.[27]

My participation in the claims I encounter from the text means entering a normative space of meaning. The text's statements and my involvement each condition and jointly provide the measure of my hermeneutical engagement.

3. RESPONDING TO THE NORMATIVE CRITIQUE

The dynamic relation between the third and first persons in hermeneutical application encourages interpretation to respond to the needs of both the past and the present, both the textual meaning at issue and the interpreter's situation. This argument finds its inspiration in Aristotle's ethics. For Aristotle, the ethical agent responds to the inchoate goal of flourishing by making it concrete in his own life, through cultivating qualities of his character that enable him to achieve *eudaimonia*. The third-person goal of flourishing inspires the ethical person to live well in his first-person life situation. Similarly, for Gadamer, only when the first and third persons work together and complement one another can application happen: "The text, whether law or gospel, if it is to be understood properly—i.e., according to the claim it makes—must be understood at every moment, in every concrete situation, in a new and different way. Understanding here is always application" (*TM*, 319–20). The third-person claim the text makes, which interpretation must begin by acknowledging, gets conditioned by the first-person situation of the interpreter to which that meaning, in turn, is applied. Hermeneutical application involves an interplay between first and third persons: "*Understanding proves to be a happening*" (*TM*, 320/314). In other words, understanding happens somewhere around the fluid margin between my situation and the claim of the text.

This mutually conditioning process recalls the hermeneutic circle and the radically anti-foundationalist structure of Gadamerian hermeneutics in general.[28] More germane to our purposes, the first and third persons show themselves as poles belonging to one *axis of normativity* that exposes the inadequacy of the normative critique. First, the normative critics argue that Gadamer permits the interpreter to impose her own first-person, subjective experience onto the object of understanding, preventing genuine knowledge of the historical artifact. But Gadamer is clear that the third-person claim to meaning of the text provides one basis of interpretation. Hermeneutical application must faithfully acknowledge and engage with the meaningful statements of the text itself. Furthermore, according to the normative critics, Gadamer permits the third-person horizon of historical tradition to threaten the autonomy of the interpreter, as well as of the object of interpretation. Tradition will erase the first-person standpoint of the interpreter and the distinctive claim to meaning of the text. But hermeneutical application, in addition to engaging with the traditionally mediated claims of the text, resolutely incorporates the first person by making the text speak directly to my situation and context.

In short, the normative critics have not adequately contended with the integration of first and third persons in hermeneutical application: "The meaning to be understood is concretized and fully realized only in interpretation, but the interpretive activity considers itself wholly bound by the meaning of the text" (*TM*, 341). Normativity arrives from both directions, from the third-person meaning of the text and from the first-person standpoint of the interpreter. For Gadamer, these two poles of normativity constantly condition the interpretive process. By contrast, the normative critics operate with a conception of normativity that is expressible in discursive rules formulated prior to the interpretive act. These critics conclude that the absence of such rules in hermeneutical application signals Gadamer's neglect of normativity in general. But this criticism reveals the one-sidedness of these critics' conception of normativity. Although he is not referring to Gadamerian application specifically, Claude Romano articulates my objection to the hermeneutical school founded by Betti clearly and succinctly:

> Hermeneutics does not reject the existence of norms and criteria, but the existence of *exact* norms and criteria that it would suffice to apply mechanically without appealing to discernment, judgment, and experience on the part of the interpreter. The rules of interpretation are *rules of experience*.[29]

We shall now deepen our response to the normative critique by further clarifying and illustrating the conception of normativity in Gadamerian hermeneutics.

Here we may draw upon Steven Crowell's groundbreaking work on normativity in the phenomenological tradition. Crowell argues that phenomenology operates with a conception of norms that he construes as a measure or standard that cannot necessarily be formulated in concepts or rules. Rather, such norms express the imprecise but binding possibility of success or failure in some enterprise: "I do not merely do certain things but commit myself to the possibility of failure. That is, for *me* being a father is a normative status. Even if I cannot define what it means to be a father, I am oriented toward that meaning as toward a measure."[30] Crowell crystallizes the relation between third and first persons that I have referred to. On the one hand, it is my actions and being that are at issue for me. I want to succeed as a father in my life. On the other, my success or failure as a father takes place against the backdrop of a standard of what it means to be a good father generally. My first-person attempt at being a father is judged *in light of* a third-person measure: "To act in light of norms, however, is to measure *myself* against a standard of success or failure, to grasp *myself* in terms of the very idea of better and worse."[31] For Crowell, such norms are not invented or determined by me, since otherwise they would have no genuine grip on me. But these norms only matter to me insofar as they show up in and condition my attempt at being a father. I take on and make a standard of my own and judge myself by that norm. I commit myself to a measure, and only in light of that norm can I even attempt to live up to that standard. I take responsibility for these norms by making them own.

The model of phenomenological normativity outlined by Crowell can further illuminate my account of hermeneutical application. Like Crowell, Gadamer thinks of norms as impossible to express definitively and finally: "As with every norm, one can always come only relatively close to it."[32] And yet such norms provide a genuinely binding measure of success or failure:

> All this [our linguistic acts] should be "correct." We must listen exactly to the word we use in such circumstances. It does not mean correspondence to a prescribed rule, but rather its opposite, the correct application of rules. What we mean everywhere by "correct" goes beyond the pregiven and prescribed, and points in this direction: to behave correctly; to make the correct judgment; to find the correct word; to give the correct advice; to understand what a correct prayer is; to read a text correctly; to carry on a correct conversation.[33]

Recall that the normative critics locate normativity in rules formulated outside of or prior to interpretation. Gadamer rejects this conception, not only because binding norms cannot be fully expressed. Furthermore, as he argues here in this passage from 1992, linguistic acts are normative *from the very beginning* and do not have normative structures imposed on them only subsequently. That is, using language entails entering a space of meaning that is already saturated with normative constraints. As soon as I use words, I subject myself to standards of success or failure for speaking as is "normally" done in the context of advice, conversation, flirtation, gossip, judgment, lecture, prayer, protest, recitation, song, or whatever linguistic situation into which I enter. In speaking, I am not beholden to arbitrary standards that are external to my existence. Rather, I judge myself by a measure with which I identify because this linguistic activity matters to me in my life. In trying to speak well, I hold myself to the standard of how one should or is supposed to speak. I employ language in light of a norm for which I take responsibility by entering into the space governed by that standard.

Hermeneutical application from *Truth and Method* mirrors this normative structure that Gadamer explicates in the later essay quoted above. In interpretation, I take a third-person measure of success or failure and make it my own. If my thesis is correct, then it becomes impossible to accept the central contention of the normative critique, which Gjesdal summarizes: "Gadamer's hermeneutics is not . . . an attempt to carve out a notion of normativity."[34] I will now crystallize the normativity of hermeneutical application with a phenomenological example.

When I read *The Education of Henry Adams*, I receive the text's transmissions from the past as they have been mediated by tradition.[35] The book's reputation as an august landmark in American letters suggests an academic dryness that discourages me from entering Adams's world. Furthermore, I am not initially compelled by the book's seemingly Victorian diction, including Adams's choice to write about himself in the third person. But when I become a reader, I am initiated into conditions of success or failure. As soon as I begin interpreting Adams, I submit myself to the possibility of getting his text right or wrong. I persist, then, in trying to read thoughtfully and charitably because I want to get the text right. I identify with the third-person standard of a successful interpretation of Adams insofar as I strive toward that success in my interpretive engagement with Adams's text.

Committing myself to understanding the text adequately, I grapple with what Adams means by "education." I recognize that my disclosure of Adams's meaning by this term must be responsive to the particularities and subtleties of his view as he expresses it. My reading, to be successful, requires an exegetically sufficient engagement with his textual statements. While his positive definition is not yet obvious to me, I conclude that Adams's account of education cannot refer to formal schooling or higher learning, both of which he criticizes explicitly. Here I discover a horizon for interpretive failure of Adams's meaning.

In confronting my continued puzzlement about how to interpret Adams's definition of education, I begin to relate to Adams's descriptions of feeling out of step with his time and struggling to understand his experience. Adams's experience of cultural alienation echoes mine. When I feel moved by Adams's expressions, I begin to care even more deeply about understanding his meaning. This resonance becomes the window through which I glimpse the vista of Adams's account in *The Education*. I have taken Adams's point of view and allowed it to speak directly to my situation and outlook. I am stepping into Adams's world picture. This relation encourages me to understand Adams as expressing the need to find one's orientation in a rapidly changing society in which one does not feel at home. I discover evidence for this interpretation in Adams's depictions of political cynicism, civilizational decline, and scientific and technological development against the backdrop of his advocacy for self-cultivation amid this alienating cultural landscape. I find Adams promoting the obligation to learn from the surprises and drama of one's experience even within a bewildering modernity.

My disclosure of Adams's view of genuine education is grounded in the text. I could only have arrived at this interpretation through my careful engagement with moments throughout his book. But I have located these features of his text by allowing them to show up for me and resonate with my experience. There can be no question of my inventing this reading or imposing it onto the text. I am neither irresponsibly creating an anachronistic impression nor am I allowing the text to recede into the expanding horizon of the tradition of its reception. Rather, I am faithfully responding to the text's claims and relating them to my experience and viewpoint. Through this engagement, the text's meaning arrives before and speaks to me, pointing in the direction of a successful interpretation and away from a failure to grasp its real content.

For Gadamer, my hermeneutical engagement with Adams is judged by the norm of *my participation in the text's claim to meaning*. As soon as I begin any interpretive process, I enter a space of meaning that draws its normative force from two directions. This normative framework receives its measure from the text's third-person statements and from my first-person involvement with the text. My reading is accountable to and balanced against both these poles, which open up a framework in which my interpretive activity takes shape and counts as better or worse as an engagement with Adams's text. I allow myself to feel moved by Adams's writing. This entry point encourages me to adopt a first-person comportment toward the text of reading it responsibly and thoroughly, which in turn means that I have taken on for myself the third-person norm of getting the text right. The first and third persons co-constitute my interpretation. Understood in this way, Gadamer's account of hermeneutical application includes a robust normative standard.

NOTES

1. Hans-Georg Gadamer, *Truth and Method*, 2nd ed., trans. Joel Weinsheimer and Donald G. Marshall (New York: Bloomsbury Publishing, 2013), 318. Hereafter cited in text as *TM*. Where the German is cited or the translation has been altered, the page number of the original is indicated after the slash. The latter refer to Hans-Georg Gadamer, *Wahrheit und Methode*, Gesammelte Werke I (Tübingen: Mohr Siebeck, 1990).

2. See David Liakos and Theodore George, "Hermeneutics in Post-War Continental European Philosophy," in *The Cambridge History of Philosophy, 1945–2015*, ed. Kelly Becker and Iain Thomson (Cambridge: Cambridge University Press, 2019), especially 408–12.

3. See Jean Grondin, *Introduction to Philosophical Hermeneutics*, trans. Joel Weinsheimer (New Haven: Yale University Press, 1994), 125–29.

4. Emilio Betti, "Hermeneutics as the General Methodology of the *Geisteswissenschaften*," trans. Josef Bleicher, in *Contemporary Hermeneutics:*

Hermeneutics as Method, Philosophy and Critique, ed. Josef Bleicher (London: Routledge, 1980), 83.

5. Friedrich Schleiermacher, *Hermeneutics and Criticism and Other Writings*, trans. and ed. Andrew Bowie (Cambridge: Cambridge University Press, 1998), 263.

6. Betti, "Hermeneutics as the General Methodology of the *Geisteswissenschaften*," 78.

7. Betti, 83. See also Grondin, *Introduction to Philosophical Hermeneutics*, 127.

8. Donatella Di Cesare, *Gadamer: A Philosophical Portrait*, trans. Niall Keane (Bloomington: Indiana University Press, 2013), 190. To focus my argument, I have omitted Di Cesare's reference here to E.D. Hirsch, Jr., who also followed in Betti's footsteps in the Anglophone context.

9. The frame of reference of the scholars I am about to discuss is avowedly shaped by Dilthey, Herder, and Schleiermacher. The importance of Betti, although he also belatedly comes from the Romantic milieu, is rarely discussed. I also provide a critical treatment of methodological hermeneutics in David Liakos, "Attitude Isn't Everything: Hermeneutics as an Unfinished Project," *Analecta Hermeneutica* XIII (2021). In the present chapter, I have been influenced by the framing of the normative critique in Theodore George, "Hermeneutics," in *The Stanford Encyclopedia of Philosophy*, ed. Edward N. Zalta (2020), https://plato.stanford.edu/archives/win2020/entries/hermeneutics.

10. Kristin Gjesdal, *Gadamer and the Legacy of German Idealism* (Cambridge: Cambridge University Press, 2009), 197.

11. Gjesdal, 3.

12. Gjesdal, 181.

13. Rudolf A. Makkreel, *Orientation and Judgment in Hermeneutics* (Chicago: University of Chicago Press, 2015), 41.

14. Makkreel, 51.

15. Michael N. Forster, *German Philosophy of Language: From Schlegel to Hegel and Beyond* (Oxford: Oxford University Press, 2011), 310.

16. Forster, 310.

17. See Peter Singer, *Animal Liberation* (New York: HarperCollins, 2009), 1–24. This is the well-known chapter "All Animals Are Equal."

18. Bernard Williams makes this point about the role of the first person in his wide-ranging critique of modern moral philosophy, especially regarding Kant. See Williams, *Ethics and the Limits of Philosophy* (Cambridge, MA: Harvard University Press, 1985), 66–70.

19. Betti, "Hermeneutics as the General Methodology of the *Geisteswissenschaften*," 58.

20. Betti, 83.

21. See also Carlo DaVia, "The Role of Aristotle in Gadamer's Work," in *The Gadamerian Mind*, ed. Theodore George and Gert-Jan van der Heiden (London: Routledge, 2022).

22. Aristotle, *Nicomachean Ethics*, trans. Robert C. Bartlett and Susan D. Collins (Chicago: University of Chicago Press, 2011), 28, 1104a1–5.

23. Linda Martín Alcoff argues that Gadamer develops "an account of knowledge that links experience and identity as constitutive features for understanding without making them all-determining." Alcoff, *Visible Identities: Race, Gender, and the Self* (Oxford: Oxford University Press, 2006), 96. I agree with this crucial insight concerning Gadamer's contribution to a theory of identity, but Alcoff does not connect this idea to application, which for me is the main site of Gadamer's account of the first person.

24. Sympathetic commentators have appealed to third-person conditions as sources of normativity in Gadamer's thinking. See Morten S. Thaning, *The Problem of Objectivity in Gadamer's Hermeneutics in Light of McDowell's Empiricism* (Cham: Springer, 2015), 160, who appeals to language; and Brice Wachterhauser, "Getting It Right: Relativism, Realism, and Truth," in *The Cambridge Companion to Gadamer*, ed. Robert J. Dostal (Cambridge: Cambridge University Press, 2002), 58, who refers to tradition. While this scholarship is important, these accounts neglect the first person, and hence application, entirely.

25. I have adopted this conception of a hermeneutical object standing over and against the interpreter from Günter Figal, *Objectivity: The Hermeneutical and Philosophy*, trans. Theodore George (Albany: SUNY Press, 2010), 1–4.

26. I distinguish Gadamer from the politics of conservative traditionalism in David Liakos, "Hermeneutics and the Conservatism of Listening," *Cosmos and History* 16, no. 2 (2020): 495–519.

27. Hans-Georg Gadamer, *Gadamer in Conversation: Reflections and Commentary*, ed. and trans. Richard E. Palmer (New Haven: Yale University Press, 2001), 40–41, emphasis mine.

28. See Jeff Malpas, "Placing Understanding/Understanding Place," *Sophia* 56, no. 3 (2017): 379–91, here 381.

29. Claude Romano, *At the Heart of Reason*, trans. Michael B. Smith and Claude Romano (Evanston: Northwestern University Press, 2015), 500.

30. Steven Crowell, *Normativity and Phenomenology in Husserl and Heidegger* (Cambridge: Cambridge University Press, 2013), 215.

31. Crowell, 187.

32. Hans-Georg Gadamer, "The Artwork in Word and Image: 'So True, So Full of Being!,'" in *The Gadamer Reader: A Bouquet of the Later Writings*, trans. and ed. Richard E. Palmer (Evanston: Northwestern University Press, 2007), 217.

33. Hans-Georg Gadamer, "Towards a Phenomenology of Ritual and Language," trans. Lawrence K. Schmidt and Monika Reuss, in *Language and Linguisticality in Gadamer's Hermeneutics*, ed. Lawrence K. Schmidt (Lanham: Lexington Books, 2000), 50. I was pointed to this important passage by Greg Lynch, "Does Conversation Need Shared Language? Davidson and Gadamer on Communicative Understanding," *The Southern Journal of Philosophy* 52, no. 3 (2014): 359–81, here 372.

34. Gjesdal, *Gadamer and the Legacy of German Idealism*, 2.

35. Henry Adams, *The Education of Henry Adams* (Boston: Mariner Books, 2000).

Chapter 10

TM II.2.3

The Finitude of Reflection

Greg Lynch

Gadamer concludes part II of *Truth and Method* with an analysis of one of the text's central concepts: historically effected consciousness (*wirkungsgeschichtliche Bewußtsein*). This is not the first appearance this concept makes in the text; Gadamer introduces it near the end of section II.2.1, but there he does not spell it out in any significant detail. Instead, Gadamer devotes the first two sections of II.2 to exploring the *implications* of historically effected consciousness for the human sciences—that is to say, exploring the way that historically effected consciousness "operates" in the enterprise of understanding what history hands down to us.[1] These implications include what is probably the most well-known thesis of Gadamer's work: that the understanding of tradition takes the form of a "fusion of horizons" that occurs through the "application" of its meaning to one's own historical situation. In the final section of the chapter—the section that I will try to unpack here—Gadamer takes a step back and attempts to justify the underlying conception of consciousness[2] on which this important thesis rests.

Two points from Gadamer's earlier discussion should be noted before we turn to the section at hand. The first is that, as Gadamer acknowledges earlier in the text, the term *historically effected consciousness* has a double sense (*TM*, xxxi). At one level, it refers to a type of explicit self-awareness that a person might, but does not necessarily, achieve. To have historically effected consciousness in this sense is to *recognize* the fact that one's understanding is radically shaped by history and to structure one's attitudes and expectations accordingly. At a more fundamental level, however, the term refers to a universal feature of understanding. All understanding, on Gadamer's account, is shaped by history, whether we acknowledge its influence or not. In this sense, *historically effected consciousness* refers not a possible achievement of understanding but to a basic structure of it, an "element in the act of understanding itself" (*TM*, 312). This second, more fundamental, sense is the one on which Gadamer's analysis of historically effected consciousness in section three will primarily (though not exclusively) focus.

Second, when Gadamer claims that all consciousness is historically effected, his claim is not simply that it is always shaped by the historical situation in which we find ourselves but that this shaping necessarily exceeds what we can bring to explicit awareness. Though we may reflect on our own historical situatedness (as we will do if we achieve historically effected consciousness in the first of the two senses above) this reflection "can never be complete" (*TM*, 313). The influence of history always occurs, at least to some extent, behind our backs. Importantly, Gadamer contends that this incompleteness is not a "deficiency" and so does not entail the skeptical conclusion that human beings are incapable of genuine knowledge (*TM*, 313). It does entail, however, that the Enlightenment dream of perfect self-possession—of an understanding that would, as Kant puts it, grow out of its "self-incurred immaturity" and rely only on principles whose validity it recognizes for itself—is illusory.[3]

Gadamer's task in the section at hand is to make good on this claim about finitude. Doing so, as we will see, brings him face to face with infinity's greatest champion: Hegel. Hegel offers reasons for thinking that consciousness simply cannot be "historically effected" in the way Gadamer claims, and these reasons, as Gadamer himself insists, cannot easily be brushed aside. To get beyond Hegel, Gadamer contends, requires no less than re-thinking the nature of experience itself. We must recognize that experience does not (as nearly all of Western philosophy has supposed) follow a progressive logic where each new experience constitutes a further step along the road to absolute knowledge. Instead, it follows a "logic of question and answer" in which we perpetually find ourselves back at the beginning.

1. THE HEGELIAN CHALLENGE

The title that Gadamer gives to the first subsection of his analysis, "The Limitations of Reflective Philosophy," is a bit of a misnomer. Though Gadamer will, by the end of the section, identify what he takes to be mistaken about reflective philosophy, he does not do that here in the first subsection. On the contrary, the central claim of the first subsection is that reflective philosophy is *not* limited in the ways it is often thought to be and thus presents a genuine challenge to philosophers who, like Gadamer, wish to prioritize finitude.

Gadamer describes that challenge as follows:

> But what sort of consciousness is [historically effected consciousness]? That is the decisive problem. However much we emphasize that historically effected consciousness itself belongs to the effect, what is essential to it as consciousness is that it can rise above that of which it is conscious. The structure of reflexivity is fundamentally given with all consciousness. Thus this must also be the case for historically effected consciousness.
>
> We might also express it thus: when we speak of historically effected consciousness, are we not confined within the immanent laws of reflection, which destroy any immediate effect? Are we not forced to admit that *Hegel* was right and regard the basis of hermeneutics as the *absolute mediation of history and truth*? (*TM*, 350)

This passage is highly compressed and presupposes a good deal of familiarity with German idealism. Since it presents the basic problem to which the rest of the section is a response, it will behoove us to take a moment to spell out some of the background needed to make sense of it.

To begin, what does it mean to say that consciousness is fundamentally *reflexive*? Part of the answer, certainly, is the familiar idea that there can be no awareness without self-awareness. I cannot be in a conscious state (say, the state of perceiving a tree) without also, in some sense, being aware of the fact that I am in that state. The sense of *reflection* that Gadamer is using here, however, includes more than just that. To reflect on a state is not merely to be aware of it, but also to recognize the *conditions* on which it depends. To reflect on a decision, for example, is not merely to take note of the fact *that* I have decided something but also to recognize the reasons *why* I decided as I did. In this sense, reflection involves "ris[ing] above" that of which one is conscious (*TM*, 350). The claim at hand is that consciousness necessarily includes at least the possibility of such rising above. Let's call this claim the *reflection thesis*.

As Robert Pippin observes, for the line of thought that Gadamer calls "reflective philosophy" (a line that begins with Kant and stretches through Fichte and Schelling to Hegel), the reflection thesis is motivated by the need to explain how our conscious states and activities can *belong* to us in the way that they do.[4] The basic underlying idea here is analogous to—indeed, it is just a more general form of—a concern that is familiar from philosophical discussions of free will. It would seem that if my actions were the mere products of external forces (like the laws of nature or inexorable patterns of socialization), then they would not really be *my* actions at all. I would not be the doer of such actions; I would at best be the vehicle through which someone or something else does them. Thus, for an action to be *attributable* to me (in the way it must be if I am to be responsible for it), it must have originated in me. I must, in some sense, be the *author* of the action. What is true of actions is also true of consciousness. For my beliefs, decisions, intentions, perceptions, hopes, fears, and so on, to be truly *my own*, the conditions that produce them must be my own as well. One of the key insights of German idealism is that at least part of what it means for a condition to be my own is that it is reflectively available to me. If we grant this plausible idea, then the reflection thesis follows.

As Gadamer notes in the second paragraph above, the reflection thesis introduces—or at least *appears* to introduce—certain "immanent laws" into our thinking about consciousness, laws that would ultimately "destroy any immediate effect" that external factors might be thought to have on consciousness. "Immediate effect" here simply means an effect that reflection has not "risen above," an influence that has shaped consciousness without its knowledge or consent. What the reflection thesis appears to "destroy" is not the idea that conscious is subject to such effects (the thesis requires only that the conditions of consciousness be available to reflection, not that they be actually reflected upon), but rather the idea that consciousness is *necessarily* subject to them. The reflection thesis, in other words, seems to entail that it is possible, at least in principle, for consciousness to leave behind all alien influences and become fully self-possessed. The claim that such self-possession—what Kant calls "autonomy" and Hegel "absolute knowing"—is possible is what defines reflective philosophy in Gadamer's sense of that term.

It should be clear from this why reflective philosophy poses a challenge to Gadamer's notion of historically effected consciousness. When Gadamer says that consciousness is historically effected, he is making precisely the claim that reflective philosophy denies. He is saying that consciousness *is* necessarily subject to immediate effects of history, that complete self-possession is impossible. To state the point differently, if reflective philosophy is right, then the very idea of historically effected consciousness is self-contradictory. Insofar as consciousness is effected (by history or anything else), it cannot be consciousness, and vice-versa.

If we narrow our focus to the specifically Hegelian form of reflective philosophy, then this challenge becomes even more pointed and more immediately relevant to Gadamer's project in part II of *Truth and Method*. Like Gadamer (and unlike Kant), Hegel thinks that the conditions that make consciousness what it is are not abstract rational principles but rather concrete norms that hold sway in particular historical communities, and those norms, Hegel famously holds, are themselves the products of a long historical dialectic. In short, on Hegel's view, *all of history* is a condition of consciousness. In Hegel's version of reflective philosophy, therefore, the claim that complete self-possession is possible entails that a complete possession of history is possible as well. For Hegel, this "absolute mediation of history and truth" is the "basis of hermeneutics," in the sense that it defines what genuine knowledge of history and tradition would amount to. Clearly, the essentially finite type of understanding that Gadamer champions falls well short of this standard. Thus from a Hegelian perspective, what Gadamer offers is not a legitimation of the human sciences but, on the contrary, an admission that no real knowledge can be achieved in these disciplines.

To vindicate the idea of historically effected consciousness, Gadamer must identify where reflective philosophy goes awry, and this is his task in the section at hand. Because the reflective challenge occurs at two different levels—as a general challenge to the idea of historically effected consciousness itself and as a more specific challenge to the conception of the human sciences that stems from it—Gadamer's response occurs at two levels as well. The text toggles back and forth between discussions of basic phenomenological structures (like experience and openness) and of activities specific to the human sciences (like interpreting texts and historical events). This can make the thread of his argument somewhat difficult to follow. What's worse, Gadamer offers no signposts to help us see how the points he makes in the second and third subsections serve to answer the challenge identified in the first. One of my main aims here will be to make the overall structure of this argument more explicit. Doing so, I hope, will give a sense of how Gadamer takes the different topics he discusses in this section to hang together.

There are many ways that one might go about challenging the basic claim of reflective philosophy, three of which are relevant here.

First, the most direct way to break with reflective philosophy would be simply to deny its starting point in the reflection thesis. Obviously, if that thesis is not true, then reflective philosophy poses no real challenge to hermeneutics. Pippin suggests that Gadamer's own response runs more or less along these lines. He explains,

> [For Hegel] one cannot ever be said simply to be "in" a state of consciousness without also at the same time *not* being wholly "in" such a state, not being wholly absorbed in the intended object, except as an occasionally contingent and always recoverable self-forgetting ... One cannot likewise just be "carrying on," at some level unavailable to reflective consciousness, the practices and rules of a community life. In Hegel's account, there is no such level unavailable to reflective life or the activity could not count as an activity belonging to us, and *therein lies the deepest disagreement between Gadamer and Hegel*.[5]

On Pippin's reading, Gadamer simply rejects the reflection thesis, presumably either because he denies that attributability requires reflexivity or because he denies that consciousness must be attributable in the first place.

This allows Pippin's Gadamer to affirm that consciousness is ultimately rooted in a "level" of reality that reflection cannot illuminate.

However, while this interpretation is certainly understandable, there are reasons to suspect that it is not quite right. Chief among these is the fact that for Gadamer the paradigm case of historically effected consciousness is *dialogue*, and dialogue would be impossible for a consciousness like the one Pippin describes. Dialogue consists precisely in the (non-dogmatic) exchange of reasons, but obviously reasons can be offered only where one has reflective access to them. As Pippin himself observes, without reflection, the only 'reasons' one could ultimately offer for one's views would be "this is traditional" or "this is the way we go on"—which is to say, one could not really offer reasons at all.[6] Furthermore, as Gadamer conceives of it, the most important insights we gain from dialogue occur when we are "pulled up short" by what the other says and thereby prompted to "foreground" and critically examine our prejudices (*TM*, 280, 316), and the consciousness Pippin describes would be incapable of such insights. If our prejudices (or at least our most fundamental ones) resided at a level that reflection cannot reach, then they would be immune to such foregrounding. In short, if Gadamer really did hold the view of consciousness that Pippin attributes to him, he would be forced to admit that human beings are simply incapable of genuine dialogue.

A second way of responding to reflective philosophy would be to try to topple it, as it were, from the outside by identifying a feature of our experience for which it cannot account. This, Gadamer notes, is the primary strategy that Hegel's nineteenth-century critics employed. Thinkers like Kierkegaard, Feuerbach, Marx, and others opposed Hegel by pointing to a residue of immediacy—be it that of "bodily nature, or the Thou making claims on us, or the impenetrable factualness of historical accident, or the reality of the relations of production" (*TM*, 353)—that, supposedly, reflection must always leave behind. These phenomena, they argued, exceed what can be captured by the rules in terms of which we make conceptual sense of them and so reveal that reflection is not all-encompassing. Influential as these critiques were and continue to be, however, Gadamer does not think they ultimately hit home. "Hegel's critics," Gadamer contends, "never really succeeded in breaking [reflection's] magic spell" (*TM*, 351). The basic problem is that, without challenging the account of reflection on which it rests, arguments against absolute knowledge can have "no starting point" (*TM*, 352). Any supposed residue of immediacy would, by definition, evade expression in concepts. But, for just that reason, it could never figure in a premise of an argument, including an argument against absolute reflection. Thus objections of this sort are inevitably "self-refuting" (*TM*, 352).

Gadamer does note that this kind of self-refutation argument is not *always* legitimate, even when it is formally unimpeachable. It is clear, he contends, that some arguments of this type are mere sophistry. Their lack of real substance is evidenced by the fact that they "rebound against the arguer" (*TM*, 353). They do not convince us of their conclusions, rather they leave us with a sense that the argument itself, perhaps in some way that is not fully clear to us, is suspect. (This, Gadamer claims, is what happened with the Neo-Kantian arguments against relativism.) Yet, important as this point is, Gadamer admits that it cannot help to answer the Hegelian challenge. Hegel is "fundamentally beyond the argumentative formalism that we, like Plato, call 'sophistical'" (*TM*, 354). Unlike those of the Neo-Kantians, Hegel's self-refutation arguments are based on more than just the formal logical properties of propositions. They are rooted in serious thinking about how an activity like making an argument is possible in the first place.

A third type of response would be to go to the heart of Hegel's account by challenging the conception of reflection on which it is based. Specifically, one could try to demonstrate that reflection, while indeed essential to consciousness, is not governed by the supposed "immanent laws" that lead to infinity. This would open the possibility that reflection can be *genuine* without being *absolute* and thereby defuse the challenge that reflective philosophy poses. This, I submit, is the strategy Gadamer adopts. He unfolds it gradually over the following two subsections, to which we will turn our attention momentarily. Before we do, however, it will be helpful to know where we are headed, so let me put my cards on the table. Contra Pippin's reading, I want to suggest that Gadamer *agrees* with the reflective philosophers that consciousness can have no conditions that are unavailable in principle to reflection.[7] Though Gadamer certainly affirms that reflection is limited, he does not conceive of this limit as a fixed boundary that separates those conditions reflection necessarily can access from those it necessarily cannot. There is no "level" of conditions that reflection cannot, in principle, reach. Instead, the finitude of reflection stems from the fact that consciousness cannot reflect on all of its conditions *at once*. This is so, not because we lack the necessary circumspection or brain power, but because the presence of any one condition to reflective awareness is possible only *on the basis of* the absence of others. The essential problem with reflective philosophy, in short, is that it misunderstands the nature of presence, and so, *a fortiori*, the nature of the presence that is achieved in reflection.

2. THE END OF EXPERIENCE

One of Hegel's many important insights, in Gadamer's view, is that reflection is not a mere looking within, but "an *experience* that experiences reality and is itself real" (*TM*, 355). Because reflection always takes the form of experience, an analysis of the nature of experience can help us better understand the nature of reflection and perhaps also point a way beyond the challenge that reflective philosophy presents. This is Gadamer's task in the second subsection, which he titles "The Concept of Experience and the Essence of Hermeneutic Experience."

Gadamer prefaces his account with a conceptual history that traces how the concept of experience has been taken up by earlier thinkers.[8] Specifically, what Gadamer is interested in here is how the tradition has conceived of the relationship between experience and *knowledge*.[9] He identifies two "elements" of this relationship that have been particularly important in the history of Western philosophy: how the accumulation of experience provides us with knowledge of universals, and how unexpected experiences negate our mistaken ideas.

The first element of experiential knowledge is so familiar to us that it barely needs to be stated. In the course of our experience, we notice certain regularities, and if they recur frequently without being contradicted, they justify us in judging that a universal law obtains. In this way, experience provides the basis for empirical science. Gadamer has no interest in disputing this obvious fact about the nature of experience, but he argues that the traditional accounts of it are problematically "one-sided" (*TM*, 358). They have tended to focus *exclusively* on scientific knowledge and so have overlooked other forms of insight that experience can yield. Gadamer illustrates this by examining the accounts of experience offered by Edmund Husserl, Francis Bacon, and Aristotle. Each of these thinkers, he argues, identifies features of experience that reveal it to be more than just a prelude to science, but in each case this insight is either downplayed or misconstrued. The moral to be drawn, as Gadamer puts it, is that "the main deficiency in the theory of experience hitherto . . . is that it is entirely oriented toward science and hence takes no account of the inner historicity of experience" (*TM*, 355).

Beside the fact that these accounts overlook the non-scientific forms of knowledge that experience generates, Gadamer argues that they also gloss over an essential dimension of the process by which it generates knowledge. Except in rare cases, experience does not lead to knowledge via a straight path but through a series of switchbacks in which "what was regarded as typical is shown not to be so" (*TM*, 361). This negative moment, in which "false generalizations are . . . refuted by experience," marks a second element of experiential knowledge, one that, in Gadamer's view, is more fundamental than the first. Negative experience constitutes "'experience' in the genuine sense" because it is in these cases that experience yields its most significant and far-reaching insights. Hegel's key contribution to the theory of experience is to bring this negative element to the forefront. His analysis highlights two distinctive features of negative experiences: their *unrepeatability* and their *reflexivity*.

Unlike positive experiences, which yield the knowledge they do precisely through their repetition, negative experiences are essentially unrepeatable. Just as you can never have a second first kiss, "the same thing cannot again become a new experience for us" (*TM*, 362). The reason this is the case, Gadamer points out, is that negative experience *changes us*. The person who experiences a phenomenon the second time is, in an important sense, different from the person who first encountered it. In the second case, we are prepared for it, and this preparation fundamentally changes the significance the experience has for us.

Most importantly for Gadamer's overarching purpose in this section, Hegel also highlights the fact that negative experiences are reflexive. What comes to light in a negative experience is not simply the fact that my prior consciousness (my belief or expectation) failed to conform to its object but that there was something amiss *within* my prior consciousness itself. Experience alerts me to the fact that there is something I had hitherto failed to think through, some possibility I failed to consider. In this way, experience does not just reveal something about the external world, but, more fundamentally, something about myself. Through experience I acquire a fuller, more explicit understanding of my own thinking, and it is in this way that negative experience changes me. That is why Hegel insists that experience should not be conceived as an episode in which consciousness is reversed *by* an object. Rather, in experience consciousness reverses *itself*, and this reversal changes both consciousness and its object (*TM*, 362–63).

Despite these crucial insights, however, Gadamer notes that Hegel's account of experience remains no less wedded to the ideal of scientific knowledge than those of Husserl, Bacon, and Aristotle.

> For Hegel, it is necessary, of course, that conscious experience should lead to a self-knowledge that no longer has anything other than or alien to itself. For him the consummation of experience is "science," the certainty of itself in knowledge. (*TM*, 363)

As we see most clearly in the *Phenomenology*, for Hegel, experience is its own gravedigger. Each experience moves us one step closer to a state of absolute knowledge, at which point reversals of consciousness will no longer be possible.

Gadamer's critique of Hegel's account of experience is somewhat different from the others he discusses. Gadamer, as we saw, does not deny that the accumulation of positive experiences tends toward scientific knowledge; he just denies that this is its *only* tendency. In response to Hegel, though, he says something stronger. Hegel's claim that negative experience leads to absolute knowing is not just one-sided; it is mistaken. "The dialectic of experience,"

Gadamer claims, does *not* find "its proper fulfillment . . . in definitive knowledge" (*TM*, 364).

Gadamer's opposition to Hegel on this point is easy to misunderstand. It is natural to suppose that Gadamer's claim is simply that finite human beings can never *actually reach* a state of total self-transparency—that we can at best approach absolute knowledge only asymptotically. Gadamer's well-known description of himself as "a defender of what Hegel called 'bad infinity'"[10] would seem to support this reading, since for Hegel the bad (or "spurious") form of infinity is precisely that of an unending succession of finite moments, in contrast to the true infinity of the completed whole. Gadamer, however, makes it clear that this is not his view. He writes,

> I have taken it on myself to restore to a place of honor what Hegel termed "bad infinity"—but with a decisive modification, of course. For in my view the unending [*unendliche*, infinite] dialogue of the soul with itself which thinking is, is not properly characterized as an endlessly refined determination of the objects that we are seeking to know, either in the Neo-Kantian sense of the infinite task or in the Hegelian dialectical sense of thinking moving beyond every particular limit.[11]

A second problem with this interpretation is that the asymptotic view cedes to Hegel the very point on which Gadamer challenges him. Such a view *grants* that the end toward which experience tends is absolute knowledge; it simply denies that we will ever reach it. Gadamer's claim, however, is that absolute knowledge does not constitute the "consummation" or "proper fulfillment" of the "dialectic of experience" in the first place (*TM*, 364).

The actual teleology that experience follows, Gadamer contends, is precisely opposite the one Hegel identifies. Experience does not culminate in an absolute knowledge that is impervious to new experiences but, on the contrary, in a recognition of our finitude that engenders an "openness to experience" (*TM*, 364). This marks a third element of experiential knowledge, one that the tradition has largely overlooked but which in Gadamer's view is the most important of all.

The openness that, on Gadamer's account, is the proper culmination of experience is double-sensed in just the way that historically effected consciousness is. Taken in one sense, it refers to something like an intellectual virtue. The "experienced person" who has come to recognize her own finitude is "radically undogmatic" and so "particularly well equipped to have new experiences and to learn from them." Surely only some people (probably not many) are like this. In another sense, however, openness is a constitutive, and so universal, feature of understanding. Someone *completely* closed-off would be unable to have experiences at all. Their horizon would be incapable of the movement that understanding requires. Even the most dogmatic person is not like this. The "reversals" characteristic of experience *cannot but* alert us to our finitude, and experience "is not something anyone can be spared." Thus some degree of openness, if only an implicit one, is the inevitable consequence of being human (*TM*, 364).

But what, exactly, does it mean to be open to new experiences? What does "openness" consist in? Gadamer offers an initial answer to this question by considering the type of openness that characterizes specifically "hermeneutic" experience—that is, the experience of trying to understand what has been handed down to us from history. Openness in general is a kind of *stance* or *posture* that one assumes toward what one experiences, and Gadamer argues that in the case of hermeneutic experience this is analogous to the posture one assumes toward a "Thou," that is, toward another person who *addresses* us (*TM,* 366). To elucidate this, he distinguishes this posture from two others that one might assume in relating to another person—the "scientific" and "psychological," to borrow Monica Vilhauer's helpful terminology.[12] Each posture, Gadamer shows, facilitates a different sort of knowledge, a different respect in which we might be said to *learn something from* the other, and these correspond to different ways of conceiving of the knowledge that is achieved in the human sciences.

To take up the scientific stance toward another person is to regard her as merely an instance of "human nature." We can see this stance, for example, in the relationship that a quantitative psychologist assumes to the participants in her studies. Certainly, the researcher can 'learn something from' the participants, but only in the sense that one can learn something from any scientific experiment: her observations of the participants can confirm or disconfirm hypotheses about what is "typical and regular" in human behavior. Though such a stance can be legitimate in certain specific contexts, Gadamer notes that it "contradicts the moral definition of man," in that it regards others not as *persons* but merely as natural objects of a special type. (*TM*, 366–67)

By contrast, the psychological stance recognizes the other's personhood. It regards the other as an individual with a unique perspective on the world, and it regards the other's words and actions as *expressions* of that perspective. Here we might think of the posture one assumes toward a speaker in a 'listening session.' The 'listener' in such a context is not concerned with the truth of what the other person says (he does not 'pass judgment'), but rather with what it reveals about how the other person sees the world. His aim is to understand the other person, where *understanding* means something like being in a position to say "I can see why you would think that." Gadamer contends that here, while we encounter the other as a person, we still do not encounter her as a Thou. By always relating the other's claims back inward to her own subjectivity, rather than outward to the subject matter about which she speaks, the occupant of the psychological posture "reflects himself out of his relation to the other and so becomes unreachable by him" (*TM*, 368). The listener quarantines the other's claims safely inside a set of quotation marks and thereby protects his own views from any challenge they might pose.

In contrast to these relationships, to be open to the other is to encounter her as a Thou—that is, to allow her to address us. It is in *dialogue* with the other that this sort of posture is most fully realized. What distinguishes the kind of 'learning from' that characterizes dialogue from the other two we have considered is a certain form of vulnerability to the other person. To have a genuine dialogue I must allow what the other says to call my understanding of myself and of the world into question. Openness thus requires me, as we noted above, to be "undogmatic." It "involves recognizing that I myself must accept some things that are against me, even though no one forces me to" (*TM*, 369). At the same time, however, openness is not a matter of mere *deference* to the other. To uncritically accept whatever the other says, no less than to uncritically dismiss it, is to fail to truly engage with them. Either way I prevent the other from calling my understanding into question: in the one case, by pretending my own understanding is unquestionable, in the other by pretending I have no understanding of my own to be questioned.

The upshot of all this is that openness is fundamentally different from, and in some respects counter to, the posture of objectivity that is typically thought to underlie knowledge. Whether pursued by way of the empirical methods of the natural sciences or the psychological-cum-historical methods recommended by romantic and historicist versions of hermeneutics, objectivity is a matter of putting one's prejudices out of play. To be open, however, is precisely to put one's prejudices *in* play, to leave them exposed to questioning by that which one aims to understand. It is this vulnerability, and only it, Gadamer contends, that makes possible the reversals of consciousness that characterize genuine experience and through which genuine knowledge of oneself emerges.

3. QUESTIONING REFLECTION

Let's pause to take stock. Reflective philosophy, particularly in its Hegelian form, argues that consciousness must be capable, at least in principle, of recovering through reflection everything that conditions it. This would imply that the only genuine knowledge—that is, knowledge in an unqualified sense—is *absolute* knowledge, knowledge that is not influenced by any unconscious prejudices. Gadamer's contention is that this line of thought rests on a misunderstanding of how reflection operates. Gadamer agrees with Hegel that reflection takes place via experiences in which consciousness is reversed and thrown back on itself, bringing previously unnoticed prejudices to the fore. Unlike Hegel, however, Gadamer does not think that this foregrounding marks a step along the road to absolute knowledge. The accrual of experience does not produce an ever-greater degree of self-transparency but rather an ever-greater awareness of our finitude. This awareness manifests itself as a posture of openness, wherein we allow ourselves to be addressed by what we encounter—by others, by tradition, and by the world in general. On Gadamer's view, it is this openness, and not transparent self-possession, that is the defining feature of consciousness and knowledge. The most genuine or authentic form of knowledge, then, is not one that is maximally free of prejudices, but one that is maximally open. When the human sciences come to genuinely understand history and tradition (which, Gadamer thinks, they regularly do) it is not because they have achieved or even approximated some state of perfect objectivity, but because they have opened themselves up to what tradition has to say. Such openness is not only compatible with the idea that consciousness is historically effected (i.e., that it is always shaped by historical prejudices); it requires it, since to be open is precisely to put one's prejudices in play.

This argument gets Gadamer to the conclusion he needs to answer the challenge of reflective philosophy. However, one of its key premises remains dubious. His argument hinges on the idea that the moments of self-transparency that occur when experience foregrounds our prejudices are, as I'll put it, *non-additive*. They do not add up with one another in such a way that with each experience I become a little *more* transparent to myself—move a little closer to a state of total transparency. Again, Gadamer's claim is not simply that we will never arrive at this final destination but that reflection does not lead us in that direction in the first place. Here it is fair to ask: *how could this be*? If reflection really does eliminate some of my prejudices by bringing them to the foreground (at which point they are no longer *pre*-judices), how could this *not* amount to a step, even if only a small one, toward a state in which I would no longer have any prejudices at all? Though it takes a little while for it to come into focus, Gadamer offers an answer to this question in the final subsection of Part II, which he titles "The Hermeneutic Priority of the Question."

Gadamer approaches the nature of openness from two different angles. The first, which we just discussed, comes at openness from the experience of being addressed. The second, which he lays out in the final subsection, comes at it from the experience of *asking questions*. Ultimately, these are two different ways of saying the same thing. As we glimpsed above, to be addressed *just is* to be called into question by the other and to respond with questions of one's own. Nevertheless, framing the phenomenon in terms of questioning highlights dimensions that have not yet come into view. Specifically, Gadamer claims, questions reveal the "logical structure of openness" that is present in all experience and knowledge.

This structure is one of a *determinate plurality of possibilities*. The essence of a question is that it presents possibilities to us. A question "breaks open the being of the object" by revealing what, for all we currently know, it might be. In opening up the object in this way, the question opens us up, as well. It reveals that the thing is not necessarily what we previously took it to be. Our pre-judgment of it is not necessarily correct; it is only one possibility. In recognizing this, we undergo the reversal characteristic of (negative) experience. We no longer naively rely on the prejudice in question but adopt a critical attitude toward it. Gadamer contends that all such reversals, at least implicitly, unfold in this way. "The structure of the question is implicit in all experience" (*TM*, 370).

Obviously, for a question to 'possibilize' our prejudices in this way, it must reveal *more than one* possibility to us. In order to discover the "questionability of what is questioned," the object "has to be brought into [a] state of indeterminacy, so that there is an equilibrium between pro and contra" (*TM*, 371). Without this, there is no genuine question at all. A question for which only one answer is possible—for example, a rhetorical question—is not really a question but only a grammatically disguised assertion. A real question is an *open* question, and this means that it admits of a plurality of possible answers.

At the same time, however, "the openness of a question is not boundless." A question must admit of more than possible answer, but if just *anything* would count as a possible answer to it, then the question is meaningless. Such a question has no "sense of direction"; it leads nowhere. Mere bewilderment becomes a determinate question only when it calls up a *determinate* plurality of possible answers, only when "its fluid indeterminacy is concretized into a specific 'this or that'" (*TM*, 371–72).

Gadamer calls this determinate range of possible answers, which every meaningful question projects, the "horizon of the question." One of the key insights that we gain from Plato's theory of dialectic, he argues, is that knowledge is possible only on the basis of such a horizon. "Discourse that is intended to reveal something requires that that thing be broken open by the question . . . The path of all knowledge leads through the question" (*TM*, 371). Gadamer cites two reasons for this.

First, without passing through the openness of the question, our knowledge would not be *justified* (and so would not be knowledge). I cannot be said to know that p if I have never considered the possibility that ~p. "It is the essence of knowledge," Gadamer claims, "not only to judge something correctly but, at the same time and for the same reason, to exclude what is wrong." Knowledge thus requires that one has considered the counterarguments to one's own position and shown them to be incorrect (*TM*, 373).

Second, an item of knowledge can have no determinate *content* apart from some question to which it constitutes an answer. Considered in isolation, a proposition like *Stan is aggressive* is not something that one can know, or even believe, to be the case, because in isolation there is nothing determinate that such a statement means. If the question is whether Stan (the coach) is likely to punt or go for it on fourth and short, *being aggressive* would amount to one thing. If the question is whether Stan (the addict) is likely to respond well to an intervention, it would amount to something quite different. What something means is always a function of what it rules out, and this is supplied by the horizon of the question. To affirm any one possibility that occupies the question's horizon is to deny the others, and it is through this mutual contrast that the possibilities become determinate. As Gadamer puts it in a later essay, "No statement simply has an unambiguous meaning based on its linguistic and logical construction as such, but, on the contrary, each is motivated. A question is behind each statement that first gives it its meaning."[13]

Gadamer credits R.G. Collingwood with having (mostly) recognized the hermeneutic implications of this point. It is not just an individual sentence whose meaning depends on an underlying question; the meaning of a text does as well. Thus "we can understand a text only when we have understood the question to which it is an answer." This is a crucial hermeneutic insight, since it indicates that the "hermeneutical horizon" in which a text must be situated to be understood is the "horizon of the question" that it answers. Collingwood, however, takes it that the question at issue here is the *author's* question (i.e., the question the author intended to answer), and in Gadamer's view, this is a mistake. We cannot assume that the question the author set out to answer is the one the text actually does answer—not any more than we can assume that the significance of a historical event aligns with the plans of those involved in it. Of course, trying to identify an author's intentions is a legitimate undertaking (often a necessary one for a historian or biographer), but it is "quite a different task" from seeking the meaning of a text. (*TM*, 378–81)

Gadamer goes on to argue that the text's question not only *can* diverge from the author's question, in an important respect it *necessarily* does so. To understand a text requires understanding the question it answers and "to understand a question means to ask it" for oneself. To grasp a question *as a* question is to encounter the possibilities it discloses as genuine possibilities, as live options. What constitutes a live option, however, depends on the questioner's own situation. "This," Gadamer tells us, "is the reason why understanding is always more than merely re-creating someone else's meaning. Questioning opens up possibilities of meaning, and thus what is meaningful passes into one's own thinking on the subject." (*TM*, 382–83)

Another way to put this is to say that, just as the meaning of every statement depends on an underlying question, so too the meaning of every question depends on an underlying situation that allows it to be meaningfully posed, a "motivated context of questioning" (*TM*, 384). As Gadamer explains elsewhere, "Every question is itself an answer . . . Every question is motivated. Even its meaning is never totally encountered within it."[14] A question becomes meaningful to me when it reveals what is questionable in *my own* situation or "horizon," when it uncovers what is possible *for me* to do or to think. This, as Gadamer here explains, is the fundamental reason why understanding involves a "fusion of horizons" and not just the reconstruction of the text's 'original' horizon (*TM*, 385).

Gadamer notes that one key upshot of this is that, contrary to the Neo-Kantian idea that we can understand intellectual history as a series of answers to timeless 'problems,' questions "do not exist like stars in the sky." The meaning of a question depends on the situation in which it is posed, and it is the nature of situations that they are always changing. This is not to deny that one can, in some sense, ask 'the same question' as was posed by someone else in another situation (denying this would destroy what Gadamer calls the "ideality" of meaning and would render genuine communication impossible), but it does mean that this sameness can never be one of simple *identity*. Just as we always "understand in a different way, if we understand at all" (*TM*, 307), we always question in a different way as well. (It is, in fact, precisely because questioning is always different that understanding is too.) The idea of a timeless problem that exists self-same through history is an abstraction, a "bastard of historicism" that ignores the historicity of questioning (*TM*, 384–85).

The dependence of meaning and knowledge on underlying questions puts us in a better position to see why, on Gadamer's view, complete self-transparency is impossible. Like all understanding, the self-understanding that occurs in reflection depends on, and draws its meaning from, the question to which it is an answer. In the course of reflection, I can make genuine progress toward answering such a question, and in principle there is no reason why I might not even answer it completely—that is, rightly identify which of the possibilities on the table is correct and back up that identification with reasons that satisfy me and my interlocutors. Even such a complete answer, however, could never amount to a complete self-understanding. The horizon of a question, as we have seen, is necessarily a limited one; it includes only those possibilities that amount to live options given the situation in which the question is posed. In other words, the horizon in which reflection takes place—the horizon of the question—is itself conditioned by the situation that motivates the questioning. This situation is not foregrounded in the asking of the question; on the contrary, it is only by remaining in the background that the situation allows the possibilities at play to come forward in the way that they do. In a later essay on Hegel, Gadamer repeats this point and notes its Heideggerian roots. For Heidegger, the reason reflection is essentially finite is that there must be an "event of being" that "opens up the space for the movement of reflection, as well as for all knowledge, in the first place."[15] Gadamer agrees, and his addition is to point out that this "event of being" transpires precisely when a genuine question occurs to us.

The event-like character of questioning also reveals why reflection is non-additive. Even when I have, on a given occasion, successfully answered some question about myself, I cannot simply cross that question off the list and move on to the next one. Because questions do not "exist like stars in the sky," what counts as a successful answer to a given question in one situation may not count as one in the next. Just as for Kierkegaard each generation must determine anew what it means to be a Christian, such that each "begins primitively" and cannot "advance further" by building on previous generations' results,[16] so too for Gadamer a question must be asked anew each time it arises, and what one discovered the last time one asked the question will not necessarily provide a head-start in this. Each situation in which reflection might occur brings with it a new constellation of possibilities that must be considered and sorted through. Thus, as James Risser observes, "the infinite dialogue" or 'bad infinity' that Gadamer opposes to absolute knowledge "is not really a matter of postponement (of an end) at all, but rather, to be precise, always a reenactment of beginning."[17] Or, as Gadamer puts it, because it "never ceas[es] to be underway . . . reflection, the movement of logic, is homeless; it can stay nowhere."[18]

Gadamer does not deny that consciousness, even historically effected consciousness, requires the possibility of reflection. On this point, he sides with reflective philosophy against materialistic and psychologistic accounts of cognition. Where reflective philosophy goes wrong, in Gadamer's view, is in its failure to recognize that consciousness is not (just) a subjective activity, but an event in which one participates. As Gadamer told us earlier in the text, this is his basic point in calling it "historically effected" (*TM*, 310). Taking this point to heart means recognizing that the inevitable opacity of human self-knowledge is not a lack or a failing-not a matter of having fallen short of a transparency that is possible in principle but unattainable for us-but a feature of knowledge *as such*. Knowledge happens in a finite way or not at all, and thus the limited knowledge that we achieve when we open ourselves up to experience is the most genuine sort of knowledge there could be.

The question remains, however, whether this conception of self-knowledge as essentially finite is sufficient to address the concerns about attributability that first set reflective philosophy on its course toward infinity. In what respect could a consciousness conditioned by history in the way Gadamer suggests be *one's own*? We do not get a direct answer to this question in the section we have been examining, nor, as best I can tell, anywhere else in *Truth and Method*. We do, however, get a glimpse of what a Gadamerian account of self-ownership might look like. As Jerome Veith observes, there is "a parallel to be traced between Kant's announcement of the social project of *sapere aude* and Gadamer's account of the task of engaging dialogically with historical effect."[19] Putting one's ideas at risk in a dialogue is *a* way of 'owning' them or 'taking responsibility' for them, and for Gadamer, it would seem, it is the most fundamental one. Whether this sort of ownership is enough to account for the sorts of normative practices in which human beings engage is not a question that can be considered here, but it is ultimately one on which Gadamer's hermeneutic account of consciousness stands or falls.

NOTES

1. Hans-Georg Gadamer, *Truth and Method*, 2nd ed., trans. Joel Weinsheimer and Donald G. Marshall (New York: Bloomsbury Publishing, 2013), 350. Hereafter cited in text as *TM*. Where the German is cited or the translation has been altered, the page number of the original is indicated after the slash. The latter refer to Hans-Georg Gadamer, *Wahrheit und Methode*, Gesammelte Werke I (Tübingen: Mohr Siebeck, 1990).

2. As we will see as we go along, *consciousness* here means something like *cognition* and functions more or less as a synonym for what Gadamer more frequently calls *understanding*.

3. Immanuel Kant, "An Answer to the Question: What is Enlightenment?," in *Toward Perpetual Peace and Other Writings on Politics, Peace, and History*, ed. Pauline Kleingeld, trans. David L. Colclasure (New Haven: Yale University Press, 2006), 17.

4. Robert Pippin, "Gadamer's Hegel," in *The Cambridge Companion to Gadamer*, ed. Robert J. Dostal (Cambridge: Cambridge University Press, 2002), 233.

5. Pippin, 233, emphasis altered.

6. Pippin, 241. Pippin here is alluding to Wittgenstein's remark that "Once I have exhausted the justifications, I have reached bedrock, and my spade is turned. Then I am inclined to say, "This is simply what I do." (Ludwig Wittgenstein, *Philosophical Investigations*, rev. 4th ed., trans. G.E.M. Anscombe, P.M.S. Hacker, and Joachim Schulte (Sussex: Wiley-Blackwell, 2009), §217.) In my view, the criticism that Pippin directs at Gadamer is more properly directed at Wittgenstein, who really does (as I read him) ascribe to the account of reflection Pippin describes.

7. Thus, unlike Pippin, I take it that when Gadamer says that "the structure of reflexivity is fundamentally given with all consciousness," (*TM,* 350), he is speaking in his own voice.

8. For an analysis of this conceptual history that goes into more detail than space allows me to do here, see Jeremiah Conway, "Gadamer on Experience and Questioning," *Philosophy in the Contemporary World* 10 (2003), and Jussi Backman, "Encountering Finitude: On the Hermeneutic Radicalization of Experience," in *Phenomenology and Experience: New Perspectives*, ed. Antonio Cimino and Cees Leijenjhorst (Leiden: Brill, 2018).

9. The connection between experience and knowledge is already built into the connotation of *Erfahrung*, but this is mostly lost in the translation into English.

10. Hans-Georg Gadamer, "Reflections on My Philosophical Journey," in *The Philosophy of Hans-Georg Gadamer*, ed. Lewis Edwin Hahn (Chicago: Open Court, 1997), 44.

11. Gadamer, 37.

12. Monica Vilhauer, *Gadamer's Ethics of Play: Hermeneutics and the Other* (Lanham, MD: Lexington Books, 2010), 75–85.

13. Hans-Georg Gadamer, "Semantics and Hermeneutics," in *Philosophical Hermeneutics*, ed. and trans. David E. Linge (Berkeley: University of California Press, 1976), 88–89.

14. Hans-Georg Gadamer, "What Is Truth?," in *Hermeneutics and Truth*, ed. and trans. Brice Wachterhauser (Evanston, IL: Northwestern University Press, 1994), 42.

15. Hans-Georg Gadamer, "The Idea of Hegel's Logic," in *Hegel's Dialectic: Five Hermeneutical Studies*, trans. P. Christopher Smith (New Haven: Yale University Press, 1976), 96.

16. Søren Kierkegaard, *Fear and Trembling* and *Repetition*, ed. and trans. Howard V. Hong and Edna H. Hong (Princeton: Princeton University Press, 1983), 121.

17. James Risser, "In the Shadow of Hegel: Infinite Dialogue in Gadamer's Hermeneutics," *Research in Phenomenology* 32 (2002): 95.

18. Gadamer, "The Idea of Hegel's Logic," 98.

19. Jerome Veith, *Gadamer and the Transmission of History* (Bloomington: Indiana University Press, 2015), 119. Veith's book is the best and most thorough exploration of Gadamer's views on freedom and autonomy that I am aware of.

Part III

LANGUAGE AND LINGUISTICALITY

Chapter 11

TM III.1

Language as Medium of Hermeneutic Experience

Carlo DaVia

This section of *Truth and Method* (III.1)[1] gets relatively short shrift, and not without reason. The main thesis, announced already in its title, is that language is the medium of hermeneutic experience. By this, Gadamer means above all that: (i) the objects of hermeneutics are linguistic and (ii) the interpretive acts by which we understand those objects are also linguistic. Such a twofold thesis does not seem terribly controversial. We read and understand texts by means of language. Who would ever deny that?[2]

Given that this thesis is hardly controversial, it is not surprising to find predecessors endorsing some version of it. In fact, Gadamer himself in section II.1.1 seems to attribute the thesis to Friedrich Schleiermacher. In that passage, Gadamer praises Schleiermacher for characterizing hermeneutics as "concerned with understanding everything cast in language" (*TM*, 201).[3] This is a clear expression of (i). Gadamer also credits Schleiermacher with affirming (ii), at least insofar as he recognizes that the "pre-given totality of language" guides the interpreter in their hermeneutic quest for understanding (*TM*, 193). This happens in what Schleiermacher calls "grammatical" interpretation. Grammatical interpretation, along with "psychological" interpretation, are his two fundamental hermeneutical methods. Both are quite nuanced, but they can be characterized roughly as follows: Grammatical interpretation seeks to understand the meaning of spoken or written speech on the basis of linguistic usage *common* to the speaker and their original audience. Psychological interpretation, by contrast, understands written or spoken speech on the basis of the *individual* thought process of the speaker. A grammatical interpretation of Sophocles' *Ajax* would accordingly involve appreciating the linguistic norms of Attic tragedy and how they work in the text to express its meaning;

a psychological interpretation would involve intuiting the distinctive thought of Sophocles himself. Both methods of interpretation are necessary for understanding the meaning of the text. This is because, according to Schleiermacher, any written or spoken speech expresses the individual thoughts of the speaker by means of linguistic practices shared by the speaker and their original audience. The *Ajax* expresses Sophocles' thoughts and does so by means of the linguistic norms shared by his classical Greek readers. Therefore, at least insofar as Schleiermacher regards grammatical interpretation as indispensable for interpretation, he would agree with (ii): understanding any text requires interpretive acts that are linguistic in character. Interpreters cannot simply transpose themselves into the mind of the author; they must also take into consideration the linguistic norms of the author's day.[4]

The necessary role of language in the interpretive process is made even more explicit by Schleiermacher in other passages which Gadamer, oddly, does not ever seem to cite.[5] Consider, for example:

> Language is the manner in which thought is real. For there are no thoughts without speech. The speaking of words relates solely to the presence of another person, and to this extent is contingent. But no one can think without words. Without words the thought is not yet completed and clear.[6]

These words have an unmistakable Gadamerian ring, and Schleiermacher intends them to hold true generally, not just for grammatical interpretation. All interpretation involves apprehending what is meant in thought, and all thinking involves language. These are claims that Gadamer would support, despite his misgivings about psychological interpretation.[7] Moreover, they show Schleiermacher's commitment to Gadamer's thesis that language is the medium of hermeneutic experience. It is therefore rather fitting for a quote from Schleiermacher to serve as the epigram for Part III of *Truth and Method*: *Alles Vorauszusetzende in der Hermeneutik ist nur Sprache* ("Everything to be presupposed in hermeneutics is language").[8]

Why, then, should we bother reading past this epigram? What does section III.1 have to offer that we cannot learn either from Schleiermacher himself or from Gadamer's earlier discussion of him? Should we just concede that III.1 is "of a rudimentary character," providing, if anything, limited reflections on language that would be further developed by Gadamer over the next several decades?[9] This chapter will address these questions by showing how section III.1 presents a coherent line of inquiry that not only builds upon the prior conclusions of II.3 but also motivates the subsequent conceptual history of language in III.2. Gadamer certainly returns in later writings to some of the concepts presented here, but that does not diminish their significance. As we will see, of particular importance are his notions of the text and the hermeneutic conversation by which the interpreter finds the language to articulate its meaning.

1. THE HERMENEUTICAL CONVERSATION

In the previous section of *Truth and Method* (II.3), Gadamer explains how the task of understanding a text is governed by the same logic of question and answer that governs a conversation. If we want to understand what a text or person states, we need to grasp the question for which the written or spoken speech is an answer. Suppose I overhear my aunt saying "That's just Noemi." Grasping what she means depends on my understanding the question to which her statement serves as an answer. Is she announcing who is at the door? On the phone? Or is my aunt affirming that Noemi's behavior in the story just told is typical of her? The meaning of my aunt's statement depends on the question it answers. The same holds for texts. In order to understand Aristotle's account of *akrasia* (weakness of will) in Bk. VII of the *Nicomachean Ethics*, we need to grasp the question to which that account serves as an answer. Does the question motivating the passage concern the essential definition of *akrasia*? Or the difference between *akrasia* and vice? Or something else? If we can identify the question to which the text is an answer, we can identify its real subject matter, what the text is really about.

While summarizing this way in which interpretation is modeled after a conversation, Gadamer indicates the next step in his argument:

> When we try to examine the hermeneutical phenomenon through the model of conversation between two persons, the chief thing that these apparently so different situations—understanding a text and reaching an understanding in a conversation—have in common is that both are concerned with a subject matter that is placed before them. . . . This understanding of the subject matter must take the form of language. It is not that the understanding is subsequently put into words; rather, the way understanding occurs—whether in the case of a text or a dialogue with another person who raises an issue with us—is the coming-into-language of the thing itself. . . . Whereas up to now we have framed the constitutive significance of the *question* for the hermeneutical phenomenon in terms of conversation, we must now demonstrate the linguisticality of dialogue, which is the basis of the question, as an element of hermeneutics. (*TM*, 386)

The process of interpreting a text, of coming to understand the answer it gives to a question, is a process that "must take the form of language." This is because understanding a text is modeled after conversation, and understanding a conversation happens only through language. The same holds for an interpreter and their text. Insofar as interpretation is dialogical, governed by the logic of question and answer, it, too, is only achieved in the medium of language. Or so Gadamer will argue in section III.1.

At the beginning of III.1, Gadamer clarifies the sense in which conversation always takes place in the medium of language. Obviously, conversation involves language. But Gadamer means something more. A genuine conversation is not merely an exchange of words, as when the participants already have thoughts that they simply wish to communicate. Relaying a message from your boss, delivering to your boyfriend a rehearsed breakup speech, or sharing with students your deep-seated views about Sophoclean tragedy—none of these are conversations in Gadamer's sense. The conversations he has in mind happen when "the partners conversing are far less the leaders of it than the led" (*TM*, 401). On these occasions, there is a shared subject matter, and the partners in conversation both seek to understand it.[10] The conversation develops as they both help one another in answering the question that is guiding them. Neither person knows what will come of their discussion. But any insight they do gain into the subject matter will have been achieved through their talking things through.

However, arriving at a shared understanding in conversation is not a matter of one participant intuiting some truth and then conveying it to the other. In order for the understanding to be *shared*, the participants need to "find a common language" in which the truth emerges for both (*TM*, 406). This is the deeper sense in which understanding in a conversation happens through language. Only by creating a common language can we truly come to a *shared* understanding.

But how is such a common language created? Gadamer explains this process by first considering cases of conversation mediated by a translator. In such cases, the translator must understand what one speaker means and then translate that meaning into the other language. For the translation to be any good, it must preserve the intended meaning and yet express it in a way appropriate to the other language. Finding the appropriate expression is always an act of interpretation, since the translator must themself not only take a stand on what the speaker is saying but also relay what was said in a manner that inevitably highlights certain aspects of the intended meaning at the expense of others. In a conversation in which everyone speaks the same language, the participants must carry out a similar interpretive task to the translator. The participants are trying to better understand some subject matter and neither yet have the words adequate to answer their shared question. In the to-and-fro of dialogue, each participant will have to interpret what the other says. This interpretive task arises for at least two reasons. First, a participant will inevitably say something that is in some respect alien or foreign to the other. After all, both participants are groping for the right words that will make evident the answer to their question. The participants are therefore bound to say things that are difficult for the other to fully understand. Just consider the countless occasions on which Socrates says something without irony and still manages to leave his interlocutors confused. The second reason why conversations involve interpretation is because no speaker can fully articulate what they mean; there is always something left unsaid. As a result, the other participant must interpret what the person means in light of their shared communicative context. Through these acts of interpretation, the participants in a conversation build a common language in which the truth they seek can become evident to both. The extent to which they build a common language mirrors the extent to which they have come to understand one another and thereby something about the subject matter under discussion.

The interpreter of a text is in a situation much like that of the participant in a conversation. The interpreter can accordingly be said to participate in what Gadamer calls a "hermeneutical conversation" (*TM*, 406). Admittedly, in such a conversation, the text cannot speak for itself; the interpreter must speak on its behalf. But even so, the interpreter and text collaborate so as to allow something meaningful and true to become evident. To accomplish this, the interpreter and text must find a common language. In a real conversation, participants develop a common language by taking the strange and unclear things that the other says and trying to understand them as true, and in their own words. "In saying . . ., do you mean . . .?" "Yes, exactly!" Or "No, not quite. I meant ..." In a hermeneutical conversation, the interpreter must similarly try to understand the text as true and in her own words. The interpreter comes to understand the text through her interpreting its meaning in language, and the language by which she interprets the text is precisely the common language shared by her and the text. In this way, "finding a common language is not, any more than in real conversation, preparing a tool for the purpose of reaching understanding but, rather, coincides with the very act of understanding and reaching agreement" (*TM*, 406).

It might be objected that Gadamer has restricted his notion of conversation so narrowly that, however convincing his account of conversation may be, it fails to show that the understanding of *all* texts is also achieved in the medium of language. Conversations, as Gadamer characterizes them, are rare. It is not often that we speak with someone about a question that we both really share and work together toward and that consequently leads us to some conclusion neither of us had foreseen. Texts, by contrast, are commonplace. On my desk sits both a copy of Sophocles' *Ajax* and a page of notes that I jotted down while reading it. Are they not both texts? And yet the process of understanding them seems different. We can grant that reading the *Ajax* is like a conversation in which we readers are compelled to ask for ourselves the questions raised by the tragedy. Why, after all, did Ajax suffer such a fate, and what does his fate teach us about the human condition? With my notes, though, things are quite different. They seem to serve merely as mementos of my prior thought processes. I see the note and immediately remember what I had been thinking. In order to understand the note, I do not need to talk it out with myself or anyone else. Moreover, it would be a rare accident if in reading the note I happened to gain some novel understanding of what it meant. Hence, the worry: if understanding a note is so different from the understanding reached in conversation, then how can the conversation serve as an appropriate model for the understanding of *all* texts?

This objection loses its force when we see that Gadamer means something very specific when he here speaks of a "text." By *text* he is not referring to anything that has been written down, typed out, or otherwise inscribed. He means, rather, a linguistic meaningful whole whose meaning does not depend upon any one particular occasion or context in order to be understood. The *Ajax*, for example, is a meaningful whole that we can all understand without having to transport ourselves—either literally or imaginatively—back to classical Athens. My notes, by contrast, do not form a meaningful whole. If I forget enough of the original context in which I took down some note, I will become unable to understand its meaning. A text, then, unlike other writings, bears a meaning that can be understood across time and place, without recourse to the original occasion for which the text was intended. A text can accordingly detach itself from its original historical context and be handed down by tradition. This is why Gadamer insists that the text is the paradigmatic object of hermeneutics.[11] In III.1.a, Gadamer will develop this notion of text in order to clarify the sense in which language is the medium in which the hermeneutical conversation between text and interpreter takes place.

2. THE NATURE OF THE TEXT (TM III.1.A)

Texts differ from other historical artifacts insofar as they are not merely "to be investigated and interpreted as a remnant of the past." Texts are not "left over" *for* us but rather "speak" *to* us (*TM*, 407–8; cf. *TM*, 163). By this, Gadamer means that texts make a claim upon us to take them as saying something true about ourselves and the world in which we presently live. Insofar as the *Ajax* is a text, it is not merely a fragment of ancient Greek life but rather something which reveals truths that still hold for us today about, say, the need for mortals to know their limitations and to moderate their ambitions. We can, of course, also study the *Ajax* as a historical document and mine it for information about ancient theatrical performances, among other things. But as a text, it is always of more than historical significance for us. This is generally not the case for other written artifacts. Inscriptions on monuments and business records on papyrus typically do not "speak" to us but instead point us toward a bygone age.

How is a text able to "speak" to us in this way? The answer, for Gadamer, lies in the fact that writing detaches language from its original communicative context. When language is put in writing, it becomes accessible to others even when the original speaker and audience are no longer present (because separated by either space or time). In this way, all language is detachable from its original context. This, however, does not necessarily imply that the *meaning* of what is written can always also be so detached. In many cases, the meaning of something written depends on the original context for which the writing was intended. The famous Dipylon inscription found on an archaic Greek wine jug reads "whoever of all the dancers plays most delicately, to him this." The meaning of the inscription depends in part on the historical context in which the ancient Greeks held contests for which wine jugs served as prizes. Without having some awareness of that original context, the inscribed meaning would be lost on us.

The meaning of a text, by contrast, does not depend on the original context in which it was written. This is because a text, as Gadamer puts it, "always express[es] a whole" (*TM*, 408). A text is not a "fragment" whose meaning depends on the historical context from which it originates. That said, the meaning of a text is not completely context-independent. Like all spoken or written language, the meaning of a text depends on some context or other. But a text is distinctive insofar as the only context on which its meaning depends is the one in which a reader seeks to understand it. That is, its meaning depends on the context in which the text and its reader participate in hermeneutical conversation. It is in that context that the reader seeks to make the text speak, and what the text has to say is something which purports to be true not just for some prior culture, but for the reader, too. In this way, the texts handed down by tradition are not relics of the past but "contemporaneous with each present time" (*TM*, 408).

Just as language can be detached from the original context of utterance by virtue of its inscribability, so too linguistic meaning can be detached from the original context because of its *ideality*: "The ideality of the word is what raises everything linguistic beyond the finitude and transience that characterize other remnants of past existence" (*TM*, 408). Meaning is ideal in the sense that it is not spatio-temporally individuated, not "real" in the Husserlian sense. In this respect, meanings differ from physical objects, which are determined in part by their belonging to a specific place and time. Meanings are not so determined. All meanings can in principle be repeated and shared across time and space.[12] The meaning of a text, however, is distinct insofar as its meaning does not depend on the original context for which it was produced. A text detaches "both from the writer or author and from a specifically addressed recipient or reader," and thereby "raises itself into a public sphere of meaning in which everyone who can read has an equal share" (*TM*, 410). All meanings are public, but not all meanings can be shared equally by everyone. Some meanings are shared only by those participating in their little private conversation. But the greater degree to which the meaning of something written can be shared by everyone (or at least everyone literate), the greater degree to which that writing comprises a text. The ideal meaning of the text allows it to be contemporaneous with every present and to speak to every reader.

Examples from literature readily demonstrate this ability of a text to be intelligible to us even when we are ignorant of the author or the intended audience. We do not know who wrote *Beowulf*, but that hardly prevents us from understanding what the epic poem is about. There are surely interpretive disputes about the poem, but those disputes can be settled by the text alone insofar as it stands as an autonomous, meaningful whole. Moreover, even if scholars were able to determine who the author was, whatever relevant information they learn about that person can only confirm what the text already gives us. For other texts, it is not the author who is unknown, but the intended audience. But once again, this ignorance does not preclude our understanding. Franz Kafka's *The Trial* was published posthumously, against his wishes, by his literary executor. It is unclear who the intended audience was, if anyone; Kafka wanted it burned. But we can read the novel today and understand it as speaking trenchantly to us about the injustices of the criminal system in the modern bureaucratic state. Whoever Kafka may have been writing for, the text is also for us.

From this brief account of the text, Gadamer already draws important hermeneutic implications.[13] The biggest implication is that the nature of the text calls into question the "sensible hermeneutical rule . . . that nothing should be put into a text that the writer or reader could not have intended" (*TM*, 413). However sensible this rule may seem, and however much it may be true for certain sorts of writing, it does not also hold for texts. Since the meaning of a text does not depend on the original context for which it was produced, neither the author nor the intended original audience determine its meaning. The written word of a text can detach its meaning from that original context, and when it does so it "makes the understanding reader the arbiter of its claim to truth" (*TM*, 412). By this, Gadamer does not mean that we readers get to decide that the text means whatever we want. He means, rather, that by participating in hermeneutic conversation with the text, we come to understand what it has to say *to us*. In section III.1.b, Gadamer will expound further upon the linguistic process by which we carry out this conversation and come to understand the text.

Before turning to that exposition, let us revisit Gadamer's relationship to Schleiermacher, since now we can better see how general points of agreement between the two belie important differences in their hermeneutic theories. Schleiermacher characterizes hermeneutics as "the art of understanding another person's utterance [*Rede*] correctly."[14] This echoes Gadamer's claim that the paradigmatic object of hermeneutics is linguistic. For Schleiermacher, just as for Gadamer, this process of coming to understand the utterance of another is modeled after the conversation. And, again like Gadamer, Schleiermacher considers the relevant model of conversation to be one in which the discussion is not guided by some "specific objective intention." Rather, the interlocutors happen to "get fixed on something" that "is striven for by both sides," with the result that there arises "a common development of thoughts."[15] The model conversation is therefore not some mundane chat about the weather.[16] However, unlike Gadamer, Schleiermacher contends that the model of conversation only *partly* characterizes the process by which we understand spoken or written discourse:

> Every text is twofold, on the one side a conversation *Gespräch*, on the other the communication (*Mitteilung*) of a particular, intentionally willed sequence of thoughts. If we think of the latter without the former, and think of the former as absent, then to this also belongs the fact that the writer is not at all determined by the ideas of the readers with which he is confronted. If we think of this, we must say that this kind of thing is not really a text, because the author would only have written for himself. However, as soon as one thinks of a particular text as a communication it is also determined by the ideas of those to whom the text is directed. Everything in this kind of text which bears a dialogical character can only be explained by what is common to the writer and his readers.[17]

According to Schleiermacher, a text is both conversation *and* communication. It is a communication insofar as every author has some "sequence of thoughts" they wish to put in writing. But a text cannot be a communication alone. A text is a recording of thoughts *for* someone, and for that reason the author must take into consideration the intended reader. Those considerations modify the thoughts which the author wishes to put in writing, since the author must consider which things the audience will already know, and which things the audience will either misunderstand or not understand at all. The result is that the text comes to represent one side of a conversation in which "a common development of thought" arises between the author and their intended audience. By participating in this conversation, the author is stimulated by the reader such that they arrive at a distinct sequence of thoughts they had neither intended nor anticipated. But even as Schleiermacher acknowledges that authorial intentions are influenced by the intended audience, that by no means diminishes the fact that, on his view, a necessary part of understanding a text is understanding the intentions of its author.

Here, we strike at arguably the deepest difference between the theories of hermeneutics defended by Gadamer and Schleiermacher. For Schleiermacher, language is always a vehicle of expression by which speakers and writers communicate their thoughts to their intended readers or hearers.[18] A text is therefore always, at least in part, an act of communication that requires the psychological method of interpretation. Fully understanding a text requires understanding what the author thinks and intends to communicate.[19] For Gadamer, by contrast, language is not always such a vehicle of expression. More fundamentally, it is a medium through which truths are made evident. Those truths can subsequently be communicated to others, but first they must be disclosed. That disclosure for Gadamer takes place in "conversation," in his sense of the term. Such a conversation can be a real one between two people, or a hermeneutical one between a person and text. As participants in hermeneutical conversation, texts can speak for themselves, not just for others.[20] They can do this because texts are special linguistic utterances that are ideal, meaningful wholes and whose meaning does not depend on the original context for which the utterance was intended by the author. Schleiermacher fails to recognize the true ideality of the text: "Schleiermacher was the first to downplay the importance of writing," but this prevented him from seeing that the meaning of a text can be detached "from both the writer or author and from a specifically addressed recipient or reader" (*TM*, 410).

3. UNDERSTANDING THE TEXT (TM III.1.B)

Remember that the main thesis of section III.1 is twofold: (i) the objects of hermeneutics are linguistic and (ii) the interpretive acts by which we understand those objects are also linguistic. In III.1a, Gadamer has clarified (i): on his view, the paradigmatic objects of hermeneutics are not just linguistic, but, more specifically, ideal texts. Now, in III.1.b, Gadamer clarifies (ii) by showing how the nature of the ideal text determines the specific sense in which we come to understand texts through language.

We have already seen that coming to understand a text handed down by tradition takes place in what Gadamer calls a hermeneutical conversation between the text and its reader. This conversation is an interpretive process whereby the reader understands the text such that it speaks to them. As an interpretive process, it differs from two naïve approaches that Gadamer finds common in the historical sciences. One of those approaches involves employing whatever concepts one has at the ready in order to interpret the text and employing those concepts "without expressly reflecting on their origin and justification" (*TM*, 414). This is especially easy to do when treating cognates. When, for example, Aristotle mentions *theōria*, it should not be presumed that he means *theory* just as modern English speakers are apt to understand the term. When readers unreflectively apply familiar concepts in this way, they run the risk of "assimilating" the meaning of the text to fit their own "preconceptions" (*TM*, 414). An alternative approach, also pervasive in the historical sciences, tries to prevent the preconceptions of the reader from leading them to misunderstand the text. This second approach accordingly insists that in understanding texts, "one must leave one's own concepts aside and think only in the concepts of the epoch one is trying to understand" (*TM*, 414; cf. *TM*, 313–15). However well-intentioned this strategy may be, it is ultimately an incoherent interpretive ideal. It is incoherent because nobody can entirely escape their own concepts; any attempt to understand a text must be in terms of the concepts by which readers themselves think. To think in terms of Aristotle's concepts is inevitably to think Aristotle's concepts *in terms of one's own*. But this ideal—to grasp as accurately as possible the concepts of past thinkers—is not just incoherent but illegitimate. The point of our reading a text as a text, and not merely as an historical artifact, is to understand what it *presently* has to say to *us*. The meaning of the text depends not on the original context in which it was produced but rather the present one in which we read it. This does not necessarily make our interpretive task any easier, for we still have to work to understand what is alien and unfamiliar to us in the text. Doing this, moreover, is not a matter of grasping the concepts of the past as they were understood by the author or original audience. We must instead "*perform the transposition* (*Umsetzung*) *that the concepts of the past undergo* when we try to think in them" (*TM*, 415/401).

What does such a "transposition" of concepts entail? Suppose we are reading Horace's *Ode* I.11, a poem about accepting the lot given to us by the gods. The end of the poem famously bids Leuconoe, its explicit addressee, to "seize the day" (*carpe diem*). What exactly does this mean? In the film *Dead Poets Society,* Professor Keating (played by Robin Williams) explains to his students that "seize the day" is an enjoinder to "make your life extraordinary." Such an interpretation, however, seems to assimilate the meaning of the expression to the preconceptions typical of American secondary education. Professor Keating wants his students to make the most of themselves and their abilities. The students themselves want to grow up to be somebody, to achieve something. But the poem is not calling upon its readers to live extraordinary lives, as the remainder of the line makes clear: "seize the day, trusting as little as possible in the next." The poem is calling upon its readers to seize the day not so that their lives may become great, but because they cannot be sure that they will live to see tomorrow. Professor Keating missed this. But his interpretation would not have been on any firmer footing if he had instead tried to determine what *carpe diem* meant for Horace or his original Roman readers. That historical past, unmediated by the present, remains forever inaccessible. The transposition of concepts therefore involves neither assimilating traditional concepts to our own preconceptions nor shedding all our preconceptions and escaping to an undistorted past. The transposition of concepts instead involves considering a concept in the context of the *whole* text in which the interpreter is with hermeneutic conversation. Failing to do so would be just as problematic as if someone were to (mis)interpret what another person has said by taking some comment out of context, without a view to the whole of their discussion. The interpreter, moreover, must come to understand that concept by articulating its meaning in their own words. This process of articulation will quite often involve "bring[ing] own's own preconceptions into play such that at least some of those preconceptions must be rethought and revised" (*TM*, 415). For Professor Keating, then, transposing the concept of "seizing the day" (*carpere diem*) as it is handed down in Horace's poem required considering the meaning of that concept in the context of the whole poem to which it belongs. And in coming to understand its meaning, Professor Keating needed to articulate what "seize the day" meant for him; if he had done so correctly, he would have grasped what it was to *count* as seizing the day in his own circumstances. He also would have thereby called into question his preconceived idea of what the poem meant by "seize the day."

This is the very same notion of transposition that Gadamer has already attributed to judges when they interpret a law promulgated long ago (*TM*, 332–33). Interpreting the law correctly does not involve merely assimilating its meaning to the judge's preconceptions. Nor is it a matter of understanding how the legislators and original public would themselves have understood the law. To interpret a law correctly is rather to understand how the whole law, as handed down by the legal tradition, is to be fittingly applied by the judge to the case at hand. It is through such transposition that laws, like other texts, "speak" to us.

Since every circumstance is different, the way in which interpreters transpose historical concepts conveyed by a text will differ for each and every interpretation. Even if Professor Keating were to interpret the Horace poem correctly, his understanding would inevitably differ from our own. This is in part because what it is to "seize the day," to make the most of the present because there is no assurance of the future, must be carried out differently in different times and places. As Gadamer puts the point more generally: "to understand a text always means to apply it to ourselves and to know that, even if it must always be understood in different ways, it is still the same text presenting itself to us in these different ways" (*TM*, 416; cf. *TM*, 307). No two interpretations of a text will therefore be the same. In this way, the interpretation of a text is like the performance of play: just as Shakespeare's *Hamlet* is performed differently by each and every production and yet remains one and the same play, Horace's *Odes* I.11 is read differently by each and every reader and yet remains one and the same poem.[21] There is no exclusively correct interpretation. There is instead a multiplicity of correct interpretations, each of which "has to adapt itself to the hermeneutical situation in which it belongs" (*TM*, 415). For each such hermeneutical situation, a different interpretation emerges from a different hermeneutical conversation between interpreter and text. Such conversations differ insofar as interpreters find different language, appropriate to their own context, through which the meaning of one and the same text becomes evident.

4. TOWARD A CONCEPTUAL HISTORY OF LANGUAGE (TM III.2)

For Gadamer, the interpreter is in principle always able to find the language by which to understand the text. Just as every conversation can, in principle, arrive at genuine insight into the subject matter discussed, so too can every hermeneutic conversation arrive at the correct understanding of the text.

Gadamer recognizes, however, that there are a number of reasons not to share his optimism. Is it not the case that "language forces understanding into particular schematic forms which hem us in"? (*TM*, 419). Will not these schematizations of language preclude us from correctly understanding anything that does not readily fit them? Are we not therefore always bound to misunderstand texts in languages other than our own? While it is no doubt true that every language possesses conventions of meaning, it does not follow that these conventions are inescapable and that we consequently cannot articulate in language our correct, even if unconventional, understanding of a text. According to Gadamer, this worry demonstrates not the limits of hermeneutical experience but rather its need. For the experience of coming to understand through hermeneutical conversation is "the corrective by means of which the thinking reason escapes the prison of language" (*TM*, 420). Hermeneutical experience is precisely that by which Professor Keating and the rest of us can overcome conventions of meaning that preclude our understanding.

Even so, the inseverable connection between thought and language, between coming to understand and articulating that understanding in language, might still seem unobvious, if not dubious. Gadamer identifies three sources of difficulty. First, language remains largely unthematic to interpreters in and through the process of their coming to understand a text: "The interpreter does not know that he is bringing himself and his own concepts into the interpretation. The verbal formulation is so much part of the interpreter's mind that he never becomes aware of it as an object" (*TM*, 412). Because language remains unthematic to interpreters in this way, they are prone to overlook the constitutive role that language plays in their interpretations.

Second, this neglect is reinforced by instrumental theories of language. According to such theories, language is a sort of tool employed by reason to express thoughts that can be developed without language. Instrumental theories of language promote the notion that interpreters can first interpret a text and then go on to convey their interpretation in language for others. Instrumental theories of language are therefore at odds with the Gadamerian view that all achievements of understanding take place in the medium of language.[22] The third and related source of difficulty is a narrative in linguistics about the historical development of the concept of language. That narrative begins with "the complete unconsciousness of language that we find in classical Greece," and then "leads to the instrumentalist devaluation of language that we find in modern times" (*TM*, 422). There is some truth to this narrative, but, even as it recognizes that the instrumental theories "devalue" language, it also wrongly suggests that we moderns do not in a certain sense share with the ancients a certain unconsciousness of language. In fact, for Gadamer, unconsciousness of language "has not ceased to be the genuine mode of being of speech" (*TM*, 423). We have not ceased being unconscious of language precisely because, as we seek to understand, the language by which we come to understand remains unthematic to us. We are so busy attending to the subject matter itself that we overlook the way in which our language brings the matter to presentation.

To help address these difficulties, Gadamer will turn in TM III.2 to develop his own conceptual history of language. That conceptual history will sketch how the phenomenon of language has come to appearance in different ways through the Western tradition. The history will, among other things, address some of these lingering worries about the claims made in TM III.1. It will demonstrate that an essential dimension of the being of language is that it always remains unthematic, at least in part. We can never be conscious of language in the way that we are conscious of, say, a physical object, since language is the medium by which we come to understand everything intelligible, including language itself. The history of language bears this truth out. That history will also offer resources, particularly from Christian medieval thought, to better appreciate how language conceals itself in the process of making evident that which we seek to understand.[23]

All this reflects the sense in which Gadamer agrees with Schleiermacher that "everything to be presupposed in hermeneutics is language." Language is *the* presupposition of hermeneutics not only insofar as the primary aim of hermeneutics is to understand the language of texts but also insofar as the process of coming to understand itself takes place in language. The degree to which hermeneutic understanding presupposes language is so great, however, that it is often overlooked. It may be readily acknowledged that texts are composed of language and can be understood by means of language.

But beneath those points of agreement are often inadequate conceptions of language, text, and the conversation through which the meaning of the text is brought to language.

NOTES

1. Hans-Georg Gadamer, *Truth and Method*, 2nd ed., trans. Joel Weinsheimer and Donald G. Marshall (New York: Bloomsbury, 2013). Hereafter cited in text as *TM*. Where the German is cited or the translation has been altered, the page number of the original is indicated after the slash. The latter refer to Hans-Georg Gadamer, *Wahrheit und Methode,* Gesammelte Werke I (Tübingen: Mohr Siebeck, 1990).

2. As Jean Grondin puts it, "In some ways, we may feel that, in their generality, they are pushing at open doors. Doubtless this is the case in the first great thesis, according to which language represents both the object and understanding's mode of accomplishment." *The Philosophy of Gadamer*, trans. Kathyrn Plant (Bucks: Acumen, 2003), 125. Grondin then suggests that Gadamer's thesis seems less banal once we "recognize that Gadamer ventured into a still unexplored jungle when he proposed his hermeneutics of language." It is certainly true that philosophy of language in both the analytic and continental traditions came to much greater prominence after the publication of *Truth and Method*. However, it seems more accurate to see Gadamer not so much as breaking philosophical ground that has since become well-trodden, but rather taking up theses about language already found in German thinkers like Schleiermacher and Herder and imbuing them with new meaning.

3. As Schleiermacher himself puts it: hermeneutics is "the art of understanding another person's utterance correctly." *Hermeneutics and Criticism*, ed. and trans. Andrew Bowie (New York: Cambridge, 1998), 5; *Hermeneutik und Kritik*, ed. Manfred Frank (Frankfurt am Main: Suhrkamp, 1977), 75.

4. There is a debate among scholars as to whether psychological interpretation really requires that the interpreter somehow "transpose" themselves into the mind of the author. Gadamer thinks it does (see *TM*, 303). For contrary readings, see, for example: Andrew Bowie, "The Philosophical Significance of Schleiermacher's Hermeneutics," in *The Cambridge Companion to Schleiermacher*, ed. Jacqueline Mariña (New York: Cambridge, 2005), 73–90; Kristin Gjesdal, "Aesthetic and Political Humanism: Gadamer on Herder, Schleiermacher, and the Origins of Modern Hermeneutics," *History of Philosophy Quarterly* 24, no. 3 (2007): 275–79; Kristin Gjesdal, *Gadamer and the Legacy of German Idealism* (Cambridge: Cambridge, 2009), 174. Regardless of whether Gadamer is right, it is clear that Schleiermacher, by regarding grammatical interpretation as indispensable, cannot agree to any such claim that the interpreter can "get in the head" of the author and understand what they are thinking without that interpretive process being mediated by language.

5. In the 1972 Afterword to *Truth and Method*, Gadamer does acknowledge in passing the significance of Schleiermacher's "discussion of the connection between thought and speaking" (*TM*, 589). Gadamer locates that discussion in

Schleiermacher's lecture on dialectic, but one can also find many similar passages in his lectures on hermeneutics (see n.6).

6. Schleiermacher, *Hermeneutics and Criticism*, 8; cf. 91, 144, 167.

7. These misgivings have already been discussed earlier in *TM* I.2.2.d. For discussion of that section, see Kevin Vander Schel's contribution to this volume. Gadamer returns to his reading of Schleiermacher in "The Problem of Language in Schleiermacher's Hermeneutic," ed. Robert F. Funk, trans. David E. Linge, *Journal for Theology and the Church* 7 (1970): 68–95.

8. Schleiermacher, *Hermeneutics and Criticism*, 38; *Hermeneutics: The Handwritten Manuscripts*, 50, trans. amended. Joel Weinsheimer argues that Gadamer's famous slogan, "Being that can be understood is language," is a paraphrase of this statement by Schleiermacher. (See *Gadamer's Hermeneutics: A Reading of Truth and Method* (New Haven: Yale, 1985), 214–16.) But that does not seem right. Schleiermacher's statement is about the conditions for the possibility of hermeneutics. That is, it is a statement about how understanding is possible, and how a *theory* of understanding is possible. Gadamer's slogan, by contrast, has ontological import; it has something to say about the role of being in the process of coming to understand in language.

9. Grondin, *The Philosophy of Gadamer*, 124. For helpful discussion of the composition of *Truth and Method*, see Grondin, "On the Composition of Truth and Method," in *The Specter of Relativism: Truth, Dialogue, and Phronesis in Philosophical Hermeneutics*, ed. and trans. Lawrence K. Schmidt (Evanston: Northwestern, 1995), 23–38.

10. For fuller discussion of Gadamer's technical notion of "conversation," see David Vessey, "Gadamer and Davidson on Language and Thought," *Philosophy Compass* 7, no. 1 (2012): 33–42.

11. In later writings, Gadamer will refer to them as "eminent texts." See, for example: the Afterword to *Truth and Method* (*TM*, 600); "Text and Interpretation," in *The Gadamer Reader: A Bouquet of the Later Writings*, ed. Richard E Palmer (Evanston, IL: Northwestern, 2007), 156–91; "The Eminent Text and Its Truth," *The Bulletin of the Midwest Modern Language Association* 13, no. 1 (1980): 3–10. Everything Gadamer says in TM III.1 is consistent with this characterization of a text, except for perhaps: "Everything written is, in fact, the paradigmatic object of hermeneutics" (*TM*, 413). However, Gadamer must here be speaking loosely, because just a few pages earlier he distinguishes literary texts from writings like inscriptions, which (at least often) are fragments of a past whose meanings can only be grasped by understanding the historical context in which they were produced.

12. Gadamer has already discussed the way in which the ideality of a work renders it "repeatable and hence permanent" earlier in section I.2.1.b (see especially *TM*, 115).

13. For a richer account of texts, see Gadamer, "Text and Interpretation." For helpful discussion of that account, see James Risser, *Hermeneutics and the Voice of the Other: Re-Reading Gadamer's Philosophical Hermeneutics* (Albany: SUNY, 1997), 163–68.

14. Schleiermacher, *Hermeneutics and Criticism*, 5.

15. Schleiermacher, 124.
16. Schleiermacher, 13.
17. Schleiermacher, 129.
18. This is different from the claim that Schleiermacher conceives of language as "aesthetic self-expression which expresses *only* the subjectivity of the person expressing himself" (Weinsheimer, *Gadamer's Hermeneutics: A Reading of Truth and Method*, 220, emphasis added). This is a misreading of Schleiermacher, since for him the grammatical and psychological methods of interpretation are complementary. Gadamer himself does not commit this misreading. He acknowledges the complementarity of grammatical and psychological interpretation, even while focusing on the latter in order to make clear its historical influence and philosophical inadequacy (see *TM*, 192). This final point has already been made by Georgia Warnke in *Gadamer: Hermeneutics, Tradition, and Reason* (Oxford: Polity, 1987), 14.

19. This seems a fair representation of Schleiermacher's hermeneutics. Andrew Bowie, for example, characterizes his theory in the following way: "Hermeneutics seeks the specific intentions of the individual in the contexts of their utterances. These intentions are obviously not exhausted by the possible general validity of those utterances." For Bowie, this follows from Schleiermacher's conception of language: "Because language results from concrete 'speech acts' the speech act is necessarily individual: it is your or my act at a particular time in a specific situation." ("The Philosophical Significance of Schleiermacher's Hermeneutics," 84–85.) Michael Forster makes a similar point: "Schleiermacher implies, very plausibly, that . . . in order to fix the linguistic meaning of words and sentences one often needs to address problems of semantic and syntactic ambiguity, and that can only be done by appeal to conjectures about the author's intentions." (*After Herder: Philosophy of Language in the German Tradition* (New York: Oxford, 2010), 374.)

20. Gadamer repeats this point in "The Problem of Language in Schleiermacher's Hermeneutics," 77.

21. None of this eliminates the possibility for correct interpretation. Gadamer does not here spell out a criterion of correctness. He does, however, describe what happens if we interpret correctly: "The interpretive concepts are not, as such, thematic in understanding. Rather, it is their nature to disappear behind what they bring to speech in interpretation. Paradoxically, an interpretation is right when it is capable of disappearing in this way" (*TM*, 416).

22. This broader claim—that we understand *being* in language—Gadamer will defend later in TM III.3. Here in TM III.1 he is primarily concerned with the narrower claim that we understand *texts* in language. He does, however, make clear his commitment to the broader claim, and he offers some preliminary reasons in support of it. Due to limitations of space, however, those reasons have been omitted from this chapter.

23. For more on this, see John Arthos, *The Inner Word in Gadamer's Hermeneutics* (Notre Dame, IN: Notre Dame), 2009, as well as Gert-Jan van der Heiden's contribution to this volume.

Chapter 12

TM III.2
Gadamer and the Concept of Language

Gert-Jan van der Heiden

To develop the basic concepts of philosophical hermeneutics, Gadamer's conversation with the history of philosophy is of utmost importance. The third part of *Truth and Method* is devoted to an analysis of the philosophical role and place of language in human thinking and understanding. The engagement with the concepts of language that have been developed in the course of Western thought is the task of the second section of this third part: "The Development of the Concept of Language in the History of Western Thought."[1]

The subject matter or *Sache* in this conversation with the history of philosophy is the mode of being of language, *die Seinsweise der Sprache*. Gadamer argues that the history of philosophy is marked by some remarkable distortions of the nature of language. Two basic, related distortions stand out. First, the philosophical understanding of language is marked by a *semiotic* conception of words as signs, and this has led to a strictly *instrumental* conception of language: words are signs of thoughts and language can be used as a vehicle to communicate our thoughts or ideas. This semiotic conception of language as a sign system obscures the *ontological* relation between word and thing (*Sache*), as well as the *epistemological* relation between language and thinking.[2] Second, the instrumentalization has led to a specific understanding of concept formation guided by the ideals of *univocity*, so that each concept expresses one and only one meaning, and of *universality*, so that different particulars can be recognized as particulars of one and the same concept. These ideals, however, tend to devalue and obscure the *logical* importance of natural concept formation, which does not meet the demands of universality and univocity.

The goal of this chapter is to analyze and comment on 1) how Gadamer aims to overcome these distortions in the historical-philosophical conceptions of language and 2) how he explicates the epistemological, ontological, and logical roles of language in such a way that they avoid the distortions to which such understandings of the mode of being of language lead. Following the order of Gadamer's own text, which follows the historical development of the concept of language, I will first discuss the ancient Greek philosophical experience of language as *onoma* or word in relation to *logos*, subsequently the patristic and medieval Christian conception of language as *verbum* modeled on the theological doctrine of the trinity, and finally the Renaissance humanist conception of language, which is marked by a characteristic interest in and account of the plurality of languages.

1. THE GREEK EXPERIENCE OF LANGUAGE

"In the earliest times the intimate unity of word and thing was so obvious that the true name was considered to be part of the bearer of the name, if not indeed to substitute for him" (*TM*, 423). Thus reads the opening sentence of "The Development of the Concept of Language in the History of Western Thought." In the Greek language, as Gadamer notes, this intimate unity is expressed by the very word for word; *onoma* means originally one's "'proper name' . . . the name by which one is called." (*TM*, 423) Each time that only one person answers to the name we call, we experience the unity of the name and the one who is named. In this sense, the proper name is the exemplary word, and the co-belonging of name and named is paradigmatic for the unity of word and thing.

The philosophical reflection on language, however, interrupts this basic trust in the word and its unity with the thing. In the pre-philosophical experience, the name exemplifies—that is, the name is the *Vorbild* of—the unity of word and thing. However, as soon as philosophers point out that names are not fixed but can be altered, it becomes clear that the name does not always and simply name the thing as it is. Thus, the name turns into a counterexample—a *Gegenbild*—of the unity of word and thing (*TM*, 424/409).[3] In the context of a reflection on language and words, philosophy thus begins by suspending the basic trust in the word. The reason for such a suspension and the reason for distrusting the word, as Plato's dialogues sufficiently show us, is found in the philosophers' struggle with the sophists. The domain of interrogation of the latter is the field of words alone. Their examinations of language, however, do not lead to the truth of the thing discussed but rather distort the thing and thus lead people astray.

It is this confrontation that led ancient philosophy to the conviction that "the proper being of language (*das eigene Sein der Sprache*)" can only be understood as "confusion (*Beirrung*)" (*TM,* 435/422).[4] Gadamer summarizes the approach of ancient thought as follows: "Thus from early on, the Greek philosophers fought against the 'onoma' as the source of the seduction and confusion of thought (*die Verführung und Beirrung des Denkens*), and instead embraced the ideality that is constantly created in language" (*TM,* 422/435). In this summarizing account, we discern two approaches to what Gadamer calls language (*Sprache*): the first one is oriented toward the sensuous word, *onoma*, of which all natural languages are composed; the second one, however, subordinates this sensuous nature of language under the authority of what Greek thought called *logos*. The latter subordination detaches language from the reign of the word and brings into play another conception of language, which since then has dominated the philosophical understanding of language.

For Gadamer, Plato's dialogue *Cratylus* is the exemplary ancient locus for this philosophical polemic with the word because it offers the main arguments on which later sources in ancient thought only vary. In order to grasp the basic thrust of Gadamer's interpretation of this dialogue, I distinguish between, on the one hand, Plato's actual argumentation and explicit goal in the *Cratylus* and, on the other hand, that which, according to Gadamer, is forgotten or kept silent in this dialogue.

1.1 The Argumentation and Goal of the *Cratylus*

The first aim of the dialogue's interrogation of the word or *onoma* is to decide between two conflicting theories of the word. The difference between these two theories basically goes back to the distinction between *phusis* and *nomos*, between nature and custom. According to the first, "*phusei theory*," word and thing are related by nature, that is to say, there is a natural resemblance or similarity between the word and the thing to which it refers. Therefore, Gadamer also refers to it as the "*similarity theory*" (*TM,* 427, 424). In this theory, the word is understood as *mimēsis* or *Darstellung*, a presentation or representation of the thing; the word is an image (*Bild*) or a copy (*Abbild*) of the thing. In this theory, modeled on Plato's conception of *mimēsis*, it makes perfect sense to speak of the truth of a word: a word is true if it is a good copy, resembling the thing and presenting it as it is; it is false if it is a bad copy, presenting the thing in a distorted way. Much of the discussion in the *Cratylus*, especially the multiple peculiar derivations of words from their resemblance with the things they present, presuppose this particular theory of the word.[5]

The second, conventionalist theory argues that word and thing are not related naturally, that there is no resemblance between the two, but that the word is added to the thing by custom and convention. The word is nothing but a *sign* of the thing. Therefore, the conventionalist theory of language ultimately implies the semiotic conception of language. In light of the question of the truth of language, Socrates offers a rather clear-cut refutation of conventionalism by arguing that a statement can only be true if its constituents, the words or names, are true. However, from a conventionalist point of view, it makes no sense to say that a name is true: it is, after all, only an arbitrary sign referring to a thing. If, indeed, the word needs to be true, a natural relation between word and thing needs to exist and, hence, the similarity theory seems to be the only feasible alternative of the two. However, the progressive demolition of the similarity theory that takes place in the course of the *Cratylus* ends up with important examples that in fact presuppose a conventional name for a thing. The name of a number, for instance, has no resemblance with the number it represents: "the whole principle of similarity falters and is refuted by such examples as the words for numbers," as Gadamer concludes (*TM*, 427). The final result of the comparison of these two theories is that the similarity theory is not sufficient and that convention needs to step in to complement it at crucial stages.

This result has important implications for the philosophical conception of language that follows from it and continues to influence our conception of language today. In fact, as Gadamer suggests, "Wedged in between image and sign, the being of language could only be reduced to the level of pure sign" (*TM*, 435). To understand why the confusion between the similarity and conventionalist theory leads to the ultimate victory of a version of the conventionalist theory, we need to turn to the specific goal of the *Cratylus*. Because of the strange mixture of theories Socrates ends up employing in order to account for language, the basic conclusion is that the word by itself does not offer us the means to get to the truth of things. For Plato, however, this conclusion is a very fortunate one because it allows him to completely break with the realm of words and with the question of their correctness, thus settling his dispute with the sophists. To examine the truth of things, we cannot limit ourselves to an inquiry of language and words alone, but we rather require dialectics.

As Gadamer emphasizes, the dialectical surpassing of the realm of words does not imply that "there really is such a thing as knowledge without words, but only that it is not the word that opens up the way to truth. Rather, on the contrary, the adequacy of the word can be judged only from the knowledge of the thing it refers to" (*TM*, 425). Knowledge of the things allows us to speak adequately about them and allows us to judge whether the statements we make about the things are true, that is, correspond to the truth of the things and their relations. The true nature of thinking is thus not found in the art of rhetoric or in the power of the word, but in the dialogue of the soul with itself by which the soul aims to attune itself to the total and rational arrangement of the ideas. The Greek name for this order is *logos* and to speak truthfully means to speak guided by knowledge of this rational order. It is in this sense that Gadamer can conclude that for Greek philosophy truth cannot be found in natural language and its words, but only in a language that is a sign-system that represents the order of the *logos*. In this sense, Gadamer concludes, "it is *not word but number* that is the real paradigm of the noetic" (*TM*, 430). The rational order in which the number has its place grants the number its exactness; the conventional sign that refers to the number is, thanks to this exactitude and order, strictly univocal. By contrast, the words of which our natural languages are composed are ambiguous and equivocal; they do not represent a strict rational order but suffer from indeterminacy; they can take on different shades of meaning when used in particular contexts or circumstances. It is in this context that language, modeled on the paradigm of the word, can only be understood as a confusion of thinking. By contrast, the semiotic concept of language becomes the preferred scientific and philosophical conception: only as a *sign system*, modeled on the paradigm of the number, can language be used as an *instrument* of thought to *represent univocally* and *adequately* the rational order of what is.

1.2 The Forgotten and Obscured Being of the Word

When reading Gadamer's account of the *Cratylus*, one notices that he does not only paint the picture of how the semiotic and instrumental conception of language is born in and from Plato's considerations; he also points out where and when in the dialogue Plato makes important, strategic decisions to gain a victory over the sophists. In and by these decisions, Plato tends to obscure and forget other important venues of investigation that might allow the being of language and the being of the word to be understood differently.

First, despite their difference, both the similarity and the conventionalist theory begin with the same presupposition, namely, that words exist and are instrumental and that things are already known separately by other means than by their names and by language. "Thus they start too late," as Gadamer concludes (*TM*, 425). These theories presuppose a *separation* of words and things and thus have already abandoned the primordial unity of word and thing; consequently, they can grasp the correctness of the word only in terms of a *correspondence* between word and thing.

Gadamer generously suggests that Plato is fully aware of this presupposition: "We must then ask if, in showing the two extreme positions to be untenable, Plato is questioning a presupposition common to them both" (*TM*, 425). Although he does not really pursue the latter suggestion explicitly, his considerations concerning the principle of similarity and the particular mimetic nature of the word that is at stake in the similarity theory might perhaps be read in line with this suggestion. In this theory, the *mimēsis* of the word is not to be understood as mere imitation; it is rather a genuine *Darstellung*, a presentation of the thing. This particular sense of *mimēsis* seems to concern an understanding of the being of language that, for Gadamer, precedes the distinction between a natural and a conventional conception of the word. Indeed, to speak of *mimēsis* in relation to the word is to say that the word is "making the thing meant apparent (*das Offenbarmachen der gemeinten Sache*)" (*TM*, 428/414). The being of the word is the disclosure and the making manifest of the thing and its meaning. Yet, by choosing the concept of *mimēsis* to account for the relation between word and thing, the similarity theory also introduces a *distance* between word and thing: after all, to say that a copy is a *mimēsis* is to say that the copy does not only present the original but also presents something else, namely, it shows itself as *not* being the original, as being different from the original.[6] This distance, however, does not do justice to the unity that is at stake when we say that the word makes the thing manifest.

At this point, Gadamer argues that by accounting for the being of the word—that is, the making manifest of the thing—in terms of the model of *mimēsis*, a more intimate unity of word and thing is hidden from view. Consider the following important citation:

> But words name things in a much too intimate and intellectual (*geistigere*) way for the question of the degree of similarity to be appropriate here. . . . Thus we may speak of an *absolute perfection of the word*, inasmuch as there is no perceptible relationship—i.e., no gap—between its appearance to the senses and its meaning. . . . [The "truth" of a word] lies rather in its perfect intellectuality (*Geistigkeit*)—i.e., the manifestness of the word's meaning in its sound. In this sense all words are "true"—i.e., their being is wholly absorbed in their meaning—whereas a copy is only more or less similar and thus, judged by reference to the appearance of the original, only more or less correct. (*TM*, 428–29/414–15)

We are so much accustomed to understanding words as representations or signs of things that the phenomenological evidence of the position that Gadamer defends here may easily escape us. He appeals to the following basic experience. If we don't understand the meaning of a word when we listen to someone speaking, we actually *don't* hear words but rather hear only empty sounds; and, vice versa, when we hear a word, we understand its meaning. This is the very being of a word: unlike the sign, the word displays no gap between its sensible appearance and the meaning it discloses. The truth of the word is this immediate manifestation of its meaning in its sensible appearance. This unity of word and meaning precedes both theories that Plato discusses in the *Cratylus* because this unity cannot be understood in terms of a correspondence. The question of correspondence can only be raised when different ways of speaking about a thing make this thing manifest in different ways, and when one of these manifestations is taken as the measure or norm for the others. It is in this sense that the phenomenological unity of word and thing is ontologically prior to the questions of representation and correspondence and, in fact, is their condition of possibility.

Second, one might object to the previous considerations that Plato's distinction between language and thinking is not taken into account here. Should one not say that there is a primacy of thinking the truth of the thing dialectically and that, subsequently, this knowledge may be represented adequately in language? Along these lines, the epistemological issue of the relation between thought and language imposes itself in the wake of the ontological question concerning the unity of word and thing. With respect to Plato's distinction between natural language and the correctness of the words versus philosophical dialectics and the truth of the ideas, Gadamer wonders why Plato forgot to reflect on the fact that also dialectics is *linguistic* in nature. Even though Gadamer appreciates Plato's struggle with the sophists, he deems this latter forgetfulness to be devastating: "The net result, then, is that Plato's discovery of the ideas conceals the true nature of language even more than the theories of the Sophists, who developed their own art (techne) in the use and abuse of language" (*TM,* 426). As Gadamer adds, Plato argues on "the basic assumption that words have no real cognitive significance of their own, a conclusion that points beyond the whole sphere of words and the question of their correctness to the knowledge of the thing" (*TM,* 426). Yet, it is somewhat curious that much later in the second section of the third part of *Truth and Method,* Gadamer actually acknowledges the epistemological importance of Plato's "flight into the *logoi,*" thus contradicting his previous statement (*TM,* 447). Perhaps we may conclude that, at this point, Gadamer exaggerates his critique of Plato because, at other places, he acknowledges that the relation between thinking and speaking is not simply absent in Plato's dialogue. Can we truly say that discourse is forgotten when Plato uses an image borrowed from the practice of human discourse—dialogue—to characterize thinking? Perhaps, to anticipate the discussion in the next section, the sensuous, outer character of language is suspended here in order to demonstrate that language has an inner dimension intrinsically relating it to thought and that speaking has an intimate connection to thinking, which therefore can be portrayed as silent dialogue?

2. THE TRINITARIAN MODEL OF LANGUAGE

For the next step in his examination of the historical-philosophical conceptions of language, Gadamer turns to medieval philosophy and theology. This part confronts his readers with two highly sophisticated concepts in Christian theology, namely, that of the incarnation, or the becoming human of God in Christ, and that of the doctrine of trinity, which aims to establish the relation between the three persona of God—that is, Father, Son, and Holy Spirit. Because this doctrine includes the relation of God the Father and God the Son, it is indispensable for a theological understanding of the incarnation.[7] The question of why the interrogation of incarnation and trinity is of importance to a reflection on the concept of language has a simple answer: in the Christian tradition, God the Son is identified with the word of God, the *verbum Dei*. Therefore, as Gadamer suggests, the Christian theological reflection on the relation between God and Christ provides a truly non-Greek understanding of the being of the word.

As the word of God, the notion of word—*logos* in Greek and *verbum* in Latin—has a particular theological significance, which indeed goes far beyond the Greek conception of the word as *onoma*. As the book of Genesis narrates, creation—an incomprehensible idea to the ancient Greek mind—is through the word of God: God speaks the word and the cosmos comes into being. Moreover, as the opening lines of the Gospel of John suggest, Christ himself is the word of God that has become flesh and thus makes God and his redemption of the world known to humans. This idea of incarnation is also non-Greek, for two reasons, as Gadamer notes. First, it needs to be distinguished from the Greek idea of embodiment. While, for instance, as Plato argues in the *Phaedo*, Greek thought conceives of the body as a prison for the soul from which it needs to be liberated because the body contaminates the soul with its lowliness, the becoming human of Christ does not reduce the divine status of Christ in any way: he is and fully remains God. Second, incarnation is completely different from the way in which the Greek gods adopt a human form: the latter do not lose but rather fully maintain their divine powers (*TM*, 436). As opposed to the Greek gods, the incarnation of Christ is a genuine *kenosis*, as St. Paul notes in Philippians 2:6–8. By becoming human, Christ gives up superhuman characteristics, such as his immortality and eternity and, hence, becomes a mortal human being living in a specific historical period of time; this *kenosis* becomes the ultimate sacrifice when he dies the most scandalous and humiliating death imaginable in the Roman era, namely, death by crucifixion.

The double role of the word in Christian theology—as the word of creation and of redemption—motivates the patristic reinterpretation of the Stoic distinction between *inner word* and *outer word*, as Gadamer notes. Rather than conceiving of the external, outer word as diminishing the divine *logos*, as the Stoics did, the theological reinterpretation points out the positive significance of the relation between these two words. For the Stoics, *logos* is the principle of the *kosmos*. Similarly, the inner word is the *logos* or word with which God created the cosmos—that is, it is also here the principle of the *kosmos*. The outer word, on the other hand, is the word that has become flesh in Jesus of Nazareth. The life, death, and resurrection of Jesus is nothing less than the divine act of the redemption of the *kosmos*. Hence, the outer word does not weaken or diminish the inner word but rather brings it to fulfillment and brings to light a new sense or dimension of the inner word: the creation of the world is fulfilled and brought to completion in and by the redemption.

The goal of Gadamer's discussion of the incarnation and the doctrine of the trinity is twofold. First, he aims to extend, by analogy, the theological reinterpretation of the relation between inner and outer word to the sphere of human language so that the outer word, the word that is actually said aloud—"speaking the word aloud in the vox (*das Lautwerden des Wortes in der vox*)"—may be appreciated for what it truly is and does, namely, to *complete* the inner word or *logos* of thought (*TM*, 437/423). Second, he aims to extend, by analogy, the doctrinal description of the relation between God the Father and God the Son, this time in terms of the inner word, to an interpretation of the relation between thinking and speaking. He notes that Latin offers two translations of the Greek *logos*: *ratio*, reason, and *verbum*, word. This double translation, he argues, suggests that medieval thought is much more aware than Greek thought of the positive role of the word in the *process* of thought: the relation between God the Father and God the Son depicts the life and liveliness of divine thought as a relation between reason and inner word. Let me, as in the previous section, try to elucidate what this means for both the ontological and the epistemological issue.

2.1 The Being of the Word as Event

Theologically, the inner word of God concerns the inner rational order of creation, which by definition marks creation from its very beginning and is, in this sense, ahistorical. The outer word, however, concerns the singular, unique event of God becoming human at a certain moment in history. In this sense, the outer word is given *in* the sensuous, temporal world of human existence and in this existence itself. Because, theologically, the historical reality of humanity begins with the Fall and being expelled from Paradise, the redemption that Christ brings into the world by his life, death, and resurrection is a genuine event in this history: it divides this history into two, a time before this event and a time after it. When Gadamer writes "the word is pure event," he definitely has the epoch-making character of the becoming flesh of the word of God in mind (*TM,* 437). Yet, it also means something more. The life, death, and resurrection of Christ is not only a revolutionary event in the course of human history, as, for instance, Alain Badiou and others insist in their understanding of St. Paul, but it is also a genuine *word* for Gadamer.[8] As the Gospel of John clearly states, Christ is the word of God—that is, he is *the event of making* God the Father *manifest,* as well as his redemptive work. To say that the word is an event is to say that it makes its subject matter manifest and that this manifestation itself defines its epoch-making character because it is only by the appearance of the word in the world that the subject matter is revealed in and to the world. The unity of word and thing is exemplified here in the figure of Christ and his redemptive work: without the word, there would be no redemption.

This characteristic of the word as event is also emphasized several times when Gadamer discusses the inner word.[9] At stake in this event of making manifest is that the word is not something in addition to the subject matter, but is the sheer manifestation of the subject matter—and this is what makes it true: "the word that is true, because it says what the thing is, is nothing by itself and does not seek to be anything: nihil de suo habens, sed totum de ilia scientia de qua nascitur. It has its being in its revealing (*Offenbarmachen*)" (*TM,* 438/425). Theologically, this unity of word and thing is the heart of the matter: Christ as the word of God is nothing else than God—simply put, Christ is God—but as word he is the event that makes God the Father known to the world and enacts the divine redemption; as creative word he makes the rationality of God the Father known in the act of creation.

Yet, there is a difference with respect to the inner word or the divine *logos* as the principle of creation and the outer word or the historical appearance of Christ that makes the redemptive work of God the Father known. The former is not only eternal but is also always already given in the cosmos as its basic principle. The latter, however, appears in history at a certain time and is now no longer present on Earth in bodily form. What does this mean for the outer word? How is it present, how does this word make its subject matter known? Does it not disappear as every historical, outer word seems to do? Is it said aloud once and then slowly dies out and is never heard again? The crucial category, as already Kierkegaard knew, is that of *repetition*: the outer word, marked by historical rather than eternal presence, has to be repeated to be present. It is in this sense, as Gadamer notes, that even the unity of the word—which is so much cherished in the medieval theological reflections on the word of God that they prefer to limit themselves to a consideration of the eternal, inner word—cannot exist without *multiplicity* and *multiplication* when it concerns the outer word. Not only the appearance of Christ but also successive proclamations make the gospel known: "The proclamation of salvation, the content of the Christian gospel, is itself an event that takes place in sacrament and preaching, and yet it expresses only what took place in Christ's redemptive act" (*TM,* 444). The unity that is thus maintained is obviously a theological one, grounded in the unity of God and the eternal inner word. The exact nature and the positive meaning of this multiplicity for human understanding in more general terms is only brought to light in the reflections on language in the Renaissance, as discussed in section 3.

2.2 Thought and the Inner Word

As noted before, Gadamer argues that the double Latin translation of the Greek *logos* as *ratio* and *verbum* reflects the medieval attentiveness to the role of language in the process of thinking; clearly, the double translation of *logos* is mirrored in the theological account of the relation between God the Father and God the Son. Gadamer is sometimes criticized for the claim that the theological notion of the inner word offers a genuinely new understanding of language that can be useful for philosophical hermeneutics; after all, the inner word is eternal and lacks true externality, so it seems rather distant from all the concerns that mark philosophical hermeneutics and its attention to the historical nature of language and its multiplicity. However, this criticism tends to overlook exactly the fact that there is a *double* translation of *logos*; hence, there is genuine multiplicity in the trinity. Although the "externality" of the inner word remains within the eternal confines of God, this multiplication does grant an inner life to divine thinking—and it is exactly the word of God that generates this life and relation between reason and inner word in the divine mind.

Whereas the Greek philosophical reflection has argued for the primacy of the *logos* of thinking over the word of speaking, the theological paradigm cannot conceive of the word of God as a devaluation—for instance, as a mere copy of a thought of God or, even worse, as a mere sign—because the Son is not lower in degree or rank than the Father. The Nicene creed clearly states this: while the creation of God is lower than God, the Son is not created by the Father; the Son is born or begotten but is of the same essence of and consubstantial with the Father. Therefore, as Gadamer points out, the church has used the Neoplatonist vocabulary of emanation in order to emphasize that the word flowing from or begotten by God does not diminish or weaken God in any way. Rather, the begetting of the Son is a process that remains immanent to God itself. Mirroring the double sense of *ratio* and *verbum*, Gadamer argues that this theological model also guides the medieval understanding of the process of thinking and its relation to the word (*TM,* 440).

How to understand this relation? One might be tempted to understand it in terms of the human incapacity to think without the word:

> Because our understanding does not comprehend what it knows in one single inclusive glance, it must always draw what it thinks out of itself, and present it to itself as if in an inner dialogue with itself. In this sense all thought is speaking to oneself. (*TM*, 440)

This "finiteness of our discursive understanding" that motivates the supplementary need of the word is indeed characteristic for human thought—and the fact that Gadamer uses Plato's image of thinking as a dialogue of the soul with itself shows that this need of the word is not foreign to the ancient Greeks. Yet, this finitude cannot have a place in the process of the internal, eternal divine relations between Father, Son, and Holy Spirit. In this sense, the analogy between the process of thinking and the process of the divine *personae* cannot be understood in terms of this finitude. In fact, if we would approach the analogy in this way, we would lose the genuine insight that the doctrine of the trinity has to offer. Rather, the analogy concerns the actual birth of the word from thinking. Just as the Son is not made or created by the Father, but born from the Father, the word is not made or created after the process of thinking when thought articulates its knowledge in language, but the word is born in the very process of thinking as an integral part of this process. This birth marks the life of the divine mind.

In this trinitarian model, the word is not the result of thinking, used by thought to express its knowledge and to make it known to others; if this were the case, the word would, for thinking, only be a reflection of itself, in which it can recognize itself. Instead, the model suggests that the formation of the word is part and parcel of the process of thinking. The Neoplatonist figure of emanation suggests that the process of thinking itself includes—not its self-expression but—its self-overflowing in the "begetting of the word (*Erzeugung des Wortes*)" (*TM*, 441/428, translation modified)[10] that makes a subject matter known to thinking itself. Hence, in thinking, I come to know a subject matter in the words that are formed. Gadamer emphasizes that this overflowing begetting or engendering of the word by thinking should not be mistaken for the description of *reflection* (*TM*, 443). The word cannot be a reflection in which thought recognizes or comes to know itself because the word does not express thought; it rather makes the subject matter known that we aim to understand.

This analogy between the human and the divine mind, however, should not obscure some substantial differences, as Gadamer notes, with the view of Thomas Aquinas. The human word is imperfect due to the finitude of the human mind, which "does not really know what it knows." Moreover, the human word does not reach completion; it cannot contain the thing "as a whole within itself" (*TM*, 443). These two aspects of the finitude of human thinking and human language, however, have a positive significance in the self-transgression of the human mind and the self-surpassing of the words that humans engender in their attempts to think a subject matter. It is this dimension that is brought to full fruition in the Renaissance humanist reflections on the plurality of human language.

3. THE RENAISSANCE HUMANIST EXPERIENCE OF LANGUAGE

In his reading of Plato's *Cratylus*, Gadamer concludes that the ancient Greek examination of language offers us the outlines of a semiotic and instrumental concept of language. The scientific and logical perfection of this concept is found in an artificial language composed of signs that are univocal and together represent and express the logical order of the world. Even though humans do not know this logical order of the world in all its complexity, this ideal does guide the scientific understanding of the logic of concept formation: in science, we always examine particular cases and conduct individual experiments, but these cases are scientifically conceived of as particulars subordinated under a universal and univocal concept. Concept formation in science thus aims at developing such universal and univocal concepts that reflect the logical order of the world and that allow us to subordinate the particular cases encountered in the world to these concepts (*TM*, 446). From the perspective of this ideal language with its universal and univocal concepts, the natural human languages are flawed because, due to their ambiguity and inexactitude, they cannot live up to the demands of this ideal language, and, therefore, they are not up to the task to represent the rational order of the world.

Gadamer's exploration of the medieval conception of language, guided by the trinitarian relation between God the Father and God the Son, allows him to point to the more intimate and integral relation between thinking and speaking than a semiotic conception of language can account for. In conversation with the Renaissance humanist Nicholas of Cusa, Gadamer subsequently aims to show how the life of natural languages and the way in which words and concepts are formed in them suggest a different logic reflecting the intimate and integral relation between speaking and thinking. The life of a natural language actually displays another epistemological model than the scientific one in which language's natural concept formation plays a constitutive role in our understanding of the world, mirroring in linguistic terms Gadamer's account of hermeneutic experience, as discussed in the second part of *Truth and Method*.

When we try to understand a specific thing we encounter in the world and when we begin to speak about it, we do not aim to subordinate our specific experience with this thing to a universal and univocal concept; rather, we are so much immersed in the singularity of the thing we encounter and the circumstances in which we encounter it that the words or concepts we use in our attempt to articulate our experience with this thing actually *enrich* their general meaning. Words and concepts have a general meaning. Yet, the fact that language allows us to use them also to articulate the singular encounter with this thing does not mean that we subordinate this experience under this general meaning, but rather that we extend and enrich this general meaning with this singular experience and articulation, "so that what emerges is a new, more specific word formation which does more justice to the particularity of that act of perception" (*TM*, 446). Hence, while to speak always means to use words with a general meaning, their meaning is further developed, specified, and changed in the process of speaking; this is the "life [of meaning] of a language" (*TM*, 446).

This account of natural concept formation indeed mirrors Gadamer's earlier descriptions of (hermeneutic) experience.[11] Experience is more than perception. While perception only offers us a multiplicity of perceptions and does not inform us about the relation between them, experience concerns the discernment of similarities between perceptions, relating and gathering these perceptions. Experience is also different from conceptual thought: the actual discernment of similarities does not offer us a universal concept that allows us to subordinate the multiple particular perceptions to the unity of the concept. In the history of philosophy, as Gadamer argues in the second part of *Truth and Method*, experience is usually understood as the intermediate stage between the multiplicity of perception and the unity of the universal and univocal concept: experience is *no longer* the sheer multiplicity of particular perceptions but is also *not yet* the unity of the universal concept. It is this latter subordination of experience to the universal concept to which Gadamer objects because there are many domains of the world in which finite human understanding can never reach a universal, divine understanding of the world. In these cases, experience is the only form of understanding available to humans. To argue that we could understand this human experience as subordinated to a concept available to us would be to transgress the boundary between human and divine thought and, consequently, to obscure the specific nature of *human* language.

The work of Nicholas of Cusa conveys a similar conviction and develops it in his conception of human language. Due to its finitude, human understanding is different from divine understanding. This finitude can be traced in the inexact, imprecise, and ambiguous nature of human languages: their words and concepts are incapable of expressing the rational order of the world, as the divine concepts do. Nevertheless, as Cusa argues, there *is* a congruence between the human word and the actual thing, but this congruence remains imprecise and equivocal. This imprecision, however, is exactly the source of the multiplicity of human languages: different experiences of the world lead to different articulations, and from this differentiation and multiplication of experience and expression, the multiplicity of human languages is born.

This has both a metaphysical and a logical implication, and to understand Gadamer's account of Nicholas of Cusa, it is important to distinguish these two. Metaphysically, the multiplicity of human languages is subordinated to the logical and rational order of divine thought.[12] Natural human languages are the result of the human encounter with this order; experiencing and understanding this order takes place in speaking and in the natural formation of words and concepts. Logically, however, the artificial conceptual language of the sciences cannot coincide with this order since it is beyond any human grasp. In fact, one cannot even claim that the artificial sign language approaches the divine logical order better. After all, the artificial language is itself a human construct based on the human experience of reality as made manifest in the natural languages and is in this sense derived from it;[13] and even though the artificial language of the sciences mimics the universality and univocality of the divine order in their concept formation, they can only do so by emptying out the specific human experience of reality to which the natural languages attest. If the human word is truly congruent to the thing in the natural languages, then moving away from the richness of this congruence by artificially imposing univocity and universality is moving away from the linguistic domain which is most attuned to the divine order. To phrase it in the Platonic terms of *mimēsis*, the artificial language of logic and science indeed imitates the univocity and universality of the divine order, but it results in a mere simulacrum—that is, a bad copy that has lost its resemblance with the life of divine thought to which the trinitarian model has made Gadamer attentive.

Analogously, the primordial task for human understanding is not the subordination of experience to a universal concept. This subordination rather empties out and renders bloodless the liveliness of the actual human encounter with reality. That the human encounter with reality concerns the understanding and knowing of the thing encountered is not demonstrated by scientific, conceptual understanding but rather by experience. In fact, because conceptual understanding begins by suspending the lively human encounter with reality, one could even make the case that it is the very ideal of mere conceptual knowledge that has given rise in the first place to the idea that the human encounter with reality is actually and fundamentally different from understanding and knowing; after all, if scientific knowledge would be genuine understanding, the human immediate encounter with the world cannot be genuine understanding and, hence, must be something else. The hermeneutic conviction, however, is otherwise: *to experience is to experience that the lively encounter with reality takes place as understanding.*

In the human life of understanding, the unity of thinking and speaking is the unity of experiencing similarities and begetting—*Erzeugung*—the words that make these similarities manifest. Therefore, linguistically, Gadamer describes the experiential form of understanding in terms of the fundamental metaphoricity of language.[14] Different experiences of the world beget different wordings that make the discerned similarities manifest to thinking.[15] While the ambiguous and imprecise nature of natural language appears as a flaw in light of the ideal of an artificial language of univocal and universal concepts, it now becomes clear that this ambiguity and inexactitude actually mirrors the human plurality of the human experience of the world as well as the human openness to encounter and experience reality in different ways:[16] "Suddenly it is of positive significance that things can be articulated in various ways . . . according to their similarities and their differences" (*TM*, 452).[17]

To experience that the world is different than I anticipated is an event of understanding; similarly, to make unprecedented, unexpected and unforeseen similarities manifest in a language is an event of understanding. As historical phenomena, languages remember and preserve the human experiences articulated in them. To those who listen to the languages handed down to them, they disclose the encounters with the world that were once expressed in them.

NOTES

1. Gadamer, Hans-Georg. *Truth and Method*, 2nd ed., trans. Joel Weinsheimer and Donald G. Marshall (New York: Bloomsbury Publishing, 2013), 409–42. Hereafter cited in text as *TM*. Where the German is cited or the translation has been altered, the page number of the original is indicated after the slash. The latter refer to Hans-Georg Gadamer, *Wahrheit und Methode*, Gesammelte Werke I (Tübingen: Mohr Siebeck, 1990).

2. Note that the English translation translates the German *die Sache* both as "thing," for example, in the expression "word and thing (*Wort und Sache*)" and as "subject matter."

3. The English translation does not really capture the striking opposition between *Vorbild* and *Gegenbild*. By paraphrasing *Gegenbild* as "substituting," the translation in fact introduces a confusion that is absent from the original: in the first paragraph of this section, Gadamer writes that in the experienced unity of name and thing, the

name is a *Stellvertreter*, which is also translated as "substitute." Yet, the name as *Gegenbild* is the exact opposite of the name as *Stellvertreter*.

4. I'm not following the reinterpretation of the English translation (see *TM*, 422/435) that renders Gadamer's actual phrasing in such a way that it says that the idea that language has its own being is a confusion; however, Gadamer's actual phrase is somewhat stronger: he writes that the proper being of language is confusion (of thinking).

5. In fact, as Gadamer argues, "The discussion stays entirely within the fundamental assumptions of the 'nature' theory—i.e., the similarity principle—demolishing it only by progressive limitation" (*TM*, 427).

6. See, for example, Plato, *Sophist*, 240a–b.

7. For an extensive study of the role played by the trinitarian model in Gadamer's hermeneutics, see, John Arthos, *The Inner Word in Gadamer's Hermeneutics* (Notre Dame, IN: University of Notre Dame Press, 2009).

8. Alain Badiou, *Saint Paul: La fondation de l'universalisme* (Paris: PUF, 1997).

9. "Certainly the word is not the event of utterance, this irrevocable handing over of one's own thinking to another, but the word still has the ontological character of an event" (*TM*, 439).

10. The decision in the English translation to translate *Erzeugung* as "creation" runs the risk of confusing the theological background of Gadamer's discussion: the Son is not made (*poieō*), but is begotten (*gennaō*), as the Nicene creed insists for the very reasons that Gadamer exposes here: to be created means to be in a lower degree of being than the creator and to be outside of the internal process of the trinity (and by analogy: the process of thinking). *Erzeugung* is better seen as Gadamer's translation of *gennēsis* in its distinction from *poiēsis*.

11. For the concept of (hermeneutic) experience in Gadamer and others, see Gert-Jan van der Heiden, "Poverty and Promise: Towards a Primordial Hermeneutic Experience," in *Phenomenology and Experience: New Perspectives*, ed. Antonio Cimino, Cees Leijenhorst (Leiden/Boston: Brill, 2019), 63–80. On hermeneutic experience, see also Greg Lynch's chapter in this volume.

12. "In the infinite there is, then, only one single thing (*forma*) and one single word (*vocabulum*), namely the ineffable word of God (*verbum Dei*) that is reflected in everything (*relucet*)" (*TM*, 454). This also implies that human language necessarily remains imprecise and incomplete; as Grondin notes, this relates the problematic of the inner word to that of the universality of hermeneutics. See Jean Grondin, *Introduction to Philosophical Hermeneutics*, trans. Joel Weinsheimer (New Haven, CT: Yale University Press, 1994), xiii–xiv.

13. Gadamer notes that both Plato and Aristotle knew this; however, Aristotle relays the linguistic expression of similarities of experience to rhetoric: "What originally constituted the basis of the life of language and its logical productivity, the spontaneous and inventive seeking out of similarities by means of which it is possible to order things, is now marginalized and instrumentalized into a rhetorical figure called metaphor" (*TM*, 449).

14. "This is its fundamental metaphorical nature (*seine grundsätzliche Metaphorik*)" (*TM*, 446/433). For a more extensive account of the notion of metaphor for the

conception of language in continental thought, see also Gert-Jan van der Heiden, *The Truth (and Untruth) of Language: Heidegger, Ricoeur, and Derrida on Disclosure and Displacement* (Pittsburgh, PA: Duquesne University Press, 2010), 124–80.

15. "The particularity of an experience finds expression in metaphorical transference, and it is not at all the fruit of a concept formed by means of abstraction" (*TM*, 446).

16. "Experience is always actually present only in the individual observation. It is not known in a previous universality. Here lies the fundamental openness of experience to new experience" (*TM*, 360).

17. "That is why it is always artificial and contrary to the nature of language to measure the contingency of natural concept formation against the true order of things and to see the former as purely accidental. This contingency comes about, in fact, through the human mind's necessary and legitimate range of variation in articulating the essential order of things" (*TM*, 453).

Chapter 13

TM III.3

On Language and the Universality of Hermeneutics

James Risser

In writing *Truth and Method*, Gadamer had always understood the perspective of hermeneutics to be all encompassing. What Gadamer often refers to as the universality of hermeneutics, or better, its universal aspect, is nothing other than this encompassing perspective of hermeneutic experience. For Gadamer, hermeneutic experience pertains not just to the interpretation of texts or the reading of history but also to any encounter in experience that presents something to understand. This means that his *philosophical* hermeneutics cannot be defined through the problem of the self-understanding of the historical human sciences alone. It cannot be defined as a hermeneutics concerned only with, what at first appears to be the case in *Truth and Method*, the recovery of the past—a hermeneutics of tradition. Why his hermeneutics has been regarded as such by commentators and critics can be explained in part by the fact that Gadamer presents the main elements of his theory of hermeneutic experience in relation to the problem of historical understanding in part II of *Truth and Method*. But as Gadamer clearly indicates at the end of part II, a further analysis is needed to adequately define his philosophical hermeneutics. The fusion of horizons that takes place in historical understanding, he tells us, "is actually the achievement of language."[1] To be more precise, what is now at issue in defining philosophical hermeneutics is demonstrating the linguisticality, the linguistic element (*Sprachlichkeit*), of dialogue, with its dialectic of question and answer, as a further element of philosophical hermeneutics.[2]

It is, of course, part III of *Truth and Method* that completes the analysis of this element, and in doing so, Gadamer demonstrates that the encompassing perspective of hermeneutic experience—the universal aspect of hermeneutics—is such by virtue of the linguistic element in hermeneutic experience. In his demonstration, Gadamer will make a subtle distinction. Hermeneutic experience does not simply take place through the medium of language, thereby constituting, as we see in the first section of part III, both the act and the object of hermeneutic experience. More than this, Gadamer emphatically claims that hermeneutic experience has ontological weight. In this regard, Gadamer is following Heidegger, who had already set hermeneutics within his fundamental ontology. In his own way, Gadamer wants to show how hermeneutic experience expresses the basic character of our being in the world, and the linguisticality of hermeneutic experience is to be understood accordingly. As we will see, Gadamer places his philosophical hermeneutics within an ontology that is more Greek than modern. This is an ontology that follows Heraclitus's saying "listen not to me but to the Logos and you will agree that all is one."[3] Heraclitus's *logos* is more than the operation of the logical, understood as the rational discourse of the knowing subject who, by virtue of such discourse, gives expression to being. The *logos* of Heraclitus is nothing less than the very intelligibility of being. It is this idea of *logos* that in the medieval philosophy rooted in Christianity comes to be conceptualized in the idea of *verbum* and, in yet a different way, in the movement of spirit (*Geist*) in the philosophy of Hegel.

As we will also see, Gadamer's version of this ontology will take some distance from the ideal intentions in Plato and Aristotle's version of this same ontology, as well as from the related ontology that we find in Hegel. This distance has everything to do with the finitude of hermeneutic experience that Gadamer first finds in Heidegger's ontology of historical life. The condition of finitude qualifies every apprehension of being within the fundamental link between *logos*, as language, and being. This link is the explicit focus of the third and final section of part III of *Truth and Method*: "Language as Horizon of a Hermeneutic Ontology." In this third section, Gadamer develops the full intent announced in the title for the whole of part III of *Truth and Method:* "The Ontological Shift of Hermeneutics Guided by Language." He captures this intent in the most succinct way with the controversial expression "*being that can be understood is language*" (*TM,* 490, emphasis in original). The expression describes just what we have been saying from the outset about the universality of hermeneutic experience—namely, that the scope of the hermeneutic perspective is unrestricted in the experience of understanding. According to Gadamer, it means "being that can be experienced and understood, and it means that Being speaks. Only via language can being be understood."[4]

How Gadamer arrives at this expression and how the experience of understanding is configured in relation to it is the explicit concern of this chapter. The analysis here follows closely the three subsections of the third and final section of *Truth and Method.* In the first subsection, Gadamer establishes that the hermeneutic experience of the world is linguistic in nature. From this, he then explains just how language articulates experience by virtue of its speculative character. And then in the final subsection, Gadamer points to the "universal ontological significance" of the being of language—namely, its ability for the *self-presentation* of meaningful reality (*TM*, 491).

1. LANGUAGE AS EXPERIENCE OF THE WORLD

In this first subsection, Gadamer is in a certain way completing his historical analysis of the concept of language (the second section of part III). In that analysis, most notably in the discussion of language and *verbum*, Gadamer indirectly makes the case for a concept of language in his own work that links thinking to language as word and links language to the thing (*Sache*) thought in language. This concept only makes sense if the word of language is more than a sign indicating a reality outside language. To designate words as signs effectively separates thinking from language and language from thinking in a fundamental way. As a mere system of signs, language is simply an instrument at the disposal of thinking to express thoughts about reality. As such, the ontological character of language is fundamentally a second-order phenomenon: there is first the reality present to thought and then, second, the assignment of language to re-present the reality in thought. Against this view, Gadamer maintains that we always think *in* a language, we always search *in* language for the right word to say what we mean. And in our thinking, it is the (objective) matter of thought (the *Sache*) that language actualizes. All this is to say that the interiority of thought is already languaged, and language does more than serve as a bridge between conscious thought and some external reality. It is this idea that Gadamer now develops more fully, and in doing so, he effectively completes his historical analysis of the concept of language. For this, Gadamer turns to a modern consideration for thinking about language and to the work of Wilhelm von Humboldt in particular.

Humboldt (1767–1835) was, among other things, a linguist who studied the language of specific cultures, most notably the Basque language and the Kavi language of Java. His work is of such significance that he is considered the founder of modern philosophy of language. Humboldt famously claims that the essence of language is not a work (*ergon*) but a living activity (*energeia*) of speech that is capable of expressing thought and through which we can perceive the historical life of the mind. Humboldt's claim is significant in at least two respects. First, Humboldt does not think that language is simply one among other human activities but regards it an essential human endeavor. It is the one activity that we take up from the beginning, so to speak, such that the human world is fundamentally a language-world. In fact, as Gadamer points out, it is on the basis of language that we have a world at all, for it is only in language that we experience the world. And second, the activity of language is distinctive as a living creation originating in what Humboldt calls the "inner activity of spirit." This activity entails an "infinite use of finite means," which is to say that language is always more than the fixed content of what we say and what has been said in it (*TM*, 457). Gadamer will soon develop this idea through the Hegelian idea of the *speculative*. He will turn to the idea of the speculative because Humboldt's way of expressing the expansive activity of language is marked by a formalism that Gadamer rejects. Humboldt, with his modernist assumptions, roots linguistic activity in a mental power, not unlike a Kantian faculty that would give form to content. But for Gadamer, this amounts to a form-content distinction—the distinction between linguistic form and traditionary content—that is, an abstraction that cannot be separated out in hermeneutic experience.

What Gadamer finds most significant in Humboldt's contribution to the philosophy of language, though, goes beyond his idea of language formation as such. It pertains rather to the connection between language and world. When Humboldt came to realize in his comparative linguistics that language mirrors the individual mentalities of nations, Gadamer sees this as an insight into the whole of language—namely, that language extends beyond the individual and is capable of disclosing a world view. Gadamer writes,

> [As a world view] language maintains a kind of independent life vis-à-vis the individual member of a linguistic community; and as he grows into it, it introduces him to a particular orientation and relationship to the world as well. But the ground of this statement is more important, namely that language has no independent life apart from the world that comes to language within it. Not only is the world world only insofar as it comes into language, language, too, has its real being only in the fact that the world is presented in it. Thus, that language is originally human means at the same time that man's being-in-the-world is primordially linguistic. (*TM*, 459)

This passage gives expression to one of the central ideas in Gadamer's phenomenology of language. That language has an independent life underscores his insistence throughout his writings that language is not a mere possession of a conscious subject and "that consciousness of the individual is not the standard by which the being of language can be measured."[5] It also underscores the precise nature of the independence: language is not a possession of an individual because it is that which one is already in, orienting one to a world that is the common ground uniting all who talk together.

To give credence to this provocative claim, Gadamer points to the distinction between the concept of world and that of environment. In general terms, the concept of world entails an ensemble of references; there is the world of business as there is the world of the ancient Greeks, and so on. Gadamer does not describe it exactly this way, but in the idea of world as meaningful references one can readily infer that world is linguistically constituted—the world as world has a pervasive linguistic element. In a more cumbersome way, Gadamer describes this element in the concept of world through a notion of freedom. To speak of freedom in this context is to acknowledge the open space of both world and language. In contrast, environment is essentially a closed space, indicating conditioning factors relating to the way in which we live our lives. It is easy to see this difference between world and environment, as Gadamer notes, as a difference between the human, who has a world, and the non-human animal, who only has an environment. But this distinction blurs the real import of the difference. The human animal also lives in an environment, but at the same time, it can rise above its environment through its ability to keep itself at a distance from what it encounters. This distance is a freedom which is nothing other than the ability to understand ourselves and to be able to see "what is." And for Gadamer, it is quite telling to then say that humans do not have the ability to rise above their world. Not only does it bring the distinction between world and environment into further relief, it also helps us understand Gadamer's claim that world, which is what it is in language, is the "common ground," uniting all who talk with one another (*TM*, 462). As a common ground, world cannot be an object of language, just as language itself cannot be an object of language without abstracting from the very act of speaking.

What then are the objects of language, given its relation to world? They are not at all objects in the traditional sense of sensible beings with properties; rather, they are, as Gadamer repeatedly tells us, the (objective) things (*Sache*) in language. In our worldly experience, we experience the linguisticality of things. The word *Sache* and its cognates *Sachlichkeit* and *Sachverhalte* used here by Gadamer do not lend themselves to an easy translation. The word *Sache* generally means *topic*, in the sense of the subject matter, and it has been translated as *the matter at issue* or even *the point of dispute*.[6] It is a word taken up in the phenomenological tradition in Husserl's cry "back to the things themselves (*Zu den Sachen selbst*)" and Heidegger's "the matter of thinking (*Zur Sache des Denkens*)." But it is also a word used by Hegel, and Gadamer draws on this as much as he does from phenomenology.[7] Clearly, the intended meaning of *Sache* is that of a thing or matter that has a being of its own, a concrete givenness to which we have to accommodate ourselves. So understood, there is an objective status accorded to it, but this objectivity (*Sachlichkeit*), as Gadamer points out, is different from the objectivity (*Objectivität*) of science. The objectivity of science eliminates all subjective elements relating to the object while keeping the object available for calculation and use by the subject (*TM*, 469). Such is not the case for the objectivity

(*Sachlichkeit*) of language in which the object is dealt with similar to the way we must 'cope' with experience. The objective thing in language is the substantive matter that one has to attend to. In Gadamer's words:

> From the relation of language to world follows its unique objectivity (*Sachlichkeit*). It is the substantiveness bound to the matter [the facts of the matter, the state of affairs = *Sachverhalte*] that comes into language. That a matter comports itself in various ways permits one to recognize its independent otherness which presupposes a real distance between speaker and the thing. (*TM*, 461/449, translation modified)[8]

Gadamer finds this same objectivity of language in Greek thought. What exists is not the object of statements, but it does come to language in statements. Gadamer's own path alters this idea only slightly—language has its true being in conversation which places the matter at issue, like a disputed object, between the dialogical partners. In language, the reality beyond every individual consciousness becomes visible; our linguistic experience of the world embraces everything.

2. LANGUAGE AS MIDDLE AND ITS SPECULATIVE STRUCTURE

In this second subsection, Gadamer will make explicit the full dynamic of the linguistic experience of the world. He begins by noting that the idea of the linguistic experience of the world, which links language and being, has been maintained by philosophy since its metaphysical beginnings. Gadamer's reference to Plato's "flight into the *logoi*" in this context is a reference to Plato's often noted remark in the *Phaedo* that the work of philosophy proceeds by a second-best course: given the difficulty in investigating things directly, the recourse of philosophy is to investigate the truth of things by means of words.[9] The structure of being is to be read from the articulation of the *logos*, which is language-bound. Gadamer claims that the metaphysical tradition that keeps this idea in place until Hegel treats the relation theologically in the sense that thinking is to take hold of the highest and most proper being (Aristotle's thought of *nous*). The articulation of the *logos*, oriented to its fulfillment, is to bring the presence of being itself, its truth, into language. In contrast to this metaphysical structure of the relation between language and being, Gadamer proposes to understand the relation under the assumption of "the finitude of our historical experience" (*TM*, 473).

Following Heidegger in this regard, Gadamer cannot get away from the finite structure of being that sustains the limit in every act of understanding.

The exact nature of this limit, though, is not immediately evident in Gadamer's acknowledgement of it. It appears at first that Gadamer is arguing for a humble version of Hegel's unity of thinking and being—a hermeneutics of finitude that holds to the infinite separation within the unity of being and thinking. Finitude assures the incompleteness in bringing being to presence in language. Gadamer actually gives support to this view when he says that his hermeneutics wants to save the honor of Hegel's bad infinity where the end keeps on delaying its arrival.[10] But this remark does not tell the whole story. The finitude of historical experience does not just acknowledge the incompleteness in our apprehension of being, it is an indication of the limit *in* being, of the very concealment of being. The finitude of historical experience means that there is an occlusion in the very fabric of being such that the word of language is itself plagued by a self-concealing tendency.[11] Our intimacy with language is an uncanny experience in which the search for the right word for understanding may never be fully attained. What comes to presence in the word is at once an absence as well. So our linguistic experience of the world will embody finite experience with its peculiar repetition: the return of experience to experience that complicates the movement toward fulfillment.[12]

Under the condition of finitude, then, the word of language is neither the perfection of the species (a reflection of a pre-given order of being) nor an instrument that constructs an objectified universe of beings. Rather, in language "the order and the fabric of our experience itself is initially formed and constantly changed" (*TM*, 473). Language is the record of finitude precisely because it is "constantly being formed and developed the more it expresses the experience of the world" (*TM*, 473).

Exactly how language is being formed in this way, that is to say, how language enacts the coming-to-word of the experience of the world, has everything to do with what Gadamer calls "the living virtuality of speech" (*TM*, 474). In speaking no one word stands alone but is related to the whole of language so that every speaking holds within itself the possibilities contained in the whole of language. In this effort of coming to word, we are not just in the medium of language; we are actually in the middle of language. The English translation fails to fully capture this subtle yet important distinction. Language is indeed the medium (*Medium*) of hermeneutic experience, as the title of the first section of part III indicates, but what is at issue in the third section is almost a different concept: language as middle (*Mitte*) and its speculative structure. The key passage reads:

> Every word breaks forth as if from a middle (*Mitte*) and is related to a whole, through which alone it is a word. Every word causes the whole of the language to which it belongs to resonate and the whole worldview that underlies it to appear. Thus every word, as the event of a moment, carries with it the unsaid, to

which it is related by responding and summoning. The occasionality of human speech is not a casual imperfection of its expressive power; it is, rather, the logical expression of the living virtuality of speech that brings a whole of meaning into play, without being able to express it fully. (*TM*, 474/462)

To say that every word breaks forth from a middle of language is to say in an obvious way that every word breaks forth from within language; we never speak from the beginning of language as if the speaking were a first word. That the word breaks forth as if from a middle also means that language does not depend on the reflections of an acting subject to generate the movement of linguistic understanding.[13] A few lines before the quoted passage Gadamer writes: "It is the middle of language alone that, related to the whole of beings, mediates the finite historical nature of humanity with itself and with the world" (*TM*, 473).

This movement of language is for Gadamer nothing less than a dialectic of the word, a dialectic different from the dialectic formally presented by Hegel, as well as by Plato. Gadamer distinguishes his dialectic of the word from the dialectic of Plato and Hegel on the basis of the generation of meaning that is possible in the living language of speech. Unlike living language in which every word stands in relation to possibilities of meaning (the unsaid in every saying), the dialectic of Plato and Hegel holds to a dialectic of statements—a dialectic that simply reflects the logical content of statements.

But exactly how are we to understand this dialectic of the word, which accords every word an inner dimension of multiplication, as dialectical? In one sense, it is a dialectic in the way that, according to Gadamer, the Greeks always understand dialectical presentation. For the Greeks, there is no inherent problem in how the knowing subject *belongs* to the object of knowledge. This is only a problem in modern philosophy when it becomes entangled in the *aporias* of subjectivism. Unlike modern philosophy, the Greeks never attempted to base the objectivity of knowledge on subjectivity; rather, as we learn from Parmenides, thinking and being are the same. According to Gadamer, dialectical thinking for the Greeks—this experience of the *logos*—was not a movement performed by thought but thought experiencing the movement of the thing itself. The same dialectic can be found in Hegel. He too presents dialectical thinking as the articulation of being. Hegel's opposition to Kant's subjective idealism is based on this affirmation of the fundamental belonging together of thinking and being. Hegel opposes what he calls *external reflection* in which the very method of dealing with a thing is alien to it.[14] For Hegel too, "the true method was the action of the thing itself" (*TM*, 479).

Hegel's dialectic is of course a grand dialectic. It intends to repeat the total mediation between thinking and being. Gadamer's own dialectic of the word adapts this mediation accordingly: the dialectical movement of the word occurs dialogically; it is a movement in which the mediation has no formal structure when compared with the movement of logical necessity in Hegel's dialectic. As Gadamer puts it, in dialogue "something happens." The knower is not in control, and that something happens is not a "progressive knowledge of what exists" (*TM*, 477). Rather, the word encounters the knower in such a way that widening possibilities of meaning are played out. And in this dialectical movement, the concept of *belonging* in which thinking and being are held together takes on new meaning. The concept of belonging now follows the dialectic of hearing. The one who hears must acknowledge the fact of being addressed: "belonging is brought about by tradition's addressing us" (*TM*, 478). And in the living language of conversation, where being addressed by the subject matter is enacted, we can say that "language speaks us rather than we speak it" (*TM*, 479).

Yet, in another sense, we are to understand Gadamer's dialectic of the word as Hegel does—namely, as having a speculative structure. The word "speculative" refers to the mirror relation (*speculum*, mirror) where something is reflected in something else. The castle is reflected in its image in the water of the lake. Such an image is not strictly speaking a copy of something but an image that is directly connected with the actual sight of the thing. The mirror image is a duplication that is still only the *one* thing. As Gadamer notes, the word *speculative* enters philosophy during Hegel's time as a way of describing thinking that is reflective in the sense of being in accord with the pure appearance of what is reflected. Such thinking opposes the dogmatism that holds fast to "the fixed determinateness" of what is meant in the appearance (*TM*, 482). For Hegel, dialectical thinking is speculative in just this sense; what is in thought is a mirror image of the appearance of the real, which is nothing less than the unity of thinking and being. How this is so, dialectically, is explained by Hegel through the speculative statement which opposes the typical logic of statements. In ordinary statements, the subject term is given a fixed position and the statement refers the predicate term to the subject; it designates a property or an aspect of the subject term. In the speculative statement, though, the very nature of what is being thought in the subject passes into the predicate; in a sense, it disappears into the predicate which then becomes the truth of the subject term. To say "God is one," for example, does not mean that oneness is simply an attribute of God along with other attributes; rather, it is God's *nature* to be one. A speculative dialectic does not simply say something about something (s is p) but intends the unity of the concept.

In an analogous way, Gadamer maintains that the dialectic of the word in hermeneutics has a speculative structure in the way that language goes into itself. In the dialectic of the word, the enactment of meaning is "speculative in that the finite possibilities of the word are oriented toward the sense intended as toward the infinite" (*TM*, 485). In seeking and finding words for what we want to say—the event of thinking—we "hold what is said together with an infinity of what is not said in one unified meaning and . . . ensure that it is understood in this way" (*TM*, 485). This dialectic of the word, as previously noted, does not occur by making statements which are cut off from the whole of language. It is certainly least of all a dialectic of the concept in which the one-sidedness of a statement is corrected by another to arrive at the unity of the concept. It is rather a dialectic of the word from the middle of language in which thinking and speaking express a relation to the whole of language. Even more so, it is a dialectic in which every attempt to let the thing itself speak in language occurs as a response to the question presented by the thing. Gadamer's earlier analysis in *Truth and Method* of the importance of the question, and with it the movement of dialogue, enters here as a way of highlighting the difference between Gadamer and Hegel on the speculative, and thus the dialectical character of their respective projects. Gadamer's dialectic is that of question and answer generated from the response to the question that confronts the interpreter. Dialectics has to be conceived from this middle of language where hermeneutics is not dialectics, but dialogue.

3. THE UNIVERSAL ASPECT OF HERMENEUTICS

Gadamer begins the third and final subsection of "Language as Horizon of a Hermeneutic Ontology" with a brief summary. Language is fundamentally a middle (*Mitte*) "where I and world . . . manifest their original belonging together" (*TM*, 490). The middle of language is speculative in nature as a finite process in accord with hermeneutic experience. The movement of the speculative, in which language goes into itself, is the coming into language of meaning—the doing of the thing itself and not the methodic activity of a subject. From this summary, Gadamer draws his conclusion about the ontological turn in his hermeneutics. The activity of the thing itself effectively claims that "being that can be understood is language" (*TM*, 490). What is to be understood in the hermeneutic experience of worldly being is understood as language. This provocative claim by Gadamer has been much discussed and often misunderstood in the commentary on Gadamer's hermeneutics.

Generally speaking, the misunderstanding centers around an implied position within the claim, namely, that everything is language, and thus Gadamer is committed to a "panlinguisticism" or a form of linguistic idealism, not unlike what one finds in Hegel.[15] Certainly, Gadamer is appealing to a broad conception of language when he makes this claim. As he notes in a later essay, "language is not only a language of words . . . [it] includes all communication, not only speaking but also gestures that come into play in the linguistic relations among humans."[16] Even with this broad conception of language, which effectively equates language with the universality of reason, Gadamer readily acknowledges that not all experiences of the world take place in language. There are those prelinguistic and metalinguistic inner awarenesses and speaking silences in which our immediate contact with the world is taking place. "Who would want to deny," Gadamer insists, "that there are real factors conditioning human life, such as hunger, love, labor, and domination, which are themselves not language or speaking, but which for their part furnish the space within which our speaking to each other and listening to each other can take place."[17] Gadamer also acknowledges the fact of these prelinguistic experiences of the world in his second Supplement to *Truth and Method*, which was written after the book's initial publication. In the Supplement, Gadamer is responding to criticism of his views on language by Jürgen Habermas. Noting Habermas's reference to Piaget's research on child learning, Gadamer admits that "our experience of the world does not take place only in learning and using a language" (*TM,* 573). Still, Gadamer argues, there is something in common in certain phenomena we experience, such as gestures, facial expression and movement, as well as laughter and tears (a reference to the work of Helmut Plessner) that are not yet language but look to an ever-possible verbalization.

Elsewhere Gadamer also acknowledges that we can have experiences so overwhelming that they leave us speechless, as if in some sense we are confronted with a wordless experience. But even in the case of speechless astonishment, it is easy to see how the experience is still on the way to verbalization. "The breakdown of language actually testifies to one's capacity to search out an expression for everything."[18] From it, we find ourselves continuing with language; we begin to search for the words for what we want to say, all the while recognizing that our language is often hemmed in by our conventional forms of speaking. Because language is not limited to the stock of words immediately available to us, but always stands in relation to the not-yet-said, "there is nothing that is fundamentally excluded from being said, to the extent that our act of meaning intends it."[19]

What does Gadamer mean, then, when he says "being that can be understood is language" (*TM,* 490)? What is most essential to the intended meaning of the claim is the fundamental link between understanding and language—that understanding is linguistically formed—and the pending issue is how this understandability correlates with the intelligibility of the world. So Gadamer offers his own interpretation, to quote again: "Above all it means: being that can be experienced and understood, and it means that Being speaks. Only via language can being be understood."[20] With the emphasis appropriately placed on the word understanding in the phrase "being that can be understood is language," we can more readily see the import of the link between language and being. As we know from his description of dialogical conversation, Gadamer thinks that the idea of speaking with another involves more than carrying one's opinion over to another; it involves being caught up in language that builds up and bears within it a commonality such that there can be a shared understanding.[21] And when these agreements in understanding sink back into the "stillness of agreement and to being self-evident," they nevertheless remain tied to the understanding that unfolds in speaking. For Gadamer, language is not just the language of words. In its broader sense, language means communication, which confirms not just our worldly being but the distinctive character of it—namely, to be in relation to a 'common,' to the condition of language as being with one another.

But, for all this, the claim "being that can be understood is language" still holds an ambiguity. As reported by Donatella di Cesare, in making the Italian translation of *Truth and Method*, Gianni Vattimo asked Gadamer about the commas that are in the statement in the original German (*Sein, das verstanden werden kann, ist Sprache*). With Gadamer's consent, the commas were omitted. In doing so, the ambiguity becomes apparent. With the commas, the statement says being *is* language and as such being is understandable. Without the commas, the statement simply "identifies the domain of beings that offer themselves to understanding with the domain of language."[22] Vattimo preferred the statement with commas because the statement could then be seen as a more radical ontology, one that fits with Vattimo's own "weak ontology" influenced by Heidegger and Nietzsche. Gadamer, though, does not want to say that being unconditionally is language. He does want to affirm what he calls "the language of things (*Sache*)," as we have noted in several places here. The thing—the matter at issue—is in being and is so in such a way that we can more readily say that Gadamer's position here is closer to realism than a (linguistic) idealism.

It is a form of realism that is actually not too far from Hegel, if given a better reading of his idealism, one that, as we have seen, draws on sources in Greek ontology to affirm the self-presentation of being. This is the self-presentation that Gadamer identifies with the doing of the thing itself. Looking back over the whole of *Truth and Method*, Gadamer tells us that this self-presentation is what he was aiming at in his critique of aesthetic and historical consciousness. *This self-presentation is the defining mark of Gadamer's hermeneutics*. The structure of play in relation to art, the opening to new experience from within experience, the undergoing of a genuine dialogical conversation, are all characterized by self-presentation. In its simplicity, self-presentation means that the being of things is not for a hermeneutic consciousness something re-presented in consciousness nor is it a being-in-itself separated from its appearance (the structure one finds in Kant). And because self-presentation occurs in the medium of language, Gadamer thinks he is able to expand his hermeneutics beyond the methodological basis of the human sciences. From this expansion, hermeneutics becomes a universal aspect of philosophy. Gadamer's hermeneutics is a philosophical hermeneutics in which it has a "universal aspect"; it has an entry into the domain of the intelligible, into the domain of what is (being), through the experience of understanding.

The precise character of this self-presentation is what Gadamer now wants to make explicit in the final subsection of *Truth and Method*. On first reading, it is a strange analysis. Not only because Gadamer presents the general theme of truth for the first time here and does so in an indirect way but also because he presents the theme of self-presentation, oddly enough, through an analysis of the beautiful. The oddity of this closing subsection quickly fades, though, when we see that it is concerned in every aspect with the ontological dimension of self-presentation.

In introducing the concept of the beautiful, Gadamer reminds us that it was not always a concept for aesthetics in its concern with the fine arts, which quite literally are the arts of the beautiful in contrast to the arts that make useful things. Originally, the concept of the beautiful was a metaphysical concept and thus related to a universal doctrine of being. Something of this broader employment of the concept can be seen in the Greek word for the beautiful, *to kalon*. We do indeed correctly translate this Greek word as *the beautiful*, but its use had a range of associated meanings, especially that of the fine in the sense of noble and good (thus fine arts). As Gadamer points out, what is *kalon* is opposed to the necessities of life and desired for its own sake, not as a means to something else. "Beautiful things are those whose value is of itself evident," and what is beautiful "is what can be looked at, what is good-looking in the widest sense of the word" (*TM*, 493–94).

That Greek thought keeps to this association between the beautiful and the good in relating the concept of the beautiful to the order of being is most evident in the philosophy of Plato. Here the concept of the beautiful has the properties of harmony and proportion. What is beautiful has an ordering arrangement, a proper measure. It is an idea expressed earlier in the work of Pythagoras. For Pythagoras, the order of being is seen in the order of the heavens, which, as harmonious and proportioned, is the order of beauty. Plato understood the beautiful accordingly, so that in his attempt to think the good as the source of being he will say in the *Philebus* that the good takes shelter in the beautiful: "The power of the good has taken refuge in the nature of the beautiful: measure and measuredness constitute what beauty and excellence are everywhere."[23] What really interests Gadamer in this connection is the special advantage that the concept of the beautiful has for Plato, an advantage that links it not just to the order of being but also to being in its self-presentation.

As we learn from Plato's *Phaedrus*, the beautiful, as measure and proportion, has an additional quality, that of radiance and luminosity. It has the character of a shining that shines forth so as to put forth a look, a letting-being-seen. This quality gives it a special status among the forms. In the elaborate myth of the soul in love in the *Phaedrus*, Socrates describes the ability of the human earthly soul to take hold of true being, which is tantamount to taking hold of the forms. While most of the forms do not shine bright enough through their earthly appearance to be readily apprehended, the form of the beautiful is the exception. The beautiful, as "most radiant and lovely," is the one form that is visible in its appearance because it is its nature to shine forth in appearance. It is the one form that effectively presents itself in its appearance, closing the gap between idea and appearance. All this is to say that the beautiful names the way in which being shines forth in the midst of the beautiful. As Gadamer tells us:

> Radiance is not only the quality of the beautiful but constitutes its actual being.... Beauty is not simply symmetry but appearance itself.... Beauty has the mode of being of light.... [This means] that the beauty of a beautiful thing appears in it as light, as a radiance. It makes itself manifest. (*TM*, 498)

What Gadamer wants to emphasize here is the reflective nature of the mode of being of light that characterizes the beautiful. It joins the very seeing, the illuminating, with being visible. Beauty, having the mode of being of light, is not something added to the appearance of something. The metaphysics of light has the character of self-manifestation. Gadamer's carefully chosen word for this self-manifestation is *einleuchtend*, which means to make clear or to become evident. And it is this metaphysics of light that Gadamer carries over into his hermeneutics. There is a close structural relation between the shining forth of the beautiful and the becoming evident of the understandable in hermeneutic experience.

Specifically, Gadamer points to two features of hermeneutic experience that follow from this close structural relation. The first is that the becoming evident of understanding has the characteristic of an event. Gadamer has described hermeneutic understanding as an event throughout *Truth and Method*. It means that understanding is not a procedure that a subject brings about through its own design but is what happens when we get involved with something. When we come to understand something of the matter at issue in this way, something *in* the matter becomes evident. This does not mean that we secure a fact in the way this is understood in empirical research. Becoming evident belongs, as Gadamer says, to the tradition of rhetoric.

What is evident is always something that is said and does not adhere to demands for certainty. The becoming evident, then, is an event in the sense that something asserts *itself*, just as the beautiful charms us "without its being immediately integrated with the whole of our orientations and evaluations" (*TM*, 501). The becoming evident in understanding, as in an event, does not mean that what is understood is, in every detail, "secured, judged and decided" (*TM*, 501).

Second, Gadamer says that hermeneutic experience "has a share in the *immediacy* which has always distinguished the experience of the beautiful, as it has that of all evidence of *truth*" (*TM*, 500). The emphasis on the word immediacy points to the fact that hermeneutic experience, even in the way it takes place in dialogical conversation, is not a mediation all the way down. That is to say, the evidentness of understanding cannot be the result of mediation, as if understanding were a matter of logical demonstration reaching its end in a mediation. In hermeneutic experience, the evidentness of understanding is an experience of truth in the same way the beautiful is linked to truth for Plato. Here truth is something not arrived at through the agency of the one who wants to understand. Rather, truth has the character of a self-revealing unconcealment. In a later essay, Gadamer describes the directness of this experience of truth when, in reading a text, we come to say, "that's right!"— an acknowledgment that the text has revealed its meaning to the reader.[24] One would think that Gadamer should have more to say about truth, given that the title of the book has the word *truth* in it.[25] Certainly for Gadamer, the issue of truth is important, as one can readily see from his discussion of art, but here at the end of the book, it seems sufficient for Gadamer to say that in understanding we come to see what is, which is precisely the mark of truth—namely, to be in accord with what is. In this context, what really interests Gadamer is what he calls "the truth of the word" where something asserts itself as true. So Gadamer ends *Truth and Method* by saying that what we mean by truth is to be found in the play of language itself where we are "drawn into an event through which meaning asserts itself . . . [where it] captivates us just as the beautiful captivates us" (*TM*, 506).

NOTES

1. Hans-Georg Gadamer, *Truth and Method*, 2nd ed., trans. Joel Weinsheimer and Donald G. Marshall (New York: Bloomsbury Publishing, 2013), 386. Hereafter cited in text as TM. Where the German is cited or the translation has been altered, the page number of the original is indicated after the slash. The latter refer to Hans-Georg Gadamer, *Wahrheit und Methode*, Gesammelte Werke I (Tübingen: Mohr Siebeck, 1990).

2. Gadamer does not explicitly discuss the difference between linguisticality (*Sprachlichkeit*) and language (*Sprache*) in *Truth and Method*, but the difference is of upmost importance. In his "Reflections on My Philosophical Journey" he describes linguisticality as the capacity of language to be "inseparably linked with rationality as such." ("Reflections on My Philosophical Journey," in *The Philosophy of Hans-Georg Gadamer*, ed. Lewis Hahn (Chicago: Open Court, 1997, 25.)) This is the rationality that is fundamentally Greek in nature. It is the rationality of *logos*, which pertains to the intelligibility of things that is brought into view by speaking. More precisely, in an essay from 1993 Gadamer says that he uses the word linguisticality because it avoids speaking of language as if there is simply a multitude of different languages. (*Nachträge und Verzeichnisse*, Gesammelte Werke 10 (Tübingen: Mohr Siebeck, 1994), 273.) In every language there is an "urge to speak," an impulse to bring to word. This is the linguistic element of language out of which languages are able to form themselves. In our thinking and speaking in the effort to understand and communicate, we are drawn back into the linguisticality of things. As we will see, linguisticality characterizes our experience of the world in general and is "prior to everything that is recognized and addressed as being" (*TM*, 466). The translators of *Truth and Method* muddle this difference and confuse the reader when they translate *sprachliche* as *verbal*.

3. Heraclitus, Fragment 50, in *The Presocratic Philosophers*, ed. G.S. Kirk and J.E. Raven (New York: Cambridge University Press, 1969), 188.

4. Hans-Georg Gadamer, "A Look Back over the Collected Works and Their Effective History," in *The Gadamer Reader*, trans. and ed. Richard Palmer (Evanston: Northwestern University Press, 2007), 417.

5. Hans-Georg Gadamer, "Man and Language," in *Philosophical Hermeneutics*, trans. and ed. David E. Linge (Berkeley: University of California Press, 1976), 64.

6. The German *Sache* is related to the Latin *causa*, the disputed matter under consideration.

7. See Hans-Georg Gadamer, "The Nature of Things and the Language of Things," in *Philosophical Hermeneutics*, trans. and ed. David E. Linge (Berkeley: University of California Press, 1976), 70–71.

8. The use of the word *fact* in the English translation of *Sachlichkeit* as *factualness* only makes sense when we consider the meaning in the colloquial expression "In fact, what I really wanted to say. . . "

9. See Plato, *Phaedo*, 96a–99e.

10. Gadamer makes this remark in several places. See "Reflections on My Philosophical Journey," 37; and *Reason in the Age of Science*, trans. Frederick Lawrence (Cambridge: The MIT Press, 1981), 40 and 59–60. Without qualification, though, Gadamer's remark can be misleading. For a more extensive treatment of this way of relating Gadamer and Hegel, see James Risser, "In the Shadow of Hegel: Infinite Dialogue in Gadamer's Hermeneutics." *Research in Phenomenology*, 32 (2002): 86–102.

11. Gadamer is more explicit about his finitude of concealment in his later essays when discussing the relation of hermeneutics to deconstruction. See Hans-Georg Gadamer, "Hermeneutics Tracking the Trace" in *The Gadamer Reader*, trans. and ed. Richard Palmer (Evanston: Northwestern University Press, 2007).

12. In an interview Gadamer says that the humanities "have their special significance in the fact that no experience they deal with can be closed; this I call *die Unabschliessbarkeit aller Erfahrung* [the unconcludability of all experience].... We are constantly learning new things from what has been passed down to us.... In them we come upon new insights. And that always means, also that we are released from the blindnesses that held us captive." *Hans-Georg Gadamer in Conversation*, trans. and ed. Richard Palmer (New Haven: Yale University Press, 2001), 53.

13. Gadamer makes this point early on in his work. Already in *Plato's Dialectical Ethics*, which is the publication of his *Habilitationschrift* from 1927, Gadamer critiques the stance of reflection in relation to successful conversation. In *Truth and Method* Gadamer highlights this point in his discussion of language and *verbum*. The incarnate word is not formed by a reflective act; the word is not generated to express the mind but the intended subject matter.

14. See especially *The Science of Logic*, II.1.1.C.

15. In the first chapter of the *Phenomenology of Spirit*, Hegel first describes language has having a "divine character" in relation to the sensible world of appearance, for it enables us to apprehend things as universal. Language effectively idealizes reality.

16. Hans-Georg Gadamer, "Boundaries of Language," trans. Lawrence K. Schmidt, in *Language and Linguisticality in Gadamer's Hermeneutics*, ed. Lawrence K. Schmidt (Lanham, MD: Lexington Books, 2000), 9.

17. Gadamer, "Reflections on My Philosophical Journey," 28.

18. Hans-Georg Gadamer, "Language and Understanding," in *The Gadamer Reader*, trans. and ed. Richard Palmer (Evanston: Northwestern University Press, 2007), 93.

19. Gadamer, "The Nature of Things and the Language of Things," 67.

20. Gadamer, "A Look Back over the Collected Works and Their Effective History," 417.

21. Gadamer does not think there can be such a thing as a private language and is in full agreement with Wittgenstein who famously states this same claim. In his interview with Carsten Dutt Gadamer says that "whoever speaks a 'language' that nobody else understands is not really speaking." Gadamer, *Gadamer in Conversation*, 56.

22. Donatella Ester di Cesare, *Utopia of Understanding: Between Babel and Auschwitz*, trans. Niall Keane (Albany: SUNY Press, 2012), 5.

23. Plato, *Philebus*, 64e.

24. Hans-Georg Gadamer, "The Artwork in Word and Image," in *The Gadamer Reader*, trans. and ed. Richard Palmer (Evanston: Northwestern University Press, 2007), 192–224.

25. The title *Truth and Method* was not the initial title for the book; it was proposed by the publisher. Gadamer's initial title is in the subtitle, which is actually omitted in the English translation, namely, *Grundzüge einer philosophischen Hermeneutik* (Fundamentals of a Philosophical Hermeneutics).

Index

Abbild, 44, 79–81, 229
Aeschylus, xxvii, xxxii
aesthetic consciousness, x, xix, xxiii, 20, 29–30, 32–33, 40, 46, 51–52, 80–81, 83, 85, 97
aesthetic differentiation, 20, 40, 51, 79–80
aesthetic non-differentiation, 81
aisthesis, 20, 29, 30
architecture, x, xx, 66, 79–81, 86, 91–95, 99–100
Aristotle, xxvi, 12, 18, 22, 29, 42–43, 56, 62, 65–66, 76, 113, 123, 173–75, 179, 184–85, 194–95, 211, 218–19, 243, 246, 250
artwork, x–xi, xv, xx, xxiii, xxxi, 4, 10, 20–21, 23, 25, 27–29, 31–36, 39–44, 47–55, 64, 66, 68, 72, 79–81, 83, 86–88, 91, 93–99. *See also* work of art

Bacon, Francis, 153–54, 162, 194–95
Baumgarten, Alexander, 25, 30, 37
beauty, xxx, 67, 71, 81, 92, 98, 177, 257–58
being-in-the-world, 60, 96, 138, 248
Betti, Emilio, 162, 165–73, 175, 180, 183–84
Bewusstsein (*Bewußtsein*), xxv–xxvi, 21, 37, 123, 146, 187, 201

Bild, 9, 44, 79–82, 98, 229
bilden, 9
Bildung, ix, xxi–xxii, 4, 8–10, 25–26, 53, 112–13

consciousness, xiii, xix, xxv–xxvi, 21, 37, 123, 146, 187, 201. *See also Bewusstsein*
contemporaneity, 53–55
copy, xviii, 9, 42, 44–45, 65, 79–82, 84–85, 97, 229, 232
Cratylus, xiv, 229–33, 239
Critique of Judgment, xxii, 19–21, 25, 31

Darstellung, xxiii, 41–42, 66, 82, 229, 232. *See also* presentation
Dasein, 21–22, 24, 31, 34, 49, 61, 66, 135, 138–40
Davey, Nicholas, 49, 84, 96
decoration (decorative), 80, 85, 91, 93–95
Descartes, René, 126, 153–54
Destruktion, 25, 37
dialectic (dialectics), 71, 73, 105, 110, 230, 233, 245, 252–54
dialectic of experience, 17, 50, 195–96
dialectic of the word, 252–54
dialogue, vii, xxviii–xxix, 50–51, 53, 55, 115, 119, 165, 177, 178, 192,

196, 198, 203–4, 211, 212, 229–31, 233, 238, 245, 253–54
dialogue of the soul, 230, 238
Dilthey, Wilhelm, ix, xvii–xviii, xx, xxiv, xxxii, 7, 62, 72, 103, 105, 107, 112, 120, 122, 127–32, 134–40, 169, 170

ekstasis (ecstatic comportment), 46, 66, 69
enactment, 82, 87–88, 98, 253
Enlightenment, xii, xxv, 13, 15, 144, 152–60, 162, 188
epistemology, xxviii, 20–21, 24, 26, 107, 110
Erfahrung, 20–23, 32–36, 38, 50, 51, 96, 205
Erfahrung-Ästhetik, x, 35, 48
Erlebnis, 20–22, 32–34, 36, 127–28, 131–32
Erlebnis-Ästhetik, 32, 34, 36
Erzeugung, 238, 242, 243
eudaimonia, 174–75, 179

facticity, 48, 127, 137
festival, 54, 59, 66
Fichte, Johann Gottlieb, 112, 189
formation, ix, 8–9

game, 40–41, 59–60, 63–66, 69–74, 77. See also Spiel
Gebilde, 11, 42–43, 48, 53, 64, 65
Geist, 96, 246
Geisteswissenschaften, xvii, xviii, xxii, 3, 5, 161, 167
genius (aesthetics of, creative, Kantian), xxii, 24, 95, 128
Gjesdal, Kristin, 110, 168–70, 182
Goethe, Johann Wolfgang von, xvii, 39, 71
Grondin, Jean, ix, 70, 223, 243

Habermas, Jürgen, 166, 255
health, x, 67, 73–74, 161, 174
Hegel, Georg Wilhelm Friedrich, xiii, xvii, xxx, 10–11, 22, 62, 67, 69, 71, 73, 96–97, 108, 113, 127, 130, 136–37, 140, 188–93, 195–96, 198, 202, 246, 249, 250, 252–54, 256
Hegel's dialectic, 51, 67, 73, 190, 196, 252–53
Heidegger, Martin, xi, xvi, xviii, xxiv, xxxi, 9, 22, 25, 31, 34, 37, 41, 48, 60–63, 69–71, 73–74, 94, 125, 127, 131, 134, 135, 137–40, 144, 147, 160–61, 202, 246, 250, 256
Helmholtz, Hermann von, xxi, 7, 11, 12
Heraclitus, 62, 73, 246
Herder, Johann Gottfried, 60, 117, 170, 223
historical consciousness, viii, xvii, 54, 97, 105, 109, 111, 119–20, 127–28, 130–31, 136, 144, 148–49, 152–53, 157–60, 163, 256
historically effected consciousness, xiii, xxv, xxvii, 187–92, 196, 203
historicism, xi, xix, 120, 125–31, 134, 136–38, 140, 149, 158, 202
historicity, xi–xii, xxiv, xxv, xxvii, xxxii, 24–25, 34–36, 49, 93, 96, 127, 134–40, 143–44, 149–50, 152, 157–60, 194, 202
history (of the concept of language), xiii
history (of concepts), 24
history (of consciousness; Husserl's constituting ego), 133
history (of effects; effective history), xix, 25, 35, 52, 86, 166, 168
history (of hermeneutics), xi
history (of humanity), 107, 108
history (of language), 210, 221–22
history (of philosophy), 60, 194, 227, 240
Huizinga, Johann, 63, 71–73
humanism, ix, xiv, xxi–xxii, 8–9, 17–18
humanities, ix, xv, xvii–xxiii, xxvi, xxx, 3, 25–26, 103, 111, 114, 128, 130–32, 134, 138–39, 167–68, 171, 177, 179, 261
Humboldt, Wilhelm von, 8, 22, 247–48
Hume, David, 19, 21, 128

Husserl, Edmund, xi, xxiv, 62, 70, 127, 131–35, 137, 139, 140, 194, 195

idealism (German), 168, 189–90
idealism (Hegelian), 120
idealism (Kantian; transcendental), 25, 120, 126, 252
idealism (linguistic), xiv, 254, 256
idealism (speculative), 134
ideality, 43, 54, 202, 215, 218, 224, 229
image, 9, 23, 44–45, 81–84, 97–98, 229–30, 253. *See also* Bild
incarnation, 234–35
increase of being, 45, 83
indication, 88, 90. *See also Verweisung*
instrumentalist (theory of language), xiv, 222, 227, 231, 239
integration, 28, 33, 49, 55, 80, 96, 113, 178, 180
interpretation, viii, xii, xxiv, xxviii, xxx, 3–4, 12, 16, 47, 49–50, 65, 69–71, 153, 157, 159, 161, 163, 167–68, 170, 172–73, 175–83, 210–13, 219–22, 225, 245
interpretation (of artworks), 4, 16, 47, 49, 51–54, 65, 69, 80, 87, 91, 220–21
interpretation (Schleiermacher), xi, 104–11, 114–15, 117–18, 120, 209–10, 218, 223, 225
interpretation (of texts), xvii, 47, 95, 153, 163, 245

judgment, xiii, xxvii, 173, 180, 181
judgment (aesthetic), 19–21, 24, 27–30
judgment (humanist concept of), xxi–xxii, 4, 12–15, 17
judgment (moral), xxii
judgment (*a priori*; Kant's notion of), xxii, 30, 33, 34, 169

Kant, Immanuel, ix, xxii, xxiii, 5, 19, 21, 22, 24–31, 33–34, 62, 69, 113, 126, 128, 136, 153, 154, 169, 188–90, 256
Kidder, Paul, 94
Kierkegaard, Søren, 66, 192, 203, 236

lifeworld, 65, 138
linger, 88, 91, 95–96. *See also* tarry
linguisticality, ix, xiii, xxviii, 104, 165, 211, 245–46, 249, 260. *See also Sprachlichkeit*
logos, xxxi, 228–29, 231, 234–37, 246, 250, 252, 260

Makkreel, Rudolph A., 169–70
Marx, Karl, 192
mediation (mediational), 28, 39, 49, 51–55, 64, 66, 72, 80, 81, 92–96, 106, 128, 178, 189, 191, 252–53, 259
Mill, John Stuart, 3
mimesis, 23, 36, 42–44, 65, 79, 81, 97, 229, 232, 241
mood (moods), 71, 139
music (musical, musician), vii, viii, 22, 32, 53, 67, 71, 74, 79–81, 87–88, 93, 99, 132

Nachbild, 9
narrative, xiii, 25, 35, 42, 61–62, 119–20, 129, 222
nihilism, 32–34

objectivity, xviii, xxiv, 7, 26, 130–31, 135, 136, 140, 146, 147, 162, 167, 168, 198, 249–50, 252. *See also Sachlichkeit*
occasionality, 80, 85–88, 91–92, 252
onoma, 228–29, 234
openness, xii, xiii, xxv, xxix, 17, 46, 50–51, 71, 91, 119, 150, 151, 177, 191, 196–200, 242, 244
original (audience), 209–10, 216, 219, 220
original (in contrast with a copy), 44–45, 48, 54, 65, 67, 79–90, 96, 98, 99, 232
original (horizon), 202
original (intentions of the author), 168, 178
original (languages), 108
original (life-world; world), 52–53, 55, 86, 96

original (meaning), xiii, 43, 61, 169
original (occasion; context), 87, 96, 214–16, 218–19
original (purpose), 91

painting, x, 35, 79–86, 93, 97–99. See also picture
Parmenides, 62, 252
Parmenides (Plato's dialogue), 70, 73
performance, viii, xi, 22, 41, 51–53, 65, 79–81, 87, 97, 214, 220
Phaedo, 73, 234
Phaedrus, 258
phenomenology, 25, 61–62, 67, 131–35, 137, 140, 180
phenomenology (of human being), 69
phenomenology (of language), 248–49
phenomenology (of play), 70
phenomenology (of understanding), 170
Philebus, 257
phronesis, xxvi, 14, 113
picture, xviii, xxiii, 9, 44–45, 48, 79–91, 97–99. See also Bild
Pippin, Robert, 189, 191–93, 204
Plato, xiv, 22, 44, 60, 65, 67, 68, 70, 73–74, 79–80, 112, 114, 117, 193, 219, 230–34, 238, 243, 246, 250, 252, 257–59
Plato (metaphysics of light), xxix–xxxi
Plato (*mimesis*), 79, 97, 229, 241
Plato (Platonic dialogues), 117, 228–29, 233
Plato (Plato's dialectic), 71, 73, 119, 200, 233, 252
play, x, xii, xviii, xxiii, 29, 39–42, 46, 55, 59–75, 80, 95, 97, 163, 165, 220, 256, 259. See also Spiel
play (of art), xxiii, 29, 39–42, 55, 69, 82–83, 85, 95, 220, 256, 259
play (of the imagination), 24
play (medial sense of), 41
portrait, xi, 45, 84–88, 91
positivism, 137
prejudgment, xxv, 200

prejudices, xii, xv, xviii–xix, xxv, 110, 143, 146–47, 151, 153, 155, 168, 192, 198–200
presentation, viii, xi, xxiii, xxxi, 41–48, 52–55, 65, 69, 79–87, 89, 91, 95, 99, 113, 222, 229, 232, 252

repetition, 33, 40, 54, 56, 63, 195, 245, 251
Ricoeur, Paul, 42, 103
Rilke, Rainer Maria, 60, 67, 75, 108
Romanticism, 137, 144, 152, 156–58, 160, 167

(*die*) *Sache*, viii, xxviii, 42, 107, 118, 152, 162, 227, 232, 242, 247, 249, 256, 260
Sachlichkeit, 249–50, 260. See also objectivity
Scheler, Max, 68, 70
Schiller, Friedrich, 63, 71–73, 77
Schleiermacher, Friedrich, xi, xiii, xviii, xxiv, 96, 103–20, 167, 170, 209–10, 216–18, 222–23, 225
Schleiermacher's dialectic, 112–16
Schmidt, Dennis, 18, 83, 97, 98
Schopenhauer, Arthur, 31
Sein, das verstanden werden kann, ist Sprache, 256
Sein der Sprache, 229
self-presentation, xiv, xxxi, 40–41, 46, 51–52, 55, 95, 247, 256–58
sign, 48, 88–90, 99, 227, 230–32, 237, 247
Simmel, Georg, 72
Singer, Peter, 172–73
skepticism, 72, 126, 140, 145
Socrates, 81, 85, 97, 213, 230, 258
solidarity, 74
Sophocles, 209, 213
Spiel, xxiii, 59, 71, 72. See also game and play
Sprache, xxviii, 210, 227, 229, 256, 260
Sprachlichkeit, 14, 27, 245, 260. See also linguisticality

Stiftung, 80, 90
subjectivity, xviii, xxiv, 24, 28, 34, 63, 65–66, 70, 132–34, 172, 197, 225, 252
subjectivization, 23, 27, 28, 34–36, 40
substitution, 88–90. *See also Vertreten*
symbol, xi, 48, 71, 88–90, 99

tarry, 81, 88. *See also* linger
taste, xxi–xxii, 4, 12, 15–17, 24, 28, 30, 62, 113
temporality, 21, 32, 34–36, 54, 68, 127, 129, 134, 137–38
Thou, 50, 130, 192, 197
tragedy, xxiii, xxxii, 10, 64, 66, 68, 209, 212–13

understanding, xi–xii, xv, xvii–xx, xxiv–xxxi, 19–21, 23, 24, 33–35, 68–70, 106–7, 111, 117–18, 130, 138–40, 144, 146–52, 160, 175, 179, 196–98, 201–2, 209–14, 217–18, 221, 241–42, 246, 250, 259
understanding (and art; of art; aesthetic), 21, 23, 30, 33–36, 50, 85, 88, 96, 97
understanding (collective; communal), 23, 26, 36, 133
understanding (Enlightenment conception), 152–56, 160
understanding (event of), 96, 179, 242, 258–59
understanding (hermeneutical), xxiv–xxxi, 20, 24–25, 85, 104, 111, 119, 138–40, 144–52, 159–61, 172, 209–14, 242, 246, 250, 258–59
understanding (historicity of; historical character of), xi–xii, xix, xxiv–xxv, 35, 104, 108, 113, 119–20, 125–27, 129–31, 133, 135, 137, 143–44, 146, 149, 152, 160, 187–88, 245
understanding (of the humanities; humanistic), xviii, 4, 127, 130, 139
understanding (limits of; finitude of), xv, 23, 238, 240

understanding (linguisticality of; linguistic character; of language), xiii, xiv, xv, xix, xxviii–xxxii, 221–22, 227–29, 232, 237, 241, 252, 255–56
understanding (nature of), ix, 68
understanding (normativity of), 166, 170, 175–76, 179
understanding (ontological), 138–40
understanding (Platonic), 79, 81
understanding (*a priori* categories of; Kantian), 26–27, 33
understanding (problem of; practical challenge of), 103, 106, 110, 116
understanding (Romantic conception of), 157–60
understanding (speculative), 134
understanding (Trinitarian model of), 234
understanding (universality of), 103, 257
understanding (of the world), 62, 83, 163, 239, 240
univocity, 227, 241
Urbild, 44, 79, 81, 98. *See also* original in contrast with a copy

Vattimo, Gianni, 256
verbum, 228, 234–35, 237, 243, 246–47, 261
Vertreten, 88–90
Verweisung, 88, 90. *See also* indication
Vico, Giambattista, 13–14
Vorbild, 9, 228, 242

Wachterhauser, Brice, 70, 161
Warnke, Georgia, 70, 225
Wittgenstein, Ludwig, 63, 204, 261
work of art, 16, 21–23, 29, 33, 35, 39–44, 46–50, 52–55, 57, 60, 63–64, 82–83, 87–88, 91–96. *See also* artwork

About the Contributors

Carolyn Culbertson is associate professor of philosophy at Florida Gulf Coast University. She currently serves on the executive committee of the North American Society for Philosophical Hermeneutics. Her book, *Words Underway* (2019), focuses on philosophy of language in the continental tradition.

Nicholas Davey is professor of philosophy at the University of Dundee. His principal teaching and research interests are in aesthetics and hermeneutics. He has written considerably on Gadamer and has published over 100 peer-reviewed articles. He is the author of *Unquiet Understanding: Gadamer and Philosophical Hermeneutics* (2006) and *Unfinished Worlds: Hermeneutics, Aesthetics, and Gadamer* (2013).

Carlo DaVia is lecturer in philosophy at Fordham University. He has published on Gadamer and Aristotle and has translated Gadamer's essay, "The Socratic Question and Aristotle." His current research focuses on Gadamer and language.

Jessica Frazier is lecturer in theology and religion at Trinity College, University of Oxford. Her work explores philosophies of self and Being in Indian thought and also post-Heideggerian philosophy. Her books include *Hindu Worldviews: Theories of Self, Ritual and Reality* (2017), *Categorisation in Indian Philosophy* (2014), and *Reality, Religion, and Passion* (2008). Forthcoming books include *Religion, Hinduism and the Sacred* as well as a philosophical exploration of the sublime in modern thought.

Theodore George is professor of philosophy at Texas A&M University. He specializes in continental European philosophy since Kant, especially contemporary hermeneutics, continental ethics, the philosophy of art and aesthetics, and classical German philosophy. His recent publications include *The Responsibility to Understand: Hermeneutical Contours of Ethical Life* (2020) and the entry "Hermeneutics" in *The Stanford Encyclopedia of Philosophy* (2020). He is coeditor with Gert-Jan van der Heiden of *The Gadamerian Mind* (2021) and with Charles Bambach of *Philosophers and Their Poets: Reflections on the Poetic Turn in German Philosophy Since Kant* (2019). T. George is also translator of Günter Figal's *Objectivity: The Hermeneutical and Philosophy* (2010), and he serves as editor of *Epoché: A Journal for the History of Philosophy* and as category editor for "Hermeneutics" on *PhilPapers*.

Jean Grondin is professor of philosophy at the Université de Montréal. He was a pupil and close collaborator of Hans-Georg Gadamer. His books include *Introduction to Philosophical Hermeneutics* (1994), *Sources of Hermeneutics* (1995), *Hans-Georg Gadamer: A Biography* (2003), and *Introduction to Metaphysics* (2004).

David Liakos is instructor of philosophy at Houston Community College. He is an assistant area editor for "Hermeneutics" and assistant leaf editor for "Hans-Georg Gadamer" on *PhilPapers*. He has published on Gadamer and Stanley Cavell and has articles forthcoming in *Epoché*, *The Cambridge History of Philosophy* (coauthored), and the *Journal of Aesthetics and Phenomenology*.

Greg Lynch is associate professor of philosophy at North Central College in Illinois, where he teaches courses on a range of subjects, including hermeneutics, the history of philosophy, aesthetics, existentialism, and the philosophy of mind. His research focuses on issues in hermeneutics and the philosophy of language, particularly as they arise in the work of Hans-Georg Gadamer, Donald Davidson, and the ordinary language tradition. His works have appeared in *Ergo, Philosophical Investigations, The Southern Journal of Philosophy, International Journal of Philosophical Studies*, and *Philosophy Today*, among others. He is also coauthor, with Carlo DaVia, of a forthcoming book on Gadamer's theory of meaning.

Cynthia R. Nielsen is associate professor at the University of Dallas, where she teaches courses in the areas of hermeneutics, aesthetics, ethics, contemporary continental philosophy, and the history of philosophy. Her articles have appeared in journals such as *Philosophy Today, Symposium:*

Canadian Journal of Continental Philosophy, *Journal of the British Society for Phenomenology*, *African Identities*, and *Philosophy and Literature*. She has published two books, the most recent of which is *Interstitial Soundings: Philosophical Reflections on Improvisation, Practice, and Self-Making* (2015), which focuses on the philosophy and phenomenology of music as well as the social and political dimensions of music-making. Her current research, *Gadamer's Hermeneutical Aesthetics: On Art as a Performative, Communal, Dynamic Event* (2023), centers on bringing Gadamer's reflections on art into conversation with the insights, contributions, and practices of twentieth- and twenty-first-century music and art, particularly those of African American artists.

James Risser is professor of philosophy at Seattle University. He has published extensively on Gadamer and hermeneutics. His books include *Hermeneutics and the Voice of the Other: Re-reading Gadamer's Philosophical Hermeneutics* (1997) and the *Life of Understanding* (2012). He also serves as the associate editor for the journal *Research in Phenomenology*.

Daniel L. Tate is professor of philosophy at St. Bonaventure University. His principal research efforts are directed toward philosophical hermeneutics and the philosophy of art, particularly in light of the work of Martin Heidegger and Hans-Georg Gadamer. He has published numerous articles on Gadamer in journals such as *Epoché*, *Philosophy Today*, and *Journal of the British Society for Phenomenology*, and he has contributed chapters to several volumes on hermeneutics.

Gert-Jan van der Heiden is professor of philosophy at Radboud University. His work examines problems from metaphysics and ontology in light of recent developments in phenomenology, hermeneutics, and contemporary French thought. He is interested in the motive of speaking for the other in hermeneutics and studies how the concept of contingency determines the landscape of contemporary ontology. With others, he investigates why the letters of Saint Paul are so often read in contemporary philosophy. His books include *Phenomenological Perspectives on Plurality* (2015), *Ontology after Ontotheology. Plurality, Event and Contingency in Contemporary Philosophy* (2014), and *The Truth (and Untruth) of Language: Heidegger, Ricoeur, and Derrida on Disclosure and Displacement* (2010).

Kevin M. Vander Schel is associate professor of religious studies at Gonzaga University. He previously taught at Villanova University, University of Houston, and Boston College. Vander Schel specializes in modern Christian systematic theology and has strong interests in theological anthropology and hermeneutics, political theology, theologies of sin and grace, and Christian ethics. He is an active member of the American Academy of Religion and the Catholic Theological Society of America. His current research focuses on questions of grace and history, method and theory in the academic study of theology and religion, and social and political understandings of sin.

David Vessey is professor of philosophy at Grand Valley State University. He was a Fullbright scholar at the Husserl Archives at Katholieke Universeitat Leuven and has been a visiting scholar at the University of Oregon, the University of Notre Dame, the University of Chicago, and the University of Minnesota. He has published extensively on Gadamer and the history of hermeneutics, especially in comparison to other philosophical traditions.

www.ingramcontent.com/pod-product-compliance
Lightning Source LLC
Chambersburg PA
CBHW020110010526
44115CB00008B/776